£3.25

THE BRITISH PRESS
AND GERMANY
1936-1939

THE
BRITISH PRESS
AND
GERMANY
1936–1939

BY

FRANKLIN REID GANNON

CLARENDON PRESS · OXFORD

1971

Oxford University Press, Ely House, London W. 1

GLASGOW   NEW YORK   TORONTO   MELBOURNE   WELLINGTON
CAPE TOWN   SALISBURY   IBADAN   NAIROBI   DAR ES SALAAM   LUSAKA   ADDIS ABABA
BOMBAY   CALCUTTA   MADRAS   KARACHI   LAHORE   DACCA
KUALA LUMPUR   SINGAPORE   HONG KONG   TOKYO

MADE IN GREAT BRITAIN AT THE PITMAN PRESS, BATH

FOR MY MOTHER

PREFACE AND ACKNOWLEDGEMENTS

THIS is a book about British attitudes towards Germany in the inter-war years, particularly in the last three years of peace, 1936–9. These attitudes, all of which found a greater or lesser body of public support, are examined through the eyes and voices of the major British newspapers. The papers chosen are the seven national dailies (*The Times, Daily Telegraph, Morning Post, News Chronicle, Daily Herald, Daily Express,* and *Daily Mail*), the two important Sunday papers (*Observer, Sunday Times*), and the *Manchester Guardian.*

This selection runs the gamut of public attitudes towards Germany, and although arguments may well be made for the addition of other newspapers, or even periodicals, while such additions would undoubtedly increase both the detail and interest of the study, it would not alter any of its conclusions.

Relative importance and manageability thus became the twin criteria, and imposed a logic of their own. To be exhaustive such a study would have to be exhausting; and in terms of the attitudes it seeks to examine, the 'psychology of appeasement' which it seeks to explain, any but a rigorous selection of source materials would risk defeating the purpose and create a situation where the facts get in the way.

At times, particularly in those sections dealing with the Anschluss, the Czechoslovak crisis, and the occupation of Prague, it may seem as if this has become a study of *The Times* or the *Manchester Guardian* exclusively. The only rule violated by such a situation is that of symmetry; newspapers here are generally dealt with in direct proportion to the amount of news and analysis they printed concerning Germany. It would be ludicrous to devote as much space or attention to Lord Beaverbrook's or Lord Rothermere's few unsophisticated and obsessive ideas as to the development of important ideas and attitudes in the columns and offices of the quality newspapers. It is not, of course, coincidental that *The Times* and *Manchester Guardian* alone of the newspapers studied had extensive archive material much of which is quoted here for the first time.

The *Manchester Guardian*, although a provincial paper of comparatively small circulation, deserved and enjoyed an international reputation as the liberal counterpart of *The Times*. The decision to include provincial papers like the *Yorkshire Post* and the *Glasgow Herald* would have made exclusion of some others more difficult, and the study would have become too long.

The inclination to include the more important periodicals had to be resisted for the same reasons. They merit a study of their own, and here I have referred to them only when, as in the case of the *New Statesman* in August 1938 or *The Week* in October 1937, they have a direct bearing upon the course of the history being related.

Each newspaper is a fascinating story in itself, and deserves telling as such. In this study, the newspapers are treated as much for the attitudes and opinions they espoused as for their particular organization or personnel.

Another problem concerns the attribution of authorship. It is true, for example, that other members of *The Times*'s Berlin staff wrote many of the articles with which Norman Ebbutt was popularly credited. Leading articles were frequently the result of several hands and minds. In the text I have tried to avoid personal attributions except where they are documented, important, or necessary to the narrative.

I have imposed a common spelling and punctuation throughout, and corrected obvious misspellings or misprints instead of using the otiose [*sic*]. This was not done through any cavalier attitude towards the source materials, but because the exigencies of producing a newspaper every day did not allow the accuracy which the authors would otherwise have shown.

The basic research for this study lay in reading the bound volumes of the ten newspapers covered, every day from January 1936 until September 1939. This was done in the Bodleian Library, the British Museum Newspaper Library, and the Senate House Library of the University of London. This reading was supplemented and extended by numerous interviews and correspondences. I am particularly grateful to the following for their help:

The late Sir Gerald Barry; Mr. Ivor Bulmer-Thomas; the late Hon. Randolph S. Churchill; Mr. Ian Colvin; Miss

Virginia Cowles; Mr. Geoffrey Cox; Mr. Aidan Crawley; the late Hon. Mrs. Cecilia Dawson; Mr. Sefton Delmer; Mr. K. T. Downs; Mr. W. N. Ewer; Mr. M. R. D. Foot; Lord Francis-Williams; Mr. G. E. R. Gedye; the late Mr. Victor Gordon-Lennox; Sir Hugh Greene; Mr. H. D. Harrison; Lord Hartwell; Mr. John D. Harvey; Mr. James Holburn; Mr. Derek Hudson; Mr. David Irving; Dr. Rolf Kieser; Mr. C. A. Lambert; Miss Hazel Neary; Lady Mander; Mr. Iverach McDonald; Mr. Malcolm Muggeridge; Mr. G. L. Pearson; Mr. Karl Robson; Mr. Robert Skelton; Mr. A. J. P. Taylor; Mr. V. V. Tilea; Mr. P. B. Wadsworth; Mr. A. E. Watson; Mr. Emlyn Williams; Miss Elizabeth Wiskemann.

The Editor of *The Times* and the Editor of the *Guardian* kindly opened their papers' Archives to me. The Archivist of *The Times*, Mr. W. R. A. Easthope, and his predecessor Mr. John S. Maywood, were most helpful in providing me with the relevant materials. The Historian of the *Guardian*, Mr. David Ayerst, gave generously of his time and advice in sorting out the hitherto unsorted papers in Cross Street for these years.

Mr. Donald McLachlan generously put at my disposal the manuscript and notes for his biography of Barrington-Ward, *In the Chair*, as well as several unpublished papers he wrote during the course of his research.

For their particular kindnesses and hospitality, I am indebted to Mrs. F. A. Voigt and Mrs. H. M. Whistler.

I am very grateful to the Principal and Fellows of Jesus College, and the Warden and Fellows of Nuffield College, Oxford. I am also grateful to the Warden and Controller of London House.

Mr. D. C. Watt of the London School of Economics first introduced the topic to me, and he followed the progress of my research with keen interest. Dr. David Butler of Nuffield College was never daunted by my erratic production of hundreds of manuscript pages which for some reason always had to be read over a week-end; his advice was always careful and perceptive. Mr. Martin Gilbert of Merton College gave much advice on many matters, and was as generous in hospitality as he was in drawing upon his many resources and contacts for people and information in the inter-war years.

Professor James Joll, both at St. Antony's and the University of London, showed a warm and constructive interest in my research and conclusions.

For their friendship and support through the years during which this study was researched and written, I am especially indebted to Mr. Rodney Bewes, Mr. Christopher Bruce, Miss Julie Félix, Mr. L. G. Parker, and Mr. and Mrs. David Wall.

Carol Murphy typed the original thesis: her great accuracy was matched by her great patience.

The greatest debt is to Professor Herbert Nicholas of New College. His encouragement, advice, direction, and insight mainly account for whatever merit the study may possess, including, most basically, its existence.

New York City   F.R.G.

CONTENTS

ABBREVIATIONS

Berlin (etc.) Corr.   from our (own) Correspondent in Berlin (etc.)

DBFP   *Documents on British Foreign Policy*, 3rd Series, H.M.S.O. (Nos. refer to volume and document)

DGFP   *Documents on German Foreign Policy*, Series D, H.M.S.O. (Nos. refer to volume and document)

Dipl./Spec. Corr.   from/by our (own) Diplomatic/Special Correspondent

ed. art.   editorial article, referring to articles other than leading articles, which appear on the editorial or leader page of a newspaper. In *The Times*, because of their position in the last right-hand column, these are known as 'turn-over' articles.

Hist. Times   *The History of The Times*

RCP   *Royal Commission on the Press*, H.M.S.O., 1947 (Nos. refer to day of sitting and page)

Propaganda makes it increasingly difficult to form any idea of what is the state of affairs in countries whose system of government has become the subject of controversy.

Accounts of contemporary Germany, for instance, range between a gruesome picture of butterless woe and non-stop jamboree.

One writer with passionate conviction describes smouldering discontent; another, also with passionate conviction, boundless strength through joy. And the camera helps all. It is one of the many ironies of our time that photography, which seemed to promise accuracy, has proved a fruitful source of deception. The fact that it cannot lie makes its lies the more impressive.

Malcolm Muggeridge in 'Books of the Day', *Daily Telegraph*, 10 January 1939.

. . . all stories are written backwards—they are supposed to begin with the facts and develop from there, but in reality they begin with a journalist's point of view, a conception, and it is the point of view from which the facts are subsequently organised. Journalistically speaking, 'in the beginning is the word'.

Claud Cockburn, *In Time of Trouble*.

I

INTRODUCTION: THE ANATOMY OF APPEASEMENT

THE late 1930s, the last years of peace, were the golden age of newspapers in Great Britain. More newspapers reached more people than ever before, or than anywhere else in the world. The random harvest of the Elementary Education Act of 1870 was methodically gathered and bundled up in the circulation war in the early years of the decade. In those days just witnessing the development of radio as a news media, and before television, the newspaper press was the only means of information about the outside world for the vast majority of people. To meet this demand there were, in 1938, 52 morning, 85 evening, and 18 Sunday newspapers published in Great Britain of which 20, 3, and 10 respectively were published in London. The Press was one of the major manufacturing industries, producing, in 1937, a total of 1,577 newspapers and 3,119 magazines and periodicals; in 1934 every 100 families bought 95 morning and 57½ evening newspapers every day, and 130 Sunday newspapers every week.[1]

All classes were permeated and served; for the industry was competitive. Although the lunacies of the circulation wars of the early 1930s had been left behind, the favour of the public had still to be sought and courted: advertising revenue still depended upon circulation. The newspaper press had become a large and important business, and its business structure developed quite separately from its journalistic structure; in the popular press, the latter became largely subservient to the former.

It was a vicious circle: if the aim was to sell newspapers, then the public must be given what it wanted. But the new mass literate public was by no means a discriminating or

---

[1] *Political and Economic Planning Report on the British Press*, pp. 3, 47.

responsible one: it preferred entertainment to information. Further, advertisers were attuned to public attitudes, and people bought more when they felt secure and contented. It is becoming clear that economic recovery in Britain after the Great Depression hit Europe in 1931 was quite rapid. There was a natural desire to foster this recovery by creating a good psychological atmosphere.

In the case of Nazi Germany, the result was that the popular press painted it in extreme and fantastic colours. The menace of the great military parades was lost in the breathless reports of their scale and excitement. The stage-management of the Nuremberg *Parteitag* seemed more interesting than the speeches made at it. When a speech was reported, it was given crisis headlines: but the crises rarely seemed to develop, and when they did, every effort was made to underplay them. None of the popular papers, except the *Daily Mail,* actually supported or condoned Nazi Germany, but they were similarly reluctant to exacerbate international affairs by adopting a hard line towards it. Both financially and intellectually it was unwise or impossible for the British Press to adopt a strongly critical line towards Nazi Germany: the readers did not want to read it, and the intellectuals did not want to write it.

Besides, there was no lack of prospective enemies. France was fading fast as the villain of Europe by 1936, mainly because its essential weakness was becoming clear and known. But there were Italy, Nationalist Spain, and Japan, to occupy the Left, and Soviet Russia and Republican Spain to trouble the Right. For all the quirks and barbarisms of Nazi Germany, the regime had produced some undeniably beneficial results, including the abolition of unemployment. And unlike Mussolini, who had invaded Abyssinia and was stirring up trouble for Britain in North Africa and the Mediterranean, or Japan which had invaded China and threatened Singapore, or Soviet Russia whose revolutionary finger seemed to be in every pie—unlike these troublesome powers, Hitler's was a stable Government based upon an obvious popular mandate and seemingly interested only in internal reform and equality of international status for Germany.

British newspapers and journalists also played an active role in the events they reported and in shaping public attitudes and reaction towards them. The 1930s were the age of the foreign correspondent. Partly because some of them showed considerable initiative which paid off in scoops or good coverage for their papers, and partly because they provided a way of personalizing great world events for British readers, the extra-special correspondent or commentator became a necessity for every popular paper; some, through their autobiographies, became the veritable ideological James Bonds of their time. The foreign correspondent became a knowledgeable, romantic, and ultimately reassuring figure. That many of these correspondents had a case to plead must not be overlooked; their pleading, reinforced during the War, which seemed to prove them right, still bears fruit today in the school of 'new revisionists' as Professor Beloff has called it. As a writer in *The Round Table* has stated, the main theses of these revisionists date back to before the outbreak of the Second War:

They originated with that brilliant school of radical foreign correspondents, mainly British and American, which dominated the international press between the wars—Dorothy Thompson, William Shirer (whose new, massive reiteration of his views of these days tops the best-seller lists of the U.S.A.), Christopher Dawson, Douglas Reed, G. E. R. Gedye, G. L. Steer, Sefton Delmer and many others were plugging the theory of the 'evitable war' from the early 1930s onwards. After the outbreak of the war they were followed by the brilliant pamphlets of Michael Foot and Simon Haxey, *Guilty Men*, and *Your M.P.*, to name only the two most successful of the series put out under the Gollancz imprint. The views inspiring the group were radical and socialist, New Deal in America, Popular Front in Europe. To them what was at issue was a civil war of European dimensions between democracy and totalitarianism—and this has been the outlook and the ideological framework occupied by all but a handful, radical conservatives of the right, of their successors.[2]

The Europe of these journalists, centred either on Moscow or Geneva or both, never had any real existence in fact; for all

---

[2] 'Appeasement Reconsidered', *The Round Table*, liii. 212 (Sept. 1963), p. 359. The author is D. C. Watt. [Other outstanding examples are H. R. Knickerbocker and Edgar Mowrer. Mowrer's book, *Germany Puts the Clock Back*, which was issued as a Penguin Special in 1937, had caused his expulsion from Germany in 1933. Sefton Delmer really should not be included in the list as a British radical of the kind described.

its relevance to the fragmented and disillusioned Europe of the late 1930s, they might as well have dated their dispatches 'Camelot' as 'Geneva'. With the increasing ideological gap over Nazi Germany as the 1930s progressed, difficulties spread throughout the communications media. Great concern arose, some of it reaching the floor of the House of Commons, over political censorship of cinema newsreels; conflicts flared up which had been long latent between radical correspondents and conservative London offices, or within editorial offices between radical editors and conservative commercial or advertising directors.

In the cases—notably *The Times*, the *Daily Telegraph*, and the *Morning Post*—where the sympathies of some of their outstanding foreign correspondents were not at all those of the newspapers they served, conflict was always possible and most often avoided by a tacit mutual restraint; after the Anschluss such restraint became increasingly difficult on both sides.

In some respects the basic problem lay in a conflict of romantics: the romantics of the Left, who went to Spain to report and stayed to fight, or who counselled the *Illegalen* parties after the Austrian civil war, or who condemned at every turn the excesses and brutality of the Nazi regime, were matched by a smaller group of romantics of the Right who glorified the civilizing mission of the British Empire, upheld the value of the *status quo*, and saw the greatest threat Western Civilization had ever faced—literally anti-Christ—in Soviet Russia.

It is one of the great ironies of the period, and perhaps the major conclusion of this study, that appeasement was in fact the product of a crisis of the liberal conscience. So much print— and newsprint—has been devoted to painting the distinction between the far-sighted liberals of the Left who understood the real nature of the Nazi menace from the very beginning, and the reactionary conservatives of the Right who welcomed Hitler not only for himself alone but also for the check he promised to deliver to Bolshevist Russia. This view, though variously assaulted, has not yet been laid low; it is hoped that this study will contribute to its timely demise.

With one or two minor exceptions, the journalists and editors of the British Press between the wars were men who thought of themselves as liberals in the broadest sense of the term: the paradox is that they were all right, or very nearly right, in so thinking. Understanding of this seeming paradox is fundamental to any proper understanding of the policy and psychology of appeasement of Germany; it is lack of such understanding which has spoiled most of our historical and critical appreciations of this period to the present day.

It was the seeming vindication of one side with the coming of war in 1939 which gave easy rise to the forgetting—and, in some cases, the deliberate obfuscation—of the common ground shared by appeasers and anti-appeasers of Germany. The war seemed to prove beyond doubt or cavil that appeasement had been a short-sighted policy from the outset; the nature of political controversy was further confounded by the exigencies of the war. It was now necessary to understand how it came about that the cream of the upper classes of Britain had gradually given way over a period of twenty years until now Britain was fighting another war with Germany in which it seemed that Germany might well win. But in fact, the Guilty Men of the Victory Book Club were really only the polemical villians of the Left Book Club a year—and a new world war—later.

The common experience of all the journalists and editors of the period was the Great War. The carnage and disillusion of the war to end wars worked upon the journalists as much as it did on the poets and the politicians. All were involved in it: fighting it, reporting it, directing it. It was a common experience of many of those who were the outstanding foreign correspondents of the 1930s to have gone first to Europe to fight. It was a radicalizing experience, after demobilization, to stay behind and see the depraved shambles of a continent in ruins. This was the period in which the only forces which seemed positive, humane, and relevant to the construction of decent life in Europe were the forces of the Left. This was the period in which many British journalists made those sympathetic contacts with Social Democrats and Social Revolutionaries and communists which, a dozen years later, led to their proscription by the Nazis and in some cases by their London editors as well. The central revelation for these correspondents was that the working class must never again allow itself to be exploited by the international financiers and arms profiteers.

But the war had, after all, been genuinely classless—indeed it had, if anything, told more heavily upon the upper classes. The genuine liberal legacy of the war was the universal determination that it must never happen again; and the realization that care and vigilance would have to be exerted to avoid such a repetition.

By an early date, then, both the Left and the Right had come to a shared abhorrence of war and a determination that it must never again be allowed to happen. Kingsley Martin has described the situation:

Some ten million men had been killed in the war, in addition to thirty-six million casualties. The first, and in many ways the best, of the anti-war books was C. E. Montague's *Disenchantment*,[3] published as early as 1924, but most of the books which profoundly affected the mind of the British public by reviving unspoken memories of the horror of the trenches appeared between 1926 and 1930. The oath of 'Never Again' which we swore at a thousand meetings was not a Labour aberration nor the soft notion of pacifists and pro-Germans. Almost everyone, Conservatives, Liberals and Labour alike, regarded the French notion of keeping Germany permanently as a second-class power as absurd, and agreed that the Versailles Treaty must be revised in Germany's favour.[4]

It was this spirit of 'Never Again' which informed the Oxford Union Debate, the East Fulham by-election (which so impressed Baldwin that he withheld information about Germany's rearmament from Parliament), and the Peace Ballot. Ironically it was the Chancellor of the Exchequer Neville Chamberlain who, in a speech at Kelso in September 1935, heralded the major increase in his defence estimates of March 1936. As long as Hitler retained at least the spurious pretext of Versailles-based grievances no one could seriously propose a war to stop him; even after he had taken Czechoslovakia, the horror of war counselled every attempt to reach a peaceful solution.

In every crisis in these years but the last we shall see that it was ultimately the dread of unleashing the dogs of war which

---

[3] Montague was C. P. Scott's son-in-law, and a leader-writer on the *Manchester Guardian* in the 1930s.   [4] Martin, *Editor*, pp. 22–3.

kept many papers from crying havoc at some earlier time. W. W. Hadley, Editor of the *Sunday Times*, summed up Press opinion at the time of Munich. After quoting relevant sections from leaders in fifty papers, Hadley concluded that:

It will be seen that these representative journals were all but unanimous in their expression of the warmest gratitude to the Government, and especially to the Prime Minister, for the maintenance of peace. In not one of them was it suggested that in the discussion with Germany about Czechoslovakia any issues were raised which justified war. In some stress was laid on the high price paid for peace and the sacrifices imposed on the Czechs; but even in the journals of the Left there was (with one exception) no anticipation of the sweeping attacks on the Government which developed in the bitter party warfare that followed. There was every reason to believe that the judgements on Munich from which we now quote faithfully represented public opinion.[5]

Although the revulsion against war was not confined to the working class or those of the political Left, its bases were somewhat different for those of the Right: these were the men who had seen the flower of their generation fall in the trenches of the Western Front and in the heat and sick squalor of the East. These were the men who read *Die Grosse Politik* and knew that for all the highfalutin rhetoric, the war had been a ghastly mistake which Europe blundered into over a weekend in August 1914. Some of these men even accompanied the British delegation to the Versailles Conference and had there to watch while blind inefficiency, sheer jobbery, and, perhaps most frustrating of all, the best of misguided good intentions, established a peace system which could only serve to draw ruin in its wake. These were the people who read Keynes's polemic *The Economic Consequences of the Peace* when it first appeared after Keynes returned from Versailles in 1921—and if they had begun to lose their fervour for the Keynesian gospel, they were reconfirmed by Harold Nicolson's memoir *Peacemaking 1919* which first appeared in 1933, the year Hitler came to power.

This common revulsion against war had, for the Left, corollaries of the greatest importance, particularly in its

---

[5] Hadley, *Munich: Before and After*, Ch. XIV, 'Judgement of the Press', p. 93 ff.

attitudes towards armaments. Tied to Geneva, collective security, and opposition to armaments as they were, the newspapers of the Left were in the curious position of reversing Theodore Roosevelt's dictum: they wanted Britain to speak loudly but carry a small stick. The newspapers of the Right, on the other hand, felt that every attempt should be made for moderation, and for cordial relations with all nations; Geoffrey Dawson, the Editor of *The Times*, wrote to a friend, 'I always hate using forcible language when I know that it will not be followed by forcible action.'[6]

It is this fact which underlines the difficulty of making 'judgements' against any of the British newspapers of the 1930s, because in terms of Nazi Germany it was precisely those papers which proved most blind over, obtuse about, or sympathetic towards Hitler's regime, which pursued the strongest line over the armaments which would be needed to fight if the others' dire predictions proved correct.

On the whole, only Voigt of the *Manchester Guardian* and the Conservative press can be said to have seen the need for armaments to protect Britain's interests and security. Voigt wrote to his Editor in February 1936: 'If we were not rearming, Germany would certainly prepare to attack France, leaving her eastern plans until later on. If war is averted at all, it will be British rearmament that will have done it.'[7] This remained a preoccupation of Voigt's—although he did not mention it very much in his diplomatic correspondence in the paper. As with the Conservative press, Voigt's view of Britain's vital interests allowed him to tolerate a multitude of sins as long as no such interests were surrendered and sufficient strength was maintained to defend whichever of them might be challenged. The day after the Anglo-French proposals were sent to Prague, 19 September 1938, he noted in his diary: 'We have chosen a shameful peace and shall have a terrible war. If only we would learn the lesson and pull ourselves together, put our industries on a war-basis and conscribe men and money. All would not be lost then. But we won't do it, we won't! Disaster is coming, hastened on by ourselves.' And on 30 September 1938, he noted, 'Today they march in. Poor

---

[6] Dawson to Brand, 17 Feb. 1938, *The Times* archives.
[7] Voigt to Crozier, 5 Feb. 1936, *Manchester Guardian* archives.

Czechoslovakia! I wouldn't mind so much if I thought we would learn the lesson—and arm, arm, arm!'[8]

Finally after Munich the *Manchester Guardian* itself was moved to a negative conviction of the necessity for armaments—'The real explanation is that, as the world, under the disastrous guidance of the Governments that had to surrender at Munich, has reverted to the system under which justice is at the mercy of power, no Government can discharge its duty or protect its interests unless its diplomacy has behind it material strength and confidence'[9]—but nothing further was done to implement this realization.

The *News Chronicle*, committed to collective security and the League of Nations, never backed up its insight into the Nazi regime by a call for British armaments. Indeed, as late as 15 March 1938, in the wake of the Anschluss, the *News Chronicle* stated in a leading article that 'Rearmament alone is no sort of answer to the grim future that faces us. Even when we have rearmed to the teeth, we cannot defend the British Empire against a league of plundering dictators. The rule of international law and decency is the most potent weapon, the only ultimately effective weapon, in the British armoury.'[10]

The *Morning Post* began a defence campaign in January 1936 with a leading article and headline story on 'what the country is not told' about the deplorable state of British arms.[11] And the *Daily Mail*, for all its admiration of Hitler's Germany, stated consistently and with such immediacy and clarity as only the *Daily Mail* could summon, that Britain must rearm, especially in the air. It initiated a campaign (ironically on the day of the reoccupation of the Rhineland), in the form of a money-prize contest for readers' ideas on increasing the number of military volunteers. 'It is madness', a leader in the *Daily Mail* stated in July 1936, 'for Great Britain to remain unarmed when Germany and Italy are armed to the teeth and able at any moment to attack our vital interests.'[12] Ward

---

[8] Quotations from the unpublished diary of F. A. Voigt, by kind permission of Mrs. Voigt.   [9] *Manchester Guardian*, 29 Oct. 1938, 1st Leader, p. 12.

[10] *News Chronicle*, 15 Mar. 1938, 1st Leader, p. 10.

[11] *Morning Post*, 16 Jan. 1936, 1st Leader, p. 10, and art., p. 11.

[12] *Daily Mail*, 7 July 1936, 1st Leader, p. 10. See also *Daily Mail*, 8 July 1936, Dipl. Corr., p. 12.

Price coined the best motto for Anglo-German relations:
'Negotiate—but arm.'[13]

The Times's attitude towards armaments was reasoned and
forthright. In June 1936 a leading article stated that

. . . the final contribution we can make to an organized peace
is the speediest possible completion of our defence arrangements,
and this lies wholly within our own jurisdiction. . . . It remains
urgently true that British leadership must have material backing
and that, in present circumstances, an adequate level of British
armament is paradoxically indispensable if the advance to agreement and disarmament is to be resumed.[14]

The question of belief in Germany's sincerity—held up against
The Times by its critics—was seen to be irrelevant in this case;
a leader in July 1936 explained that

In the quest for this cooperation there is no need to profess either
trust or distrust of Germany's sincerity—and least of all to abate
for a moment the resolute restoration of British armaments to an
effective level. Every one is agreed in these days that British foreign
policy must have the backing of far greater strength to enforce it.
We cannot afford to depend for our existence upon the views of this
or that Minister about German intentions, and all that need be
said on that point here is that professed distrust can only breed
distrust and is taken for a sign of weakness.[15]

This had been summed up in a leader on 3 April: 'British
rearmament is more necessary than ever if Germany is insincere, and by no means unwelcome to her if she is not.
Limitation of armaments, when it comes, must be a collective
operation and the index of collective security.'[16]

If the revulsion against war created the psychological situation in which another war was unthinkable, the discrediting
of the Treaty of Versailles made it virtually certain that no war
would be fought against a Germany trying to revise that Treaty.
As late as 1938, *The Times* stated that German complaints
against the Treaty of Versailles were 'still the most universally
potent force in modern Germany'.[17] If the *Daily Mail* and the

---

[13] *Daily Mail*, 16 June 1936, ed. art. by Ward Price, p. 12.
[14] *The Times*, 4 June 1936, 1st Leader, p. 13.
[15] *The Times*, 6 July 1936, 1st Leader, p. 15.
[16] *The Times*, 3 Apr. 1936, 1st Leader, p. 17.
[17] *The Times*, 3 Oct. 1938, ed. art. by a Corr., p. 13.

Observer were only the most outspoken critics in the British Press of the Treaty and its consequences for Britain and Europe, supporters were nowhere to be found. Lloyd George's *The Truth About The Peace Treaties*, which gave a further fillip to criticism at a critical time, was published in October 1938, and serialized in the *Daily Telegraph*. The *Manchester Guardian* asserted, in a leading article noting publication of this book, that the Treaty of Versailles had been wrong, especially in its economic provisions.[18] The *Daily Herald* bluntly affirmed in November 1937 that no Treaty was sacrosanct or could last forever, especially the Treaty of Versailles.[19]

Desire for revision of Versailles was no new phenomenon. As Barrington-Ward, the Deputy Editor of *The Times*, wrote to the Master of Balliol:

May I add two things more at the risk of seeming egotistical? I am one of those who campaigned against the Treaty of Versailles from February 1919 onwards. No reasoning that has yet come my way can convince me that what was inexpedient and immoral then—in Czechoslovakia and elsewhere—has suddenly become both moral and expedient merely because we have brought the Nazis to power in Germany. My last credential is that in those same years I was also doing my humble best to resist the foolish plan of a *cordon sanitaire* round Russia and to secure the recognition of the Soviet.[20]

By the middle of the 1930s, the Treaty of Versailles itself was a dead letter for the British Press: criticism was so widespread and so well accepted that it was simply taken for granted. This criticism informed current judgements, however, on subjects like France (as the villain of the Versailles system), Czechoslovakia (as its most splendid work or disastrous pomp, depending upon one's point of view), Austria (whose union with Germany was forbidden by the Treaty of St. Germain), the League of Nations (as its futile attempt to perpetuate and ensure the values which were a sham in the Treaty itself), and most basically on the futility of war (which after years of carnage had only managed to produce this tawdry document).

---

[18] *Manchester Guardian*, 17 Oct. 1938, 1st Leader, p. 8. The point being made was that Munich had not corrected the injustices of Versailles but had only established the rule of force in Europe.

[19] *Daily Herald*, 25 Nov. 1937, Leader, p. 10.

[20] Barrington-Ward to the Master of Balliol, 7 Oct. 1938, *The Times* archives.

Largely on the basis of Keynes's indictment, opinion in the 1920s and early 1930s held France responsible for the instability and unrest in Europe. Clemenceau had used his white gloves to hide his sleight-of-hand techniques which had succeeded at Versailles in establishing French hegemony on the Continent. Instead of enshrining the noble principles for which the war had been fought, France turned the Treaty of Versailles into a gambit in the traditional Franco-German rivalry. Regardless of the consequences for the future, France had done everything possible to hobble Germany by reparations and then to surround her with a ring of hostile states.

Anti-French feeling reached a peak when French troops used a technicality about non-payment of reparations to occupy the Ruhr in January 1923; of the British Press, only the anti-German *Morning Post* supported this action. As late as 1936 the *Manchester Guardian* considered that at Locarno France had cleverly secured promises from Britain which were one-sided and not at all in Britain's interests.[21] Large residues of this ill-feeling still remained at the time of the Franco-Soviet Pact in 1935–6.

G. E. R. Gedye, of the *Daily Telegraph*, affords a good example of the kind of thinking about France widespread after the Great War. The burden of his reporting from 1923 until 1933 was that France was the conscious and underhand cause of European instability. His book, *Heirs to the Habsburgs*, published in 1932, surveyed post-Versailles Europe and concluded that the inheritance was arranged not according purely to the principle either of nationality or of economic necessity, but rather to enable France to pursue her great aim of hemming in Germany by a ring of neighbours who were to be made as hostile to her as possible.[22] As early as 1930 he had written that 'the criminal follies of Poincaré-imperialism' during the occupation of the Ruhr and the attempted establishment of a dummy separatist Republic had caused 'a desperate nation to raise an obscure fanatic like Adolf Hitler to the threshold of a Fascist dictatorship under the device of "force to meet force" '.[23]

---

[21] *Manchester Guardian*, 1 Feb. 1936, 1st Leader, p. 12.

[22] Gedye, *Heirs to the Habsburgs*, p. 276.

[23] See Gedye, *Fallen Bastions*, p. 158. After 1933, as we shall see, Germany replaced France as Gedye's *bête noire*.

French perfidy was seen as the reason for the spread of financial crisis in Europe after the failure of the *Kredit-Anstalt*, and for the failure of the proposed Austro-German Customs Union three months earlier. The prevalent attitude in Britain in February 1935, as W. P. Crozier, the Editor of the *Manchester Guardian* saw it, was clear: 'I do not know whether any reference has been made in the Paris press to one point which seems to me important,' he wrote, 'and that is that disapproval of the carping criticisms in the French press was expressed equally in *The Times*, the *News Chronicle*, and the *Manchester Guardian*.'[24] A year later, after the Rhineland coup, Crozier restrained Voigt's enthusiasm by reaffirming that the paper adopted a 'questioning line' towards the Anglo-French alliance, and the wisdom of tying Britain so irrevocably to France.[25]

Conservative circles in Britain watched as the insult of the *Front populaire* was added to the injury of the Franco-Soviet Pact which had been concluded in May 1935 but awaited ratification in France until February 1936 when Hitler used it as his pretext for reoccupying the demilitarized zone. Ebbutt, *The Times* Berlin Correspondent, reported German feeling thus:

The hostility to the proposed Pact . . . is compounded of indignation, fear and genuine regret that France, by linking herself with an Eastern and a Communist State, is making an understanding in Western Europe more difficult. . . . All these arguments might be summed up in a French phrase: *La Russie, voilà l'ennemi*. And by this is meant not only the enemy of Germany, but of all European civilization. So—today—says the Germany of Herr Hitler.[26]

It is important to remember that in 1936 and 1937 every British newspaper extended at least some credence to Hitler's sincerity in believing in the basic tenets of Nazism: the grievances against Versailles, the anti-Bolshevism, and the Aryan principle. Everything seemed to point to the incompatibility of Nazism and Communism—only philosophers like Voigt could understand the essential similarities. There was, further, the tendency to see Hitler as either totally insane and

---

[24] Crozier to Werth, 19 Feb. 1935, *Manchester Guardian* archives.
[25] Crozier to Voigt, 25 Mar. 1936, *Manchester Guardian* archives.
[26] *The Times*, 22 Feb. 1936, Berlin Corr., p. 11. See also *The Times*, 12 Feb. 1936, Berlin Corr., p. 14.

irresponsible over the Bolshevik and Jewish questions, or to see him as simply fitting the traditional Austrian pro-Polish as opposed to the Prussian pro-Russian syndrome.[27]

The Times, particularly, accepted Hitler's protestations on this point. 'No Englishman in German shoes would consent to accept the commitments of a new treaty while the Franco-Soviet Pact and the Russian pact with Czechoslovakia were still in full force. They are incompatible with a full political settlement.' Indeed, even if Russia were governed otherwise, 'the pacts would still sound the same alarum in the German mind.'[28] The Pact had only been ratified, according to *The Times*, when, 'thanks admittedly to M. Barthou', Germany had

taken the bit between her teeth and had begun to head for unknown objectives with unlimited rearmament. For all that, it was regarded by at least half of France with lukewarmness or positive antipathy. Britain viewed it as, at best, a confession of international failure which a successful conference for the re-establishment of security would certainly render nugatory and possibly expunge.[29]

After 1936, as France's weakness became clearer, the tendency in the British Press as in the British Government was to ignore French opinion or to take it for granted. In the meantime, however, attitudes towards France had smoothed Hitler's way and no small part of many of the resentments of Czechoslovakia was that it had been the linchpin of the French encirclement system in Eastern Europe.

Several factors influenced the British Press in its treatment of Austria. The Conservative press saw the ultimate confirmation of Hitler's argument that Austria was German in the Austrian Chancellor Schuschnigg's acceptance of it. The first paragraphs of *Mein Kampf* proclaimed the necessity, the inevitability, of Austria's inclusion in, or return to, the Reich, and opinion was thus conditioned for it.[30]

[27] Many found reinforcement of this view in their reading of *Mein Kampf*.
[28] *The Times*, 28 Jan. 1938, 1st Leader, p. 15.
[29] *The Times*, 21 Dec. 1936, 1st Leader, p. 13.
[30] See *Manchester Guardian*, 15 Feb. 1938, Dipl. Corr., p. 6. Voigt wrote that 'What Hitler wrote in *Mein Kampf* on the subject of Austria is German foreign policy today'.

The Liberal and Labour press had little sympathy for the Austrian dictatorship which had smashed the Socialists in the brief but bloody civil war of Februrary 1934. Even as the real nature of the German threat became known, it required some tortuous reasoning before support could be put behind Schuschnigg. In the wake of the Anschluss the *Daily Herald* identified the issue:

It is true enough that the Austrian regime was no democracy. It was Fascist. It was built on the ruins of bombarded Vienna, and on the suppression of all political and industrial freedom.

The last moment concessions were no conversion, but a desperate attempt at self-preservation. The Schuschnigg of 1938 is still the Schuschnigg who was Dollfuss' lieutenant in the bloody days of 1934 that established Fascism.[31]

When it was announced after the Anschluss that Schuschnigg would be brought to trial, the *News Chronicle* wrote that 'Though Dr. von Schuschnigg was himself a dictator and had been guilty of repression, the world must give him full credit for high qualities.'[32]

For the British Press as a whole, however, there were four overruling considerations. First, the separation of Austria and Germany was generally considered to be among the most obvious and foolish mistakes of the Versailles system. Many felt that revision would have come about long before except for French obstructionism, especially over the proposed Austro-German Customs Union in March 1931. The distinction was made between pre- and post-1933 Germany but it did little to abate the force of the basic argument, which, in the event, the general enthusiasm throughout Austria for the Anschluss would support. There was, second, just this fear that were the Western democracies (with or without Italy) to go to Austria's aid, they might find half the Austrian nation fighting for Germany.[33]

Third, Austria was considered to be under Italy's protection. From July 1934 when Mussolini moved troops to the Brenner Pass, until the Stresa Conference in April 1935, it was expected that Italy would prevent the expansion of

[31] *Daily Herald*, 12 Mar. 1938, Leader, p. 10.
[32] *News Chronicle*, 28 Mar. 1938, 1st Leader, p. 10.
[33] See *The Times*, 21 Feb. 1938, 3rd Leader, p. 15.

German power to her own frontiers, at the expense of a friendly State which was also a signatory of the Rome Protocols. When it became clear that Mussolini had disinterested himself in Austria's fate (he had done this long before Schuschnigg precipitated the crisis by announcing the plebiscite), columns were filled in bitterness at what was considered to be Mussolini's perfidy. *Quid pro quo* became the catchphrase, and everyone speculated as to what Mussolini had been given or promised to hold his hand.

Whether Mussolini's inaction caused genuine surprise or was seized upon as a welcome excuse—or both—the fourth consideration was the most important: it was that, as in March 1936 and September 1938, there must not be a war. No reason whatever would justify the unleashing of a war upon Europe. The question of going to Austria's support had thus been settled in the British Press, on the basis of its attitudes towards the Versailles system, three weeks before the crisis over the Anschluss began and before Mussolini refused to answer his telephone. It was the combination of all these factors which led Voigt to his perceptive and resigned judgement in June 1937 that 'I do not think Germany will begin on Czechoslovakia (the conquest of that country would take months) but on Austria.'[34]

Czechoslovakia was an entirely different case. As Voigt wrote to Crozier in November 1937, 'The strength of Germany is tremendous, but Poland, Yugoslavia, Rumania, Hungary and Austria are like a rotten apple with one hard pip, Czechoslovakia. Germany has only to push east and south-east and she goes through mush.'[35] By the mid-1930s Czechoslovakia was obviously the most successful but clearly the most controversial part of the Versailles system. Depending upon the political complexion of the paper, Czechoslovakia was viewed as democracy's bastion in Central Europe or as an indefensible amalgamation of races under Czech domination in patent contravention of the principle of self-determination.

As Geoffrey Dawson wrote to a friend shortly after Munich,

---

[34] Voigt to Crozier, 19 June 1937, *Manchester Guardian* archives.
[35] Voigt to Crozier, 16 Nov. 1937, *Manchester Guardian* archives.

'I have the notes now of my talk with Beneš in 1920 when I ventured humbly to press upon him the view that the Anschluss[36] was less of a peril to Czechoslovakia than the denial of it.'[37] The merit of this case was such that despite their anti-Nazism, both Voigt and the *Manchester Guardian* had to allow that Britain should exert sufficient pressure upon Prague to ensure that if Germany genuinely wanted a settlement, one could be reached without war.[38] Crozier wrote to Voigt in July 1938:

I don't myself object, and I have never objected, to the British Government advising the Czechs to give way to the utmost degree that they can without endangering their existence. They ought to do so, not only because of the danger of a European war but because in my opinion the Sudeten Germans have a moral claim to certain self-governing powers which we should certainly admit if Czechoslovakia were not, politically and strategically, what she is. But the British Government should not push Czechoslovakia to a point where the Germans can get all they want by shaking Czechoslovakia to pieces from within.[39]

Indeed, the *Manchester Guardian*'s sole objection to the fulfilling of the German demands against Czechoslovakia was on strategic grounds.

So weighty an opinion as Winston Churchill's was expressed in the *Daily Telegraph* that 'Without the championship of armed Germany, Sudeten wrongs might never have been redressed.'[40] *The Times* pointed out that 'Between 1919 and 1923 there was no self-respecting Liberal and Labour publicist or politician who did not, like most other Englishmen, condemn as futile and even as immoral the policy upon which the composite Czechoslovakia was founded.'[41] Even Churchill, 'that formidable critic', as another leader in *The Times* pointed out, had written in *The World Crisis* about the Versailles settlement of Czechoslovakia that 'to exclude the German-speaking population was deeply and perhaps fatally to weaken the new

[36] In this context Dawson was referring to the annexation of the Sudetenland by Germany.   [37] Dawson to Nigel Law, 4 Oct. 1938, *The Times* archives.
[38] *Manchester Guardian*, 9 May 1938, Dipl. Corr., p. 14. See also *Manchester Guardian*, 10 May 1938, ed. art. by a Corr., p. 11.
[39] Crozier to Voigt, 26 July 1938, *Manchester Guardian* archives.
[40] *Daily Telegraph*, 23 June 1938, ed. art. by Winston Churchill, p. 16.
[41] *The Times*, 4 Oct. 1938, 1st Leader, p. 15.

State; to include them was to affront the principle of Self-Determination.'[42]

J. L. Garvin, the Editor of the *Observer*, was the British Press's most virulent Czechophobe; he felt that any defence of Czechoslovakia would be 'a war of foredoomed futility in the vain attempt to preserve a state of things which never ought to have been created by the purblind and botching statecraft of Versailles in 1919. The result is not a national unit, such as the soap-box warriors suggest, but a medley ruled by a minority.'[43] 'Scrutator' pursued a Garvinian line in the *Sunday Times*:

> But we have no alliance with Czechoslovakia, no interest of our own to serve except the remote contingency that later if Germany won and turned to invade France we might be fighting alone on her side without Eastern allies. For both England and France participation in a war for the defence of Czechoslovakia would be a preventive war; but with this important difference, that whereas France, rightly or wrongly, has persuaded herself that her interests are continental, ours quite definitely are not.[44]

Lord Rothermere's correspondence with Wickham Steed in the summer of 1938, printed in the *News Chronicle*, is a compendium of the numerous kinds of attitudes we have been considering, as brought to bear upon Czechoslovakia.

> From the day Czechoslovakia came into existence it has opposed the German, Hungarian, Slovak and Polish minorities. It has done so without protest, because the League of Nations, until lately, was entirely controlled by France and her allies, including Czechoslovakia.
> I am afraid that you are one of those journalistic Bourbons of whom there are many. You seem to have forgotten nothing and learned nothing. You seem to think that 1938 is still 1914. You do not seem to know that today Great Britain, instead of being largely invulnerable as she was in 1914, is, owing to the development of aircraft, the most vulnerable country in Europe.
> If you and your friends had your way, you might provoke a war infinitely more disastrous than the Great War of 1914.
> I suppose you do know, but I should like to impress it upon you, that the day Great Britain goes to war in pursuit of some aim or

---

[42] Quoted in *The Times*, 23 Sept. 1938, 1st Leader, p. 13.

[43] *Observer*, 6 Mar. 1938, Garvin, p. 16. See also *Observer*, 20 Mar. 1938, Garvin, p. 14 and 27 Mar. 1938, F. Yeats-Brown, p. 21.

[44] *Sunday Times*, 20 Mar. 1938, Scrutator, p. 16.

design in Central Europe two or three of our most important Dominions will declare their neutrality and, by doing so, will bring an immediate end to the British Empire.[45]

The *Observer* and the *Daily Mail* shared the conviction that Czechoslovakia had become a six hundred mile long corridor through which Soviet Russia could strike at Germany. In 1936 Garvin stated that 'The question then, for us, is whether we are to have another Anglo-German War for the sake of Soviet Russia or any interest in Eastern Europe. The answer undoubtedly is "No".'[46] Two years later, in the week before Munich, the opinion had not changed: 'At present Czechoslovakia is a corridor for Russia against Germany.'[47] Rothermere affirmed in July 1938 that 'If Czechoslovakia becomes involved in war, the British nation will say to the Prime Minister with one voice: "Keep out of it".'[48]

Not even Czechoslovakia's most ardent defenders could deny that the nation was in fact an essentially unhomogeneous union of different and differing ethnic, linguistic, and political minorities which the Czechs had come to dominate. The ultimate application of the principle of self-determination—a plebiscite—was thus precluded in Czechoslovakia's case; for it could not be denied that it would mean the end of Czechoslovakia. Not only would the Sudetens overwhelmingly vote to go to Germany, but other minorities could then demand the same rights—the Poles, Hungarians and Ukrainians as well as the Slovaks—and dissolution would be the result.

From the point of view of British public opinion, Poland was the least attractive of the succession States. Pilsudski's dictatorship, which had been imposed following his coup in 1926, was not very much to the taste of conservatives in Great Britain, and was utterly abhorrent to British liberals. After 1933 the dictatorship was carried on by the army clique which added anonymity to the repression. The Foreign Minister, Colonel Beck, had a not altogether undeserved reputation for being crafty or even shady. Poland's treatment

---

[45] Lord Rothermere to Wickham Steed, 3 Aug. 1938, printed in *News Chronicle*, 16 Aug. 1938, p. 7.   [46] *Observer*, 1 Nov. 1936, Garvin, p. 20.
[47] *Observer*, 18 Sept. 1938, Garvin, p. 14.
[48] *Daily Mail*, 18 July 1938, ed. art. by Rothermere, p. 10.

of her minorities was appalling, especially of the Jews, who were forced into the most degrading ghettoes. As Crozier wrote to Voigt in 1936, 'I don't see why, if we trounce the Germans for their abominable behaviour, the Poles should be allowed to get away with it.'[49]

Poland's composition at Versailles had given over large numbers of Russians, Ukrainians, and Germans to Polish rule which was oppressive. The Polish Corridor, separating the Reich from East Prussia, and admittedly inhabited by a German majority, and Danzig, clearly a German city and virtually Nazi since 1935, were two of the strongest German claims against the Versailles system. The Poles, after twice suggesting preventive war against Germany in 1933 immediately Hitler came to power, had turned full circle and concluded the German-Polish ten-year Treaty of Friendship in January 1934, thus removing Poland from much Western strategic thinking until, after 1938, aggressive German revisionism seemed unlikely to stop short of Danzig or the Corridor.

From the various reactions to Poland generally, and especially to Britain's commitment to her in the Anglo-Polish Guarantee in 1939, it is very likely that had Hitler forced a settlement with Poland before the Prague coup, he would have met with little, and probably with no resistance from Britain or France. Indeed, had Beck informed the British or French Governments of the nature of Hitler's several approaches to him after Munich, and of his refusal to consider them, it is unlikely that the Guarantee would have been so precipitately extended. Hitler seemed willing, for the time being at any rate, to reach an amicable agreement with Poland, involving a corridor across the Corridor and union of Danzig with the Reich in return for special trade considerations for Poland in the city and port.

Poland's conduct at the time of Munich, its coveting of Czech territory, did little to raise it in the estimation of the British Press. The *Manchester Guardian* admitted the strategic difficulties involved in not offending Germany but still thought Poland should abandon 'the hostile attitude she has of late been taking up against the Czechs and to refrain from anything that might in the least help to bring disaster on all

⁴⁹ Crozier to Voigt, 16 Feb. 1936, *Manchester Guardain* archives.

Europe, herself included'.[50] After Munich Voigt was so exasperated at Polish conduct as to say that the Poles, if anything, were worse than the Germans.[51] It was Polish intransigence (quite understandable in many ways) against allowing Soviet troops rights of passage which frustrated the inclusion of Soviet Russia in a Peace Front after March 1939.

It is a measure of the extent to which British opinion changed after the occupation of Prague that despite all these facts, the unilateral guarantee was extended to Poland. When *The Times* ventured to say that the guarantee was not meant to preclude any German-Polish negotiations, the furore was enough to cause the Government to issue inspired denials through the *Daily Telegraph* and the *Sunday Times*.[52] Still, as Voigt wrote to Crozier in April 1939:

I am not at all happy about the Polish alliance. I admit that the elimination of Poland would tilt the balance of power against us in a most dangerous fashion. Nevertheless, I should have preferred a defensive policy in the west and an *offensive* policy in the Mediterranean. The Polish alliance condemns us to an offensive policy in the west—if we are attacked Poland will not, in my opinion, be able to do much except to immobilize a considerable number of German troops and aeroplanes. If Poland is attacked, we can only help her by a direct attack on Germany—and for that we are simply not prepared.[53]

Aside from attitudes towards individual countries or succession States, and even independent of feelings towards the Treaty of Versailles, there was a widespread feeling in the British Press that German predominance in Eastern and Central Europe was geographically and economically inevitable. Britain and the Western Powers would be quite powerless to hold back the waves of German economic and commercial expansion to the east. This was especially true now that old empires had been carved to pieces and old nations reconstituted with new boundaries; Germany's size and location as a natural market would act as a magnet for these new States lacking trade outlets and investment capital and experience.

---

[50] *Manchester Guardian*, 17 Aug. 1938, 2nd Leader, p. 8.
[51] *Manchester Guardian*, 19 Oct. 1938, Dipl. Corr., p. 9.
[52] See p. 278.
[53] Voigt to Crozier, 10 Apr. 1939, *Manchester Guardian* archives.

The Times expressed this feeling in a leading article on 4 March 1939:

In this country at any rate there is not the slightest desire to block the natural expansion of German influence, as such, whether in Europe or elsewhere. In so far as it implies the application of an innate capacity for organisation to the new problems of the post-War age, there is complete agreement that, economically at least, it should be given fullest scope. But it is bound to rouse opposition, which must in the long run be fatal to it, if it is for ever to be joined with a consuming desire for political domination and the suppression of racial and individual liberties. If the use that is made of great strength is to help others in a spirit of cooperative leadership, then its benefits may be general and permanent. It is when strength is used to coerce free peoples into uncongenial ways that it cannot hope to endure.[54]

Barrington-Ward had developed the corollary argument in a letter in December 1938:

Assume, as I do, that the better cause would triumph [if, as the Opposition seems to wish, a Franco-British-Soviet front fought Fascism] and leave out of account for the moment all the other consequences for civilization that a world war might be expected to have at the moment: what would we do with Germany at the end of such a war? Is it back to 1919 and then on again to 1938? Germany under any rulers will demand *Lebensraum* and, despite all the perversions of Nazi propaganda, the Germans are not to be safely or wisely denied their historic mission of organizing the trade and raising the standard of living of the backward agricultural peoples of eastern Europe. If they overplay their hand, if they try to convert economic leadership into political dominion, they will weaken and defeat themselves.[55]

Even so critical an observer as Voigt felt the weight of these arguments and consistently maintained that, while German domination was undesirable and Nazi domination dangerous, the one was always geographically inevitable, and the other politically unavoidable for the time being. 'That Germany will make herself master of central and eastern Europe seems to me as certain as anything in politics can be. ... We, by being strong, can keep war at arm's length and can,

[54] *The Times*, 4 Mar. 1939, 1st Leader, p. 12.
[55] Barrington-Ward to G. V. Ferguson, 13 Dec. 1938, *The Times* archives.

perhaps, mediate or exercise pressure in the new and very shifting situation that will develop out of the accomplished Anschluss.'[56]

The question of British interests was very relevant here. A line had to be drawn between those political and economic situations and events which Britain would not like to see happen and those which Britain would fight to prevent. As the stakes of modern warfare became ever greater, an even finer distinction—between interests and vital interests—had to be made. Writing to the Editor again in November 1937, Voigt concluded that Eastern and Central Europe were lost; Britain could turn the situation to her advantage if proper use were made of the time; 'for while Hitler is devouring his spoil, we may be able to gain sufficient time to make ourselves secure'.[57]

Although by 1937 the Webbs had removed the question mark from the end of the original title of their massive volume *Soviet Russia, A New Civilization*, many people remained doubtful. Censorship of the foreign press was extremely rigid in Russia; this was the reason why *The Times* refused to have a correspondent in Moscow. Far from being attributable to an anti-Soviet bias in Printing House Square, *The Times*'s position, as explained in a letter to the Foreign Office in 1932, was that:

The Times is and always has been perfectly ready to send a correspondent to Moscow, provided that:
1. The correspondence shall be free and unfettered;
2. We send a man of our own choosing;
3. The facilities open to us are equally open to the rest of the British Press.
. . . The Editor adds that in the last eight years he has been approached on this subject repeatedly, has always made the same conditions, and has never had any assurance of their fulfilment.[58]

As *The History of The Times* explains,[59] despite criticisms (especially from the *News Chronicle*) of both the practice and the correspondent's person, *The Times* was very likely better

[56] Voigt to Crozier, 19 June 1937, *Manchester Guardian* archives.
[57] Voigt to Crozier, 16 Nov. 1937, *Manchester Guardian* archives.
[58] Kennedy to W. Strang (F.O.), 1932, *The Times* archives.
[59] See *Hist Times*, iv. 911–12.

served by its Riga correspondent who kept up with all the
Soviet journals and papers and was able to send uncensored
reports, than those papers with correspondents actually in
Russia. *The Times* finally sent a correspondent to Moscow
along with the Anglo-French mission in the summer of 1939.[60]

Voigt's position on the Soviet Union combined both insight
and foresight:

> We ought, I think, to be critical of Russia. We need her and it
> isn't the time for polemics against her. But we must not, in my
> opinion, refer to her as a democracy—she is more tyrannically
> governed than even Germany is. The number of people done to
> death in Germany runs into thousands—in Russia into tens of
> thousands. Altogether, the terror in Russia is such that persons
> living even under the Nazi terror could hardly conceive of such a
> thing. But we cannot afford to be particular about our allies,
> though we must, I think, always remain particular about our
> friends.[61]

Soviet Russia was a basic issue between the Left and Right
in Britain. The Left, as mirrored in papers like the *Daily
Herald, News Chronicle,* and less so the *Manchester Guardian,*
tended to see it in far more ideological terms than the Right.
The Left generally looked eastward towards the glowing red
dawn of a new civilization arising from a noble—if occasionally somewhat rough—social experiment. Admiration was
not unbounded, however, and in some respects these attitudes
were more against those considered to be anti-Soviet than
actually pro-Soviet thesmelves.

The basis of the fictional 'Cliveden Set', invented by Claud
Cockburn in his weekly newsletter *The Week,* was that it was a
plutocratic conspiracy based upon property interests which
prompted giving Hitler a free hand in the east so as to secure
the west against his encroachment. Cockburn coined the
concept of the 'One-Way Gun': the west would be packed
with alliances and then Hitler set loose to do his worst—or
best, as one looked at it—in the east and south-east; with

---

[60] Even then, although the correspondent was allowed to visit Leningrad or
Odessa from Moscow whenever he wished, he was allowed no contact with sources
of political news other than a spokesman of the Soviet Foreign Office who was sometimes accompanied by a silent watchman from the secret police. See *Hist. Times,* ibid.

[61] Voigt to Crozier, 21 Mar. 1939, *Manchester Guardian* archives.

luck the packing would protect the west from any recoil. *The Times* in fact stood, and defended itself, against these charges. Not only *The Week* and the popular Left-wing papers, but even the *Manchester Guardian* occasionally slipped into this kind of Marxist analysis. A leading article in March 1938 placed blame for the Anschluss on the shoulders of the upper classes who had been moved from the traditional defence of British interests,

. . . for a new and blinding fear has come upon them, destroying their judgement and paralysing their will. This is the fear of Communism . . . in this case the fear of Communism has reconciled the English upper classes to the prospect of the complete loss of British power in the world, for Hitler and Mussolini stand in their eyes for the defence of property . . . this view of Hitler and Mussolini has reconciled the upper classes to the loss of power and prestige in the world and has allowed them to accept insults that in any other age would have provoked an explosion. . . . Men who will not protect British interests against the dictators are in no mood to protect the liberty of Europe. Indeed, the sympathies that draw them to Hitler and Mussolini determine their whole conception of policy. Somebody, they argue, must give order and stability to Europe, and who will do it better than these strong men with their hatred of Communism? Moreover, if we are polite to them, they will leave us alone, and we can settle down to a quiet life on our own estates.[62]

The Right tended to be less ideological in this respect and to favour detachment from all systems. As Barrington-Ward wrote to Dawson on 26 August 1936,

The German line against the Franco-Soviet Pact and 'encirclement' is obviously going to be the appeal to anti-Communism generally and an effort to form *blocs* accordingly. We shall clearly have to avoid countenancing either the Franco-Soviet Pact or the anti-Communist stunt. I wish it were possible to get the French to trade their unhappy Pact for, say, an arms limitation agreement; but this is a little distant and chimerical at the moment.[63]

The *Morning Post* was violently anti-Soviet, as were the *Daily Mail* and the *Observer*. Lord Rothermere was very near to being unbalanced on the issue of communism, and

---

[62] *Manchester Guardian*, 21 Mar. 1938, 1st Leader, p. 8.
[63] Barrington-Ward to Dawson, 26 Aug. 1936, *The Times* archives.

constantly importuned Ward Price to write articles like that of 21 September 1936 in which he stated that Bolshevism was a greater threat to the British Empire than National Socialism, and said that if Hitler did not exist, 'all Western Europe might soon be clamouring for such a champion'.[64] Garvin, in the *Observer*, was concerned lest Russia use Britain to gather Soviet chestnuts from European fires: 'The question then, for us is whether we are going to have another Anglo-German war for the sake of Soviet Russia or any interest in Eastern Europe. The answer undoubtedly is "No".'[65]

Some other factors figured in assessments of the value of Soviet Russia as an ally of the Western Powers against Germany. First, the piously maintained distinction between the Soviet Foreign Ministry and the Comintern fooled no one, and it was understood that the aim of the Soviet policy was to hasten world revolution wherever convenient by the means nearest to hand. Even the Popular Front agitation in France had to be measured against Soviet intervention in Spain, which was far better known than Germany's though not Italy's; and there was the feeling in some quarters that unlike Germany and Italy, Russia was trying to subvert Britain even on its own ground.[66]

Second, there were the purges which began in 1936 and continued intermittently through 1939. They claimed untold lives including almost all the old Bolshevists who were made to confess to the most ludicrous trumperies. Not only the Party organization, but also the Army, was hard hit, most of the General Staff being among those liquidated. Even those British newspapers, like *The Times*, the *Daily Telegraph*, and the *Manchester Guardian*, which would have accepted if not welcomed Russia as an ally gainst Germany, were thus cast into doubt over the actual value of the Russian Army, whose equipment was not very modern and most of whose officers and leaders had been recently executed for treason. Dawson wrote in October 1938 of the Russians 'immobilized by the murder of their leading generals and admirals',[67] but a correspondent in

[64] *Daily Mail*, 21 Sept. 1936, ed. art. by Ward Price, p. 12.
[65] *Observer*, 1 Nov. 1936, Garvin, p. 12.
[66] *Observer*, 30 May 1937, Garvin, p. 18.
[67] Dawson to Brand, 2 Oct. 1938, *The Times* archives.

the *Manchester Guardian* insisted that a State-controlled force like the Red Army would be as strong as necessary whenever it was called upon; he reached the somewhat cynical conclusion that after all, 'this was not the first crop of executions in Russian history'.[68] Generally, however, opinions were divided, and sure knowledge impossible.

There was, third, an ethical question. All the newspapers except the *News Chronicle* and the *Daily Herald* (and even the latter was not without reservations in this regard) felt very deeply Voigt's worries about the propriety of not discriminating among dictators. Russia sitting in judgement of Germany at Nuremberg has been likened to a trial of Don Juan with Casanova on the bench, and there were those in the late 1930s who thought it ludicrous to talk of a democratic front against Germany if that front included—as it must to be sufficiently strong—Soviet Russia. As Barrington-Ward asked a friend, 'Are we to commit ourselves to an ideological campaign in the untrustworthy and compromising company of Stalin?'[69] *The Times* had the most sensible attitude: associate with Russia only to the minimum extent necessary to hold Germany in check; but common sense is rarely the measure in international politics.

The Soviet demands during the negotiations with Britain and France in the summer of 1939 served to confirm those who felt that Russia's interest was in territorial aggrandisement in the Baltic and Poland. Even so the British Press on the whole was willing to countenance an agreement, especially after March 1939, and if mistakes were made they were mistakes of over-confidence. On 14 August 1939 *The Times*'s first leader affirmed that 'This country and other countries— among whom may certainly, in principle, now be included Russia—are determined to resist the arbitrary pronouncements of the German leaders that such and such a European question is one for Germany alone and must be settled as Germany desires.'[70]

To whatever extent it was relevant, public opinion generally favoured Russia. In answer to the British Institute of Public

[68] *Manchester Guardian*, 9 Nov. 1938, ed. art. by a Corr., p. 11.
[69] Barrington-Ward to J. A. Stevenson, Feb. 1938, *The Times* archives.
[70] *The Times*, 14 Aug. 1939, 1st Leader, p. 11.

Opinion's question 'If there were a war between Germany and Russia, which side would you rather see win?' 59 per cent preferred Russia, 10 per cent Germany, and 31 per cent had no opinion. The very slight sympathy for Germany was 'most pronounced among Government supporters, the rich and the elderly'. Eight out of ten of the opposition to the Government, the young, and the poor, favoured Russia.[71]

The British newspapers which concerned themselves with the two overwhelming practical questions involving Russia during the late 1930s—whether Russia would have gone to the aid of Czechoslovakia in September 1938 and whether the British and French Governments really wanted Russia as part of the Peace Front in the summer of 1939—split along roughly predictable lines.

The *Manchester Guardian* placed great faith in the importance of Soviet Russia as a factor in the Western Powers' favour in defending Czechoslovakia and keeping Germany in line in 1938. It was particularly upset at the exclusion of the Soviets at Munich, and took issue with *The Times*'s report[72] that Maisky, the Soviet Ambassador, had seen the British Foreign Secretary, Lord Halifax, and been satisfied with his explanations for it. In the *Manchester Guardian*'s London Correspondence the very next day, it was stated as coming from 'a good Russian source' that during Maisky's visit the subject had never arisen.[73] Cummings in the *News Chronicle* was particularly insistent upon Russia's value and reliability; he hoped that some day *The Times* would 'even develop sufficient nous to stop the practice of sneering at Soviet Russia, without whose support and cooperation at the moment the Western Powers could not stand for a day against German aggression'.[74] On 14 October 1938 a leading article absolutely stated that Russia would have acted in support of Czechoslovakia had she been given the opportunity.[75]

As far as wanting an agreement with Russia after March 1939 was concerned, conditions had so changed that it was

---

[71] *News Chronicle*, 9 Jan. 1939, p. 7.

[72] *The Times*, 3 Oct. 1938, Dipl. Corr., p. 12.

[73] *Manchester Guardian*, 4 Oct. 1938, Our London Correspondence, p. 10.

[74] *News Chronicle*, 13 Sept. 1938, Spotlight on Politics, p. 10.

[75] *News Chronicle*, 14 Oct. 1938, 1st Leader, p. 12. See also *News Chronicle*, 10 Oct. 1938, Leader, p. 6.

only a case of relative degrees of enthusiasm. The general inability to conceive of a Nazi-Soviet alliance led most papers to assume that agreement with the Western Powers was only a matter of time and must come about.

It was the issue of colonies which showed how very deep and bitter these Left-Right differences could be. In 1937 the *Manchester Guardian* said that Germany had lost her colonies because she had lost the war, and 'Just as it was useless to disarm Germany if the Allies refused to disarm, so it was useless to make Germany's colonies League mandates if the other empires remained a species of private property'.[76]

At *The Times*, several disparate elements produced a balanced outlook. The British Empire was perhaps the most important and basic element of Geoffrey Dawson's outlook. Sir John Evelyn Wrench states in his Life of Dawson that 'the really vital factor in Geoffrey's mind, which for diplomatic reasons could not be argued at the time, was his deep misgiving lest the United Kingdom Government should be led into war in circumstances in which the Empire might not support us'.[77] Dawson and *The Times* did not propose a straightforward restoration of colonies to Germany, but felt that any general settlement of outstanding questions must take into account the Versailles strictures against the German colonial Empire. As Dawson wrote in May 1937 to H. G. Daniels, the paper's Geneva correspondent, 'But let me add that in my opinion the worst possible way to an understanding is to clamour for the retrocession out of hand of all the former German colonies. I do not believe that this is what Germany really needs most, and in any case I should regard it as no more than an item for reasonable discussion as part of a comprehensive settlement.'[78]

Daniels replied four days later, saying that he had reason to know what Dawson had said about returning the colonies 'accurately represents what they themselves think. To make

[76] *Manchester Guardian*, 1 Nov. 1937, 1st Leader, p. 8. Also, *Manchester Guardian*, 6 Feb. 1937, 1st Leader, p. 12.

[77] Wrench, *Geoffrey Dawson and Our Times*, p. 374.

[78] Quoted in *Hist. Times*, iv, p. 907.

any attempt to return them out of hand would be a great
mistake, and would have the worst possible effect.'[79]

For the *Manchester Guardian* and the newspapers of like
mind, however, the question was much more basic; it was,
indeed, unfortunate that a Nazi Germany was raising it,
since abhorrence for that regime necessarily obfuscated 'the
greater question of plain right and wrong' as related to
colonies.[80] It was apropos of colonies that the paper stated
in a leading article on 2 January 1937: 'It is not easy to remember in face of the frequently violent speeches of the Nazi
leaders with their complete contempt of truth and reason that
Germany has any grievances at all, though not so many years
ago this was generally admitted by progressive thinkers in this
country.'[81]

The most remarkable statement of all, however, was made
earlier, in September 1936, when a leading article stated that
the National Government should return to an Open Door
policy and extend the mandate principle to all its colonies.
The article concluded: 'Would not the British people accept
such a policy and its consequences if only they were told the
reason why? And, even if the offer failed to avert war, it
would at least free many men and women in England from
the feeling that, when war comes, they may be as guilty as
those whom they are sent to kill.'[82]

Thus it was that when Hitler came to power in January 1933,
he and his new regime were simply slotted in amongst the
already important and mainly divisive issues which in fact
determined the reactions of the different British newspapers to
the new leader and Government itself. Hitler did not appear
as a cataclysmic turning-point or in a vacuum: he appeared
to each British newspaper in a well-defined context which had
little or nothing to do with himself. By the time he had proven
himself fully as evil as his strongest critics had warned, the
initial attitude of wait-and-see tolerance had turned into

[79] Daniels to Dawson, 16 May 1937, *The Times* archives.
[80] *Manchester Guardian*, 6 Feb. 1937, 1st Leader, p. 12.
[81] *Manchester Guardian*, 2 Jan. 1937, 5th Leader, p. 8.
[82] *Manchester Guardian*, 16 Sept. 1936, 1st Leader, p. 8.

reluctant acceptance of his stable and undeniably popular regime.

Hitler and his demands were like a funnel into which British attitudes on every question from armaments to xenophobia were poured: what emerged from the funnel was the single policy of appeasement. One of the best, and certainly the most compendious, sources for these different attitudes and this single policy is the British Press. Newspapers had to deal daily, often at length, and, depending upon the paper, with varying degrees of consistency and coherence, with all the important national and international issues. The newspaper was also like a jeweller's setting in which foreign and domestic news were only two of several stones, and in the case of the popular press, not even those of the greatest importance.

The factors and forces which made for appeasement in Britain are still too recent, too deeply felt, to be ready for detached reappraisal. Appeasement of Nazi Germany was, as we have seen, as much the result of a complex of attitudes and susceptibilities which divided the Left and Right in Britain, and split them within themselves, as it was the result of reaction to the Nazi regime. Many of these basic problems about what life in Britain and what Britain's place in the world should be were not settled by the War in which Germany was so utterly defeated; and so, despite that defeat, they continue today to bedevil both contemporary politics and the possibility of a detached consideration of the inter-war period.

2

THE BRITISH PRESS:
1936–1939

1. DAILY MAIL

THE *Daily Mail* was the largest paper of the most complete newspaper combine in Great Britain. In 1937 its circulation was 1,580,000; it was the only popular daily paper which had a predominantly upper- and middle-class readership.[1] Until his retirement in 1937, Lord Rothermere dictated the paper's policy; he was succeeded by his son, the Hon. Esmond Harmsworth.

From the very outset, the *Daily Mail*'s attitude toward the Nazi regime was one of admiration for its internal accomplishments, both spiritual and material. Rothermere's editorial article of 10 July 1933, 'Youth Triumphant', was used for Nazi propaganda throughout the 1930s. With a dateline 'Somewhere in Naziland', the article stated that

As a sexagenarian myself I welcome the example that has thus been set to the world. I maintain that youth has a right to rule. Mussolini succeeded to supreme authority in Italy at the age of 39. His collaborators were even younger. Together they have made their country the best-governed state in Europe.

I confidently expect to see similar results achieved by Hitler, who has come to power at the age of 43.[2]

The *Daily Mail* had no patience with 'the old women of both sexes' who filled British newspapers with hysterical reports about Nazi 'excesses'. Hitler had retrieved Germany from the hands of its alien elements, 'Israelites of international attachments', and if excesses existed, 'the minor misdeeds of

---

[1] In this Chapter circulation figures and technical information about the newspapers' production is mainly from *Political and Economic Planning Report on the British Press*, and Lord Camrose's *British Newspapers and Their Controllers*.

[2] *Daily Mail*, 10 July 1933, ed. art. by Rothermere, p. 10.

individual Nazis will be submerged by the immense benefits that the new regime is already bestowing upon Germany'.[3]

Along with Rothermere's admiration of Nazi Germany went an almost obsessional concern for British air rearmament. His book *Warnings and Predictions*, published in 1939, traced the story of his concern for Britain's air strength which began in print on 7 November 1933, and included founding the National League of Airmen in 1935, and financing the design of an advanced bomber aircraft which he then donated to the nation—the 'Britain First'. A reviewer in the *Sunday Times* summed up the paradox of Rothermere's position:

. . . he combined awareness of the danger to Britain implicit in German rearmament with a belief that a rearmed Britain could be firm friends with a rearmed Germany. He saw Hitler as a sincere man who had defeated Communism in his own country and whose programme was now to reverse the *Diktat* of Versailles. He did not see him as a conqueror whose ambitions for world power inevitably mean, if not conflict with, then hostility to, the British Empire.[4]

A. J. Cummings took a rather more critical view: he wrote in the *News Chronicle* in August 1937 (after the *Daily Mail* had been the only paper virtually to justify Norman Ebbutt's expulsion from Berlin)[5] that 'There is nothing in modern politics—not even in German politics—to match the crude confusion of the Rothermere mentality as revealed in the Rothermere Press. It blesses and encourages every swash-buckler who threatens the peace of Europe—not to mention direct British interests—and then clamours for more and more armaments with which to defend Britain, presumably against his lordship's pet foreign bully.'[6] Even the *Daily Express* criticized the *Daily Mail*, in May 1938, when the latter claimed that the *Daily Express* was playing the German game by under-estimating Britain's need for air strength. It was the *Daily Mail*, the *Daily Express* stated, 'that has spent the last five years assuring us that 'Dolfie Hitler is a wonderfully good fellow and is very fond of Britain'.[7]

The *Daily Mail* during this period was indeed a remarkable pot-pourri of prejudices. Rothermere dismissed editors he did

[3] Ibid.   [4] *Sunday Times*, 26 Mar. 1939, p. 7.
[5] See below, p. 121 ff.   [6] *News Chronicle*, 31 Aug. 1937, p. 10.
[7] *Daily Express*, 12 May 1938, Opinion, p. 12.

not like. His overriding fear was a communist invasion of England, against which event he set about preparing vast estates in central Hungary. On balance, however, the paper must at least be credited with promoting British armaments. Also to its credit was the outstanding special correspondent of the 1930s, George Ward Price.

Unlike his colleagues of the time, Ward Price was almost totally unideological. Although he was clearly impressed with what he considered the positive aspects of Hitler's and Mussolini's regimes, he abhorred their brutality and excesses. Privately he held a deep conviction of the superiority of everything English, but as a reporter his interest was to get the best story. 'Since I reported [Hitler's] statements accurately, leaving British newspaper readers to form their own opinions of their worth,' he wrote in his autobiography, 'I had many opportunities of observing him under different sets of circumstances. He appreciated having a foreign auditor for the long harangues in which he tried to justify himself and his policy.'[8] Hitler once told Göring that Ward Price was the only foreign journalist who reported him without prejudice. The reader must decide whether this was a compliment or an indictment of a working journalist.

The *Daily Mail*'s Berlin correspondents included Ralph Izzard, Paul Bretherton, and Rothay Reynolds, who had been a minister and was particularly interested in the Church conflict in Germany; little of such news appeared in the *Daily Mail*, however, which dealt with a bare minimum of German news and placed emphasis upon descriptive or human interest articles and the special interviews with Hitler and Nazi leaders for which Ward Price became famous and infamous.

2. DAILY EXPRESS

In the period 1936–9, Lord Beaverbrook's *Daily Express* had, as its masthead proclaimed, the 'World's Largest Daily Sale,' of 2,329,000 copies. Readership of the *Daily Express* was evenly spread over all income groups although nearly two-thirds of its sales were in the next-to-lowest group. A. J. P. Taylor

---

makes a somewhat extreme—not to say frightening—claim for the *Daily Express*:

The *Daily Express* was distinguished not only by its circulation. It was unique also in the universality of its readership. All other newspapers were associated with a particular social level from *The Times* at the top to the *Daily Herald* for trade unionists. The *Daily Express* drew its readers impartially from every group—about a third from each of them. Beaverbrook, its Canadian proprietor, was not confined by the English social system and had the New World view that there was no difference between rich and poor except that the rich had more money. The *Daily Express* was what England would have been without her class system.[9]

Beaverbrook's other papers were the *Sunday Express*, which he founded in 1918, and the quality evening paper, the *Evening Standard*, which he acquired in 1923 in conjunction with the Daily Mail Trust and Lord Rothermere from the estate of Sir Edward Hulton.

The *Evening Standard* served up good political and social gossip in the 'Londoner's Diary', and provided a forum for the brilliant political cartoons of the New Zealand cartoonist David Low. Individual cartoons have become classics, particularly the 'Shivers Sisters Ballet' which appeared in the *Evening Standard* on 3 January 1938. It pictured J. L. Garvin, Lady Astor, Geoffrey Dawson, and Lord Lothian doing ballet class to a gramophone labelled 'Foreign Policy' under the baton of a tiny, malevolent Dr. Goebbels. The florid-faced betowelled Blimp and the twin figures of Taint Necessary and Sno Use ran through the weekly cartoons and the 'Low's Topical Budget' pages.

Even Beaverbrook occasionally figured in Low's cartoons. It is a testimony both to Beaverbrook's respect for Low's talent and to his recognition that the competition would snap him up in a minute, that a lucrative contract guaranteeing complete freedom of subject was arranged. Even at that, Beaverbrook would frequently try to influence the witty pen. Many of Low's *Evening Standard* cartoons were reproduced weekly in the *Manchester Guardian*.

The personality and character of Lord Beaverbrook

---

[9] Taylor, *English History*, p. 310.

fascinated, confused, and repelled observers during his lifetime; but this is not the place to consider him. It is to be hoped that Mr. Taylor's official biography will contain much material about Beaverbrook's conduct of his papers, especially the *Daily Express* in which his interest and control were greatest and most direct. There are some delightful passages in Beaverbrook's testimony to the Royal Commission on the Press when he disarmed his interlocutors with his answer to why he owned a newspaper. 'I ran my paper', he said, 'purely for the purpose of making propaganda and with no other object'.[10]

The Editor of the *Daily Express*, Arthur Christiansen, described the technique of editing the paper: 'make the news exciting even when it was dull. Make the news palatable by lavish presentation. Make the unreadable readable.'[11] His job and his outlook were entirely non-political: 'But I was a journalist, not a political animal. The policies were Lord Beaverbrook's job, the presentation mine, and when, for example, a decision was taken to use the slogan "There will be no war", I projected it so violently that there was no escaping it.'[12]

Thus, despite its distinguished array of correspondents, which included Sefton Delmer, William Forrest, Sydney Morrell, Geoffrey Cox, O'Dowd Gallagher, Alan Moorehead, and Selkirk Panton and Noel Monks in Berlin, Beaverbrook's policy of determined isolationism kept reporting of European conditions, aside from the Spanish Civil War, to the absolute news minimum although there were frequent human interest stories. As Lord Beaverbrook stated his policy at the time, 'My sole and only object is to serve the public interest and advance the cause for which I stand—the united British Empire, strong, resolute and determined in the pursuit of peace.'[13]

Splendid Isolation from the world and cultivation of the Empire and ties with the United States were the paper's policy. The paper could understand France's feelings, faced with Nazi Germany, but France must try to understand Britain's determination too: 'It is impossible that the British Government should pledge us to fight to hold together the

---

[10] *RCP* 26th, p. 4 ff.   [11] Christiansen, *Headlines All My Life*, p. 144.
[12] Ibid.   [13] *The Times*, 23 Sept. 1937, advertisement, p. 7.

ramshackle State of Czechoslovakia.'[14] Splendid Isolation should mean 'exactly that': 'It means that Britain does not undertake to look after Abyssinia, Austria, China, or Czechoslovakia. And we are very happy to inform the *Daily Herald* that the first three clients are already off our books, and the fourth may be off, too, at any time now.'[15]

In addition to Splendid Isolation, indeed as corollaries to it, the paper stood for food tariffs, against Fascism in Britain, and for 'public works and a policy of expansion'![16]

Germany was treated as a good reason for having nothing to do with Europe. Hitler was only slightly more unpleasant than most foreigners, although his well-staged rallies and demonstrations provided striking and dependable copy. Lloyd George's celebrated article about Hitler was written for the *Daily Express*.[17] Any tendency towards caution would have been strongly reinforced by the embarrassing and expensive loss of the Hanfstaengl libel suit.[18]

Aside from the Lloyd George interview, the most famous Beaverbrook feature was the 'There Will Be No War' slogan. Although Beaverbrook later claimed that the decision to print this slogan on the masthead was taken after a 'referendum' of the paper's twelve European correspondents,[19] if such a thing was in fact done it was purely perfunctory. The slogan was widely used, and widely held against the *Daily Express*. Beaverbrook was perhaps most furious over Noël Coward's ironic use of it in his film *In Which We Serve*. Still, as Christiansen, who apparently thought of the refinement 'or next year either' for its second appearance, later wrote, 'I certainly did not seek to suppress publication of the slogan. It seemed to me to suit the spirit of the time and the spirit of the people.'[20]

Beaverbrook himself, testifying before the Royal Commission on the Press, put the slogan in the wider context of the *Daily Express*'s other policies:

[14] *Daily Express*, 29 Apr. 1938, Opinion, p. 12.
[15] *Daily Express*, 21 May 1938, Opinion, p. 12.
[16] *Daily Express*, 12 May 1938, Opinion, p. 12.
[17] See below, pp. 103–4.
[18] See *New York Times*, 3 Dec. 1935, p. 20; also *RCP* 34th, p. 15.
[19] See *RCP* 26th, p. 3.
[20] Christiansen, op. cit., p. 145.

The *Daily Express* at the same time that they were carrying on a prediction about no war, which they made in 1938, when they were right, and in 1939, when they were wrong, were carrying on a most determined and continuous campaign for more arms, more aircraft and more tanks. It was such a campaign as I think equalled any campaign the *Daily Express* had ever carried on. Strange to say, the more violent critics of the *Daily Express* today for the mistaken view that there would be no war, are the very persons who opposed more arms, more aeroplanes and more tanks. Then again the *Daily Express* carried on during that period a most determined campaign for conscription. They began in March, 1938, when not another newspaper supported them and no public man supported them. It was a most unpopular policy just then, but the campaign was vigorously conducted. There were seventeen leaders on the subject in 1939, I think it was.[21]

Christiansen, however, understood full well why the *Daily Express* more than many others who made a similar 'whopping error of judgement', was castigated in so many quarters. The reason was simply 'because the *Express* banged the drum the loudest'.[22]

3. NEWS CHRONICLE

The *News Chronicle* had a distinguished Liberal pedigree, being the result of a merger in 1930 of the *Daily Chronicle* and the *Daily News*, the latter having itself already swallowed two venerable Liberal journals, the *Morning Leader* and the *Westminster Gazette*.

In 1937 the *News Chronicle* had a circulation of 1,324,000. The paper was owned by the Cadbury family trust, and Lawrence Cadbury represented the family's interests.

Although it was considered by many to be journalistically and ideologically inconsequential and light-weight, the *News Chronicle* emerges most creditably from a critical reading over the Nazi years. To a certain extent the casual atmosphere which seemed to pervade the *News Chronicle* was necessary to avoid the conflicts which seemed inevitable from its structure. The Cadburys were an old Liberal family, but many of the staff felt that by the late 1930s they had become Tory

[21] *RCP* 26th, p. 3.   [22] Christiansen, op. cit., p. 145.

wolves in Liberal sheep's clothing, representing an almost Tory determination to keep the paper from taking a really radical stand. Lawrence Cadbury delegated most of his interests in this respect to the executive head of the Cadbury Group, Sir Walter Layton, who was also Editor of *The Economist*. When Vernon Bartlett phoned from Munich in September 1938 to say that the news was as bad as it could be, that Chamberlain had sold out the Czechs, Gerald Barry, the Editor, wanted to do a strong leader to this effect. Layton refused, saying 'If that's the news, it's too yellow to print.'[23]

There were no open conflicts between the Chairman and the Editor and staff, but he represented, backed by Cadbury as he was, a restraining influence.

This disparity between radical staff and moderate directors was especially true in the City and business departments of the paper. The City Editor was Oscar Hobson; he exercised a strong restraining hand. In the spring of 1939, for example, he refused to print a story from Ian Colvin who had learned the amount of the Reich's internal indebtedness from special contacts with the German Finance Minister Schwerin-Krosigk. The amount given (which was in fact an underestimate) was so high that Hobson said 'I cannot allow that figure', and no story appeared despite complaints from Harrison and Colvin.[24] Hobson was after all a typical City man who always came down on the side of caution.

The *News Chronicle* was a popular paper, and circulation was thus a major consideration, especially since it had lost the race with the *Daily Mail* for third place after the *Daily Express* and the *Daily Herald*. The business and advertising staff were opposed to anything controversial or depressing

---

[23] Interview with Sir Gerald Barry, 30 Nov. 1967. The paper's Berlin Correspondent, H. D. Harrison, only recalls one case of something being withheld from the paper because of its political content during his time in Berlin. He had received information in September 1938 about plans in the Brown House in Prague for a Nazi take-over of Czechoslovakia and other territories. 'We sent these by special messenger to London and they arrived just when Chamberlain returned from Munich, I think it was. Lord Layton asked Chamberlain, "Shall we publish?" and according to the report I heard later from colleagues in London got the reply "For God's sake don't." He did not.' (H. D. Harrison to the author, 31 Jan. 1968.) This report, as Harrison points out, is hearsay; it may refer to the information summarized in *DBFP* 3rd Ser., in which case the date is around the end of November, two months after Munich.

[24] Private information.

which might discourage advertisers. 'Why all this foreign news?' asked the Advertising Manager at one point.[25]

Gerald Barry, as Editor, wrote many of the paper's leaders; the chief leader-writer was Ivor Bulmer-Thomas. The Diplomatic Correspondent was Vernon Bartlett. Bartlett had gone from journalism into the London office of the League of Nations Union. He became an influential broadcaster on behalf of the League; the importance for British public opinion of his broadcast counselling calm after Germany's withdrawal from the League in October 1933 has not been fully appreciated. He adopted a similarly sympathetic line in a book *Nazi Germany Explained* which was published in 1933. His conversion to anti-Nazism did not come until later, but it was that much stronger when it came. As early as 1937, quite against the prevailing tide of optimism, he wrote that unless there occurred an unlikely radical shift in German foreign policy within the next few months, 'there is a virtual inevitability of war.'[26]

He was elected to Parliament for Bridgwater in September 1938 in opposition to the Government's German policy and was, thus, 'the only man to win a seat in parliament before the war solely on the strength of his talks on the radio'.[27]

The Political Editor of the *News Chronicle* was A. J. Cummings. He was probably the most influential, important, and well-informed radical journalist of the 1930s. He had joined the *Daily News* in 1921 and built a reputation around special coverage of stories like the Reichstag trial and the Metro-Vickers trial. His 'Spotlight on Politics' in the *News Chronicle* was a combination of political and diplomatic speculation, gossip, anecdote, and scandal. He was extremely pro-Soviet and received a lot of information from the Soviet Ambassador Maisky. An item on the possibility of a Nazi-Soviet Pact, written purely as speculation, was used by the Soviets as part of the *post facto* justification to the various Communist parties. He had some contacts with Attlee and Churchill and the Foreign Office; other special British sources included figures like Harry Pollitt, Aneurin Bevan, and Arthur Greenwood.

John Segrue served the *News Chronicle* in Berlin from 1933

[25] Interview with Sir Gerald Barry, 30 Nov. 1967.
[26] *News Chronicle*, 3 Feb. 1937, editorial by Bartlett, p. 1.
[27] Taylor, op. cit., p. 436.

until 1936. He was succeeded by his assistant P. B. Wadsworth who was also the *Observer*'s correspondent. When H. D. Harrison was expelled from Yugoslavia in 1937, he was moved to Berlin from which the German Government ordered his removal in March 1939. Ian Colvin moved between Berlin and London, acting after 1937 as a contact between the German civilian opposition and the British Government. He arranged for Carl Goerderler to see Gerald Barry and Cummings at the *News Chronicle* in 1939. Douglas Reed joined the *News Chronicle* in December 1938 after resigning from *The Times*.

For a popular paper, the *News Chronicle* maintained a good critical balance. H. D. Harrison recalls: 'When I went out to Berlin I was told that I could safely report any kind of political news without fear and that if I was on the "left wing" that would make no difference. In general the *News Chronicle* staff was very progressive and anti-dictatorship but I do not think they consciously influenced news this way except perhaps by the selection of the news they published.'[28]

Whatever the *News Chronicle*'s internal conflicts and problems over the treatment of German news, the finished product was the British newspaper which most annoyed the Nazis. Göring complained to Ashton-Gwatkin of the Foreign Office about it, and Ribbentrop railed against the *News Chronicle* 'as a notorious mischiefmaker'.[29] Nevile Henderson concurred with this judgement.[30] Only the *News Chronicle*'s reporting of the Night of Crystal in November 1938 caused resentment in Berlin although the entire British Press was strongly critical of this pogrom.[31]

On 2 and 3 January 1939 the *News Chronicle* printed editorial articles by H. G. Wells containing his predictions for the New Year.[32] The German Government protested strongly against the second article; Halifax wrote about the German Ambassador's visit:

He said that during recent months he had drawn the attention of the Department to certain press attacks on, or caricatures of, Herr Hitler, but that this last article, of which he complained today, was far more objectionable than anything which had preceded it. To describe Herr Hitler as a certifiable lunatic and to suggest that it

---

[28] Harrison to author, 31 Jan. 1968.   [29] *DBFP* 3rd Ser. iv, App. II (2).
[30] Ibid., App. I (vi).   [31] *DBFP* 3rd Ser. iii, doc. 291.
[32] *News Chronicle*, 2, 3 Jan. 1939, ed. art. by H. G. Wells, p. 8.

would be a patriotic act if he were to be put away was going far beyond any legitimate criticism, and he was bound to register the strongest objection to it.[33]

At the end of January, Dirksen met Chamberlain at a party and again protested; 'Chamberlain deplored these attacks and admitted that the *News Chronicle* was in fact the most dangerous British newspaper and that it had even attacked the King, the Queen, and the British Government in an irresponsible way.'[34]

4. DAILY HERALD

The Labour Party newspaper, the *Daily Herald*, had first appeared in 1912. In 1929 it was purchased by the head of Odhams Press Ltd., J. S. Elias. Odhams took 51 per cent of the shares, and the remaining 49 per cent were held in the names of thirty-two Trades Union Officials as trustees of the Labour Party. In 1939 the representatives of the Trades Unions included Sir Walter Citrine, A. A. Findlay, William Kean, and Ernest Bevin. The *Daily Herald* had no associate paper, although Odhams printed the Sunday paper *The People*.

The *Daily Herald* was predominantly a lower-middle and working-class paper: 95 per cent of its readers came from the two lowest income groups. Special attention was paid to industrial news, and great attention was given to the City Page which was less narrowly financial and more of a general economic review than in the other popular dailies. Circulation in 1937 was over two million.

Under the constitutive agreement, Odhams, in the person of Elias, held all but political control of the paper. Although the articles of agreement called for arbitration if the paper took a different line from that of the Labour Party, it was disputes over the definition of the limits of political and commercial control, as well as conflicts between these sides of the paper, which resulted in the Editor's resignation in 1940.

The Editor, Francis Williams, and his staff were faced with several and conflicting responsibilities. The Labour

---

[33] *DBFP* 3rd Ser. iii, doc. 518. For Dirksen's account of this visit, see *DGFP*, Ser. D. iv, doc. 290.   [34] *DGFP* 3rd Ser. iv, doc. 300.

Party, whose annual conference each year devoted a private session to the *Daily Herald*, was very much a house divided against itself on important issues like the Popular Front, the League of Nations, armaments, pacifism, and policy towards Germany generally. Ernest Bevin had been fighting communist infiltration of the Party, and this was one of the reasons that the *Daily Herald* was not more enthusiastic for an alliance with the Soviet Union in 1939. Conflicts within the Labour Party were not so important, however, as those with Elias and Odhams over the tone of the paper as a popular commercial property. Consistent hardline criticism of Germany was thus impossible, as Francis Williams told the Royal Commission on the Press, because just as 'It was necessary . . . to keep within the general framework of Labour Party policy, it was necessary also to remember that there was a substantial body of non-Labour opinion which would be critical of that sort of comment and therefore that it ought to be modified to some extent or cut out; and it was the culmination of a clash of that kind which in fact led to my own resignation.'[35]

Much of the paper's strength was thus wasted, and as Lord Camrose put it in 1939, 'Except for its political contents, which are not so extensive or pronounced as many members of the Party would like them to be, the *Daily Herald* is no different in its treatment of news and the doings of the world from its more plutocratic contemporaries.'[36]

The paper's diplomatic correspondent was W. N. Ewer who had remarkably wide-ranging contacts and sources for a Labour paper journalist. The Berlin correspondent was Wallace King.

5. DAILY TELEGRAPH

When the *Daily Telegraph* was taken over by the Berry Brothers' Group in 1928, Lord Camrose (Sir William Ewert Berry), who had been Editor of the *Sunday Times* since 1915, set about putting the paper back on its feet. Mainly by lowering the price to 1*d.* on 1 December 1930, Camrose made circulation soar. Sales rose 75,000 in the first month (from 100,000 to

---

[35] *RCP* 3rd, p. 2.
[36] *Daily Telegraph*, 13 June 1939, ed. art. by Lord Camrose, p. 14.

175,000) and another 25,000 in January 1939. In October 1937 the *Daily Telegraph* amalgamated with the *Morning Post*, which had been founded in 1772; it was estimated that the combined paper retained the bulk of the *Morning Post*'s 117,000 readers. The continuous rise in circulation marks the importance of the *Daily Telegraph* as a quality organ of opinion:

1931	226,324	1935	417,584
1932	274,250	1936	489,568
1933	320,000	1937	565,262
1934	353,648	1938	662,730
		1939	763,557

The *Daily Telegraph* was a quality paper with a large circulation, thanks to its price of 1*d.*; its readership was mainly of the upper and middle classes, the bulk being in the middle income group.

The *Daily Telegraph* was a Conservative and Imperialist paper which supported the National Government. The only major area of disagreement was Germany and the proper treatment of the Nazi regime. Camrose was very close to Chamberlain socially, and there were instances, notably over Lord Halifax's visit to Hitler in November 1937 and repudiation of rumours of a return to appeasement in mid-1939, in which Government inspiration was clear. Generally, however, the paper was more sympathetic to the Eden–Churchill line on Germany. Churchill, indeed, would often ring the News Editor at 2 a.m. to get the latest news. Victor Gordon-Lennox, the Diplomatic Correspondent, was particularly close to Eden. The Editor, Arthur E. Watson, acted largely as an organizer, overseeing operations generally; the news was left to Robert Skelton, the News Editor, under Camrose's supervision, and the leaders were all written, under Camrose's supervision, by some distinguished Fleet Street figures like J. B. Firth and J. C. Johnstone. It was the latter who, having come to the *Daily Telegraph* from the *Morning Post* when they merged, wrote the original uncompromising draft leader rejecting the Munich conference.

The idea is fairly widespread that the *Daily Telegraph* was the only British newspaper to condemn the Munich Conference. As a reading of the paper shows, however, it was only the most critical in its comments before as well as after; the only paper to oppose Munich out of hand was *Reynolds News*. In September 1938 Lord Camrose was away on his yacht, sailing off the coast of South Africa, and his son Seymour Berry (now Lord Camrose) was left in charge of the paper. When news of the invitation to Munich arrived, J. C. Johnstone wrote an uncompromising leader rejecting the idea of negotiations under such conditions. Seymour Berry, undoubtedly very much under the influence of his friends, including Duff and Diana Cooper, and reinforced by the sentiment in the office, including Watson, Skelton, and Lord Burnham, was inclined to publish the article as it stood.

At this point, Berry was summoned to 25 Park Lane, where Sir Samual Hoare was having his weekly luncheon with Sir Philip Sassoon. After waiting for two hours, Berry was finally received by the Home Secretary who said that the Government would be very angry if the *Daily Telegraph* were naughty and criticized the latest attempt at an Anglo-German settlement. Berry was infuriated both by the wait and by the tone of Hoare's intervention, and returned to the office set upon publishing the leader as Johnstone had written it. At the office, however, Gordon-Lennox arrived, apparently from high-level talks, and insisted that the paper must not prejudice such delicate and important negotiations by prior criticism. His urgings and calmer consideration must have prevailed, for Johnstone's leader was softened considerably although it still afforded only a minimum of aid and comfort for the Munich Conference.[37]

The *Daily Telegraph* had a number of distinguished contributors and correspondents dealing with German affairs. Austen Chamberlain and Winston Churchill both wrote occasional editorial articles, the former (until his death in 1937) refusing to admit Germany's colonial claims, and the latter writing critically on various topical events concerning Anglo-German relations. Gordon-Lennox's contacts in London were first rate, many of them based upon his social position. The chief Berlin correspondent until 1938 was Eustace B. Wareing; he was succeeded in August of that year by his assistant, Hugh Carleton Greene, who remained until his expulsion in May

[37] This version of the events is based on two separate and reliable sources.

1939. Anthony Mann also worked for the paper in Berlin. There does not appear to have been any conflict between Berlin and London over the printing of critical articles. The case was very different with the paper's Vienna correspondent, G. E. R. Gedye, who was finally fired in April 1939 because of his book *Fallen Bastions*.

Gedye is an interesting journalistic figure, in many ways the prototype of the leftist British foreign correspondent between the wars. Although he did not have much to do with Germany until the Anschluss when he was expelled, his insight into the Hitler regime, based upon his ideological abhorrence for it, was early and clear.

Gedye's career began soon after the Great War. The burden of his reporting and writing from 1923 until 1933, as we have seen, was that France was the conscious and underhand cause of European instability. After 1933, Nazi Germany replaced France and the Clerical-Fascist Austrian Government as Gedye's *bête noire*. He contributed an article of his 'Impressions of Hitler's Germany' to the *Contemporary Review* of June 1933. In it he explained that the worst French excesses were not sufficient excuse for Hitler or his regime: 'Condemnation of those who tease and torture an animal until it loses normal control and flies at the nearest victim in a passion to be free does not involve approval of the maddened animal.' Enthusiasm for Hitler in Germany could not be denied, but unity was only being achieved 'by cramming the German prisons so that huge concentration camps (one of which I have visited)[38] had to be created for the overflow and ringed around with live electric wires, barbed wire and machine guns'.[39] A German in Munich told Gedye that Nazism would last 'because it suits the Germans like a Savile Row suit an Englishman. Our people can be divided into three: One part wants to be kicked, another part to kick. These make up 90 per cent. The remaining 10 per cent looks on at the spectacle and weeps.'[40]

The relations between Gedye and the *Daily Telegraph* show clearly how deeply divisive the Left-Right political issues which we considered in Chapter One could be: not even

---

[38] Gedye had visited Dachau on Hitler's birthday in 1933.
[39] Gedye, 'Impressions of Hitler's Germany', *Contemporary Review*, No. 810, June 1933, p. 670.   [40] Ibid., p. 676.

a shared anti-Nazism could bridge the gap. The *Daily Telegraph*, while generally giving its complete support to the National Government, maintained a hard-core criticism of the Government's policy towards Germany. Although they led him to similar conclusions about Germany, however, Gedye's politics were something quite different. His outstanding abilities as a journalist were never doubted, but there were times when his enthusiasm or indignation would have to be toned down.

It was undoubtedly with the recent and unfortunate example of Douglas Reed in mind (another radical journalist who published a political book[41] while working for a conservative newspaper), that when *Fallen Bastions* was advertised in Hodder and Stoughton's 1939 spring list as telling 'the uncensored truth', Watson wrote to Gedye that such a book seemed 'very undesirable'. He was summoned to London and told to charter his own plane if no regular flights were immediately available. No agreement seemed possible, and he was given six months' severance pay. He then returned to Prague, and thence to Warsaw and Moscow for *The New York Times*.

Fallen Bastions was probably the most influential journalist's book of the 1930s. So extensive was Gedye's knowledge of Austrian politics that even in the light of the captured documents it is virtually impossible to fault the Austrian sections of the book. Of its five hundred pages about three-quarters are devoted to Austria and form in large part an autobiographical history. Although Gedye's sympathies are entirely and obviously with the Socialists against both the Austrian Clerical and German Nazi regimes, he only occasionally ventures, in the Austrian sections, into polemics.[42] The style throughout is assertive and authoritative. Conversations are reported verbatim which it was impossible for Gedye to have heard or known about; as a result some parts—particularly those concerning the Hitler–Schuschnigg meeting at Berchtesgaden—are quite incorrect in detail. The chapters dealing with Czechoslovakia

---

[41] *Insanity Fair*, in October 1938.
[42] He states (p. 105) that 'Fascism is the international form which reactionary capitalism has employed everywhere where it proved impossible to deprive the masses by other means of power which they had legally obtained at parliamentary elections'.

are strongly polemical, completely critical of British policy. Chamberlain was stifling freedom and selling out to Hitler, 'and when the leader of His Majesty's Opposition ventures to say that some action of the Premier . . . has been a disaster, Führer Chamberlain accuses him of fouling his own nest and enviously remarks that in a Nazi country this would be impossible'.[43]

The book was published at 18s. in February 1939. The following month, with the occupation of Prague, it was taken over by the Left Book Club and sold at 7s. 6d. As might be expected, the reviews varied greatly. Philip Jordan in the *News Chronicle* heartily recommended it, as did F. A. Voigt in the *Manchester Guardian*. Herbert Sidebotham, in the *Sunday Times*, thought the book was often ruder to Chamberlain than the argument required—as when it referred to 'Gauleiter Chamberlain'[44] and to the 'criminal folly' of his surrender at Munich. Sidebotham objected to Gedye's alternative policy as well:

Mr. Gedye is an attractive writer, a man of keen conscientiousness and of great industry, but he can never see any question from any point of view than that which is immediately under his eye. The distress that he sees moves him to pity, and often to very eloquent writing. The distress that his own policy would have caused is outside his imagination, as it is outside his sight.[45]

The reviewer in *The Times Literary Supplement*[46] gave the most cogent and balanced assessment: in the part on Austria, the 'breathless narrative knows nothing of half-tones. Every Socialist is pure White; and there are few nuances in the depth of black reserved for Clericals, Heimwehr men and Fascists. Given this over-simplified approach, unstinted praise may be given to Mr. Gedye's vivid sketch of the last twelve years of Austrian history.' The part about Czechoslovakia, however, was something else altogether. Albeit written in haste and under great pressure, it should have been rewritten or omitted:

An arguable case can be made out against British policy last September, particularly if every factor but one in the problem be ignored. But this case cannot be built on wild hearsay statements, extravagant innuendos, crude vituperation of the Prime Minister

---

[43] *Fallen Bastions*, p. 505.   [44] *Ibid.*, p. 307.
[45] *Sunday Times*, 12 Feb. 1939, p. 7.   [46] *TLS*, 18 Feb. 1939, p. 99.

and savage attacks on Lord Runciman. In two or three years, when Mr. Gedye has had time to discover that Lord Baldwin was not driven from office because he was too democratic for Mr. Chamberlain and that Great Britain is not passing through a 'pre-Fascist' epoch, he may perhaps be induced to give a fresh edition. . . .

The *Morning Post*, which merged with the *Daily Telegraph* in October 1937, was the oldest London newspaper. Throughout the 1930s circulation dwindled rapidly while costs and competition increased, and finally on 30 September 1937, H. A. Gwynne, Editor since 1911, wrote his final leading article.

The *Morning Post* maintained an extreme right-wing Tory line towards international affairs. The object of such affairs was the preservation and protection of Britain and the British Empire. Bolshevism was as repugnant as Nazism; the paper was openly and virulently opposed to what it deemed the pawn-of-Moscow Spanish Republican Government.

It was difficult not to admire this idiosyncratic integrity and forthrightness. The *Manchester Guardian* lamented the demise of its frequent antagonist:

So the *Morning Post* is gone, dying of principles in the last ditch. . . . Now something of the sparkle and of the courage even to offend for conviction's sake goes out of journalism. The cavalry dwindle as the mechanical battalions grow.[47]

Antagonism was, indeed, provoked left and right; when it became clear that something drastic must be done or the paper would have to be sold, Lord Lloyd went to Chamberlain pleading 'Don't let this great Conservative organ sell out.' Chamberlain reportedly told him that he had no use for independent conservative criticism, and that accommodation with Germany was of the utmost importance and would only be hindered by the *Morning Post* continuing as in the past.[48]

Both the *Daily Telegraph* and the *Morning Post* represented British conservative opposition to Nazism. Their reservations about the policy of appeasement could not be implemented because they supported the Government on other seemingly equally important issues, and also because they realized that there was no possible acceptable alternative to Chamberlain.

[47] *Manchester Guardian*, 1 Oct. 1937, 3rd Leader, p. 10. See also *The Times*, 30 *Sept.*, 1937., 2nd Leader, p. 13.   [48] Private information.

The *Morning Post* had no more use for British Socialists—the Labour Party—than for Soviet ones; and although the *Daily Telegraph* opened its columns to Churchill, both Camrose and Gordon-Lennox surely knew that Eden (the only possible replacement, according to public opinion polls) was not the ideal exponent of this line, and was not really preferable to Chamberlain.

The *Morning Post* was edited by H. A. Gwynne. The Foreign Editor was Alastair Shannon, and the chief foreign leader-writer J. C. Johnstone. The extreme right-wing attitudes of the paper made it subject to frequent criticism from readers who did not share its anti-Nazism; some of them were those few Tories whom Ribbentrop *had* managed to charm—the ones popularly thought to be running *The Times*. Karl Robson, the paper's Berlin correspondent, recalls that despite such pressure,

I cannot remember that they ever discarded a single story. They interrogated me closely and intelligently whenever I was in London, and once arranged (their suggestion) for me to meet Vansittart, who was then Permanent Secretary to the F.O. After my expulsion they sent me out to look into Nazi agitation beyond the frontiers of Germany—in Austria and Tyrol south of the Brenner, Danzig, Poland, the Memel, Riga, Czechoslovakia and regions south-east as far as Ankara.[49]

Malcolm Muggeridge described the reasons for the demise of the *Morning Post;* its circulation had dropped since the Great War, and as its readers died there were none to take their places:

Its point of view was unfashionable, and the honesty with which it was stated, uncongenial. In its last years, before its absorption by the *Daily Telegraph*, it was a stranger in a strange land; with no ideological affiliations, finding MacDonald as unpalatable after he had formed the National Government as before, Hitler as unpalatable as Stalin. Its correspondent was among the first to be expelled from the Third Reich. With a final burst of energy, it attacked Sir Samuel Hoare's Indian Bill, and the subterfuges adopted to gain support for it, and then expired. Its lonely but spirited existence in a world in which Colonel Blimp was funny and Litvinov on the side of the angels, could not be protracted.[50]

---

[49] Robson to author, 14 Apr. 1968.   [50] Muggeridge, *The Thirties*, p. 168, n.

6. THE OBSERVER

The *Observer* was the oldest of the Sunday newspapers, founded in 1791. It had long fallen upon bad times when Northcliffe bought it for less than £5,000 in 1905, and it did not become successful until Northcliffe prevailed upon J. L. Garvin to take the editorship. Political differences soon arose between the two, and in 1911 Northcliffe told Garvin that he would sell his interest if Garvin could find a purchaser. Garvin found the first Viscount Astor.

As soon as Garvin had complete control, the paper began to flourish. He effected a newspaper revolution on the editorial page. His leading articles, carefully set so as to lead the reader on without taxing his attention or concentration, skilfully headed and sub-headed, spreading across three, four, or even five columns, were the main selling point of the paper. He also engaged the most reputable critics available for the paper's book and arts review pages.[51]

Although political differences with the second Viscount Astor finally led to Garvin's resignation in 1942,[52] during the 1930s he was very much in unfettered charge of the paper, and its policy was his policy. As one of two quality Sunday papers, the *Observer*'s influence was undoubtedly great. Its circulation, however, grew very little during the 1930s, while that of the *Sunday Times* rose and overtook it. In 1930 the *Observer*'s circulation was 201,000, and in 1936 it was 214,000.

Garvin was the British Press's most outspoken Czechophobe. His contempt for the Treaty of Versailles was boundless: the whole kind of system of international affairs it represented—based upon British involvement with France in Europe—seemed to him repugnant and dangerous to British interests. Although Garvin by no means condoned the racial policies of the Nazis, he clearly felt that agreement between Germany and Britain was possible and desirable; its importance was paramount. Along with this policy of Anglo-German co-operation he stressed the need for British rearmament.

Until Munich, Garvin was reasonably sure that Germany

---

[51] For Garvin's writing and lay-out technique, see A. M. Gollin, *J. L. Garvin and The Observer*.

[52] See Oliver Woods, 'Garvin's Last Years', *The Times Saturday Review*, 6 Apr. 1968, p. 1.

wanted peace. The Rhineland and the Anschluss were unsettling but explicable; Munich was frightening although it might well mean peace for ten years. Above all, Britain must arm. In a review of 1938 in the paper on New Year's Day 1939, Garvin saw 'a moral as heavy as pile-driving': that equal power could be assured only by equal exertion. During the rest of January he wrote on conscription and rearmament in the air.

Although Garvin welcomed Munich—'Mr. Chamberlain was a thousand times right in saving peace at Munich, even at the price exacted'—he did so cognisant of the price. How strange it seems to read of his concern, after years of vituperation against Czechoslovakia, that not only the Germans in Czechoslovakia but in effect ten million Czechs were given over in effective control to Germany at Munich.[53] This said, an uneasy interval followed until Hitler marched into Prague. Garvin wrote four days later that 'The last rag of human decency was discarded this time'.[54] The road to Prague would be the road to Hitler's own ultimate destruction, 'but the issue may convulse mankind'. Henceforth there was no more ardent anti-Nazi in the British Press. Adam von Trott zu Solz recorded a conversation with Garvin at Cliveden in June 1939 in a report for the German Foreign Office; Garvin, he said, was deeply depressed and pessimistic, and let it be understood 'that it was better to end an honourable history of 800 years with a desperate struggle, rather than "allow oneself to be kicked around like a fool and a coward" (Garvin evidently believes war with Germany to be inevitable) . . .'[55]

Garvin was a controversial figure. Keynes dismissed him by stating that 'Garvin at least has the merit that he makes the worse cause appear the worser.'[56] But even his political and ideological opponents paid tribute to his long-standing independence by never labelling him with the Cliveden stamp although it was 'his' Astor who owned the house. In terms of his actual influence, it is likely that he had become so well known that although his articles were read, they were taken on a wholly personal basis without the weight which might otherwise

---

[53] *Observer*, 1 Jan. 1939, Garvin, p. 12.
[54] *Observer*, 1 Mar. 1939, Garvin, p. 16.
[55] *DGFP*, Ser. D. vi, doc. 497.   [56] Quoted in Martin, *Editor*, p. 244.

attach to such specific and insistent editorial comment in a major national newspaper.

The *Observer*'s Berlin Correspondent was P. B. Wadsworth, who also contributed to the *News Chronicle*; indeed it was considered that his work for the former kept him from being expelled because of his work for the latter. Garvin gave him no instructions, and only once or twice altered very minor things in his reports.[57]

7. SUNDAY TIMES

The other Sunday quality paper was the *Sunday Times*. The Berry brothers bought the paper in 1915 when its circulation was only 50,000. Lord Camrose was Editor for twenty-two years during which time the circulation grew prodigiously, passing its rival, the *Observer*, in the early 1930s. *The Sunday Times*'s circulation was 187,000 in 1932 and 270,000 in 1937.

In January 1937 the Berry brothers decided to separate their affairs. Lord Camrose, as we have seen, took the *Daily Telegraph* and retained control of the Amalgamated Press interests and the *Financial Times*. Lord Kemsley (Sir Lionel Gomer Berry) bought his share in Allied Newspapers which was a vast network of provincial papers and the London morning *Daily Sketch* and the *Sunday Graphic* and *Sunday Times*.

Lord Kemsley was firmly convinced of the possibility and desirability of an Anglo-German rapprochement, and did not hesitate to use his influence with his newspapers to make smooth its path. The Royal Commission on the Press heard an example of direct interference from him in London in the presentation of news in his provincial papers. The Editor of the Manchester office of the *Daily Sketch* stated:

A direct instance of the imposition of 'policy' from London in journalistic judgement came at the time of Hitler's Nuremberg speech on the Czech situation before the Munich agreement. I personally took over the telephone from the London office an instruction that we were to put out a contents bill containing a reproduction of one of the more agreeable photographs of Hitler, with the one word 'Peace'. The comment of the chief sub-editor when he received this 'directive' was 'Well, that's not my reading of

[57] Interview with P. B. Wadsworth, 10 Sept. 1967.

Hitler's speech' and that was the general opinion. But we had to put out the bill just the same. It was another instance of journalistic knowledge, experience and sense of responsibility to the public being overridden by the fiat of a Press Lord.[58]

The Hon. Lionel Berry defended his father's practice by asserting that the Editor decided the contents bill of the paper as part of his job, and that there was no question of a special directive or dictation in this case. Further, the word 'Peace' was not meant to describe the contents of the speech but to make the point that despite the ominous predictions about what Hitler might do at Nuremberg, he had chosen at any rate not to go to war.[59]

R. J. Minney told the Royal Commission about his conversation with Lord Kemsley after he had taken over the *Sunday Referee* of which Minney was Editor.

When the *Sunday Referee* was absorbed by the Kemsley Group, Lord Kemsley asked me what features were 'pulling'. I said 'Madame Tabouis is always certain of a sale of 40,000 copies in the streets.' He said 'I will not have that woman in my paper at any price.'[60]

Minney felt that Kemsley's motives were clearly more personal and political than commercial:

I think he is a little ignorant about circulation, and at that time politically was flying high in the Fascist sky; he was very much with the Hitler group, and carried on his cooperation and appeasement after Chamberlain had abandoned it. He was still in Germany a few days before war broke out, seeing Dietrich, the head of the Press. He felt he would get a circulation of nearly 500,000 anyhow, and Madame Tabouis was a pernicious influence from his point of view. There was a politcal motive in trying to suppress Madame Tabouis whose influence he did not want in this country.[61]

Kemsley did indeed feel that if he could only get to see Hitler he would be able to straighten out many of the rough patches in Anglo-German relations. At the end of July 1939 he went to Bayreuth to meet the *Reichspressechef* Otto Dietrich to discuss exchanges of articles. The *News Chronicle* remarked: 'It is feared

[58] *RCP* 9th, p. 2. [59] *RCP* 36th, p. 24.
[60] *RCP* 10th, p. 9. [61] Ibid.

that only the most milk and water statements by British appeasers stand any chance of acceptance by the Reich Press Chief.'[62]

The Editor of the *Sunday Times* was W. W. Hadley. In many respects his functions were similar to those of Watson on the *Daily Telegraph*. Beyond supporting the Government, and favouring an Anglo-German settlement, the paper did not have a particularly sophisticated editorial policy regarding Nazi Germany. The *Sunday Times* was served in Berlin by the *Daily Telegraph*'s correspondents there, E. B. Wareing and then Hugh Greene; the editorial page was quite separate in interpretations and conclusions from its news page.

The major spokesman for the *Sunday Times* on foreign affairs was 'Scrutator', from the 1920s until 1940 Herbert Sidebotham. Sidebotham had gone down from Balliol to the *Manchester Guardian* as a leader writer in 1895. He stayed there for twenty-two years, the while developing his interest in military history and contributing pieces from a 'Student of War' during the Boer War. In 1918 he went to *The Times* as Military critic, but the war soon ended and he wrote as a 'Student of Politics' until 1921. Briefly in 1922–3, on Lloyd George's suggestion, he was political adviser to the *Daily Chronicle*. In 1923 he joined the Berry organization as 'Scrutator' on the *Sunday Times*, 'Candidus' on the *Daily Sketch*, and a 'Student of Politics' on the *Daily Telegraph*.

Sidebotham's successor as 'Scrutator', R. C. K. Ensor, wrote of him that 'In the "Scrutator" articles he reached his highest level; they combine a style of brilliant maturity with a wealth of knowledge and often an almost uncanny insight; no others then written were more widely and attentively read by influential people.'[63]

In the light of events, however, the Scrutator articles on Germany and Anglo-German relations seem examples of the most extreme kind of appeasement, ignoring not only the menacing external actions of the Nazi regime, but also the internal policies and barbarisms which even most of the ardent appeasers found repugnant.

[62] *News Chronicle*, 27 July 1939, Berlin Corr., p. 2.
[63] R. C. K. Ensor, *Dictionary of National Biography*, 1931–40, London, 1949, pp. 810–11.

8. THE TIMES

The Times was incomparably the most important British newspaper of the 1930s. Despite its price of 2*d*. and its daunting 'quality press' outlook and layout, its circulation rose steadily from 187,000 in 1930 to 192,000 in 1937 and 204,491 in 1939.

After the vicissitudes of the Northcliffe years (1908–22), the paper was controlled by Major the Hon. John J. Astor, with the original proprietorial family, the Walters, retaining a nominal number of shares. A Trust was established in 1924, comprising the Lord Chief Justice of England, the Warden of All Souls College, Oxford, the President of the Royal Society, the President of the Institute of Chartered Accountants, and the Governor of the Bank of England. Any future sale of the paper would have to be subject to approval of these trustees, and it was thus expected that *The Times* would become legally established as a veritable national institution.

Geoffrey Dawson was Editor of *The Times* from 1912 to 1919 and again from 1923 to 1941. From 1914 to 1944 he was Editor of *The Round Table*. Born in 1874, a deeply rooted Yorkshire-man, he was educated at Eton and Magdalen. He entered the Civil Service and was elected a Fellow of All Souls in 1898; he was transferred to the Colonial Office in 1899 and became assistant private Secretary to Joseph Chamberlain in 1901; he became Lord Milner's private Secretary from 1901 to 1905 in South Africa, and after Milner returned home, he stayed on as Editor of the *Johannesburg Star*, 1905–10. He met Northcliffe in 1908 and from that meeting came an invitation to work on *The Times* in 1910 and the Editorship in 1912. After quarrels with Northcliffe over the latter's increasingly irresponsible personal interventions in the paper, he resigned in 1919 and was replaced by Wickham Steed. When, after Northcliffe's death on 14 August 1922, Astor and Walter became the new owners of *The Times*, they decided on a change of editor. Walter told Steed that 'Astor and I wished to keep the policy of the Paper in our own hands, that he, Steed, had impressed his own personality so strongly on the Paper's policy and had impregnated it so thoroughly with his own views that the risk of disagreement with him on some important question, at any moment, was greater than we were willing to incur, and that a change could be made more easily and appropriately now than later.' Dawson was then invited to return as Editor which he did after obtaining agreement to his almost unfettered authority.[64]

Thus by the beginning of the 1930s, Dawson was firmly entrenched with virtually complete authority as Editor of *The Times*. Neither the Walters nor the Astors intruded very often, and then only by way of comment. Criticism for the aid and comfort which *The Times* gave to the policy of appeasement has therefore centred largely upon Dawson.

The criticisms are of four different kinds although the critics often overlap one into the other. It is firstly maintained that Dawson was not really or primarily a journalist, but rather a politician and an *éminence grise*. Typical expression of this attitude is found in Francis Williams's *Dangerous Estate* and Dr. Kieser's book in which he quotes A. L. Rowse, the major proponent of it:

Der Hauptgrund für die immer deutlicher sich abzeichnende pro-deutsche Haltung der *Times* ist in der Person des Herausgebers, Geoffrey Dawson, zu suchen. Er besass bedeutenden Einfluss in den obersten Gesellschaftsschichten, war der Vertraute der Premierminister MacDonald, Baldwin und später Berater Neville Chamberlains. Trotz der engen Beziehung zwischen Whitehall und Printing House Square stellten Dawsons Leitartikel nicht einfach das Echo seiner Gespräche mit den verschiedenen Ministern dar. Der Editor of the *Times* [sic] betrachtete es als seine Aufgabe, 'to mould public opinion'. Er war ein politischer Autodidakt und meinte trotz mangelnder Kenntnisse und Voreingenommenheit, ausgerechnet auf dem schwierigen Feld europäischer Probleme seinen Einfluss auf die Öffentlichkeit geltend machen zu müssen: 'Dawson was by instinct a pro-German: he could not help it . . . he was deeply and invariably anti-French in prejudice . . . Without any knowledge of European history, still less of German history, without knowing one word of the language or having the slightest insight into the German mind, he threw all his influence—which was immense—into undermining Versailles and doing the business of the Germans for them.' Dieses harte Urteil eines ehemaligen Bekannten Dawsons entbehrt nicht der Grundlagen.[65]

[64] See *Hist. Times*, iv, 769.
[65] Kieser, *Englands Appeasementpolitik*, pp. 75–6. The quotation at the end is from Rowse, *All Souls and Appeasement*, p. 6.

There are, second, those who treat of Dawson as an autocrat
running the paper according to his ambition or whim, regardless
of the counsels of precedent, of prudence, or of others. For
The History of The Times, his failure to appoint a Foreign
Editor at any time after Harold Williams's death in 1928
assumes almost monumental proportions of arrogance and
wrong-headedness. Third, there are those who present Dawson
as a man of limited intellectual reserves if not resources, whose
limited knowledge of many important things—like Europe—
led him to a cavalier dismissal of the things themselves or to
reliance upon a limited circle of advisers. Fourth, there are
those for whom Dawson seemed a sinister figure, exercising
vast anonymous and irresponsible power—for whatever
reasons—against the best interests of his own country.

Dawson died in 1944, and was thus unable to defend
himself or his paper when, after the War, both were thoroughly
blanketed with ill-repute for having supported appeasement
in the 1930s. Perhaps it was because this attitude was so strongly
ingrained that the author of *The History of The Times* made no
attempt, with the material at hand, to 'rehabilitate' Dawson
or the paper; and Sir John Evelyn Wrench's biography
Geoffrey Dawson and Our Times failed to strike an adequate
balance between piety and the necessity to answer rigorous
criticism.

It is true that the linchpin of Dawson's thought was the
British Empire. He had, after all, been tutored in the school
of Empire by Lord Milner himself; for them the concept did
not mean the strident, commercial ideal of Beaverbrook and
Rothermere, but the calm and grandeur of the *Pax Britannica*.
For Dawson it was not the illiberal blot on British history,
holding colonial people in its exploiting grasp, as it appeared
to the *Manchester Guardian*, the *News Chronicle*, or the *Daily
Herald*, but the embodiment of the British and Christian
values of order and decency. It was also a defensive entity, and
Dawson quoted Milner in a leading article 'Youth and Empire'
on Empire Day 1934.

The British Empire, keeping the peace within its own borders,
bound in its own interest, by the very nature of its constitution, to
'seek peace and ensue it' everywhere, is the most powerful bulwark in
the world today against the spread of international discord. The

maintenance of the strength, the preservation of a unity of the Empire is not the only contribution, but is by far the greatest and most practical contribution, which British statesmanship can make to the welfare of mankind.[66]

Dawson was indeed a journalistic Editor who took great interest in all parts of his paper, and would frequently exercise the editorial prerogative of emending contributions or adding 'impish' notes to articles (hence the myth of his addition to Anthony Winn's Lobby correspondence of 3 October 1938, describing Duff Cooper's resignation speech as having the effect of 'a damp squib').[67] By 1939, Dawson's second editorship had covered seventeen years. His first contribution to the paper had been made thirty-three years earlier, in 1906.

Dawson was not, then, either an inexperienced, dilettante journalist, or a man unaware of the realities of world politics. He is too complicated a character, and the issues concerning him are too important, to pretend, as does, for example, Rowse, that if Dawson's 'First' had been in History instead of 'Mods' and 'Greats', he would have been a fire-breathing anti-appeaser. Although his primary interest lay in the British Empire, he was certainly aware of European problems and events; his diary is full of meetings and consultations with various visitors and authorities from the Continent; he read his own correspondents' background letters and saw them when they came to London; and there are indications that during certain times—for example during the Czech crisis in September 1938—he had access to the Government's diplomatic correspondence.

He was not really an *éminence grise*, and his fixing in the public mind as such, along with Montagu Norman and the Archbishop of Canterbury (which was understandable at the time of the Abdication on the part of the popular press, but consciously invented by *The Week* along with its Cliveden fiction) was not based on fact. It is true that after 1937 the two main officers of the British Government were men with whom he had the closest personal *rapport* and sympathy, and one of them was his old friend and Yorkshire neighbour. *The History of The Times* is partly correct therefore when it states that Dawson was more concerned with finding the right man for the job than

---

[66] *The Times*, 24 May 1934, 1st Leader, p. 13.   [67] See below, p. 66 ff.

with knowing what he would do in the job; his intimate knowledge of Halifax and Chamberlain confirmed his own personal
convictions and gave him the assurance that the Government
would work along these proper lines. *The Times* considered
itself an independent newspaper, and the Deputy Editor
wrote to a friend in July 1938 expressing surprise that it
should be considered otherwise:

I wonder why you describe *The Times* as an organ of High Tory
opinion. It was not so when it led the attack on the Hoare–Laval
agreement, for example, or when it was putting the Special Areas
on the map. I do not think that you would find many High Tories
to agree with you or many Labour members either. The coal-
owners would certainly repudiate your suggestion in heated terms
at the moment.[68]

Although he ran a taut ship at Printing House Square,
and was clearly aware of all that his exalted position entailed,
Dawson was no thoughtless autocrat.

Much is made of Lord Milner's influence over Dawson—so
determinative as to be responsible for his having gone into
journalism in the first place. It is surprising that no one has
thought to consider his journalistic influence—or ferreted out
W. T. Stead's description of Milner as journalist (he was Stead's
assistant Editor on the *Pall Mall Gazette* for a number of years)
in the *Review of Reviews* for July 1899:

He would squirm at an adjective here, reduce a superlative there,
and generally strike out anything that seemed calculated need-
lessly to irritate or offend. He was always combing out the knots in
the tangled mane of the P.M.G., and when the lion opened his
mouth, Milner was always at hand to be consulted as to the advisability of modulating the ferocity of its roar. . . . He stood as
guardian armed with ruthless pen, ever on guard against any
expression that seemed strained, or any utterance that rang false
by excess of vehemence.

Dawson kept in cordial touch with his correspondents,
including Ebbutt.[69] He was certainly never isolated from the
paper or any aspect of its operation. The archives of *The Times*

---

[68] Barrington-Ward to G. V. Ferguson, 27 July 1938, *The Times* archives.
[69] Dawson also saw Ebbutt whenever he came to London. See below, p. 62.

and his own diaries and papers provide ample indication and evidence of the vitality of his role and involvement.[70]

It is difficult to understand *The History of the Times*'s almost obsessional criticism of Dawson's decision not to appoint a new Foreign Editor when the position fell vacant in 1929. This was 'the most important decision of Dawson's second innings and most deliberately reached'.[71] Such criticism, however, is based upon two very great assumptions. First the explicit assumption that there was available 'a man of mature judgement, versed in foreign affairs, eastern and western, able and willing to write leading articles at short notice and capable of instructing leader-writers and revising their articles'.[72] The conditions of foreign and imperial politics were such by the 1930s that such men were not to be found. On 18 July 1936 Dawson wrote to his friend Lord Brand, 'A really good Foreign Editor would be a great support' but that no one good enough was around at present.[73] Second there is the tacit assumption that such a man, when found, would have directed *The Times*'s policy otherwise than Dawson did.

In a lengthy Memorandum to the Manager of the paper in July 1929, Dawson set out his reasons for 'abandoning the idea and title of a "Director of the Foreign Department", which has become an anachronism and dividing the various functions rather more precisely between the half dozen members of the staff who nowadays carry on what used to be one man's task when the title was originally invented for Sir Donald Mackenzie Wallace'.[74] Responsibility for receiving and supervising foreign articles and telegrams would be divided between a morning and evening man with an extra in reserve. The writing of foreign leaders—'that is, the expression of the opinion of the paper in foreign affairs'—would be roughly divided as it had come to be in practice, according to the knowledge and experience of the writers available. 'It is impossible to attain perfection in this respect,' Dawson realized, 'and it will often happen that we shall all have to write on

---

[70] He even lately—and reluctantly—allowed a telephone to be installed in Langcliffe Hall so that he could keep up with the paper when in Yorkshire.

[71] *Hist. Times*, iv. 815.   [72] Ibid.

[73] Dawson to Brand, 18 July 1936, *The Times* archives.

[74] Dawson Papers, 'Copy of the Editor's Memorandum to Mr. Lints Smith,' July 1929, p. 1.

subjects on which we know very little', but the division of labours according to abilities seemed inevitable:

The old theory of the 'foreign leader-writer'—someone who was prepared to write on any subject or briefed by someone else—seems to me to be as obsolete as that of a 'Foreign Editor'. As a matter of fact most of the really effective foreign leaders even in the old days were written not by so-called 'leader-writers' but by successive 'Directors of the Foreign Department' e.g. Chirol and Williams. I am quite convinced that the only chance of keeping up the standard is that everyone should write as far as can be arranged on the subjects which he knows best and on which he has himself kept up close personal contact with the people concerned.[75]

In this Memorandum Dawson dealt with other practical matters like the arrangement of calls upon the Foreign Office and the various Embassies. Whoever would be working in the office in the evening should always be at the 4.15 Conference, 'which is his one opportunity for seeing the state of the paper as a whole and for expressing his opinion about what is essential or optional on the foreign side'.[76] He also wanted to keep in closer touch with the paper's correspondents not only at their foreign stations, but when they came to London. Hitherto it seemed to be the tendency for visiting correspondents to go from room to room in search of the most agreeable advice and instructions. Correspondents, he felt, should have regular opportunities for meeting the office as a corporate body. The Archives of *The Times* and Dawsons' own papers show that throughout the 1930s he kept in touch with the paper's correspondents both by post and when they were in London. He saw Ebbutt in June 1936 when he was on his way back to Berlin after a lengthy convalescence in the south of France, and in May 1937 (three months before his expulsion) both as a guest at lunch in the Boardroom and privately the following day.[77] He corresponded frequently with Douglas Reed, when he was Ebbutt's assistant in Berlin until 1935 and then as Vienna correspondent until 1938; with James Holburn both as Ebbutt's assistant and successor; with H. G. Daniels in Geneva; and with A. L. Kennedy.

The conclusion of Dawson's Memorandum might have been

---

[75] Ibid., pp. 4–5.   [76] Ibid., pp. 5–6.
[77] Dawson Papers, Diary 1936, 5 June; Diary 1937, 20, 21 May.

addressed to the author of *The History of The Times*, so well does it set out the commonsense reasoning behind Dawson's decision:

. . . namely, that the editorial staff of a newspaper cannot be organized in a rigid hierarchy like a bank or a Government Department, that the positions and duties in it must be far more elastic and must depend on individual interests and capacities, and that the fewer permanent titles there are about it the better. So far as the foreign side is concerned it seems to me that everyone should be prepared to write on his own subjects—which after all is the first and most important business of journalism—and that everyone should have in addition his allotted share of routine duties, which should in no case be so heavy as it has sometimes been in the past.[78]

Although 'everyone' was a group of about half a dozen carefully selected senior men, it will be seen that Dawson was far from being an autocrat, and his decision to allow the Foreign Editorship to lapse was far from being an autocratic one.

That the actual practice at Printing House Square tended away from the idea of this Memorandum was very largely due to the return of Robert M. Barrington-Ward to *The Times* in October 1927. He had been Dawson's Private Secretary during the first part of the 'first innings', and after service in the Great War he had gone to the *Observer* where he became Garvin's Assistant Editor in 1919. Rejoining *The Times* in 1927, he was appointed Deputy Editor in 1934, and finally succeeded Dawson as Editor (1 October 1941–8).

B.-W., as he was known because of his 'cumbrous' surname, was a man of wide-ranged knowledge and deep-seated conviction. Despite his almost determinative complicity in *The Times*'s policy of appeasement ('By the spring of 1936 he [B.-W.] had become almost solely responsible for the treatment of Anglo-German relations'), he receives kind, even generous treatment from the author of *The History of The Times*.[79] Although it is put to his credit that in the 1920s he read *Die Grosse Politik*, and knew German, French, and Italian, it is concluded that

Those in authority over the subject of foreign affairs, the Editor and his Assistant-Editor (Barrington-Ward), were in no sense

[78] Ibid., p. 9.   [79] *Hist. Times*, iv. 904–5.

specialists on the subject; in any event, they were unable to spare more than a portion, relatively small, of their time to its study. It was impossible for anyone in B.-W.'s position to read sufficiently and mark well enough the course of diplomacy as revealed in the published documents, and thus lay the basis for a judgement that would be truly independent.[80]

B.-W. was especially interested in European affairs. The keystone of his view of them was the perniciousness of the Treaty of Versailles; he was a strong Czechophobe. Hitler reaped the benefit of Barrington-Ward's long-standing attitudes, for it was his, and *The Times*'s, contention that justice did not become injustice because a dictator demanded it.

The most fundamental bases of their outlook upon post-Versailles Europe were thus the same, and in practice Dawson had confidence in Barrington-Ward's ability to express it for the paper. Dawson, however, was the Editor and this office and his social position gave him a wide range of contacts and sources. It is not true to say that he was ignorant of or simply turned European affairs over to Barrington-Ward. Further, *The Times*'s policy towards Germany was subjected to constant criticism both professional and personal. Dawson's defences of it, in letters and in leading articles, are fully as reasoned and thoughtful as are Barrington-Ward's.

A fourth criticism is that Dawson was a sinister figure, the villain of the appeasement piece. His position at the head of one of the crustiest and most infuriating organs of the Establishment was enough to make him such for radical newspapers, leftist dons, and communist propagandists. The *News Chronicle* and *Daily Herald* especially, and the *Manchester Guardian* rather more decorously, liked to sink their teeth into Dawson and *The Times*. At one point, in 1939, J. B. Priestley wrote an article for the *News Chronicle* which stated *inter alia* that, 'Nearly every day in *The Times* there are persuasive letters, from good addresses, telling us that it is all a slight misunderstanding, and that if we knew the Gestapo better (as we may do soon) we should discover that they are fine, stout fellows . . .'[81]

Dawson took offence at this article and must have written very strongly to Priestley who stated, in a prominently placed

---

[80] Ibid., p. 904.   [81] *News Chronicle*, 10 July 1939, p. 10.

box on the editorial page of the *News Chronicle* on 14 August that 'As I have received a protest from the Editor of *The Times*, and as a detailed examination of the correspondence columns of that journal does prove that this was a rash over-statement of mine, I am gladly withdrawing it, with a frank apology to all concerned.'[82] Commenting on this incident, the *News Chronicle* said that Priestley's original statement had been 'in the nature of exuberant hyperbole'.[83]

Such public activity was quite unusual for Dawson; indeed for those inclined to see it as such, his apparent imperturbability must have been one of his most maddening characteristics. Perhaps he felt the need, as the atmosphere became increasingly fevered around and after the Munich crisis, to make clear the certain limits of controversy that must not be overstepped. It is very likely that the threat of severe legal action was used against Claud Cockburn whose newsletter *The Week* had claimed in a special number of 8 September 1938 that *The Times*'s famous leader of 7 September had been sent to the German Embassy in Carlton House Terrace for approval before publication, and on 14 September that it was in fact a long-standing rule at Printing House Square that all editorial items relating to Germany be sent there for vetting.[84] There was also the affair of the Spender Letter in July 1939[85] in which the *News Chronicle* had played the devil's advocate.

There remain two particular incidents which have been widely held against Dawson and which ought to be explained. The first, his alleged censoring of Norman Ebbutt's Berlin correspondence, will be dealt with at length below.[86] The second involves the resignation of Anthony Winn as Parliamentary Correspondent in October 1938.

After an apprenticeship on the *Yorkshire Post*, the Hon. Anthony Winn, youngest son of the 2nd Baron St. Oswald, became *The Times*'s Parliamentary Correspondent at an unprecedentedly early age. Dawson clearly thought of him as a protégé, and his diaries contain several references to 'young Winn'. There are almost paternal sounding entries in November

[82] *News Chronicle*, 14 Aug. 1939, p. 8.   [83] Ibid.
[84] See *The Week*, 8, 14 Sept. 1938.   [85] *Hist. Times*, iv. 969 ff.
[86] See below, p. 121 ff.

1937 about talks with Winn who was 'very undecided about an offer from Esmond Harmsworth'.[87] He was killed at El Alamein. In his memoirs *Old Men Forget*, Duff Cooper writes bitterly about his friend who died fighting the war the appeasers brought about.

Regarding Winn's resignation, Duff Cooper says, 'He duly reported the speech [Duff Cooper's resignation speech of 3 October 1938 after Munich], and what had been thought of it. I never saw what he wrote, but it did not accord with the policy of the paper. Not only did the editor suppress it but he inserted a concoction of his own in which the speech was described as "a damp squib" and headed it "from our lobby correspondent".'[88]

This version, which has been widely accepted (by, among others, Harold Macmillan who mentions it in his first volume of autobiography *Winds of Change*) has become firmly entrenched in the syllabus of appeasement's errors. In fact, it is based upon several misrepresentations. Duff Cooper's speech was fully reported in two columns on the Parliamentary pages. The speech was also summarized on the Bill page under the usual heading 'Westminster'; thus it was attributed to the reporting staff in the Gallery and not to the Parliamentary Correspondent. Dawson had been in the House for Duff Cooper's speech, so it is possible that he influenced or even emended the comment from Westminster. But it was certainly not attributed to the 'Lobby Correspondent' (a title which was, in fact, never used in *The Times*), and nowhere does the phrase 'damp squib' appear.[89]

Winn's own letter of resignation indicates that Duff Cooper's speech was not the real reason, or at any rate the only reason, for his resignation: 'I would like to emphasise that this incident only confirms a more general belief. The Duff Cooper episode apart, my distaste for what I frankly regard as a silly and dangerous policy has been hardening for many weeks.'[90] The issue was thus more fundamental than a point of editorial privilege in changing or emending anything in the paper:

[87] Dawson Papers, Diary 1937, 9, 10 Nov.

[88] Duff Cooper, *Old Men Forget*, p. 227.

[89] The author is grateful to Mr. Donald McLachlan who made available to him an unpublished paper on the Winn resignation.

[90] Winn to Dawson, 4 Oct. 1938, *The Times* archives.

In normal times it is neither necessary nor customary for a political journalist to agree with the opinions expressed in the editorial columns of the paper by which he is employed. But these are not normal times, and the dividing line, as Mr. Eden pointed out in his speech yesterday, is fundamental.

Winn concluded that 'since, rightly or wrongly, I hold these views, it is impracticable for me to be the Parliamentary Correspondent of a paper which was the first responsible advocate of secession, and which still has hopes of a genuine friendship with the Nazi regime'.

This then was the honourable and, as events proved it to be, right course Winn felt he must follow. It was caused not by any censorship on the part of Dawson, but because of the policy of the paper generally. Dawson appears to have been hurt by this somewhat summary condemnation by one of his own protégés (hence the bitter description of the letter in his Diary as 'long and pompous'), and took great pains to answer Winn's objections in a long letter on the following day:

Your account of the attitude of *The Times* to Germany is almost fantastically wide of the mark. . . . [*The Times* does not] cherish the smallest 'hope of a genuine friendship with the Nazi regime' as it exists at present. Its hope, on the contrary, is of a genuine friendship with the German *PEOPLE*, whatever form of Government they may choose; and its conviction, often expressed during the last few days, is that the Prime Minister's efforts have for the first time made popular German sentiment as vocal as it can be made under the Nazi regime.

I do not myself believe that the system will last for ever. But in any case I am convinced that the best way to consolidate and perpetuate it would be by staging a worldwide war on an issue that would be profoundly misinterpreted, not only in this country and in Germany, but in the Dominions and the United States. Similarly I am convinced that British rearmament and organization must go forward with redoubled vigour if we are ever to make the German people cry halt to an insane competition.[91]

There is a note of disappointment in Dawson's letter to Lady Astor three days later when he notes that 'I hear that our young friend AW had secured a job on the DT [*Daily Telegraph*] before his convictions were allowed to ruin his

[91] Dawson to Winn, 5 Oct. 1938, *The Times* archives.

career on *The Times*.[92] Barrington-Ward noted Winn's resignation in his diary: 'GD came to see me at 11. Anthony Winn has resigned on grounds of disagreement with the paper's attitude towards Germany and the Czechs and of an alleged sneer at Duff Cooper in the political notes (interpolated by GD into Winn's stuff) on Sunday. He is no loss. He would never have become a member of the team. Too slapdash and viewy'.[93]

There are several valid criticisms of *The Times* in this period; most of them involve basic judgements about the real nature and function of a newspaper. If the duty of a newspaper is to provide its readers with sufficient, relevant, and uncensored information with which to form independent judgements, it cannot be maintained that *The Times* was derelict in this respect. Quite sufficient to each day's evils in Germany were *The Times*'s reports thereof. None the less the paper was definitely conscious of its role as the most important newspaper in the British Empire and felt the grave necessity of avoiding inaccuracy of any kind; if there were sins at Printing House Square, they were of omission but not commission. Dawson and B.-W. were well aware of the many failings and partisan enthusiasms of some of their outstanding correspondents. The former was schooled and interested in the as yet unplumbed resources and problems of the worldwide British Empire beside which age-old European problems seemed much reduced in proportion; the latter was almost the prototype example of how the issues discussed in Chapter One affected and determined attitudes towards Nazi Germany.

The great virtue of *The Times*'s editorial columns was consistency. Never once was admiration expressed for Nazi Germany, although that it had made some positive achievements was neither denied nor begrudged. Still, the Nazi regime was *de jure*, well established, and based upon an undeniably popular mandate the basis of which was seen to be quite justified grievances against the Treaty of Versailles, both in its political and territorial provisions. A. L. Kennedy, who by this time had resigned from the paper to write his exposé of German intentions, wrote to Dawson that Europe needed a new settlement,

---

[92] Dawson to Lady Astor, 8 Oct. 1938.
[93] Barrington-Ward, Diary, 5 Sept. 1938.

'or *re*-settlement, I would prefer to call it, because I do think it is very important to do it as an admission that the 1920 settlement was one-sided, and to regard this as an *agreed* and final settlement—so far as anything can be final. Change seems to be a law of history! and what we have got to do is to make the method of change less ruinous than a war of bombing.'[94]

Unlike many of the Nazis' most ardent critics, *The Times* consistently urged the necessity for armaments against the day when Germany or any other aggressor overstepped the traditional limits of British interests. The paper was aware not only of the differing defence needs of the British Empire, but of its different attitudes towards European problems. If Dawson had not learned, along with Chamberlain at the Imperial Conference of 1937, that South Africa would not fight in a war over Czechoslovakia, he read it in Ebbutt's report from Berlin, because the South Africans told the Germans at the same time: 'The Germans are understood to have learned that at the Imperial Conference the Dominions, while ready to bear their share of rearmament and to support the Mother Country in case of need, have been inclined to press for a more negative formulation limiting to a minimum commitments which might involve Great Britain in a Continental warfare.'[95]

It had been a conscious decision by Dawson, at the beginning of his second innings that *The Times*, just recovering from its Northcliffe vicissitudes, would adopt the most serious demeanour possible. After fifteen dynamic years, Dawson felt that the paper could do with a year or two of steadiness—'even of stodginess' as he put it.[96] 'The public now required soothing,' *The History of The Times* describes his attitude, 'and Dawson espoused a policy of "giving fair play to the Government", without necessarily following them at every point. This became a permanent principle of his editorship as long as a Conservative or National Government was in power.'[97] The ideas both of general support for the Government of the day and of absolute impartiality of news reporting were thus established in 1923 as prerequisites for Dawson's resumption of the editorship.

[94] Kennedy to Dawson, 9, 17 Oct. 1937, *The Times* archives.
[95] *The Times*, 3 May 1937, Berlin Corr., p. 14.   [96] *Hist. Times*, iv. 793.
[97] Ibid., p. 794.

In his memorandum of conditions at this time he stated that
'In my opinion the first business of the Editor of *The Times*
at the present moment is . . . the restoration of the reputation
of its news columns for absolute accuracy and impartiality . . .'[98]

To think that Dawson would intervene to censor news he
found disagreeable from his own or the paper's point of view
is to understand neither the paper nor the man. It also neglects to take into account the journalistic integrity of the people
whose work would thus be censored for policy, and, especially
in domestic affairs, a well-informed readership which would be
immediately aware of any such tendentiousness.

By the mid 1930s *The Times* had gained the reputation of
being an official spokesman for the British Government. Its
quality circulation, the closeness with the National Government and, mainly through Dawson, with Halifax and Chamberlain, seemed to confirm this as fact. This reputation, which
had been built up over a number of years, seemed most prominent and important in relation to Germany. Especially
outside Britain it seemed that the paper's reputation for expressing official opinion was taken very seriously. On 9 June
1938 the German Embassy in London reported to Berlin
(apropos of *The Times*'s leader of 3 June)[99] that 'it is well known
that *The Times* is utilized for such semiofficial *ballons d'essai*,
while, on the other hand, it is also quite certain that *The Times*
would not oppose the views and intentions of Prime Minister
Chamberlain in questions of foreign policy'.[100] When, through
the quite independent ways which we have outlined, *The
Times* came to the conclusions about Germany which it did,
those who opposed these conclusions saw the double danger
of *The Times* having a grave influence on foreign opinion.
This was the basis for Anthony Eden's memorandum on *The
Times*'s leader of 4 April 1935, 'The British Role':

Sir E. Phipps' telegrams show how much harm that leader of the
4th April has done in Berlin. I can undertake that it will have done
as much, or more, harm in Moscow, Warsaw and Prague, to say
nothing of Paris and Rome. It is of little use for members of the
Government to make long journeys if a part of the confidence they

⁹⁸ Ibid., p. 780.   ⁹⁹ See below, pp. 179–80.
¹⁰⁰ *DGFP*, Ser. D. ii, doc. 247.

have striven to create is thus to be destroyed. If we are to pursue
an effective foreign policy in Europe, it is essential that it should
be made clear that *The Times*, with its defeatist leaders, does not
represent His Majesty's Government. If this is not done, all our
efforts will be in vain. I suggest a question and answer in the
House as the best method of doing this.[101]

In June 1937 there was a singular exchange of correspondence
between the Foreign Secretary Anthony Eden and Geoffrey
Dawson. On 16 June, Eden sent Dawson a copy of a letter
he had written to Lord Lothian disapproving publication of
some articles on the colonial question which Lothian had
written for *The Times*. Eden felt that the articles might affect
the Government's position in the impending talks with von
Neurath, the German Foreign Minister. Dawson replied that
Lothian's articles should help rather than embarrass the Government since they were a signed personal statement rather than
an anonymous leading article. On 18 June, Eden replied that
it was essential to withhold comment in view of von Neurath's
visit, because *The Times*'s views were taken by most of Europe
as representing those of the British Government.[102]

This was the problem to which the *Manchester Guardian*
referred in November 1938 when it called it 'a misfortune,
not an advantage, for a journal to become too "influential",
"authoritative" or too closely connected with any particular
party or Government, for in this way there are responsibilities
thrust upon it which are not of its calling'.

The irony of the situation is that *The Times* in fact derived
virtually no journalistic advantages from its 'special relationship' with the Government—certainly none commensurate
with the disadvantages of fact and reputation both at the time
and to our own day. From many sources today we know that
the British Government did not have very much information of
an important nature about Germany which might be leaked
to any newspaper; this was particularly true after Nevile
Henderson went to Berlin as Ambassador in May 1937.
Typical of this is Barrington-Ward's letter to Dawson (who

[101] Avon, *Facing the Dictators*, p. 177.

[102] Eden to Dawson, 16 June 1937; Dawson to Eden, 17 June 1937; and Eden to
Dawson, 18 June 1937, *The Times* archives. Unfortunately these letters are missing
from *The Times* archives, but their contents were noted in a Letter Index prepared
by John S. Maywood for the Historian of *The Times*.

had been away in Yorkshire since the beginning of the month) at the end of August 1938, with the Nuremberg *Parteitag* and the Czech crisis looming just ahead. He wrote that:

I saw Halifax this morning at the necessary, but unseasonable, hour of 10. I found him rather more impressed than before, though still not wholly convinced, by the stream of information coming in from many quarters to the effect that Hitler intends to have the Czech situation mopped up, whether by Czech compliance or by force, before the end of September. As we all know, the difficulty of gauging the value of reports like these is that both Czechs (and their sympathisers) and Germans have an interest in making our flesh creep. He, Simon, and the P.M. talked all this over yesterday and feel that the moment has come for a little counter-pressure to keep the Germans straight. At the same time he said that the P.M. was against activities that would suggest too much alarm here.

Naturally Hitler wants something to show before Nuremberg, but I continue to doubt, as I think you will, whether Hitler will really be ready to take all the risks implicit in forcible action but there can be no harm, at all events, in doing what can be done to discourage any such inclination provided we are not at the same time encouraging the Czechs to offer less than they ought. He told me that they were continuing the Franco-British pressure on the Czech Government.

He asks me to keep wholly to myself the next move which is being made to keep the Germans guessing. They are getting Henderson back at the week-end and there will be a meeting of Ministers next Tuesday. I see my way to some comment which should be helpful and steadying but I think it had better be deferred— and will be more useful and natural if deferred—until Henderson's return or Simon's speech on Saturday gives us a perfectly open occasion for making it.[103]

In many ways the British newspapers had far better sources of news from Germany than had the British Government itself.

Where its Government connections might have assisted *The Times*, in the area of inside information about the British Government's thinking or intentions, two factors stood in the way. The first was the obvious fact that there were many things which would not be told to outsiders however close—even assuming that motives which we readily attribute today had been formulated at the time. For example, it is difficult to

---

[103] Barrington-Ward to Dawson, 25 Aug. 1938, *The Times* archives.

credit a Government–*Times* cabal against anti-appeasers when Barrington-Ward could write to Dawson on 2 January 1938, apropos of the announcement of Vansittart's appointment as Chief Diplomatic Adviser on the 1st, that 'The more I ponder over Vansittart's appointment the more I feel disposed to think that he has been kicked upstairs or promoted out of the way. I cannot think that the P.M. would wish to give him, with his known prejudices, a position of still greater influence at this moment.'[104] Dawson's main contacts were with Halifax, not with Chamberlain. The Editor wrote a leader in October 1937 suggesting that public opinion was ahead of the Government in seeking an agreement with Germany,[105] and his diary for 28 October records a scene which hardly indicates a close conspiratorial relationship:

My leader produced a good deal of attention and approval. One sentence in it suggesting that public opinion was ahead of the Government in seeing the urgency and importance of a settlement with Berlin caused the P.M. to ask me to come and see him (in bed with gout but otherwise extremely well) so that he might tell me what he at any rate had been trying to do. He went through the whole story of overtures and rebuffs and told me some extraordinary things about the Aga's recent talks with Hitler and the prospect of Edward [Halifax] going to Berlin as a guest [for?] the Sports Exhibition. Nevile Henderson was emerging from the bedroom as I went in.[106]

In addition, it must be assumed that in those things to which Dawson and *The Times* were made privy, there was an inherent discretion which operated to obviate such information being used for the paper's advantage.

All these factors and relationships are summed up in Dawson's diary entry for 14 September 1938. Halifax told him about Chamberlain's plan to fly to see Hitler, but enjoined secrecy about it. Dawson then went on to lunch privately with Horace Wilson at the Travellers' Club: 'He goes with N.C. tomorrow, but of course said nothing of this.'[107]

The Times was an independent conservative newspaper which

[104] Barrington-Ward to Dawson, 2 Jan. 1938, *The Times* archives.
[105] See *The Times*, 28 Oct. 1937, 1st Leader, p. 17.
[106] Dawson Papers, Diary 1937, 28 Oct.
[107] Dawson Papers, Diary 1938, 14 Sept.

had independently and characteristically arrived at a policy towards Nazi Germany which happened to coincide with that pursued by the Baldwin and particularly the Chamberlain Governments. The paper's Editor was an old friend and neighbour of Lord Halifax and both men were members of Eton's Governing Council (for meetings of which it was frequently convenient to spend the night at the Astors' nearby home Cliveden). There is no apparent case of any information gained from such personal contacts having been used to the paper's exclusive advantage. More importantly, because of its earned reputation for being discreet, accurate, and dependable, and because of the calibre of its personnel, *The Times* enjoyed unique advantages of access to men and offices.

Largely because of the way things had worked out by the 1930s, *The Times* had a reputation for official guidance and inspiration which appearances conspired to support, but which, to the extent that it did in fact exist, was regarded as a matter for the utmost discretion and secrecy. For the researcher today, *The Times* remains the best and most complete source of reliable contemporary information about, and assessments of, events in Germany.

9. MANCHESTER GUARDIAN

When C. P. Scott left the *Manchester Guardian* in July 1929, he had served the paper as its Editor since January 1872. That half-century had compactly seen the full-flowering and fall of Liberalism; and the paper had played a not unimportant part in these fortunes. The great days of the *Manchester Guardian* were those of the 1906 Liberal Government when the paper reaped the reward of its constancy (which had taken great courage, especially over issues like the Boer War), and to which it had made an important contribution. Although Scott left Parliament, in which he had sat since 1895, just before the great Liberal victory, his contacts with Ministers could only be likened to Dawson's after 1937, and his interventions in, and influence upon, Government thinking are without parallel.

Under Scott's leadership the *Manchester Guardian* was transformed from a provincial Lancashire Whig newspaper to an internationally known and respected Liberal journal of news and opinion. As the Liberal Party disintegrated in and after the First World War, the paper became increasingly independent in its thinking, and correspondingly isolated. Although it lamented the purblind Liberal policy of standing aloof from the waxing Labour Party, the paper was unable to bridge the gap itself, both because of its old Party connection and its new intellectually independent position. In the 1930s it was never a vessel of Liberal policy like the *News Chronicle;* and of course the *Daily Herald* officially served the Labour Party. The Liberal pedigree of the *Manchester Guardian* was thus based upon the kind of people and intellectuals it attracted both as staff and as readers.

The *Manchester Guardian*'s circulation was always within the 25,000–50,000 provincial category along with papers like the *Yorkshire Post* and the *Glasgow Herald.* The *Manchester Guardian Weekly* was the source of the paper's great reputation in America; a very influential German edition of the *Manchester Guardian Weekly* was printed in Berlin until the Nazis suppressed it in 1933.

While Scott had certainly succeeded in his ambition of 'making righteousness readable', his policy of carrying on the paper 'as a public service and not for profit' was more problematical since profit was never one of the *Manchester Guardian*'s strong points. Scott had acquired full financial control of the paper in 1907. Although profits were never large and ever-increasing capital costs swallowed them, there were sufficient reserves to purchase the successful popular *Manchester Evening News* over the years 1923–30. In the 1930s the *Manchester Guardian*, even on an extremely small and rigorously observed budget, ran at a loss. When E. T. Scott, C. P. Scott's eldest son and successor as Editor, lost his life in a boating accident on Windermere, his half-share in the paper passed to his brother J. R. Scott, who thus became the sole owner. The Inland Revenue, in valuing E. T. Scott's half-share for death duties, pointed out that the *Manchester Guardian* had been running at a considerable loss and the *Manchester Evening News* at a considerable profit; it was contended that continuing the *Manchester Guardian* in such circumstances was a personal whim, since many large offers had been made for the *Manchester Evening News* alone. In 1936, J. R. Scott divested himself of all beneficial interests and formed a Trust to which all the ordinary shares of the *Manchester Guardian* and the *Evening News Ltd.* were assigned; dividends would be paid to the Trust and must be used to further the interests of the papers.

As the liberal quality paper, the *Manchester Guardian* was very much committed to a number of attitudes in international affairs. Among the most basic were the iniquity of the Treaty of Versailles, and the villainy of France; the paper was also deeply opposed to what it deemed the ruthless exploitation involved in colonies and the Imperial idea. We have seen that the paper considered even Locarno to have been a bit of French trickery, and its abhorrence for colonies led to extreme lengths of expression.[108] To these convictions was added the overriding determination that war must never again be the arbiter of men's affairs. This liberal intellectual British newspaper had the greatest interest in, and enthusiasm for, that German intellectual exercise, the Weimar Republic. The gradual dissolution of that enlightened experiment left much disillusion in its wake. Reactions differed according to personality, but there was everywhere a certain disappointment with the German people who were obviously not of sufficiently stern stuff to make a success of their constitution and their Republic.

When the Weimar Republic not only crumbled but was replaced quite legally by Hitler, the blow was doubly hard. Hitler, basing his case on grievances against Versailles, caused a kind of schizophrenia in the *Manchester Guardian* which opposed him ideologically but could not consistently oppose most of his political demands. From the very first there was no doubt but that the *Manchester Guardian* abhorred the Nazi regime, its racial theory and barbarous practices. The paper's Editor from 1933 to 1944, W. P. Crozier, deemed it the *Manchester Guardian*'s special mission to keep the issues of the Jewish and Christian persecutions and the concentration camps before a public eye which grew too easily weary when news was not sensational or exciting. Crozier, indeed, was bitter against those newspapers, especially *The Times*, which he felt ignored or did not pay sufficient attention to these issues. One of the very reasons Crozier was anxious for Voigt to become

108 See above, p. 12.

diplomatic correspondent working in London was that, as he explained in a letter, 'I think we can do with a little more of the spirit of Milton and Cromwell in respect of German topics, and as you and I think, I believe, pretty well on common lines as to what we could do and the duty of the *Guardian* to do it, I am looking forward to some interesting cooperation.'[109] It is interesting that much of Crozier's determination in this regard sprang from the conviction that the *Manchester Guardian* had been lacking, in the years before the Great War, in exposing the danger of the militarist and pan-German characteristics of the most important people in Germany. He wrote to Voigt in January 1934 that:

C.P.S. had such a profound belief in the goodness of human nature, everybody's human nature, that he would just not believe that there was any important section of opinion in Germany who were a real danger to peace; at any rate he would not have it said. I always remember that at the beginning of the war, when the Germans first dropped bombs or shells on undefended places, he said in so many words that that accusation against them must be untrue, that it was incredible that they should have violated international under-takings in that way; and actually he sent a reporter to investigate and find out for his private information that there were military defences at which the German attack must have been aimed. I want so far as ever possible to work for peace and good under-standing, but at the same time to be quite realistic in describing the situation. We shall get into trouble with many people, but we are bound to do that anyway.[110]

The *Manchester Guardian*'s leaders and articles on all aspects of the Terror in Germany, and Voigt's reports as 'Our Diplomatic Correspondent' and especially as 'Our Special Correspondent', stand as humanitarian and journalistic monuments to the men who wrote them and the paper which printed them. Otherwise the paper's coverage of Germany, through C. A. Lambert's dispatches and Reuters reports, was adequate and unexceptional. Although money was a constant concern at the time, we can see today that the paper's precarious finances were not really so great a disadvantage since scoops or special stories were all but non-existent in Nazi Germany. Still, the

---

[109] Crozier to Voigt, 3 Aug. 1934, *Manchester Guardian* archives.
[110] Crozier to Voigt, 25 Jan. 1934, *Manchester Guardian* archives.

paper was vulnerable since Lambert was its only correspondent in Germany. He appears to have been naturally phlegmatic, and had to be prodded constantly by Crozier; he was, moreover, prone to long vacations and inopportune illnesses, and the *Manchester Guardian*'s German correspondence at several crucial times was from H. D. Harrison or P. B. Wadsworth of the *News Chronicle*, Howard Siepen of Reuters, or Wallace King of the *Daily Herald*.

The *Manchester Guardian* provides an excellent example of how the pre-existing attitudes towards the issues discussed in Chapter One could affect a paper's treatment of Germany: the *Manchester Guardian* could not deny the justice even of a dictator's 'just' demands. The *Manchester Guardian* was in the complicated position of knowing what the Nazi regime and its ideas must lead to, but being unable conscientiously to oppose various demands based upon what it deemed genuine grievances in which Britain had complied at Versailles or was even guilty of in 1939. After the frenetic Nuremberg *Parteitag* of 1936, a leader in the *Manchester Guardian* recalled that 'After a week of Nuremberg it is difficult for us to remember that we too may be responsible for the present state of Europe. In the violence of Hitler and Goebbels we forget the arguments of Stresemann and Brüning, and do not stop to ask whether any great nation would behave like Germany that had not some cause to do so.'[111]

Crozier felt that however abominable the Nazis might be, and however much it was a bounden duty to upbraid them constantly, there was not a *casus belli* in this situation. On 15 September 1936 a leader affirmed that 'However unprofitable it may seem, it is necessary to answer unreason with reason and to remember always that the German people are still the same as they were five years ago.'[112] Crozier wrote in 1935 to Robert Dell, the paper's Geneva correspondent, and a vehement anti-Nazi:

But it simply won't do, in my opinion, to treat Germany as an outlaw, or a mad dog; she is entitled to have 'equality', whether she is run by Nazis or Communists or anyone else, and she has to be given the opportunity of coming into the Pacts that are being made

[111] *Manchester Guardian*, 16 Sept. 1936, 1st Leader, p. 8.
[112] *Manchester Guardian*, 15 Sept. 1936, 5th Leader, p. 10.

around her. It does not follow that his policy will succeed, but it seems to me to be the only course that is politically wise.[113]

Germany was, for better or worse, an integral part of any meaningful European settlement, and with war as the stake, no one could rightly risk it by simply writing Germany off as beyond the pale of all civilized dealings. This was, clearly, the only line Crozier could pursue as a responsible Editor.

Any evaluation of Crozier's attitude towards Germany must take into account the brilliant and distinguished but partisan, opinionated, and somewhat erratic staff of editorial writers and foreign correspondents with whom he had to deal. As he wrote to Voigt in 1936, 'We have at the present time about five correspondents and one Long Leader, and between them, like the famous meeting of six economists, they have at least seven policies.'[114] Most of the leading articles about Germany between 1936 and 1939 were written either by Crozier or by Voigt. Other writers and occasional contributors were J. L. Hammond, who was C. P. Scott's biographer, and C. E. Montague, Scott's son-in-law, who wrote under Crozier's direction, for example, the editorial articles opposing British participation in the 1936 Olympic Games in Berlin. A. P. Wadsworth, Crozier's Assistant and successor as Editor, appears to have had little hand in the formation or expression of the paper's attitude towards Germany, although he saw— and initialled—all the correspondence between Crozier and Voigt. Lewis Namier, then Professor of History in Manchester University, had been a very active editorial contributor to the paper in the early 1930s, but after 1936 there is no evidence of his influence, save for a voluminous correspondence with Crozier concerning Zionism.

Robert Dell was in Geneva, in succession to 'A Student of the League', Konni Zilliacus; Alexander Werth, who succeeded Voigt in Berlin in 1933, was in Paris from 1934 to 1939. M. W. Fodor was the paper's Vienna and central European correspondent. A Hungarian Jew, Fodor knew his territory and its languages well. His book *South of Hitler* is a useful and comprehensive study of the area. Its impact and sales were presumably blunted by the fact that when it appeared

---

[113] Crozier to Dell, 12 Mar. 1935, *Manchester Guardian* archives.
[114] Crozier to Voigt, 24 Apr. 1936, *Manchester Guardian* archives.

in April 1938 it made the basic mistake of predicting that Hitler would not invade Austria.

C. A. Lambert, the Berlin correspondent, had started out in the Manchester office. His main interests were German law and economics, and these are accordingly prominent in his reports. As we shall see, his reporting in no wise partook of the fervour which characterized his colleagues' work; this was very likely due to the tense conditions under which he had to work. Although it never came, expulsion was always considered imminent, and there seemed no more precarious journalistic position in Nazi Berlin than that of *Manchester Guardian* correspondent.

The outstanding figure on the *Manchester Guardian*, and undoubtedly the greatest British political journalist of the 1930s, was F. A. Voigt. Frederick Augustus Voigt was born in Hampstead in May 1892. In 1915 he received a First Class Honours degree in German from the University of London. He served on the Western Front with the Middlesex Regiment in the Great War. In May 1919 he joined the *Manchester Guardian* and was sent to Berlin the following year as assistant to the paper's distinguished correspondent there, J. G. Hamilton. From 1928 to 1930 Voigt returned to Manchester as a leader writer. His left-wing sentiments and associations were little to the taste of the German Governments of 1930–3 when he was once again in Germany, now as the paper's correspondent there. Already in 1932 Crozier had to temper Voigt's zeal in exposing German rearmament. In 1926 Voigt was Philip Scheidemann's source of information for his famous but ineffectual Reichstag speech exposing the Reichswehr's secret rearmament.[115] In 1932, however, Crozier pointed out that if the *Manchester Guardian* did an exposé of this kind, the French would use it as a pretext for some kind of extreme reaction—perhaps even an invasion of Germany. 'It seems to me, therefore', Crozier wrote to Voigt, 'that we ought to be careful while exposing the character of the present Government[116] to urge that we must take some such steps as will put them in the wrong if they then go on with their plans for rearming.'[117]

[115] Wiskemann, *The Europe I Saw*, p. 15.   [116] Papen-Schleicher.
[117] Crozier to Voigt, 26 Sept. 1932, *Manchester Guardian* archives.

From an early date Voigt made himself objectionable to the Nazis; his first personal recorded impressions of the regime and its leader indicate how and why this was so:

That situation [the German situation] is so abnormal—or at least must seem so to English people—that I fear the driest account of it must seem like a piece of sensationalism. I cannot conceive of a Hitler in England, though Bottomly had something of the Hitler in him. . . . I have described him as mildly as possible in my article, simply because I want to avoid raising incredulity. I have watched him at close quarters and have often heard him speak. I have also met people who know him well and have studied all the more serious Hitlerite literature, but unless I toned down my real impressions of him, I doubt whether I would be believed. Several times I have taken people who were incredulous to his (and other Nazi) meetings and in every case they have been astounded, especially at what I have referred to as the lynching spirit. A meeting addressed by Hitler, Goebbels, or the other leaders is simply a mob that lynches in imagination. Ebbutt, of *The Times* (a first rate man, by the way) went to such a meeting for the first time a few weeks ago, and told me that it made him physically sick.[118]

At the end of 1934, after he had come to London from Paris as Diplomatic Correspondent (a position created for him), Voigt wrote to Crozier about the Gestapo's conclusions concerning the paper's 'German service': a 'Bureau Voigt' was thought to have been established in Paris with considerable staff and agencies in France and Germany; its financial resources appeared to be considerable but their sources doubtful (there was 'good reason to suppose that it is financed by the Quai d'Orsay although it is possible that the Vatican is not disinterested'); after some time in Paris the Bureau had now been moved to London where it could work less obtrusively.

Voigt left France in December 1933, after the French Foreign Office had been apprised of plans for an attack upon his life; three Sûreté officials accompanied him to Calais.[119] Even in London, Crozier continued to worry about Voigt's safety. As 'Our Diplomatic Correspondent' but more particularly as 'Our Special Correspondent', Voigt

[118] Voigt to Crozier, 14 July 1932, *Manchester Guardian* archives.
[119] See memo, 12 Jan. 1934, and Crozier to Permanent Under-Secretary of State, Home Office, 25 Jan. 1934, *Manchester Guardian* archives.

published stories of the Terror, the persecutions, and the concentration camps; his article on the Gestapo, in February 1936—'something of a scoop' as he wrote to Crozier[120]—was the first such analysis to appear in the British Press.[121] The enraged Nazis were unable to uncover his sources of information, but as Crozier wrote to him: 'One has only to consider your stuff about the camps, which is going in tomorrow. No one but yourself could have got that for the paper. The S.S. know perfectly well that you are the author and, in general, are the most serious opponent of Nazi Germany in the English Press, and, further, as you yourself know, they conspired against you in Paris.'[122] This was true, and there can be no doubt that the Nazis would have rejoiced at Voigt's removal even if Crozier's concern was somewhat melodramatic:

In any case what is important for you to remember is this: that you are the channel through which practically all the damning exposures of what goes on in Germany get into the paper, and it must long ago have occurred to these people—what, by the way, is true—that if they could get rid of you they would stop off the supply of damning stuff to the M.G. I hope, therefore, that you will distrust everybody and everything, and take great care not to be alone in lonely places.[123]

Voigt is a fascinating and complex character who deserves a far deeper analysis than can be given here. A philosopher journalist who had begun as an extreme but anti-communist leftist, he was disillusioned by the failure of the Weimar Republic and had to re-think his entire position. Nowhere in Britain or in Germany could he find the requisite understanding of the Nazi menace. In December 1933 he noted in his diary: 'Grey depression, grey as the London fog. A whole world foundering before the onslaught of Hitler. Where there is understanding there is no will; where there is will, there is no understanding.'[124]

As a philosopher-theologian, Voigt wrote *Unto Caesar*, a

---

[120] Voigt to Crozier, 5 Feb. 1936, *Manchester Guardian* archives.
[121] *Manchester Guardian*, 17 Feb. 1936, Spec. Corr., p. 9.
[122] Voigt to Crozier, 31 Mar. 1936, *Manchester Guardian* archives.
[123] Crozier to Voigt, 12 Jan. 1936, *Manchester Guardian* archives.
[124] From the unpublished diary of F. A. Voigt, quoted by kind permission of Mrs. Voigt.

study of Communism and National Socialism, which was completed in February and published with great success in April 1938. The book argued, cogently and persuasively, that both Communism and Nazism were revolutionary secular religions backed by revolutionary religious fervour which was quite incompatible with any co-existence with other religions or philosophy.

Marxism and National Socialism are incompatible with Christianity. They have much in common with one another, but they have nothing in common with Christianity. There cannot be peace between Christianity and any State—but between Christianity and the Marxist or National Socialist State there cannot even be that armistice which is the only relationship between Church and State that is not a corruption of either.[125]

Whereas the communist threat was made obvious by the blunt intolerance of the Soviet regime, the German menace was more sinister and sophisticated because it sought to undermine Western institutions from within. Lest there be any mistaking, however, Voigt asserted that Hitler's revolution, like those in France and Russia, was not 'a purely domestic affair, but a matter of universal concern. All Europe, indeed the world, and not least the British Commonwealth, will pay heavily for failure to see that this is so.'[126]

It was his philosopher's foresight which enabled Voigt to see that both Communism and Nazism were threats to the West; in the *Manchester Guardian* he wrote that 'the word "Communism" is, in fact, no more than a cover for Germany's expansionist policy.'[127] He saw the Anti-Comintern Pact as a smokescreen against the West and understood that Russia and Germany were not unlikely partners on the basis of their common interests.[128]

In addition to *Unto Caesar*, Voigt contributed notes to each issue of *The Nineteenth Century and After* which he edited from 1938 to 1946, and wrote and published his own newsletter, *The Arrow*, from January to June 1939.

---

[125] Voigt, *Unto Caesar*, p. 71.   [126] Ibid., p. 70.

[127] *Manchester Guardian*, 26 Nov. 1936, Dipl. Corr., p. 6. See also *Manchester Guardian*, 8 Nov. 1937, p. 13.

[128] See, for example, Voigt to Crozier, 16 Nov. 1937, *Manchester Guardian* archives. *The Arrow* was largely informed by this understanding.

As a working journalist, Voigt poses several interesting problems. On a newspaper which admittedly pursued an ideological line, Voigt favoured a policy of 'hard sell' while, as we have seen, Crozier's inclinations were towards the 'soft sell'. Voigt brought what *The Times Literary Supplement* described as 'great knowledge and a burning sincerity' to all his writing.[129] No one on the *Manchester Guardian* ever doubted his knowledge or his insight, but there were often doubts about the prudence, wisdom or common sense of giving unfettered expression to his burning sincerity. As the Acting Editor wrote to Voigt in November 1936, there was no objection to the accuracy of his views, 'merely that it may in the present circumstances be more effective to assume that Hitler is not both so bad and so small-minded as I have not the faintest doubt that he really is'.[130]

The unswerving character of Voigt's convictions made a difficult time for the Editor. The few surviving letters show that in 1936 alone, Crozier had to counsel prudence in or even refuse to publish parts of the Diplomatic Correspondence at least thirteen times.[131] In mid-March, Crozier wrote about the necessities of observance *vis-à-vis* Germany:

I am sure that you must have become tonight very angry with the British Government, public opinion, probably the 'M.G.', and perhaps the world in general, but I don't think you would expect us possibly to print the latter half of your article. I think you know that we have to make the best, and not the worst of this business of dealing with Germany. Don't think that I am deluded about Hitler and his aims and methods, but I do think there is at least as much to be said for taking him at his word, or, if you like, calling his bluff, as for refusing to have any doings with him at all.[132]

This kind of running battle only once seemed to tell on Crozier's composure: in June 1936 he wrote bitterly to Voigt who had unfavourably compared the *Manchester Guardian*

[129] *TLS*, 2 Apr. 1938, p. 225.

[130] Gordon Phillips to Voigt, 17 Nov. 1936, *Manchester Guardian* archives.

[131] Crozier to Voigt, 14 Jan., 12, 13, 25 Mar. 1936; Crozier to Voigt and Voigt to Crozier, 27 Mar. 1936; Crozier to Voigt, 24 Apr., 13 May 1936; J. R. Scott to Crozier, 2 June 1936; Crozier to Voigt, 15, 16 June 1936; Gordon Phillips to Voigt, 17 Nov. 1936; all in *Manchester Guardian* archives.

[132] Crozier to Voigt, 18. Mar. 1936, *Manchester Guardian* archives.

to the *Daily Telegraph* of the previous day.[133] Otherwise the
Editor simply withheld things that went beyond the bounds
of taste or legal expediency. It is impossible not to sympathize
with Crozier, faced as he was with the practical necessity of
softening the cries, with which he was in basic agreement, of a
respected colleague who yelled 'Wolf!' for half a dozen years
before the wolf suddenly revealed itself to the whole world in
March 1939.

This insight into Hitler and Germany on Voigt's part often
served to override the fact that it was only part of a complex
of attitudes on other issues. Like the *Manchester Guardian*,
Voigt never considered very seriously the defence logistics
which might become involved in implementing in fact their
theoretical resistance to Hitler. For the paper this was largely
attributable to the expediency of avoiding facing the serious
splits in the *Manchester Guardian* and liberal intellectual ranks
generally which would follow upon any detailed treatment of
issues like armaments, war, and pacifism. Voigt, on the other
hand, delimited a very basic concept of vital interests which
Britain would fight for; although he lamented that Britain
was not arming in the face of the ever-increasing German
aggressiveness, it must be considered an oversight if not a
failing in his thinking that he never in his book and very
rarely in his Diplomatic Correspondence dealt with the
practical questions of men and weapons.

Three bases underlay Voigt's correspondence in the *Manchester Guardian* in the late 1930s: first, he held that Germany's
real hatred was for England no matter how much this was
camouflaged; second, he insisted that given the dynamic
nature of the Nazi regime, German expansion must continue;
third, he believed that Britain's only vital interests lay in the
Mediterranean and in Western Europe. All these views, and
especially the 'Mediterraneanocentric' view, were given
expression in his newsletter *The Arrow* in the first six months of
1939; in April 1939 he saw the situation in Europe developing
in such a way 'that may soon compel the Western Powers to
consider a preventive war very seriously'.[134]

---

[133] Crozier to Voigt, 16 June 1936, *Manchester Guardian* archives. The issue was
the ending of sanctions against Italy.
[134] *The Arrow*, 14 Apr. 1939, p. 56.

Voigt was not shackled to any of the liberal and Left panaceas of post-Versailles Europe: he had no use for the League of Nations as it existed; collective security must almost perforce become in practice a string in the French bow thus involving Britain in unwarranted obligations; and communism was as great a threat as Nazism, and the Red Terror in Russia was so bad that even people who had lived under the Brown Terror in Germany were shocked by it.

Voigt's theological vision added a unique element to his analysis. He looked out upon a world after the Fall; Britain was the best, but no nation was perfect, and 'no Government in the world had the right to declare war for principle'. He saw that war was endemic to fallen human nature and that man would fight the war to end wars no sooner than he could produce gold from dross. 'There is no universal remedy for war. No League of Nations, indeed no system that man can devise, will remove the causes of war, because these causes are inscrutable. They lie deep in the nature of man, and not in any specific economic or political system (though some systems may be more conducive to war than others).'[135]

Despite the fact that the Nazi regime's iniquities and barbarisms must be constantly publicized, he felt, at least until March 1939, that 'a general anti-German policy would be excessively dangerous and costly';[136] that 'the material interests of Italy and England are not in conflict',[137] and even that Russia was 'no longer a threat to the Pax Britannica. The English can afford to wish the Russian people well . . .', to hope that they might recover their pre-communist brilliance and achieve some measure of individual freedom.[138] Evil must be resisted everywhere, but it could only be eradicated in its individual forms, and this would require literally endless wars. The only possible criterion for British policy, then, was Britain's vital interests:

The purpose of British foreign policy, is, or should be, to promote the well-being, defend the security, and uphold the honour of the British people. Vital interests have to be defended in all circumstances. But beyond the defence of vital interests and without

---

[135] Voigt, *Unto Caesar*, pp. 269–70.   [136] Ibid., p. 236.
[137] Ibid., p. 237.   [138] Ibid., p. 262.

prejudice to them, it should be an object of foreign policy to counteract every warlike trend and to assist in averting situations that may contain the menace of war, for not only is war fearful in itself, but there can, in the modern world, *NEVER* be any certainty that if war begins at one end of the world, it will not spread to the other. But the defence of vital interests must *ALWAYS* come first.[139]

Voigt held the conviction that Germany had ultimately aggressive intentions towards Britain, which, by being determined to meet the challenge—and by presumably having sufficient arms to do so—could thwart or repel the attack. In the meantime, only Britain's traditional vital interests should be defended by arms.

The all but daily expressions of these complicated views in the *Manchester Guardian* often brought Voigt and Cross Street into conflict. There were occasional ruffled tempers, but generally if a piece by Voigt was cut, he made no fuss. In this way, but not without the building up of some tension, Voigt and the *Manchester Guardian* presented a valuable picture of what life in Germany was like for those sections of the German population which were subject to Nazi persecution. It was not really a balanced view, despite Crozier's desire to report the 'positive side' of the Nazi regime as well. The paper's intellectual credentials were unquestionable, and it undoubtedly had a significant readership in important circles. Halifax stated that of the provincial papers he read the *Manchester Guardian* and the *Yorkshire Post* each day.[140]

But it is not only without vision that people perish; for unless vision is supported by a strength of will to face its implications and enforce it, then the vision is only frustrating. From 1933 to 1939 the *Manchester Guardian* had a clear conception of what Nazi Germany was and what it meant. Because of other commitments and ideals, however, it was unable to draw the logical conclusions of this insight and was forced, each time it was confronted with the continual German heinousness it had always predicted, suddenly to urge tolerance and moderation

---

[139] Ibid., pp. 268-9.
[140] Crozier to Voigt, 28 July 1938, *Manchester Guardian* archives.

either because war was unthinkable, or because no one's conscience was wholly clear, or for whatever reason. One cannot help but think: if only the *Manchester Guardian* had cut aside everthing else and enforced the consistency of its convictions about Germany!

3

1936 AND 1937:
THE GATHERING CALM

ON 30 January 1936, Hitler celebrated the third anniversary of his coming to power. The event stirred up different reactions in the various British newspapers. Watching the snaking columns of torch-bearing storm troops who marched past Hitler's window that night, Wadsworth wrote to the *Observer* that the event was covered by the German Press 'with an enthusiam perhaps not entirely shared by the people as a whole'.[1] Ebbutt wrote that 'Not everyone is so confident as the Storm Troops who marched through the streets singing [*Deutschland Über Alles*].' That three years of contact with hard realities had brought 'a certain amount of disillusionment to the party and to the country at large' was not to be denied.[2] A writer in the *Daily Herald* reported that 'the abnormal of 1933 has become the normal of 1936. . . . And the most powerful and most brutal machinery of oppression which has ever been created rules ruthlessly over a disappointed, impoverished and powerless people.'[3] The *Morning Post*'s leader commemorating the event shared these sentiments.[4] Only the *Daily Mail* was enthusiastic:

This is a memorable date in the history of Europe. . . . Germany by [Hitler's] magnetic influence and the strenuous exertions of her people, has been placed once more in the forefront of the nations. Communism, which in 1933 was such a menace to the States of Central Europe, is dead and is not likely to return to life so long as his vigorous hand is in control.

The enemies who so persistently predicted his early fall have had to confess their complete want of foresight. At the end of three

---

[1] *Observer*, 2 Feb. 1936, p. 21.
[2] *The Times*, 31 Jan. 1936, p. 14.
[3] *Daily Herald*, 30 Jan. 1936, p. 10.
[4] *Morning Post*, 31 Jan. 1936, p. 10.

years of power he is stronger than ever and more popular with his countrymen.[5]

A leading article in the *Manchester Guardian* assessed the three years of Nazi rule during which time the doctrines in *Mein Kampf* had transformed Germany into an oppressive police State, whose vast armaments in the service of those doctrines were now a European problem. All this had followed upon Hitler becoming Chancellor: 'Truly a momentous event followed by prodigious achievement. For good or evil? Again, final judgement is impossible, but so far at least the evil is glaring and bears many a future menace in store, while the good is indiscoverable.'[6]

It was generally anticipated that one of the first uses Germany made of her new power would be to reassert her strength in the demilitarized Rhineland Zone. Although demilitarization had originated with the Versailles *Diktat*, it had been freely accepted in the Locarno treaties of 1925. By February 1936, it was seen clearly that if Germany really wanted to reoccupy the Zone, nothing could stop her,[7] and it was very confidentially hinted to A. L. Kennedy that the Foreign Office had some special plan for the Rhineland.[8]

British opinion expected the main difficulties in negotiations about the Zone to come from France. Crozier wrote to Werth that the French would repeat their performance over the disarmament conference: 'Month after month and year after year the French refused any idea of compromise; they refused specific proposals made by the Germans until finally the Germans took matters into their own hands and proceeded to rearm. The result is that when the process is completed the Germans will be, in a military sense, much stronger than the French.' Just as in that situation Britain had taken hold of events and concluded the Anglo-German Naval Treaty—'in

[5] *Daily Mail*, 30 Jan. 1936, 1st Leader, p. 10. Even Ebbutt had to admit in his correspondence of 2 February that 'the movement can claim to have achieved much that appeals to the patriotic instincts of every German, to have instilled a spirit of self-help in the face of economic and other difficulties, and to have set in motion positive efforts to lead the nation out of the wood of defeat'.

[6] *Manchester Guardian*, 31 Jan. 1936, 1st Leader, p. 10.

[7] Voigt to Crozier, 30 Jan. 1936, *Manchester Guardian* archives.

[8] Kennedy to Deakin, 16 Feb. 1936 (written after a talk with Leeper), *The Times* archives.

spite of the flagrant violation of the Peace Treaty that it involved'—so now she should take the initiative and suggest that the danger be taken out of the situation by considering whether a new voluntary agreement ought not to be made.[9] As Crozier had written to Voigt a week earlier: 'I don't see how she can be expected to observe the demilitarized, which means undefended, zone indefinitely. . . . It is neither physically possible nor morally right to deny her self-defence indefinitely, and simply to go on doing nothing until she takes the risk of war, would, it seems to me, be the reverse of statesmanship'.[10]

During February, while tension slowly mounted, the British newspapers seemed concerned to avoid a *fait accompli* in the Rhineland. For most of the British Press there were two controlling factors in the situation. The first was a determination not to become involved in the French machinations surrounding the Franco-Soviet Pact. 'Of course', Crozier had written to Werth, 'I understand the idea of the French: that they can build up such a containing wall round Germany that she will never even try to break out. That, of course, is a matter of speculation.'[11]

The other and more important factor was the widely held conviction in the merit of Germany's case. Voigt had written that:

Germany is dissatisfied and we cannot dismiss her dissatisfaction as a mere piece of Hitlerite aggressiveness. Nor can the insolence of Dr. Goebbels do away with the feeling present in the minds of every objective observer that Germany has a case. Nor should the menace of German rearmament and of National Socialist Imperialism deter us from examining the German case in the light of the general European situation.[12]

Since the confrontation of Europe by a *fait accompli* would mean a serious crisis, a leading article confirmed, even though war might not be the consequence, 'there is no telling what the result of crisis piled up on crisis would mean.'[13]

[9] Crozier to Werth, 3 Feb. 1936, *Manchester Guardian* archives.
[10] Crozier to Voigt, 29 Jan. 1936, *Manchester Guardian* archives.
[11] Crozier to Werth, 3 Feb. 1936, *Manchester Guardian* archives.
[12] *Manchester Guardian*, 11 Feb. 1936, Dipl. Corr., p. 6.
[13] *Manchester Guardian*, 1 Feb. 1936, 1st Leader, p. 12.

On 29 February the *Daily Mirror* printed the text of an interview Hitler had given to the French publicist Bertrand de Jouvenel.[14] In the interview Hitler pledged himself and the German people to a Franco-German rapprochement, but warned France of the effects a Soviet alliance would have on such possibilities.

The *Daily Mirror* introduced its scoop: 'Passionately . . . fervently . . . in the plain words of a Man of the People, Adolf Hitler, Leader and Master of Germany, in an exclusive interview with the *Daily Mirror* yesterday, pleaded with the world: "Let's Be Friends".'[15] De Jouvenel described the scene:

In the room where the destiny of Germany is planned her Man of Destiny sat to receive me.

Simply dressed, sitting at his desk, he unburdened his heart . . . his hopes . . . his fears.

He eyed me keenly for a moment . . . this man who sees into the mind.

Hitler placed the responsibility for the future on France:

Today France can, if she will, put an end for ever to that 'German peril' which your children, from generation to generation, learn to dread. . . . The chance is given to you: if you do not seize it, think of your responsibility towards your children. You have before you a Germany nine-tenths of whose people have complete confidence in their leader, and this leader says to you· 'Let us be friends.'[16]

This interview caused a flurry of comment in the British Press, after which news of Germany seemed to disappear until it was reported on 6 March that the Reichstag had suddenly been summoned for the following day. This interview was, then, the last 'impression' of Hitler and German policy before the Rhineland coup.

Reaction to this interview varied from critical disappointment to great enthusiasm. The *Daily Mail* represented the latter.[17] The *News Chronicle* counselled that despite the inhuman excesses of the Nazi regime, Hitler had made a 'categorical offer of friendship—not the first. The French people, who

---

[14] Maurice Edelman unaccountably neglects to mention this great scoop for the *Daily Mirror* in his book, *The Mirror*.

[15] *Daily Mirror*, 29 Feb. 1936, p. 1.

[16] Ibid.

[17] *Daily Mail*, 5 Mar. 1936, 1st Leader, p. 12.

stand most to lose and least to gain by war, cannot afford to let it pass. They must give him a chance to prove what he says.'[18] The *Manchester Guardian*, however, pointed out that Hitler had in fact said nothing and had begged all the important questions: Werth wrote from Paris that 'This interview appealed to the emotion, but could not stand the test of a logical examination'.[19]

The reoccupation of the Rhineland was one of Hitler's 'Saturday Surprises'. On the evening of Friday 6 March, he summoned a meeting of the Reichstag for noon on the next day and invited the diplomatic representatives of France, Belgium, Britain, and Italy to come to the Wilhelmstrasse before the meeting. On the morning of the 7th the Ambassadors were handed copies of a memorandum and informed by the Foreign Minister, von Neurath, that the reoccupation of the Rhineland had begun. The memorandum, which Hitler read to the Reichstag, stressed Germany's unequal treatment and set out once again the German objections to the Franco-Soviet Pact which was held to abrogate Locarno. Hitler then set out a peace programme of seven points including a twenty-five year non-aggression pact between France, Germany, and Belgium, with Britain and Italy as guarantors, and the return of Germany to the League of Nations.

By Monday morning when the British daily papers appeared, the reoccupation had been effected peacefully and was already two days old; Hitler's peace offer was fresher news than the moving of his troops. The Sunday papers, however, had already set the tone which the dailies, with one exception, would follow. Scrutator stated that 'Grave as is the news from Germany that is beginning to come in as this article is written, it also bids us hope . . .'[20] The *Observer* stressed rather more the fact that the occupation involved a violation of the freely entered Locarno Treaty, but its conclusion was the same: Britain must consider Hitler's proposals 'in a spirit of sympathy and goodwill'.[21]

[18] *News Chronicle*, 2 Mar. 1936, 1st Leader, p. 10.
[19] *Manchester Guardian*, 2 Mar. 1936, Paris Corr., p. 12.
[20] *Sunday Times*, Mar. 1936, Scrutator, p. 18.
[21] *Observer*, 8 Mar. 1936, 1st Leader, p. 18.

The *Dail Mail* was the most enthusiastic about the opportunity the reoccupation offered:

Germany's latest stroke may be said, indeed, to have cleared the air. Like a fresh breeze from the mountaintops it has swept away the fog and shown exactly where she stands. . . . This is a moment when it is most important to be beware of the Bolshevik trouble-makers. Their aim, as French critics have pointed out in the debates on the unfortunate pact with the Soviet, is to involve the great Powers of Euope in a suicidal war.[22]

The paper scorned excited talk of sanctions, and stated that 'The country wants none of them and none of the school-master tone which some of our British Ministers seem to think proper for such occasions.'[23] The *Morning Post* found itself in unaccustomed agreement with the *Daily Mail*: 'Indeed', a leading article said, 'Herr Hitler may have performed a real service to the future peace of Europe by creating a situation which shows the futility of the whole sanctions policy.' War, for the *Morning Post*, was not 'a possible even if it were a reasonable proposition'.[24]

'Is it War?' the *Daily Express* asked itself; and there was no uncertainty about the answer: 'The Germans have reoccupied the Rhineland. What does that mean to US? . . . The question is WILL BRITAIN BE INVOLVED IN WAR? The answer is NO.'[25] The *News Chronicle*, which had only urged consideration of Hitler's 'offers' to de Jouvenel, now insisted that: 'Herr Hitler's invitation must be taken up without a moment's delay. . . . Condemnation of methods must not be allowed to stand in the way of an acceptance of the new Locarno or of the attempt to rebuild upon it an international system of peace and security.'[26] The *News Chronicle* saw two reasons why the invitation must be accepted: first the realization that there could be no European peace without German co-operation and no German co-operation as long as Germany was suffering from a sense of grievance. 'We cannot pretend that equality exists as long as she, alone of all the Great Powers, is denied the right to maintain troops in an integral part of her

---

[22] *Daily Mail*, 9 Mar. 1936, 1st Leader, p. 12.
[23] Ibid.   [24] *Morning Post*, 9 Mar. 1936, Leader, p. 10.
[25] *Daily Express*, 9 Mar. 1936, 1st Leader, p. 10.
[26] *News Chronicle*, 9 Mar. 1936, Leader, p. 10.

own territory. . . . The second reason is that refusal to accept must in the end mean war.'[27] The *Daily Herald* saw the same alternatives: negotiate or fight. 'War', it stated firmly, 'is out of the question . . . to drive, or seek to drive, her troops out of the Rhineland and to enforce demilitarisation again as a condition of peace . . . to prevent German troops from garrisoning German towns.'[28] W. N. Ewer wrote that to follow the French lead and not take up Hitler's offer would be to 'have bitten off our noses to spite the Führer's face'. To be sure, he added, 'Germany must not complain if, when the new system is built, she is still for a period looked at a little dubiously and regarded as in some measure on trial.'[29]

In terms of its previous policy, the most surprising reaction to the crisis was that of the *Manchester Guardian*. We have seen some of the inter-office tensions between Crozier and Voigt, Werth, and Dell, but the leading articles during the crisis must have surprised and shocked many readers. After stressing the unpleasantness of 'hammerstroke' politics, the paper said that everyone knew all along that the demilitarization could not last indefinitely and that Hitler's offers of peace were indeed far-reaching. Further, even if German troops were expelled by warlike measures, 'the zone could no more be kept "demilitarised" permanently than Germany can now be prevented from having aeroplanes and tanks'.[30] The paper concluded that:

If we cannot overlook a repudiation which was as wicked as it was unnecessary, neither can we forget that for Germans to insist on defending their own territory with arms is not the same heinous moral offence, nor deserving the same penalties, as waging war, like Mussolini, on an unoffending country or preparing a base for an actual invasion. . . . On the one hand not to pass over or condone the German breach of faith; on the other not to lose the chance, if there should be the chance, of cleaning up the horrible mess of suspicion and fear which has poisoned these last few years, and to do it somehow with Germany, since it is obvious that it cannot be done without her: that is the aim we have to keep in view.[31]

On Monday 9 March *The Times* printed its famous leading article, 'A Chance to Rebuild', of which the paper's official

[27] Ibid.   [28] *Daily Herald*, 10 Mar. 1936, 1st Leader, p. 10.
[29] Ibid., ed. art. by W. N. Ewer, p. 10.
[30] *Manchester Guardian*, 9 Mar. 1936, 1st Leader, p. 10.
[31] *Manchester Guardian*, 10 Mar. 1936, 1st Leader, p. 10.

history says, 'It included several strongly worded phrases of
reproof, but any intimidating effect that there may have been
intended to convey in Berlin was destroyed by the sentences
among which they found themselves in print.'[32] In fact it
sounded very much like the *Manchester Guardian*:

The more sensationally minded have described it also during the
week-end as an act of 'aggression'. If it be that as well, there is still
a distinction to be drawn between the march of detachments of
German troops, sent to reoccupy territory indisputably under
German sovereignty, and an act which carries fire and sword into a
neighbour's territory. Anger and panic would, at the best, be over-
hasty interpreters of the event. No one in this country can or will
wish to dispute that the engagements of Locarno have been grossly
violated and that the obligations of the guarantor may now be
invoked.

. . . There are glaring gaps [in Hitler's seven-point peace offer]
to be filled, deep obscurities to be examined. But the questions
for statesmanship are whether the Locarno Treaty is to be made
the means or the bar to the exploration of this offer, and whether
Europe will be safer and its economic recovery nearer according as
the Locarno Powers agree to examine or determine to reject it.
. . . There cannot indeed be two minds about the objective,
for all the difficulties with which the method of its presentation has
hedged it at the moment. British opinion will be nearly unanimous
in its desire to turn an untoward proceeding to account and, far
from weakening the regime of treaties, to seize the opportunity of
broadening and strengthening the collective system which opens
with the German offer of re-entry. . . . It is one of the self-evident
facts of Europe, over and above specific undertakings, that any
threat to French or Belgian territory engages Britain . . . the whole
meaning of collective security has gained through experience . . .
France and Britain alike have reason for indignation and food for
suspicions. But, since neither stands alone, they have the more
power, even while they are faced with an admitted offence against
the law of Europe, to take a steady measure of the undertakings
which Germany has offered in extenuation. The old structure of
European peace, one-sided and unbalanced, is nearly in ruins.
It is the moment, not to despair, but to rebuild.[33]

Only the *Daily Telegraph* insisted upon facing the challenge
Hitler had posed, and dismissed his peace offers as camouflage:

[32] *Hist. Times*, iv. 899.   [33] *The Times*, 9 Mar. 1936, 1st Leader, p. 15.

The challenge is pointed, direct and deliberate, such as the signatory
Powers of Locarno cannot possibly overlook . . . for the moment
the act remains the most important thing. . . . The specious
offer of a German demilitarised zone equal in depth to similar
zones to be marked out by France and Belgium is of no value to
either. France, for example, would have to scrap the chain of
fortresses on which she has spent £35 million in the last few years
and rebuild them farther back. . . . The offer to France and
Belgium of a non-aggression pact for twenty-five years, with Great
Britain and Italy as guarantors if they choose, but containing no
provision for mutual assistance, would be a very indifferent sub-
stitute for Locarno . . . Great Britain herself in other circumstances
would have welcomed unreservedly the suggestion of Germany's
return to the League. But the actual circumstances are what they
are—the flagrant repudiation of treaties, the assertion of glorifica-
tion of overpowering military strength, and the promise of good
neighbourliness—except, indeed to Russia—within the League,
with a hope that her Colonial demands will be 'fully recognised'.
Herr Hitler's action and his speech have created a new and most
difficult situation in Europe, and on the British Government's
next step—carefully considered and, whatever it may be, we hope
it will be firm and unmistakable—the course of future events must
largely depend.[34]

Even this article, complemented by Major-General A. C.
Temperley's assessment, did not propose active resistance to
the German move. Temperley pointed out that 'If [Germany]
meant peace, the continuance of demilitarisation was a demonstration of her pacific intentions and a guarantee of security
to her neighbours. It is only if she is intent on war that reoccupation confers on her any material advantage.'[35]
Apart from the *Daily Telegraph*, only F. A. Voigt pursued
a hard line. Unlike his own paper, he saw that unless Britain
supported the French in opposing reoccupation, 'the Germans
will have attained what Hitler has in his book *Mein Kampf*
(p. 757) declared to be one of the chief aims of German foreign
policy—namely, "the possibility of achieving the overthrow
of France"'.[36] He perceived that Hitler's peace offer was
'cleverly attuned to the weakness of the collective system and

[34] *Daily Telegraph*, 9 Mar. 1936, 1st Leader, p. 12.
[35] Ibid., ed. art. by Maj-Gen. A. C. Temperley, p. 12.
[36] *Manchester Guardian*, 9 Mar. 1936, Dipl. Corr., p. 14.

is at the same time a most skilful piece of demagogy'.[37] The
next day, while his paper was proposing that Hitler show
good will by withdrawing his troops, Voigt exploded Hitler's
claims (and one of the tacit assumptions of the *Manchester
Guardian*'s editorial argument), that the German reoccupation
was merely symbolical.[38]

Within a week it was clear that nothing would be done
about the reoccupation of the Rhineland—except talk. With
the first fear of war past, the different newspapers began
gradually to return to their old attitudes, and by the time of
the German 'election', which Hitler had called to vote judgement on his policies, at the end of March, things had almost
returned to their abstract pre-March plane. The British
Government at length formulated a questionnaire for the
German Government which basically asked whether Germany
would ever honour *any* treaties. Eventually the Germans replied that they would, but failed to specify anything further,
and the matter rested there. *The Times* considered this questionnaire tactless in the extreme and always referred to it in
italics: whether to indicate French linguistic or political origin,
or to demonstrate disdain, was not clear. Disillusioning as this
process might have been, the general attitude was that, as the
Daily Herald put it: 'There is in Herr Hitler's proposals at least
a chance. And can any sane man remember, without regret
and without shame, how in the past years chance after chance
has been recklessly thrown away? Here then is another. What
reason can there be for rejecting it out of hand? Whither would
that rashness lead Britain and lead Europe?'[39]

Virtually without exception the British Press had accepted
the logic of *The Times*: 'It is no condonation of the method by
which the first of these moves was effected to say that they were
inevitable sooner or later.'[40] To understand everything was to
forgive a good deal, and 'What British opinion seized upon
was the opportunity of wresting good out of evil, of proceeding
to a comprehensive liquidation of all reasonable German
claims, and of securing for the first time the full partnership
of the National Socialist Government in a settlement of Europe

---

[37] Ibid.   [38] *Manchester Guardian*, 10 Mar. 1936, Dipl. Corr., p. 14.
[39] *Daily Herald*, 3 Apr. 1936, Leader, p. 12.
[40] *The Times*, 3 Apr. 1936, 1st Leader, p. 17.

upon the principle of mutual concessions and mutual tolerance.'[41] Hitler's plan, further, contained much that would have been common to any French or British plan.[42]

The French Government, under Flandin, adopted a very strong line, insisting upon German withdrawal from the Rhineland before any kind of discussions could begin. The British Government, as suspicious of the French as of the Germans, and determined to grasp this chance to rebuild, opposed such impossible preconditions and arranged that the League Assembly would meet in London instead of in Geneva to consider the French charge of violation of the treaties of Versailles and Locarno. Dawson wrote to Kennedy on 16 March:

I should be very sorry myself to place any confidence in the present regime in Germany. Their occupation of the demilitarised zone was a characteristically stupid blunder, as a great many Germans seem to have realised. At the same time I think it sheer folly to refuse to get the utmost out of the professions which accompanied it, whether they are sincere or not.[43]

And Barrington-Ward wrote to Kennedy a week later about the reaction to the 9 March leader:

I think that the welcome that was given to the first leader here was largely due to the effort which it made . . . to put the event into perspective and to distinguish between the illegal and the catastrophic. As to British opinion generally, our difficulty has been to find enough letters stating what might be crudely called the anti-German view to balance the correspondence.[44]

Voigt supported the French line, as did the *Morning Post*. The Conservative paper stated that a British-French-German guarantee pact was all very well but that Germany only wanted it to secure the west and assure a free hand in the east. Once German hegemony had been established from the Baltic to the Adriatic and from the Rhine to the Black Sea, it would be impossible for Britain or France to oppose any German desires or demands, and the value then of the highly

[41] *The Times*, 21 Apr. 1936, 1st Leader, p. 13.
[42] *The Times*, 4 Apr. 1936, 1st Leader, p. 15.
[43] Dawson to Kennedy, 16 Mar. 1936, *The Times* archives.
[44] B.-W. to Kennedy, 24 Mar. 1936, *The Times* archives.

vaunted Western pact would be moot indeed. 'It is not so
surprising that France refuses to walk into such a trap as this
without further ado. The immediate danger is that Germany
should succeed in capturing the acquiescence of Great Britain.
No effort is being spared to court British good will and to
appeal to sentiment.'[45] But the *Manchester Guardian* itself
stated quite frankly in May that if ever the French line had
been adopted, it had now quite definitely been dropped. The
British Government's Note 'rightly assumes that what we have
to do is to discover without more loss of time what sort of
formula exists on which to build "general negotiations" '.[46]

Hitler's election, supposedly to give the German people
a chance to pass judgement on the Nazi Government thus far,
was held on 29 March. In the event it was so run as to make
negative voting virtually impossible, and was based almost
entirely on the issue of support for the Rhineland *coup*. Those
who wished to vote against the Nazi Party list of candidates
could only do so by defacing the ballot; thus 99 per cent of the
electorate went to the polls, and 98·9 per cent voted for the
Party list.

Of the British Press, *The Times* was the most shocked by
the proceedings: 'As an election they were a farce. . . . As a
test of the nation's confidence in its present leaders, they were
vitiated from the beginning by the impossibility of giving an
adverse vote.'[47] Since Goebbels's propaganda had managed to
make the Rhineland the only issue, 'on Sunday even the opponents of the regime can go to the polls with a clear conscience,
which is the more satisfactory in that it would be inconvenient
to stay away'.[48] On the eve, Ebbutt summed up the situation:

It may be taken for granted, however, that the number of Germans
who do not vote for Herr Hitler tomorrow is far short of the total
which has misgivings about the present regime. Its work has been
done at the expense of freedom, truth, and justice as these are
conceived in the Western world, and some who feel bound to
support the Führer tomorrow on the patriotic issue will do so in

---

[45] *Morning Post*, 20 July 1936, p. 10.
[46] *Manchester Guardian*, 9 May 1936, 1st Leader, p. 12.
[47] *The Times*, 30 Mar. 1936, 2nd Leader, p. 13 (quoted from *The Times*, 21
Mar. 1936, Berlin Corr., p. 11).
[48] *The Times*, 28 Mar. 1936, Berlin Corr., p. 12.

fear and trembling that they are delivering Germany over to a new wave of National-Socialist fanaticism.[49]

The *Morning Post* gave a similarly clear appraisal of the election; Robson wrote that it would earn Goebbels a niche as 'the biggest organiser of public deception the world has ever seen'.[50] The *Daily Herald* headlined the 'German Election Farce' on the front page,[51] and the *News Chronicle* stated that the results were a 'foregone conclusion: the monstrous size of the majority is in itself a proof of its unreality'.[52]

The *Daily Express* defended the result: 'The choice is Hitler—or trouble. . . . Allowing for all—Hitler's eloquence, Goebbels' "arrangements" and Göring's secret police, it is still true that the Germans are behind their Führer.'[53] Another, unexpected, defender was the *Manchester Guardian* which stressed not the procedure but the rightness of the result: 'What other answer would the English people have made had they been asked, after a war which had led to their disarmament, whether they maintained their right to fortify the coasts of Kent and Sussex? Without propaganda and compulsion we should have produced a striking result'.[54]

In fact, Hitler got what he wanted from the election: a victory and time. By the end of March it was clear that nothing would come of the French determination to resist, and although Germany was censured by the League Council, this was the kind of sanction Hitler fed upon. Immediately the election was over, Goebbels proposed a three-week moratorium on political speeches; the suggestion enraged French opinion, but *The Times* found it admirably suited to the political climate.[55] It is clear from Geoffrey Dawson's diary that plans were under way for Lord Halifax to go to Germany in mid-1936.[56] By

[49] Ibid.
[50] *Morning Post*, 12 Mar. 1936, p. 10, ed. art. by K. Robson. Also *Morning Post* 26 Mar. 1936, Berlin Corr., p. 15 and 30 Mar. 1936, Berlin Corr., p. 11.
[51] *Daily Herald*, 30 Mar. 1936, p. 1.
[52] *News Chronicle*, 30 Mar. 1936, 1st Leader, p. 10.
[53] *Daily Express*, 30 Mar. 1936, 1st Leader, p. 12.
[54] *Manchester Guardian*, 31 Mar. 1936, 3rd Leader, p. 10. Also *Manchester Guardian*, 28 Mar. 1936, 1st Leader, p. 12.
[55] *The Times*, 3 Apr. 1936, 1st Leader, p. 17.
[56] This is corroborated by information Kennedy had from the British Ambassador in Berlin, Sir Eric Phipps. See Dawson Papers, Diary 1936, 22, 30 Apr., 4 May; Voigt to Crozier, 29 June 1936, and Dell to Crozier, undated but the same time, *Manchester Guardian* archives.

the end of April, the 'Olympic Pause' had imposed itself upon the scene, and there seemed to be little sense in disturbing it and possibly queering Halifax's pitch. April was a cruel month, with the Abyssinian war reaching its bloody climax when Addis Ababa fell in May, and sanctions and the League were the main international concern. In London the moderate German Ambassador von Hoesch died in his bath, and the Nazis showed no interest in replacing him for several months.

The 1936 Olympic Games were held in Berlin in June. The world watched with awe and apprehension as the Nazi talent for spectacle was turned to sport. The hiatus of political activity in Germany during the months surrounding the Games became known as the Olympic Pause, and[57] despite some carping (the *Manchester Guardian* pointed out in a leading article the irony that the 3,000 torches used in the 2,000 mile run between Mount Olympus and Berlin had been provided by Krupps),[58] the Games themselves passed impressively and without major incident. The Jews particularly benefited from the Olympic Pause which very likely forestalled a major pogrom over the murder of the Nazi leader of Switzerland, Gustloff, in February. Despite dire predictions in the *Manchester Guardian* about the wrath that would beset them and the Catholics as well once the Games were over, the hope that the Pause might be continued was widespread,[59] and this was in fact what happened. As the Nuremberg *Parteitag* approached, things looked hopeful for Anglo-German relations. Dawson wrote to Barrington-Ward on 11 August: 'I lunch with Edward Halifax today and shall get the low-down on the Foreign Office. It is surprising how many converts there are in these days to what may be called *The Times* point of view about Foreign Policy.'[60]

Each Nuremberg *Parteitag* had a specific theme: in 1934 it had been the justification and minimizing of the Röhm Purge; in 1935 the Nuremberg Decrees were announced; there was speculation whether, after the Olympic Pause, the Jews might not be singled out again in 1936, but in the event anti-Bolshevism was the central theme, with the demand

---

[57] See *The Times*, 18 July 1936, ed. art. by Berlin Corr., p. 13.
[58] *Manchester Guardian*, 13 July 1936, 5th Leader, p. 8.
[59] *Sunday Times*, 2 Aug. 1936, 2nd Leader, p. 8.
[60] Dawson to Barrington-Ward, 11 Aug. 1936, Dawson Papers.

for colonies running a close second to it. Hitler and the Nazi leaders delivered virulent diatribes against Moscow-directed world Communism. Barrington-Ward wrote to Dawson on 17 September that 'The Germans have played the Russian business rather too far, but their internal necessities have to be considered, and they may be more amenable now that Nuremberg is over.'[61] The demand for colonies was treated according to the different newspapers' attitudes toward the colonial question in general. All the British newspapers, however, saw and stated clearly that whatever reasons Hitler might adduce for the demand, the real reason that Germany wanted colonies was for the prestige they involved.[62]

The 1936 *Parteitag* was thus a comfortable one for the British Press. Hitler's barbs were directed eastward, and colonies were not made to seem a pressing or an anti-British issue. Further, substantiation seemed to be given to the ever-present rumours of Germany's economic difficulties, by Hitler's announcement of the Four Year Plan on 9 September.

Shortly before Nuremberg, Hitler had been visited at Berchtesgaden by Lloyd George; compliments were exchanged, and the atmosphere was most amicable. Lloyd George's impressions of his journey and his meeting with the Führer were written into article form for the *Daily Express*.[63] The first draft of the article was completed at Heidelberg on 13 September. Later in London, on the 16th, Tom Jones and Lord Dawson of Penn, who were travelling with the former Prime Minister, went over it. They objected to a section on the situation of the Protestant Church in Germany which they were afraid might cause trouble for the two Churchmen who had supplied the information; the passage was excised. On the 16th, Tom Jones tried to get Lloyd George to tone down the sentence: 'The Germans have definitely made up their minds never to quarrel with us again', but he held firmly to it and it was printed.[64] The article was published in the *Daily Express* on 17

[61] Barrington-Ward to Dawson, 17 Sept. 1936, *The Times* archives.

[62] See *The Times*, 10 Sept. 1936, 2nd Leader, p. 13.

[63] Full notes of the Berchtesgaden conversation were published for the first time in Gilbert, *The Roots of Appeasement*, pp. 197–221. Other notes may be found in T. Jones, *A Diary With Letters*, p. 241. For the exigencies of producing the *Daily Express* article, see ibid., pp. 262, 265, 267.

[64] See Jones, op. cit., pp. 260–2, 265, 267.

September. Lloyd George stated that the Germans idolized Hitler. Although criticism was officially forbidden, he had heard much of it but never in reference to the Führer. Hitler was considered the George Washington of Germany, the man who won for his country independence from all her oppressors; this description would not be considered an exaggeration by those who had seen the change. And the change had been peaceful; the Third Reich was no resurrection of the old Imperial Germany: 'The idea of a Germany intimidating Europe with a threat that its irresistible army might march across frontiers forms no part of the new vision. . . . The establishment of a German hegemony in Europe which was the aim and dream of the old pre-war militarism, is not even on the horizon of Nazism.'[65]

German rearmament was not being kept secret. Quite the contrary; it was being vaunted for all to see, but especially Russia, for it was Russia which Germany feared. Everywhere in Germany there was an intense opposition and hostility to Bolshevism. Unfortunately, blame for Bolshevism was thrust upon Russian Jews, and this was leading to a resurgence of anti-Semitism which had otherwise been dying out: 'The German temperament takes no more delight in persecution than does the Briton, and the native good humour of the German people soon relapses into tolerance after a display of ill-temper.' Still, Germany did not intend to go to war with Russia; there was no real quarrel between Germany and France, and Hitler's mind was made up never to quarrel with Britain again.[66]

It is interesting that the leading article in the column next to this was not uncritical. It lamented that Lloyd George and other tourists returned from Germany with no words about the persecution of the Christian Churches: such silence would seem curious from this leading Nonconformist: 'What a pity that when our distinguished travellers are abroad so many of them see nothing of the suppression that goes on. Enjoying liberty themselves at home, they forget to praise it as the greatest boon that man can receive.'[67]

After the post had remained vacant since 10 April, Hitler's

---

[65] *Daily Express*, 17 Sept. 1936, ed. art. by Lloyd George, p. 12.   [66] Ibid.
[67] *Daily Express*, 17 Sept. 1936, Opinion, p. 12.

friend von Ribbentrop was appointed Ambassador to the Court of St. James on 11 August. *The Times* thought this a wise choice because he was a man who knew England; the paper was not carried away, however, and made an unmistakable point in its leading article: 'On our side we believe no less that the key to a durable peace system in Europe lies chiefly in the relations of Germany with her neighbours. Our friendship with France is axiomatic; we do not falter in that; but we believe that the friendship could only be strengthened by a clear understanding with Germany.'[68] The *Daily Telegraph* felt that the appointment was an honour since the new Ambassador was so close to Hitler, and that his appointment meant the end of 'the period of rather distantly correct relations with London, and that a phase of closer diplomatic activity between the two capitals is about to open'.[69] The *Daily Mail* thought Ribbentrop 'A Welcome Ambassador' whose 'moderation and tact have been greatly appreciated' in Britain.[70] The *Observer*'s notes on the appointment were written by Voigt, who had been given permission to write for the Sunday paper during Garvin's vacation.[71] Voigt stated that Ribbentrop was Hitler's 'friend' only to the extent that they understood one another and were mutually useful.[72]

When Ribbentrop finally arrived in Britain in October, he caused several sensations by greeting the King with the Nazi salute at various official and social occasions. Then it began to be noticed that he was absent for long periods of time and performed none the less a more active role than his position called for. Already by the end of November Voigt wrote in the *Manchester Guardian*:

. . . for it is only by a kind of fiction that Herr von Ribbentrop enjoys that title to the full. An Ambassador who is only here by fits and starts, who is more concerned to teach this country what its policy ought to be than to inform himself what its policy is, who in addition to his special activity as a leading functionary in the National Socialist party is one of the principal promoters of a semi-romantic, semi-serious, holy war against what he imagines to

[68] *The Times*, 12 Aug. 1936, 3rd Leader, p. 11.
[69] *Daily Telegraph*, 12 Aug. 1936, 2nd Leader, p. 10.
[70] *Daily Mail*, 12. Aug. 1936, 1st Leader, p. 8.
[71] See Crozier to Voigt, 3 July 1936, *Manchester Guardian* archives.
[72] *Observer*, 16 Aug. 1936, by a Corr., p. 10.

be Communism—such an emissary can hardly be called an Ambassador in the ordinary sense of that term.[73]

Voigt went particularly strongly after Ribbentrop, and on 20 December the acting Editor had to write to him: 'Badly as the man behaves, he is still an Ambassador accredited to what is still a friendly Power, and I don't think that the "M.G." can go outside its own traditions so far as to attack him so uncompromisingly on the particular point of his personal expenditure.'[74]

Early in December the biggest story of the year, which had been simmering beneath the surface for some time, finally broke. King Edward, whose reign had begun so auspiciously, abdicated and began the life of an exile. Unlike the American and continental Press, the German Press had not printed the many and lurid rumours and stories which grew in number and strength as the British Press pushed discretion to its limit and beyond while waiting for a solution or a suitable opening. This German restraint must have been appreciated in Fleet Street.

THE BRITISH PRESS
AND GERMANY IN 1937

In many respects 1937 was very much like 1935. They were the only years in which really major news stories or events did not come out of Germany; years in which wars between dictatorships and democracy broke out, neither of them involving Germany; years in which Britain's wearied gaze was drawn homeward from the depressing sights of international difficulties and dilemmas to the prideful calm and dignity of royal occasions—the Jubilee and the Coronation. There was, however, a major difference between 1935 and 1937: the difference of two years' time. By 1937 the critics and the prophets had been confounded and the Nazi regime had fully consolidated itself upon an undeniable mandate from the majority of the German people, and had entered the ranks of stable governments. The character and conduct of the Nazi dictatorship continued to be distasteful to most of the

---

[73] *Manchester Guardian*, 28 Nov. 1936, Dipl. Corr., p. 13.
[74] Gordon Phillips to Voigt, 20 Dec. 1936, *Manchester Guardian* archives.

British Press; but the things that had been novelties in 1935 had become institutions by 1937.

For better or worse, Hitler was here to stay. As the brutalities of the Nazi movement and regime were either increasingly taken for granted or else attributed to extremists, its undoubted accomplishments (the virtual ending of unemployment, the fine new buildings and roads, and its seeming spiritual and physical regeneration of the German people) were more often commented upon, even in the anti-Nazi British papers.

The main events of 1936 were now seen to be the beginning of the Spanish Civil War and the Abdication. Neither involved Germany directly. Indeed Germany's intervention in Spain was generally considered to be on a very small scale, and it was Italian or Soviet intervention which was seized upon by the opposite sides for propaganda and thus tended to cancel each other out. The rumours of Mrs. Simpson's German friends never amounted to very much in the public eye. In retrospect, the reoccupation of the Rhineland appeared a minor, almost peaceful incident, and in the nine months which followed it, although Hitler had avoided answering the British note about the conclusion of a Western Pact, he had not indulged in any further adventures, and seemed indeed to be settling down for a consolidation of his victories over the limitations of the Treaty of Versailles.

As far as the Western Pact was concerned, many people felt that it was better to let events follow their own course than to insist upon negotiations only to find that Hitler had refused or posed impossible terms. When on 30 January 1937 he announced to the Reichstag the satisfaction of his territorial ambitions, renounced further claims, and proclaimed the end of the 'period of surprises', this trend in British thinking was confirmed.

Ebbutt had predicted that the speech might be 'in general of a soothing nature calculated to keep public opinion abroad, especially in Great Britain, occupied for some weeks or even months arguing about its merits and its meaning'.[75] The *News Chronicle* had even higher hopes, since Hitler 'for all his frothy rhetoric and his crude ideologies', had in 1936 at least and at last shown himself to be a realist. 'He knows,

---

[75] *The Times*, 28 Jan. 1937, Berlin Corr., p. 14.

as well as Mr. Baldwin himself, that the next great European war will be the end of civilization as we know it. He has said so.'[76]

The speech was made on a Saturday, so the Sunday papers were the first to report it. The *Sunday Times* considered it the kind of speech one had become accustomed to from Hitler: heavy in form but slight in content. Still, he had shut no doors, and Britain was always willing to talk things over. At the same time, 'something more is required than phrases. Who wills peace as an end, must also will the means to it.'[77]

The Times was glad that after four years Hitler was at last mouthing the right platitudes—but was quite aware that they were only platitudes and must be acted upon to become anything else. The *Daily Telegraph*'s Diplomatic Correspondent reported that the tone of Hitler's speech had been set by Army moderates who warned him against any adventures which might lead to a major war.[78] The paper drew up a balance sheet for the speech. On the negative side, it had offered no constructive proposals, no economic concessions, and found no good word for the League of Nations. More positively, it offered assurances that Germany would pick no quarrel in Western Europe, though this at the price that it be allowed to pursue its quarrel with Bolshevism.[79] Overall, Hitler's emphasis upon each nation deciding its own strength was ominous, since German armaments were the greatest threat in Europe. Hitler must therefore go beyond mere words and demonstrate his desire for peace; the British Government was trying its best, but 'It cannot for ever pursue a will-o'-the-wisp if there is no response beyond assurances of good will.'[80]

Curiously, the *Manchester Guardian* was perhaps the least critical of Hitler's speech. Its leading article stated that once the rhetoric was cut aside, after months of ignoring the British questionnaire which asked whether he would honour a treaty if he signed it, Hitler had at last said that he would not sign a treaty unless he intended to honour it. Further, he denied that Germany sought isolation, either political or economic: 'Since, then, he says, in answer to Mr. Eden's recent question,

[76] *News Chronicle*, 30 Jan. 1937, 1st Leader, p. 8.
[77] *Sunday Times*, 31 Jan. 1937, 1st Leader, p. 16.
[78] *Daily Telegraph*, 1 Feb. 1937, Dipl. Corr., p. 13.
[79] Ibid., 1st Leader, p. 12.   [80] Ibid.

that he is for co-operation, he should, in every disputed European field, be taken at his word.'[81] The leader was generally quite pleased with Hitler's speech although its appreciation of Hitler's point that the period of surprises was over now that he had liquidated the Treaty of Versailles was tempered by the thought that 'the "surprises", the lightning strokes, have not in fact all arisen out of the treaty. . . '.[82]

Voigt did not share the paper's optimism, and reported in his diplomatic correspondence that second thoughts in London about the speech classified it as generally negative: it had settled what few remaining illusions there might have been about any possibility of a Western settlement, and from a doctrinal point of view, no speech of Hitler's had ever stated the racial principle so clearly.[83]

The *Morning Post*'s assessment was that the speech was 'Mainly Negative', for Hitler had challenged 'what must remain the unalterable foundation of British policy when he insisted on the division of Europe into two irreconcilable camps . . .'. And the end of surprises presumably meant that Hitler no longer recognized the validity of the passages in *Mein Kampf* stating that it was necessary to destroy any State which might have become a potential threat. 'Neighbours who are not unnaturally disconcerted by the knowledge that the unexpurgated original is still compulsory reading for loyal Nazis may perhaps derive some comfort from the implicit contradiction of it in Herr Hitler's latest pronouncement.'[84]

The *News Chronicle* thought that Hitler's speech fell a little flat on European ears because they had become accustomed to expecting something exciting on Saturdays!—but also because he had not proposed any co-operation either. Colonial claims would have to be met squarely but blackmail would never be paid; and Hitler clearly was not ready for disarmament yet.[85] This was doubly unfortunate because 'Until Germany is ready for that [co-operation for disarmament] there can be little hope of any real appeasement. It is the scale and pace of German rearmament, which are the cause of apprehension and unrest in Europe today.'[86]

[81] *Manchester Guardian*, 1 Feb. 1937, 1st Leader, p. 8.   [82] Ibid.
[83] *Manchester Guardian*, 2 Feb. 1937, Dipl. Corr., p. 12.   [84] Ibid.
[85] *News Chronicle*, 1 Feb. 1937, 1st Leader, p. 10.   [86] Ibid.

The *Daily Herald* saw that the speech left Britain 'As We Were': 'For the Führer's oratory is of a nature to which precision is alien. He cannot, or will not, be precise, even though he knows that the world wants to learn, not vaguely, but with some certainty, the views and intentions of his Government.'[87] Despite such reservations and objections the speech had after all been mainly pacific, and for the next few months a period of quiet ensued, during which Germany seemed for the first time 'to have come to a virtual standstill in her policy of diplomatic "shock tactics" '.[88] This lasted until the brief uproar over the bombing of Guernica in April and then re-asserted itself as part of the general euphoria surrounding the Coronation. A component of this period of quiet was the belief that Hitler's more moderate advisers had at last been heard.[89] The bellwether of the change was an article by W. N. Ewer in the *Daily Herald*. 'I am tired of those reckless prophets who keep on assuring us that war is inevitable,' he wrote. 'They have been at it so long; they have been wrong so often: but they go on undeterred, enthusiastically determined to foretell the worst.' The times were dangerous and difficult to be sure, but if 1937 could only be got through peacefully, then war might well be avoided altogether; and if the joint policy were instituted of impressing upon Germany that aggression would be resisted while at the same time working to remove her genuine grievances and fears, then the prospects for a peaceful 1937 were far from gloomy.[90]

A dissenting view was expressed by Vernon Bartlett who had just returned from his first visit to Berlin in six months. He wrote on the front page of the *News Chronicle* of his conviction that unless there occurred an unlikely radical change in German foreign policy within the next few months, 'there is a virtual inevitability of war'.[91] The thing that most impressed him during the visit, he wrote, was the way everyone there had come to accept war 'as one of the few certain events of an uncertain future'. Very few people believed that any number

[87] *Daily Herald*, 1 Feb. 1937, Leader, p. 10.
[88] *The Times*, 10 Mar. 1937, Berlin Corr., p. 13.
[89] See *The Times*, 10 Mar. 1937, Berlin Corr., p. 13, and 14 Apr. 1937, Berlin Corr., p. 13.
[90] *Daily Herald*, 21 Jan. 1937, ed. art. by W. N. Ewer, p. 10.
[91] *News Chronicle*, 3 Feb. 1937, Vernon Bartlett, p. 1.

of concessions could satisfy German demands, but only the Germans believed that war could be localized.

Other commentators, however, did not hold conditions to be so dire. Gordon-Lennox wrote that an Anglo-German 'holiday' was likely now: Baldwin would be retiring soon after the Coronation and Chamberlain would not want to commit himself until at least after the Imperial Conference. The Government could be expected to turn its attention towards consolidating its present position and concentrating on and financing rearmament; in general European matters, concrete proposals would be awaited from others.[92] The *Morning Post*'s Diplomatic Correspondent wrote that after a visit to the Foreign Office, Ribbentrop left the impression there 'that Germany had no immediate plans in the foreign field and will be concentrating for the next few months on her economic self-sufficiency'.[93]

For the next few months news of Germany generally disappeared from the British newspapers, except for *The Times*. Ebbutt reported that Göring's trip to Poland, von Neurath's visit to Vienna, the Prague negotiations with the Sudetens, the British debates on armaments, and German colonial claims were all subjects of a 'cautious though gradually more confident, discussion in Germany. Together they would seem to mark the beginnings of a new, or interim, phase in European affairs, of which only the mistiest of outlines is taking shape yet.'[94]

In mid-April, with the period of quiet about to come to an abrupt end—as abrupt as the sudden appearance of bombers over an ancient Basque town—Ebbutt wrote that it was the growing strength of British rearmament and the closer co-operation between France, Britain, and America which were giving pause to Hitler. The cumulative effect of these factors had been to narrow the field of possible expansionist adventure and strengthen the case of those more moderate advisers 'who sought to curb the spirit of reckless calculation which, not many months ago, insisted on pressing forward at all costs with the rearmament and self-sufficiency policies and refusing to listen to suggestions for a general settlement'.[95]

[92] *Daily Telegraph*, 8 Feb. 1937, Dipl. Corr., p. 14.
[93] *Morning Post*, 12 Feb. 1937, Dipl. Corr., p. 13.
[94] *The Times*, 24 Feb. 1937, Berlin Corr., p. 13.
[95] *The Times*, 14 Apr. 1937, Berlin Corr., p. 13.

Some of the few waves troubling these three halcyon months came from the ebullient figure of the new German Ambassador. Von Ribbentrop, thought to have been appointed with an eye to improving Anglo-German relations, was, as we have seen, a controversial figure from the very beginning. In March he made a speech on the colonial question at the Leipzig Fair. One was bound, felt the *Morning Post* (albeit especially sensitive to the colonial question), 'to read into Herr von Ribbentrop's words a direct threat to this country uttered in a public speech by the German Ambassador to the Court of St. James'.[96] Ribbentrop's lengthy absences from London soon became as objectionable as his conduct when there. That his manner was quite conscious was clear from a remark attributed to him in the *Manchester Guardian*'s 'London Letter': 'The English do not understand the significance of National Socialism and the grandeur of the National Socialist State. But it is quite useless to explain it to them in mild and courteous words—they must, if they are to understand, be spoken to sternly; roughly even.'[97]

In April, shortly before Guernica, George Lansbury had an interview with Hitler in which the Führer agreed to attend an economic conference if it were convened by President Roosevelt or someone similar. British Press comment was cool. Lansbury had gone seeking peace but was offered economics, the *Daily Telegraph* complained; and the *Manchester Guardian* used an unaccustomed light hand to show the practical impossibility of a meeting such as Hitler suggested. The *Morning Post* said that the overture from Hitler was welcome but chided him for using such a situation to make it: surely Hitler must know that 'such an unofficial and unaccredited mission from a private gentleman, on matters of international politics, is not to be taken seriously'. Hitler should go through the proper channels, the *Morning Post* felt, for 'Germany may lack Colonies; but she does not lack Ambassadors'.[98]

[96] *Morning Post*, 3 Mar. 1937, 2nd Leader, p. 10.

[97] *Manchester Guardian*, 6 Mar. 1937, London Letter, p. 12. Voigt wrote to Crozier that he had picked this up from Mr. Hanna Hudson of the Ministry of Health, to whom von Ribbentrop had made the remark, and had it included in the London Letter. (5 Mar. 1937, *Manchester Guardian* archives.)

[98] *Morning Post*, 20 Apr. 1937, 1st Leader, p. 12. See also *The Times*, 20 Apr. 1937, Berlin Corr., p. 16; *Daily Telegraph*, 20 Apr. 1937, 1st Leader, p. 14; *Manchester Guardian*, 21 Apr. 1937, 2nd Leader, p. 10.

The *Daily Herald* appeared somewhat embarrassed but defended Lansbury by saying that just as Arthur Henderson had been criticized for going to Germany, so Lansbury must expect criticism. Still, Fascist dictatorships were facts and could not be ignored.[99] Like the rest of the British papers, the *Daily Herald* concluded after the meeting that Hitler had spoken fair words before, and the problem was not in summoning a conference but in improving international relations to a point where a conference could do some good.[100] Many of the papers obviously refused to take Lansbury seriously and found it impossible to believe that Hitler would either.

On 26 April, planes bombed and destroyed the undefended Basque town of Guernica. Two days later *The Times* published, as an editorial page article, a report from its Special Correspondent (G. L. Steer) which stated that the planes were part of the *Luftwaffe* squadrons which were fighting for the Nationalists. The article was accompanied by a strongly worded leader.

The Times was the only British newspaper thus to implicate Germany directly in the bombing of Guernica. The German Government and Press reacted immediately. On 4 May Daniels wrote from Berlin that 'A wave of Anglophobia is running through the German Press based on the account of the bombing of Guernica published in *The Times* of 28 April.' Although *The Times* had immediately admitted that it had been over-hasty in printing Steer's uncorroborated article, and although the charges against Germany had been taken up by other British newspapers, the continued virulence of the German campaign stirred *The Times* to its own defence. Ebbutt wrote that such outbursts indicated a readiness to accept unexamined the most wild accusations and to discern the most fantastic motives, 'which suggests that the path to an understanding will be remote indeed while Germany remains under the influence of her present political prejudices'.[101] The following day the paper supplemented Ebbutt's report with a leading article, '*The Times* Bombs Guernica'. This article voiced the confusion and frustration at German conduct which was to receive a more concrete—and notorious—formulation in

[99] *Daily Herald*, 17 Apr. 1937, 1st Leader, p. 12.
[100] *Daily Herald*, 20 Apr. 1937, 1st Leader, p. 10.
[101] *The Times*, 4 May 1937, Berlin Corr., p. 16.

Dawson's letter to Daniels the following week. Admittedly
The Times had acted hastily, and undoubtedly some embarrassment had been caused by the article; this was hardly sufficient
cause for the kind of attacks unleashed against *The Times*. The
paper forgot its own defensive position and exclaimed 'What is
the destiny of the world in which no responsible organ of the
Press can tell the simple truth without incurring charges of
Machiavellian villainy?'

But another question seemed even more to the point: '. . .
where is the wisdom, from Germany's point of view, in allowing
her embarrassment to inspire a press campaign which is
calculated to damage her relations with Great Britain and which,
consisting as it does of a series of chimerical accusations, in-
temperately made, can only discredit her powers of self-
control and—incidentally—arouse suspicious of her complicity
in the bombardment?'[102]

Dawson's letter of 23 May 1937 to Daniels, who was then in
Berlin substituting for the ailing Ebbutt, has become widely
known. In the offending sentences, Dawson said:

But it would interest me to know precisely what it is in *The Times*
that has produced this antagonism in Germany. I did my utmost,
night after night, to keep out of the paper anything that might hurt
their susceptibilities. I can really think of nothing that has been
printed now for many months past which they could possibly take
exception to as unfair comment. No doubt they were annoyed by
Steer's first story of the bombing of Guernica, but its essential
accuracy has never been disputed, and there has not been any
attempt here to rub it in or to harp upon it. I should be more
grateful than I can say for any explanation and guidance, for I
have always been convinced that the peace of the world depends
more than anything else on our getting into reasonable relations
with Germany.[103]

Writing of this letter, Colin Coote, who was a leader-writer
for *The Times* in the 1930s, says that 'Not only is the tone plaintive—almost whining—but also it would not be gathered from
the wording that the bombing of Guernica was a revolting
horror. It was carried out by German airmen lent to Franco

---

[102] *The Times*, 5 May 1937, 2nd Leader, p. 17. See also *The Times*, 4, 5 May
1937, Berlin Corr., p. 16 (both days). For Steer's Guernica article, see *The Times*,
28 Apr. 1937, Spec. Corr. in Bilbao, p. 17. See also, ibid., 2nd Leader.
[103] Quoted in *Hist. Times*, iv. 907–8.

in the Spanish Civil War, against an undefended town; there was much damage and great loss to life. This was scandalous butchery which, according to the appeasers, was not to be "rubbed in or harped upon".' Coote continues, quoting another letter written by Dawson on the same day, 'Dawson did even worse than keep things out; he actually dropped things in. On May 23 1937 he wrote to Lord Lothian, "I spend my nights . . . dropping in little things which are intended to soothe them".'[104] The important point one discovers from reading the various British papers day by day at the time of Guernica is that responsibility for the attack was never definitely known or apportioned. Steer's original article was, indeed, the only direct accusation of Germany at the time, and the leading article accompanying it was clearly written in white heat over the feeling of outrage Steer's story engendered. The rest of the British papers could only report that nothing was known for certain: everyone involved was accusing everyone else. As late as 1939 the *Daily Telegraph* commented upon German boasting about the number of towns their returning legionaries had bombed in Spain: 'Why, then, all the bother about Guernica, even if German airmen did happen to be innocent of that affair?'[105]

At this time, therefore, it was precisely not the bombing but *The Times*'s reporting of it which was unusual and controversial; *The Times* was singled out for the wrath which so upset Dawson because *The Times* was the only paper which had stated at the very outset that Germany was responsible for the destruction of Guernica.

It is perhaps necessary, further, to consider Dawson's two letters of the 23rd in light of an earlier one—also to Daniels—written on the 11th. It may go some way towards explaining what he meant both by 'keeping things out' and 'dropping things in'. He wrote:

Yes, I have seen Philip Lothian and heard what he had to say. He may write something about it for *The Times* when the Coronation

---

[104] Coote, *Editorial*, p. 169. Here, as elsewhere in his book, Coote mirrors an incorrect judgement from Gilbert and Gott, *The Appeasers*, p. 66, where it is stated that 'It was not the *reporting* of Guernica that caused the friction, but the *bombing* itself. German airplanes had bombed a defenceless Spanish town.'

[105] *Daily Telegraph*, 7 June 1939, 2nd Leader, p. 16.

is over. One of his points is that, even in small things, the Germans have a feeling that we never hold out a hand of friendship or sympathy from this country. But for my own part, I lose no opportunity, when I see it, of trying to mitigate this sort of grievance, which is mainly psychological—witness (only within the last week) a leader of sympathy with the loss of the Hidenburg [airship] and a welcome to Blomberg as representative to the Coronation.[106]

Dawson's letters make much more sense in terms of his own personal views if they are read in this context and with the unique atmosphere of the spring of 1937 in mind. Daniels had been in Berlin substituting for Ebbutt, and he wrote to Dawson about the ludicrous extremes of misunderstanding and misrepresentation of which the Nazis were capable. On 16 May, he wrote that 'The German Press has been savage about *The Times*, in fact worse than at any period I remember. The latest discovery is that if you spell it backwards it spells SEMIT, which leads them to deduce that we are a Jewish-Marxist organisation and that nothing else can be expected of us. Such are the childish results of a sheltered public opinion. The worst of it is that it renders honest efforts helpless.'[107]

The general hope for Anglo-German relations at this time was that they would undergo a welcome period of quiet as the Olympic Pause of 1936 had been extended by Hitler's speech of 30 January. The tendency to credit this hope was reinforced by the already rapidly mounting Coronation fever. Perhaps it was the conjunction of these two factors which made German complicity in, much less responsibility for, Guernica seem unlikely. The German uproar and vociferous protests of innocence of *The Times*'s accusation were added to the fact that as the days passed no official report of any kind alloted blame for the bombing. Attention soon turned to the Coronation and its attendant excitement and good will. Following the political change-over between Baldwin and Chamberlain and the Imperial Conference, favourable interest and attention were focused upon von Neurath's impending visit; Guernica was already 'dead' as news by the time of the incidents of the *Deutschland* and the *Leipzig*, when even anti-Nazi papers wrote

106 Quoted in *Hist. Times*, iv. 907. These Lothian articles must be the ones Eden succeeded in getting suppressed. See above, p. 71.
107 Daniels to Dawson, 16 May 1937, *The Times* archives.

sympathetically that these ships had been improperly attacked by Spanish Government submarines, and deplored—but did not condemn—Germany's resort to retaliation at Almeria.[108]

In May the Coronation occupied—and in some cases and at some times almost monopolized—the attention of the British Press; General von Blomberg headed the official German delegation. At the end of May, Stanley Baldwin stepped down as Prime Minister and was succeeded by Neville Chamberlain, one of whose first official acts was to preside over the Imperial Conference. There he learned of the South African Premier's direct and outspoken refusal to support Britain in a war with Germany over Czechoslovakia. Canada's support was half-hearted at best, and Australia and New Zealand were unenthusiastic about anything which would distract attention from the Far East and the still incomplete base at Singapore.

Great hope centered around the visit of the German Foreign Minister, Baron von Neurath, to London, scheduled for 23 June. Earlier in the month Spanish Government planes had bombed the German battleship *Deutschland;* when the battleship *Leipzig* was allegedly torpedoed, the German Government claimed that such intolerable violations could not be permitted, ordered the town of Almeria to be bombed in retaliation, and cancelled von Neurath's visit. Though it achieved little else, the abortive von Neurath visit produced the correspondence between the Foreign Secretary Anthony Eden and Geoffrey Dawson which we have discussed above.

Just as the Coronation euphoria began to abate, another series of purge trials began in Moscow. Most of the accused were labelled 'wreckers', allegedly in league with Germany to bring about the downfall of the Soviet State. It is possible that the fantastic charges levelled against Germany in these trials led to an even more pronounced reluctance in the British Press to report any but the best-substantiated stories. In September the Far East boiled over at the Marco Polo

---

[108] Witness, for example, the *Daily Herald*'s reaction to the bombing of Almeria: 'At the very best, Germany's intentions MAY be excellent: but her emotions and nerves are obviously still uncontrollable, her reflexes unpredictable and violent. . . . If Herr Hitler desires equality of status and equality of treatment, he must first give proof of equality in civilization and equality in behaviour.' *Daily Herald*, 2 Jan. 1937, 1st Leader, p. 10.

bridge, and yet another war demanded attention: a Japanese plane strafed the car in which the British Ambassador to China was travelling, and the wounded diplomat was a bigger story than the Axis summit meeting.

Mussolini visited Germany at the end of September; it was widely held in Britain that little could be expected of— and that little came of—the visit. Barrington-Ward minimized the importance of the Axis: 'The presentation of the new "front" as a sinister conspiracy of predatory Powers may serve the propagandist but is too melodramatic for ordinary currency.' He retained his sense of humour and found in the Field of the Cloth of Gold the only apt historical parallel to this spectacular meeting, 'though Henry and Francis were unassisted by Ministries of propaganda, uniformed populations, bullet-proof trains, and all else that may guide or stimulate the imaginations of the no less modern Press'.[109]

The visit passed off impressively but uneventfully and was generally interpreted at its face value. 'There can be no doubt that the desire for peace proclaimed at Berlin was genuine', stated the *Daily Telegraph*, and this desire was shared in fully equal measure by the Western Powers; 'The means to appeasement are in co-operation.'[110] *The Times*, too, noted that the speeches in Berlin, despite their tone ('. . . the Duce's obiter dicta belong to the idiom, and the reader may take them in his stride without a change of temperature') were all strongly for peace, and 'only inveterate alarmists could quarrel with the main purport of the speeches . . .'.[111]

October passed quietly. Lambert had only just returned to work in Berlin after three months' absence when Crozier wrote to him to 'keep messages fairly short in the near future. We have been having a tremendous lot of foreign and want to reduce the quantity a little.'[112] When the seal appeared to be put on the September visit when Italy adhered to the German-Japanese Anti-Comintern Pact in November, there was little surprise and little comment in the British Press. Voigt had claimed from the very first that the Pact was really aimed

109 *The Times*, 25 Sept. 1937, 1st Leader, p. 11.
110 *Daily Telegraph*, 29 Sept. 1937, 1st Leader, p. 12.
111 *The Times*, 30 Sept. 1937, 1st Leader, p. 13.
112 Crozier to Lambert, 7 Oct. 1937, *Manchester Guardian* archives.

against Britain, and quoted *Mein Kampf* again to support this claim.[113]

It was an issue rather than any particular event which most occupied the British Press in 1937: the persecution of the Christian Churches, which came to a head with the arrest of Pastor Niemöller in July. It was as incomprehensible to the *Manchester Guardian* as to *The Times* why the Nazis attacked what should, at the very least, have been looked upon as the most natural ally in the self-proclaimed Nazi crusade against Bolshevism.[114] As Crozier wrote to Voigt in August 1937, 'I must say that it seems to me that Hitler and his friends are very foolish in stirring up all this trouble in the one sphere where they will find other people as obstinate as themselves.'[115] A leading article in *The Times*, otherwise insistent upon the necessity of dealing fairly with the Nazis despite 'the sentiment of dislike, which is almost universal in this country, for many of the internal aspects of the German dictatorship', made this important exception: 'Except indeed in the matter of religious persecution they are rightly held to be no one else's concern.'[116]

Here was an issue which touched, uniquely and at a level deeper than left-right political differences, an essential part of the liberal conscience in Britain. Devout Christians of as different doctrinal and liturgical convictions and of such different political persuasions as Dawson and Crozier, were united against any attack upon what both considered to be the most essential part of Western civilization. Even the non-devout Liberal could appreciate the Nazi challenge at this level: as Gordon Phillips, Acting Editor in Crozier's absence, wrote to Voigt upon receiving news of Niemöller's arrest:

I myself incline to be a bit of an Erastian; I no more believe in the divine right of priests than I do in the divine right of kings, but I have absolutely no belief whatever in the divine right of führers, and this latest and gathering assault upon the German Protestant Church's independence within its own sphere looks as though it

[113] *Manchester Guardian*, 8 Nov. 1937, Dipl. Corr., p. 13.
[114] *The Times*, 7 Sept. 1936, 1st Leader, p. 13.
[115] Crozier to Voigt, 9 Aug. 1937, *Manchester Guardian* archives.
[116] *The Times*, 28 Oct. 1937, 1st Leader, p. 17.

should be well worth full length leader treatment for Saturday's paper.[117]

Niemöller was arrested on 1 July 1937 and held without trial until March 1938. In the meantime, after the initial uproar in the British Press, the two usual tendencies had to be fought: not to forget Niemöller as the secrecy of his captivity removed him from the front page, and secondly, not to endanger his safety or life by angering the Nazis with critical commentary. The *Manchester Guardian* was particularly concerned lest Niemöller become out of sight out of mind; the *News Chronicle* was only second in this concern.

There are several factors to be taken into account in a consideration of the Christians' persecution. There was, first, a difference between the German Catholics and Protestants both in terms of the kind of persecution suffered and in the mind of the British Press.[118] The authoritative hierarchical structure of the Catholic Church, its spiritual allegiance to the Pope, and the diplomatic situation between the Holy See and the German Government served to place the Catholics on a very different footing.

One of the most important considerations for Catholics at this time was Hitler's pose as leader of a European crusade against Bolshevism. From 1936 to 1939 the one place in which Catholics were not only being killed, but tortured and mutilated, was in Spain, by a militantly atheistic, 'communist' Republican Government. The theme of the 1936 Nuremberg Rally was the 'struggle against Bolshevism', and it must have posed many crises of conscience to Catholic clergy and laity in Germany. The solution of approving the foreign but condemning the domestic Nazi policy was foredoomed to failure. Catholic unity was thereby damaged by those who could not go along with such a decision; the Nazis gained by the division, and the British Press was unable to give unreserved support to such an equivocal line.

In the case of the Protestant Churches, there was a more basic, though almost entirely unexpressed, difference between those newspapers which seized upon Niemöller and the other Confessional Pastors as symbols of resistance to the Nazi

[117] Gordon Phillips to Voigt, 1 July 1937, *Manchester Guardian* archives.
[118] *The Times*, 3 Sept. 1936, 3rd Leader, p. 13.

regime, and those which considered the state of Protestant Christianity in Germany. The Confessional Church only formally opposed Nazi anti-Semitism, concentration camps, and treatment of the Christian churches, as late as Whitsuntide 1936. Voigt never really seemed to consider Niemöller theologically, although he did arrange for Karl Barth to write an article for the *Manchester Guardian* in January 1936 which was so heavily theological that Crozier feared no one might be able to understand it. Ebbutt's reporting of the Christian Church news was, perhaps as befits *The Times*, exhaustive but uncritical (although the very reporting was perhaps criticism enough). *The Times* itself, however, thought that the Nazi leaders' claims were 'not without justification, that the Protestant Church in Germany was rather slack in the out-of-church practice of Christianity which consists in charitable work among parishoners, and that the National Socialists themselves have been far more active in distributing relief, helping the sick, and organizing recreations'.[119] This distinction did not inhibit the paper from condemning the Nazi persecution, however: 'But that is certainly no reason why the activities of the pastors should now be restricted, their liberties curtailed, and their organizations deranged. Still less is it a reason why men of religious conviction should be expected to accept the doctrine that the State can do no wrong and that its every act is therefore imbued with authority from on high.'[120]

Shortly after Niemöller's arrest, the Nazis expelled Norman Ebbutt, *The Times*'s Senior Correspondent in Berlin. Ostensibly the expulsion was by way of retaliation for action the Home Office had just taken against some German 'correspondents' in London. Ebbutt, as a liberal of the old style who had known and loved the Germany of the Weimar Republic, was clearly unpopular with the Nazis; his intimate knowledge and exhaustive reports of the Church conflict undoubtedly riled the Nazi authorities. That he was expelled because of his reporting, however, is not very much more likely than that he was expelled in simple retaliation.

Ebbutt has remained a controversial figure, and has probably

---

[119] *The Times*, 4 Aug. 1936, 3rd Leader, p. 11.
[120] Ibid. See also *The Times*, 24 Aug. 1936, Berlin Corr., p. 9, and 1 Sept. 1936, Berlin Corr., p. 11.

taken the real story of his expulsion to the grave with him: an end consistent with his thirty-one years of determined silence and retirement after his return to England in October 1937.

Ebbutt's successor in Berlin, his assistant there, James Holburn, has written about the incident:

There is a danger, I think, of complicating unnecessarily the motives both of the Germans and *The Times* throughout this Ebbutt affair. Ribbentrop . . . was successively special adviser to Hitler on foreign affairs, Ambassador to London and Foreign Minister. His particular assignment in the lesser roles had been to create goodwill in Britain for the Nazis' foreign policy. His work was offset by the estimates of Nazi foreign policy and its implications for Britain which appeared from Ebbutt in *The Times*, a newspaper read and taken seriously by everyone concerned in the making of British foreign policy. So when a plausible excuse offered—the three German journalists—Ribbentrop saw to it that Ebbutt would be got rid of. In any case, I expect Ribbentrop personally disliked Ebbutt, as Ebbutt did him.

If I were asked to put the matter in a nutshell that is how I think I would do it.[121]

Barrington-Ward saw the hand of the Minister of Propaganda in the affair; in September he wrote to Dawson: 'Oddly enough I was in Germany when the great affaire took place, and watched it as a spectator from the wings. It looked to me as if the whole thing was the work of Goebbels. He was certainly responsible for the communique. It bore the hall-mark of his narrow, cunning and spiteful little mind.'[122]

Ebbutt's position in Berlin was made tenuous, at least in the eyes of *The Times*, by the vagaries of his private life which made Dawson reluctant to encourage publicity about him personally. Further, Ebbutt had been ill for the last few years, and, as Dawson wrote to a friend early in 1938, his assistants had in fact 'been sending a good many of the messages with which Ebbutt was popularly credited'.[123] It is unlikely that Ebbutt would have been able to continue in Berlin for much longer, and there is some indication that plans were already under way to replace him at the time of his expulsion.

[121] J. Holburn to the author, 30 Oct. 1967.
[122] Barrington-Ward to Dawson, 14 Sept. 1937, *The Times* archives.
[123] Dawson to Brand, 17 Feb. 1938, *The Times* archives.

It seems most probable that in this particular case, maddened by *The Times*'s article on Guernica, and annoyed by the expulsion of the three German journalists for clearly non-journalistic activities, the naturally high-handed reaction was to go right for the top and demand *The Times* correspondent's removal. No sooner demanded, it became a question of German honour not to back down.

It remains an integral part of the demonology of appeasement that Ebbutt's dispatches from Berlin were censored by Dawson with an eye to appeasing the Nazis. This seems most unlikely for several reasons, the most important being Dawson himself; with his conception of the honour and responsibility of his position as Editor, as well as his conception of the prerogatives of the office, he would not have tolerated a situation in which he was suppressing or changing a distinguished correspondent's dispatches because he disagreed with their content. If such were the case, he would simply have dismissed Ebbutt and replaced him with someone more amenable.

That Ebbutt's dispatches were cut, however, often and considerably, cannot be denied. As early as 1931 the Foreign News Editor Ralph Deakin wrote to Ebbutt:

Your complaint about the lopping off of the last sentence in nearly every paragraph is all a matter of space. From your own experience you will know that if an article is already set up in type and has to be cut to a straight column the Sub-Editors sometimes have to cut paragraphs where they can be cut conveniently and avoid slashing out passages in such a way as would necessitate a complete resetting of the article.[124]

Again in April 1933, after Hitler was in power, Ebbutt wrote defensively to Deakin:

I fear that, as usual, the articles will be found too long; and I realise that Barrington-Ward made this point clear enough in a recent letter. Yet I feel incapable of doing anything more about it than I have done, even if you give me up as a bad job. The articles have been written under considerable difficulties; not only because of the very rapid changes which occur even as one is writing, but

---

[124] Deakin to Ebbutt, 7 June 1931, *The Times* archives. See also Ebbutt to Deakin, 2 June 1931, *The Times* archives.

also because, since I spoke to you last on the telephone, I have had a long bout of unfitness.[125]

Donald McLachlan, who was a Sub-Editor and also worked with Ebbutt in the early 1930s, has recently written that:

Ebbutt tended to overwrite at times. That is to say he wrote a heavily qualified style, intended to reflect his own uncertainty about some German developments and determination to weigh everything carefully. It was the effort of the subs to simplify this material in any way possible that led sometimes to what Ebbutt could only regard as mutilation of his copy. But it was normal journalistic practice that anything that was not clear to the sub-editor must be made clear to the reader. (The sub-editors in question were not below the educational standard of the ordinary *Times* reader.)

At one time, the best way of analysing Nazi Germany was to write about the struggle between Hitler and the Protestant church. Ebbutt's concentration on this was mainly due to his having a first-rate contact in Church matters such as could not be obtained inside the Nazi Party or the Nazified Government departments. This contact had friends in the *Reichswehr* who helped him and also in the German Foreign Office. It is fair to say that detailed presentation of the German Church struggle was partly the price paid for having good inside information. The fact remains that the Church story was not every reader's meat and it had to be kept within bounds.[126]

Iverach McDonald, who worked both as a correspondent in Berlin and a Sub-Editor in London during these years, and who was made Diplomatic Correspondent in 1938, has recently written about the paper's policy that 'We always had it as a very strict rule that messages should not be "improved" and especially not "rewritten". We could cut, and indeed we did; and we could remove or touch up ugly phrasing on occasion. But it was always dinned in to me and others at the subs table that we were not to change in any way the sense of a message, either for reasons of policy or because we thought we knew better than the man on the spot. It is true that Geoffrey Dawson felt that the political notes were, like the leaders, his special province and those he would sometimes

---

125 Ebbutt to Deakin, 1 Apr. 1933, *The Times* archives.
126 Unpublished note by D. H. McLachlan. Chapter XIII, 'Berlin unappeased' of McLachlan's *In the Chair* deals at some length with the particular case of Ebbutt's correspondence and with the general question of editorial prerogative.

alter. But I really do not think that he rewrote any messages from abroad. There were agonised cries from correspondents if ever the cutting of a message seemed to alter the sense; and always Pearson would support the correspondent.' And the Chief Foreign Sub-Editor during the 1930s, G. L. Pearson, has recently stated about the cutting of Ebbutt's copy that: 'Space and clarity were what one had to consider. I am sure there was never an occasion when the Editor intervened to alter a message from Ebbutt so as to give a false picture of the situation. That would be tinkering with facts, and it was not done. Ebbutt's stuff was NOT modified.'

Iverach McDonald points out that:

Ebbutt was thrown out of Germany for what *appeared* in *The Times*. The excisions could not therefore have been damaging. A second point is that Ebbutt, for all his great gifts, was a very verbose and often difficult-to-follow writer; he also was given to speculation at times. Very often he had to be cut for purely journalistic reasons in order to make his copy clear and digestible. I think that such cuts cover about 90 per cent of the cases. . . . On the other hand Dawson did not like correspondents setting themselves up as editorial writers, especially if their tendency was against the policy of the paper. It is therefore probable that he *did* cut some of Ebbutt's opinionative pieces. I cannot give instances; I should say it was likely, but only on rare occasions. Having said so much, I must add that I would be utterly surprised if any *hard news* had ever been cut from a piece by Ebbutt or anyone else.[127]

James Holburn does not recall his chief's reports ever being censored for their contents.[128] Karl Robson, who was friendly with and encouraged by Ebbutt, does not recall any such censorship; 'But I know he was sometimes drastically cut, treated as something of a bore (especially when he wrote about the Confessional Church), and reproached with losing his "sense of perspective".'[129]

After the expulsion, plans then in progress for a special interview with Hitler had to be postponed, but aside from neglecting to raise Holburn to the rank of 'Our Own Correspondent', *The Times* took no action as a result of the expulsion.

127 Unpublished notes by G. L. Pearson and Iverach McDonald.
128 Interview with J. Holburn, 20 Mar. 1967.
129 K. Robson to the author, 14 Apr. 1968.

Many of its critics hold this fact against the paper, citing it as yet another example of how the appeasers gave in to the Nazis. More likely the real reason is to be found by looking ahead to November—and the biggest story to come out of Germany in 1937.

As the weeks of waiting for a German reply to the British Government's questionnaire had turned into months and then a year and months, the idea of a visit to Hitler by Lord Halifax seemed to become more attractive and more urgent. When he reoccupied the Rhineland, Hitler had proposed a twenty-five year non-aggression pact and Germany's return to the League; eighteen months later the offer was still there, untouched. Now, at the end of 1937, events seemed to be moving uncomfortably fast, and Hitler seemed to be falling increasingly under the sway of Ribbentrop and his extremist advisers. When it was announced that Lord Halifax had accepted an invitation from Göring to the International Hunting Exhibition in Berlin and would meet Hitler at Berchtesgaden, many hopes were raised.

Halifax was at this time Lord President of the Council. He had a long and distinguished career of public service, and was known to be close to Chamberlain who considered him 'the most important statesman and politician England had at the present time'.[130] As Lord Irwin, Halifax had been Viceroy of India, and had accomplished the seemingly impossible feat of breaking the deadlock between the British Raj and the Indian Nationalist Movement by seizing a striking personal initiative and entering into personal conversations with Gandhi. Now it seemed that at long last (the visit to Hitler had been mooted as early as April 1936) he would have the opportunity to work the same kind of personal magic on Hitler. For, as Arnold Toynbee explained in 1938:

In the minds of his countrymen, peers and colleagues, Lord Halifax was regarded at this time with a certain pride and awe, not unmingled with a spice of sceptical amusement, as a characteristically English exponent of some simple but noble virtues who at the same time had the gift of charming the most outlandishly un-English 'wild men' by the unconscious exercise of an intuitive art which was capable of surpassing the Machiavellian triumphs of cleverer and less scrupulous politicians. To the average Englishman s eye Mr. Gandhi and Herr Hitler were two hardly distinguishable specimens of the same species of foreigner in virtue of their being, both of them, superlatively exotic . . . [131]

Halifax met Hitler on 19 November. The Führer was churlish and at one point Halifax exclaimed that if Hitler's exposition really represented his thinking then they had both wasted their time, Halifax by coming to Berchtesgaden and Hitler by receiving him. Hitler inveighed against the British Press which he claimed stood in the way of any settlement. The unseemly Press scandal attending Halifax's visit to Germany was a case in point. At the conclusion of their meeting Hitler returned to this and said that in the few remaining problems between Britain and Germany, 'It was only the part played by the press which was sinister . . . . A first condition of the calming of international relations was therefore the co-operation of all peoples to make an end of journalistic free-booting.'[132] Halifax stood up against this point: if Hitler's premises were correct it would mean that there could never be any agreement between the two countries, since England would not quickly modify her present democratic system of government.[133]

More practically, Hitler refused to be pinned down in formulating his colonial demands, and Halifax listed Danzig, Austria, and Czechoslovakia as among those European questions which might see alterations with the passage of time; 'England was interested to see that any alterations should come through the course of peaceful evolution and that methods should be avoided which might cause far-reaching disturbances, which neither the Chancellor nor other countries desired.'[134] Thus, without achieving any positive result, the Halifax visit served to confirm Hitler's conviction that Britain would not fight for the status quo in Central or Eastern Europe.

Living as we do now in a world which accepts without second thoughts the need for secrecy as part of national security, it is difficult for us to understand the hopes and fears which the announcement of Lord Halifax's intention to visit Hitler aroused in November 1937. Those who disliked the Government or its policy of appeasement, and those who

---

[131] Royal Institute of International Affairs, *Survey of International Affairs, 1937*, i. 339.   [132] *DGFP*, Ser. D. i, doc. 31.   [133] Ibid.   [134] Ibid.

still sought the open covenants promised by the League of Nations, saw the impending visit as a damaging and potentially dangerous blow to the international system—a return to 'hole-and-corner diplomacy'. For those who were impatient for a return to 'practical politics' in Europe, however, this meeting between a responsible British official and the all-powerful German Führer seemed to be the first sensible move since the conclusion of the Anglo-German Naval Agreement more than two years earlier. The middle stream of opinion—probably the great majority—was indifferent or felt that the meeting could at least do no harm as long as Halifax remained noncommittal and only felt out the German demands. The *Daily Telegraph*, which would emerge as the most active and vocal supporter of the visit, felt that even if nothing came from it, 'no harm can be done by private, friendly, and face-to-face discussion of the difficulties. If it should prove that there is an essential and incurable incompatibility of purpose, then at least misunderstanding and illusion will have to be removed. We shall all know more clearly where we are.'[135] And as Crozier wrote to Voigt: 'I don't myself see much objection to Halifax's visit. . . . At the best he may come across some means of diminishing the trouble, though that is certainly unlikely; at the worst he may find out rather more exactly what we have to guard against.'[136]

The Times greeted the announcement of the visit with great enthusiasm: 'To say the least, the right kind of opportunity has come at last.'[137] The *News Chronicle* felt that everything would depend upon Halifax's tone; the paper's analysis was practical and interesting:

But if Lord Halifax takes a firmer and more long-sighted line, his visit may do great good. For the Germans have listed him in their minds as a pro-German, and if they find that he is no more prepared than anybody else to surrender Britain's security, and with it her honour, they may realize at last that they will be able to get more for Germany by genuine cooperation than by the methods of bluster and bully.[138]

135 *Daily Telegraph*, 15 Nov. 1937, 1st Leader, p. 12.
136 Crozier to Voigt, 12 Nov. 1937, *Manchester Guardian* archives.
137 *The Times*, 13 Nov. 1937, 2nd Leader, p. 13.
138 *News Chronicle*, 13 Nov. 1937, 1st Leader, 'Halifax and Hitler', p.8.

Scrutator felt that each side had much which needed explaining to the other (on the German side he mentioned the Spanish Civil War and the Anti-Comintern Pact but not the religious persecutions) and therefore welcomed the visit.[139]

Through whatever contact, Vladimir Poliakoff, who was only in the midst of a long and chequered journalistic career, had scooped the story of the Halifax visit. At this time the Diplomatic Correspondent of the *Evening Standard*, Poliakoff wrote that Halifax would visit Hitler three days before it was officially announced in the House of Commons. This must have added considerable weight to his report printed the day after the announcement, when he wrote that: 'The British Government have information from Berlin that Herr Hitler is ready, if he receives the slightest encouragement, to offer to Great Britain a ten-year "truce" in the colonial issue. During the "truce" the question of colonies for Germany would not be raised. In return for this agreement Hitler would expect the British Government to leave him a free hand in Central Europe.'[140]

This article caused a great uproar; for no one could swallow the kind of cynical dealing—and at German dictation—it was immediately taken to indicate. The Foreign Office denied it, and the German Press was furious at the insinuation that the Führer would deal with the colonial issue in such a manner.

On 15 November Halifax spoke to von Ribbentrop and suggested moving up the date of his departure so that he might visit Berlin before going on to see Hitler at Berchtesgaden. Von Ribbentrop reported, however, that 'According to a report from Halifax's circle of acquaintances, the reason for advancing the date of the meeting is the desire not to have the trip jeopardized by renewed press manœuvres.'[141] The *Daily Telegraph* particularly deprecated the *Evening Standard*'s action in printing Poliakoff's piece and stated that it 'may serve at least as a warning to the over-officious of the need for caution and reserve in a business which cannot be assisted, as the Prime Minister suggested, by public declamation'.[142] As the German Press became even more violent, the *Daily Telegraph* was

[139] *Sunday Times*, 14 Nov. 1937, Scrutator, p. 20.
[140] *Evening Standard*, 13 Nov. 1937, p. 1.   [141] *DGFP*, Ser. D. i, doc. 24.
[142] *Daily Telegraph*, 15 Nov. 1937, p. 12.

moved to remark that 'We deplore that minatory tone as much as the inexcusable indiscretion which provoked it.'[143]

That was not the end of it, however; the *Daily Telegraph* found the *Evening Standard*'s attempts to extenuate the original publication no less deplorable than the 'mischief making statement' itself. It was useless to cite similar statements from other papers since they all appeared *ex post facto* and 'might well be mere paraphrases and elaboration of the original "exclusive" announcement'.[144] Sir George Ogilvie Forbes, the British Chargé d'Affaires in Berlin, considered that the British Press had stabbed the Government in the back.[145] Chamberlain was about with the article and caused inquiries to be made as to its author: a German report of a conversation with Chamberlain's chief Press Officer George S. Stewart stated that:

These [investigations] had revealed that the author could only be Poliakoff. The article had not been inspired by the Foreign Office, by members of the Cabinet, or by parliamentary circles. An inquiry at the French Embassy had had the same negative result. It was a known fact that Poliakoff wrote in the interest of whatever power paid him the most. Stewart very clearly hinted that he suspected Italy, without, however, alluding in any way to the Embassy here.[146]

Voigt's version of the story, sent to Crozier before the storm broke, is also interesting. On 17 November, he wrote:

It is generally assumed that Poliakoff got his information from the Italians (he is well in with Mussolini). But that is not so. He got it from a high official in the F.O. who told him that this was the actual German plan for talks but did not reveal the fact that the plan had been accepted as the basis for the conversations in Berlin (as far as I am aware, Poliakoff does not know this even now).

The fight against Lord Halifax's trip became desperate about a week ago. Vansittart has had a terrific fight—the pro-Nazis really want to get rid of *him*, the attack on Eden is really an attack

---

[143] *Daily Telegraph*, 16 Nov. 1937, p. 14.

[144] *Daily Telegraph*, 15 Nov. 1937, p. 12. See *Evening Standard*, 15 Nov. 1937, p. 6. Apropos of this line, *The Week* stated that 'The excuse offered in the *Daily Telegraph* to the effect that if other newspapers on Sunday and Monday reproduced this "lie" so wicked and thumping, they only did so by way of elaboration on it and because the Foreign Office forgot to deny it, is thought to be inconclusive though none the less unfortunate in the light it would seem to throw on the conduct of said newspapers.'

[145] *DGFP*, Ser. D. i, doc. 25.   [146] *DGFP*, Ser. D. i, doc. 29.

on Vansittart, who is the real champion of the association with France and the 'general settlement' in this country.

The F.O. rarely resorts to a scheme so desperate (desperate as judged by English standards) as to counteract a dangerous political move by making a disclosure to a stunt newspaper. But this is what happened—Poliakoff was told about the German plan so that it would receive stunt publicity and be denied by the Germans. The denial was vehement beyond expectation—it was Hitler's own (Hitler acted in one of his fits of fury). It destroyed the proposed basis of the Hitler–Halifax conversations. If the Germans had not issued a denial, they would also have been in an awkward situation, for they would have been pressed for an answer about the truth or untruth of the story in the *Evening Standard*.

I don't understand Chamberlain's part in the affair, for he usually gives Eden more support than Baldwin did. But perhaps he was guileless and saw no harm in 'non-committal' talks on no matter what basis. Of course, if Halifax had come back, saying that we could have permanent peace with Germany on such terms (which would, no doubt, be wrapped in cloudly language) there would have been a strong movement in support of such a peace.

Chamberlain's defence is partly that we had to send someone to Berlin because we get nothing out of Ribbentrop (and Henderson doesn't understand Germany—though I don't suppose Chamberlain would say this even if he knew it). Chamberlain and the rest of the Cabinet are trying to cover the whole affair in fog. Yesterday's long leader in the *Daily Telegraph* was inspired by Chamberlain himself.[147]

The Times saved its comment until after the event, when it spoke of those people 'who refuse to be contented with any explanation which has nothing complicated or sinister about it, and decline to believe that Lord Halifax can have meant exactly what he himself has said about his visit. Even within the past twenty-four hours, for example, the newspaper reader has been offered a mushroom crop of comment bedded in a mass of solemn but insubstantial speculation.' Speculation is always easy, and 'A parting of the ways is always journalistically acceptable.' But no honest end was thus served, and 'It

---

[147] Voigt to Crozier, 17 Nov. 1937, *Manchester Guardian* archives. Whether this is the true story or not will await confirmation from further papers or memoirs of the period. Although Vansittart undoubtedly opposed the visit, and was aware of the manœuvrings around himself, it still seems a 'desperate' step indeed to give such a story to so notorious a figure as Poliakoff. Ian Colvin's *Vansittart in Office* offers no elucidation.

will be time enough to protest against the Government's crooked or criminal intentions when there is some evidence that they actually possess them.'[148]

It was information from Poliakoff concerning Halifax's proposed trip to Germany which led Claud Cockburn to discover—or invent—the Cliveden Set. Although the visit had in fact been planned long in advance, Cockburn's newsletter, *The Week*, portrayed it as a part of a Cliveden–Printing House Square ramp of the weekend 23–24 October, aimed at bringing about a rapprochement with Germany by meeting the demands for colonies and a free hand in Eastern Europe. In his most persuasive and abrasive behind-the-scenes tone, Cockburn wrote that Eden had been invited so that even though he disagreed with the plan, Chamberlain might be told that he had been informed of it—guilt by association was the essence of his invitation.

Eden was furious when Chamberlain approved the plan, and, still according to *The Week*, resigned on 8 November. This, however, 'like so many of Mr. Eden's political gestures', was 'a political event without consequences', and when it was agreed that Halifax would report to him first upon returning and only afterwards to the Cabinet, Eden agreed to withdraw his resignation.

On the German end of this campaign were two Englishmen—Nevile Henderson, Lord Londonderry and, intermittently, the Aga Khan, together with one German, Göring. The whole idea was to circumvent von Ribbentrop who had made such a botch of things in England and who, according to *The Week*'s intelligence, 'the titled British and Anglo-Americans' of Cliveden considered 'nothing but a common little ex-champagne salesman anyway . . .'

Everything went as planned until the *Evening Standard* scooped the planned announcement. Von Ribbentrop was livid, and personally dictated over the telephone from the German Embassy in Carlton House Terrace the virulent article suggesting that Halifax had better not make the visit in view of the high feeling in Germany. Thus although events had gone too far to cancel the visit, the best-laid plans of

---

[148] *The Times*, 25 Nov, 1937, 1st Leader, p. 15.

Cliveden and Printing House Square had gone awry, and the visit itself turned out to be a 'resounding defeat'.

Such, shorn of infinite numbers of spurious and scurrilous details, is the version according to *The Week*.[149] Only its most basic flaw is that the uproar in the German Press was over Poliakoff's *second* article, published the day after Simon's announcement of the visit, not after Poliakoff's scoop five days earlier. The picture of Ribbentrop shouting down the phone to some trembling stenographer at the *Völkischer Beobachter* loses much of its drama when one realizes that von Ribbentrop had already had five days in which to rant and rage.

This was perhaps the moment of *The Week*'s greatest glory. The natural reticence of the Government surrounding Halifax's visit seemed to lend support to Cockburn's inventions, and the Cliveden Set became an epithet heard round the world.[150]

Voigt added fuel to the controversy a week after Halifax's visit by writing a diplomatic correspondence which was printed as the paper's main news story on 24 November. In it he stated, in effect, that there was great concern in London because Halifax had done exactly what Poliakoff and *The Week* had said he would. When Chamberlain was asked about Voigt's article in the House of Commons, he replied, 'I should like to make it clear that these statements are not only irresponsible but highly inaccurate.'[151]

Voigt was obliged to take note of this, but his self-defence can only be termed tortuous.[152] Although the *Manchester Guardian* supported him, Crozier wrote privately saying that he knew, from a private source beyond doubting, that neither Chamberlain, Halifax, nor Eden had ever had any discussions or received any information of the kind reported in the *Evening Standard* or *The Week*. Indeed, Crozier even slightly changed one of Voigt's articles to coincide with a leader to this effect.[153] On 29 November, the acting Editor wrote to Voigt for the ailing Crozier:

[149] See *The Week*, 17, 24 Nov. 1937, Nos. 239, 240.
[150] For delightful but totally unreliable reminiscences of these events, see Claud Cockburn, *In Time of Trouble*, and Patricia Cockburn, *The Years of 'The Week'*.   [151] 329 H. C. Deb. 5*s.*, col. 1215.
[152] *Manchester Guardian*, 26 Nov. 1937, p. 11.
[153] Crozier to Voigt, 22, 25 Nov. 1937, *Manchester Guardian* archives.

He asks me so say that his feeling is that we can't very well write about the Cliveden group as having been responsible for the emergence of the colonial issue, for he himself heard some considerable time ago (before the Halifax visit) that the British and French Governments were considering precisely the possible ways of satisfying Germany on this issue. Besides—we have frequently argued in leaders that it should be taken up and discussed.[154]

The British Government maintained its silence and very shortly attention shifted elsewhere. The meeting's supporters had as little to go on as its opponents. 'Well begun is half done, and it is indeed eminently satisfactory to know that Lord Halifax, though his lips are sealed, is so well pleased with his reception in Germany' was all the *Daily Telegraph* could say.[155] Regarding the questions in the House of Commons, the paper complained that such conduct could defeat the very purpose of the meeting: ' "open convenants, openly arrived at" may be a good democratic principle; but conversations, it may be remarked, are not covenants.'[156] *The Times* commented vaguely that '. . . excited interpretations in the Press and anxious questions in the House are genuine evidence of the very uncertainties it is the aim of the Government to approach and to dissolve.'[157]

The *Sunday Times* stated that the conversation had apparently gone according to plan and that any opportunities resulting from it would undoubtedly be pursued. The leader added significantly: 'But in an armed world we, too, must be armed, if our voice is to be heard; and it is only on that condition that we can hope to make peace-advocacy effective.'[158]

Voigt, in the letter to Crozier quoted earlier, concluded with a pessimistic survey of the situation and the British Press:

The incident is over—but the forces that are trying to change our foreign policy remain. They are sure to renew their attempts.

I wish the Labour Party were more on the alert in the House. But it never seems to have any inkling of what goes on anywhere.

It is a calamity that there are only two free papers left in the country—the *Manchester Guardian* and the *Yorkshire Post. The Times*

[154] Wadsworth to Voigt, 29 Nov. 1937, *Manchester Guardian* archives.
[155] *Daily Telegraph*, 22 Nov. 1937, 1st Leader, p. 12.
[156] *Daily Telegraph*, 25 Nov. 1937, 1st Leader, p. 16.
[157] *The Times*, 25 Nov. 1937, 1st Leader, p. 15.
[158] *Sunday Times*, 21 Nov. 1937, 2nd Leader, p. 18.

and the *Observer* are in with Lothian and the Astors. The *Daily Telegraph* is stodgy and accepts dictation from the Government. The others don't count except for stunts (which are useful only one time in a hundred—as the *Evening Standard*'s has been).[159]

The visit, the controversy, and the quiet of 1937 were shortly left behind; 1938 was to be the most active and alarming year of German rearmament and expansion.

[159] Voigt to Crozier, 17 Nov. 1937, *Manchester Guardian* archives.

4

1938:
ON THE BRINK

NINETEEN THIRTY-EIGHT was the most important peacetime year in Anglo-German relations. After almost two quiescent years, Hitler suddenly invaded Austria over a week-end in March. As with the Rhineland two years earlier, there was a case to be made for the German claims; there was also a case to be made against the Austrian Chancellor's sudden precipitation of the crisis by announcing a plebiscite based upon a loaded question for which 'No' ballots would not be provided. The Anschluss of the two nations was effected quickly and peacefully. While Goebbels called it a *Blumenkrieg* because the populace met the German army with flowers instead of weapons, *The Times* ran a headline, 'The Rape of Austria'. Hitler was intoxicated by the tremendous enthusiasm of his reception as he moved through Austria to Vienna. After addressing a tumultuous crowd from the balcony of the Hofburg, he met Ward Price on one of the building's marble staircases. '*Nanu, Ward Price*', he asked challengingly, '*Ist das eine Vergewaltigung?*'[1]

After the Anschluss, there could be little question but that of Hitler's major remaining grievances—the Polish Corridor and the Sudeten Germans—the latter would be the next cause for revision. The complicated attitudes of the British newspapers towards Czechoslovakia were the determining factor in this regard. These attitudes emerged clearly in the false alarm of the Week-end, or May crisis. The May crisis also provides an interesting example of how the subsequent legend differs from the actual event.

The late spring and early summer brought a deceptive calm. Of course we now know that Henlein and his Sudeten

---

[1] Price, *Year of Reckoning*, p. 148.

German Party were under orders from Berlin always to demand more than the Prague Government could concede to them. The conciliatory mission of Lord Runciman, universally welcomed by the British Press, was thus foredoomed to failure; it did however serve the inadvertent negative purpose of somewhat clarifying and improving the Czech case by demonstrating Prague's willingness to make concessions.

The nine months following the Anschluss saw both the full-flowering and the end of appeasement as a viable European policy: Munich was both its highest point and the beginning of its end. The stages of this progression may best be followed in the *Observer*, where Garvin's weekly articles exhibit them step by step.

At last the need to develop adequate powers of resistance was recognized. What the British Press was now waiting for was the next German external aggression. Early in 1939, the newspapers reflected diplomatic fears for Holland and Switzerland. When the move came suddenly and unexpectedly against the rest of Czechoslovakia in March, the indignation was tempered by the realization that Czechoslovakia had been written off at Munich. The frustration of this realization led to the British Government's spate of unprecedented unilateral guarantees in March and April 1939.

Since 1938 is the most important year for our study, we shall consider it at some length. For the crises over Austria and Czechoslovakia, we shall analyse each newspaper's policy separately. This treatment, especially in the case of the crisis over Czechoslovakia, does not necessarily lead to a satisfying symmetry of presentation. The various papers' coverage and analyses differed greatly in depth, detachment, sophistication, and interest. This imbalance will seem especially obvious around the time of Munich. The *Daily Telegraph*, presumably trying to support the Government while disagreeing with its policy towards Germany, restrained its comments to the barest minimum. The *Manchester Guardian*, torn between the desire to halt Nazi aggression and its realization that Czechoslovakia was not the place to force the issue, was reticent and reserved. These difficulties are indicated and underlined by the absence of almost any important correspondence in the papers' archives for this period.

Even aside from the attention given to the famous leader of 7 September 1938, it may seem that *The Times* receives undue attention. It is rather the case that *The Times* (and in some respects the *News Chronicle*) was the only important paper whose attitude towards Germany and European problems, whether it was right or wrong, was at any rate consistent. Far from observing a discreet silence or reserving its comment during this crisis, *The Times* set out the daily exposition and development of its policy of appeasement. The archives of the paper burgeon during this period with long series of correspondence explaining and defending the paper's policy. When events proved that the German good will necessary for appeasement was lacking, the paper faced the consequence and prepared itself and its readers for war. Although war was averted at Munich, the paper saw that this was a respite but not a relief of the essential problem, and continued to counsel increased arms.

Each paper, then, is treated here with somewhat proportionately the same amount of attention and space as the paper itself devoted to Germany and German news.

The year began quietly enough. Nineteen thirty-eight was the only year in which Hitler did not make a speech to commemorate the anniversary of his coming to power on 30 January 1933. He had not made a public address since Mussolini's visit to Berlin in September 1937, and there had been little news from Germany in the New Year apart from Hitler's 'peace address' to the Diplomatic Corps on 11 January. When plans were made to assemble the Reichstag for its annual meeting, there was speculation in the British Press as to the probable tenor of the Führer's remarks. At the last minute it was announced that no meeting would be held, and the newspapers were left on their own to wonder why, and to assess the five years of Nazi rule.

The Times was enthusiastic. A leading article, 'Five Years in Germany', directed attention to 'those internal changes which even the strongest critics of the regime do not deny', namely the dispersion of the air of defeatism 'which brooded too long over Republican Germany'; the fact that 'nothing is more extraordinary about Herr Hitler's rise to power than his opponents' failure to go down fighting and their ability to quarrel among themselves to the last'; and that 'today—even if full account is taken of the suppression of the other political parties and the trade unions, the deplorable conflict with the Churches, and outlawry of the Jews—it is clear enough that Hitler's unchallenged position does not rest on mere force. Millions of Germans regard him with burning devotion as the saviour of his country. In particular the Nazis of the rising generation would gladly lay down their lives for him.'[2]

The Times frankly admitted its attitude towards Nazi Germany in the same article when it said that 'Herr Hitler might reasonably have claimed, as his enthusiastic supporters marched in torchlight through the streets, that he who seeks the new Germany's monument has only to look around.'[3]

In an editorial article in the Daily Telegraph, H. P. S. Matthews analysed the practical foundations of the Nazi regime. Hitler, he wrote, was the only alternative to chaos, he had made Germany strong, and he had liquidated unemployment. There was in Germany, too, pride in the Four Year Plan.[4]

The Manchester Guardian felt only repugnance for the new Germany. The paper opposed National Socialism on the broadest ideological level; it had done so from the first emergence of Nazism in the late 1920s. Now in 1938, however, this evil system had held sway in Germany for five years and, despite isolated and unorganized pockets of resistance, had vast popular support. Unemployment had been almost wiped out. This was an impressive achievement in a world still reeling from the effects of the Great Depression and it was not true, as a correspondent, probably Voigt, wrote, that 'the same miracle has been performed in other countries with less drastic methods'. This was tacitly admitted when he stated that it was impossible to dismiss moral considerations from judgements of Germany simply because she had 'renounced all Christian and liberal standards', or because, judged by the 'lower spheres of material life' alone, the Nazis had an impressive record.

On the eve of 30 January, a leading article formulated two (somewhat loaded) questions to test the Nazi regime's

[2] The Times, 31 Jan. 1938, 2nd Leader, p. 13.   [3] Ibid.
[4] Daily Telegraph, 31 Jan. 1938, ed. art. by H. P. S. Matthews, p. 10.

success. Had it, firstly, made for a happier and better Germany and Europe, established a political and social order that could be a model for Britain, further enriched the rich civilization of Germany and set up, as all social revolutions profess to set up, higher standards of equality and justice? Secondly, did it work—that is, did it fulfil the practical purpose of its chiefs, whether that purpose be good or ill by Western European standards, had it made Germany great, and had its first five years witnessed constructive achievement regardless of its ethical character? The answer to the first question was mainly 'no'; to the second, mainly 'yes'. In some ways Germany was undoubtedly happier but the price had been high. Terrorism had tamed chaos but when the chaos disappeared, the terrorism still remained. The reduction of the unemployed from six millions to about half a million was the result of rearmament, made possible by the reduction of real wages and the destruction of the trade unions. The leader admitted, however, that the reduction of unemployment, regardless of the methods used, was a real achievement and was recognized as such 'even by the German workmen who remain implacable enemies of the regime'.

Still, nothing could compensate for the frightful persecution of the Jews,

. . . which has not abated for one moment, or for the constant maladministration of justice, the secret and terroristic trials, the torture of prisoners, the concentration camps, the lowering of ethical and aesthetic standards, the habits of servility that have grown up amongst the ruled under the arrogance of the rulers, the incessant propaganda that is killing truthfulness in the German people, who used to be, above all, truth-seekers, the militarisation of old and young, and the new educational ideals that threaten to produce a new generation animated by a barbarous and militant nationalism.[5]

In addition to speculations about what Hitler would have said had he spoken, considerable conjecture was devoted to his reasons for not speaking at all. 'Since it is inconceivable that Herr Hitler's oratory can have dried up,' the *News Chronicle* stated, 'is it possible that there is nothing to put in the window this year? Rumours come from Germany of party

---

[5] *Manchester Guardian*, 29 Jan. 1938, 1st Leader, p. 10.

dissensions over the Jews, of trouble with the industrialists, and so on. Perhaps Herr Hitler thought the day would be more profitably spent in a study of his domestic problems.'[6]

The Times too saw domestic problems as the reason for the postponement of the speech, but felt that 'it must also be regarded as showing a wise self-restraint from the international point of view. In the past, oratorical phrases intended for internal consumption have too often caused unnecessary anxiety abroad, or else such speeches have conveyed the impression of being part of a long-range debate and thereby intended to obstruct diplomatic progress.'[7]

The *Manchester Guardian* wrote that Hitler was concerned especially with the delicate balance needed to be struck between China and Japan. But a deeper reason for the cancellation of the speech was Hitler himself. He was thought to be gradually withdrawing from the scene. The *Observer* was not surprised at Hitler's decision since he only used such occasions for major policy statements: no news was therefore good news.[8]

On 12 February, after having announced that he was going skiing in Tyrol for the weekend,[9] the Chancellor of Austria Kurt von Schuschnigg took a train for the German frontier and then motored with Guido Schmidt, his Foreign Minister, and Franz von Papen, the German Ambassador in Vienna, to meet Hitler at his mountain home at Berchtesgaden. Expecting to discuss various difficulties which had arisen in the application of the Austro-German agreement of July 1936 and to confront Hitler with the plans for a Nazi *putsch* which had been discovered in a raid on the Brown House in Vienna—the so-called Tavs Plot[10]—Schuschnigg instead found himself confronted with a raving Hitler, an ultimatum demanding the inclusion of Nazi ministers in his Cabinet, and the presence of three

---

[6] *News Chronicle*, 31 Jan. 1938, 5th Leader, p. 10. See also ibid., Berlin Corr., p. 15.   [7] *The Times*, 31 Jan. 1938, 2nd Leader, p. 13.

[8] *Observer*, 30 Jan. 1938, Berlin Corr., p. 15.

[9] See *Manchester Guardian*, 12 Feb. 1938, p. 12 and *Daily Telegraph*, 12 Feb. 1938, Reuter, p. 13.

[10] For the Tavs Plot, see *Manchester Guardian*, 27 Jan. 1938, Vienna Corr., p. 6, 28 Jan. 1938, p. 7 and 29 Jan. 1938, p. 15.

generals. Schuschnigg had in fact conceded all the ultimatum called for two days earlier in the Zernato *Punktationen* the contents of which (representing the limits of concession) had been treacherously revealed to Hitler by Zernato, Secretary-General of Schuschnigg's Fatherland Front.[11]

Frightened as he had been at Berchtesgaden, and quite convinced, as Hitler had told him, that he could expect help from no one,[12] Schuschnigg decided that the best policy was to maintain silence about the nature of his reception by the Führer, and to try to get the Federal President Miklas to accept the changes which had been demanded. The meeting was two days old (it had taken place on a Saturday afternoon and evening) when the Monday papers carried surprised reports of it. Initial panicky rumours were belied by Schuschnigg's demeanour and soon scotched.

Two things seemed to bode well for the meeting: it had been called on Hitler's initiative, and there was no publicity given to it in Germany, which would indicate that it was not a German 'victory'. In the British Press these facts were recorded and the meeting was generally considered an Austrian success. 'Herr Hitler seems to be steering a middle course', Holburn wrote. 'The change-over on February 4th may be said to have been a victory for the party over the cautious group within the army. The conversations begun yesterday may reassure the more prudent group again.'[13] The *Manchester Guardian* printed a leading article which emphasized that such a meeting was unlikely to produce a lasting result, 'but there are certain immediate questions which could usefully be discussed by these two men, and which, indeed, could hardly be well discussed by their subordinates'.[14] But just as the leading article had stated that 'there are few men in Europe who hold such divergent views on the subject of Austria's destiny as Herr Hitler and Dr. Schuschnigg', Fodor wrote to the *Manchester Guardian* from

---

[11] See Brook-Shepherd, *Anschluss;* and Gehl, *Austria, Germany and the Anschluss 1931–1938.* [12] See Schuschnigg, *Austrian Requiem*, pp. 12–19.

[13] *The Times,* 14 Feb. 1938, Berlin Corr., p. 12. The change referred to is Hitler's announcement of von Blomberg's resignation as Minister of War and Commander-in-Chief of the Armed Forces, and of von Fritsch's resignation as Commander-in-Chief of the Army—and that he, Hitler, would himself succeed von Blomberg.

[14] *Manchester Guardian,* 14 Feb. 1938, 1st Leader, p. 8.

Vienna that while the results were generally considered favourable there, 'the two headstrong men must have had a strenuous time together when they were arguing for almost eleven
hours about the future relations of their countries. It is certain
that neither could convince the other'.[15] The *Daily Telegraph*
printed Gedye's assessment: 'The general interpretation of
the Berchtesgaden interview in responsible political circles
here is that the balance is definitely in Austria's favour.'[16]

The *News Chronicle*'s Vienna correspondent reported a version of the meeting (which he termed 'less authoritative' than
his 'well-informed version') characterizing it as a 'fiasco from
the Nazi standpoint': there was believed to have been 'some
robust speaking from Dr. Schuschnigg'.[17] The *Daily Express*
headlined that Hitler was 'Baulked On New Pact' by Schuschnigg's insistence that Federal President Miklas was the
ultimate constitutional authority.

This attitude of calm analysis—on the basis of almost no
known facts—prevailed for another day. Then the real story
began slowly to emerge.[18] Gedye wrote later, 'I knew that this
official optimism was not genuine, but I was far from guessing
at the real truth, which I learned only on the following Tuesday.'[19]

On Wednesday the story broke. The *News Chronicle* stated,

---

[15] *Manchester Guardian*, 14 Feb. 1938, Vienna Corr., p. 10. See also Lambert's
report, *Manchester Guardian*, Berlin Corr., p. 12.

[16] *Daily Telegraph*, 14 Feb. 1938, Vienna Corr., p. 13.

[17] *News Chronicle*, 14 Feb. 1938, Vienna Corr., p. 1.

[18] On 15 February the story expanded somewhat: Schuschnigg had been
presented with a document, 'extremely favourable', for signature in return for
one 'little' thing: Seyss-Inquart's inclusion in the Cabinet. The generals made
their first appearance: 'An interesting light on German methods of negotiation is
thrown by the fact that during the interview between Herr Hitler and Dr. von
Schuschnigg three German Army generals were waiting in the next room.'
(See *Manchester Guardian*, 15 Feb. 1938, Vienna Corr., p. 11.) According to a
Reuter and B.U.P. report printed in the *Daily Mail*, the presence of the generals
was 'authoritatively revealed in the official gazette, the *Wiener Zeitung*'. (See
Daily Mail, 15 Feb. 1938, p. 12.) From Vienna Reed wrote to *The Times* that if
Seyss-Inquart were taken into Schuschnigg's Cabinet, 'it would, in the general
view of anti-Nazis in Austria, mean that before long the words "Finis Austriae"
would be written across the map of Europe'. (See *The Times*, 15 Feb. 1938, Vienna
Corr., p. 14. Reed's use of the phrase 'Finis Austriae' caused great diplomatic
commotion. See Reed, *Insanity Fair*, pp. 380, 384.)

[19] Gedye, *Fallen Bastions*, p. 231. Gedye claims that Schuschnigg had decided
to tell the foreign press the truth, but that Guido Schmidt instructed the head of
the Press Bureau that on no account must any press learn of the real situation.

'Now that the veil is being gradually lifted from the historic meeting at Berchtesgaden, the reasons for the Chancellor's change of front become less obscure. From the very start of the interview Chancellor Schuschnigg found himself subjected to great pressure. . . . At times the discussion was extremely blunt.'[20] *The Times* reported cautiously that Schuschnigg had gone to Berchtesgaden with great expectations but that 'in the event he underwent a very trying ordeal. Herr Hitler used the plainest language in stating his demands and it is understood that he indicated grave consequences if they were not accepted. . . . It is understood that he recommended compliance to Herr von Schuschnigg in the most emphatic terms, and expressed the view that the Austrian Government had no backing to hope for in any third quarter if they were obdurate.'[21] Gedye wrote to the *Daily Telegraph* that after upbraiding von Schuschnigg for an interview the latter had given to the *Daily Telegraph* in January,

The Führer went so far—and I can assert this positively, in the face of any subsequent denials—as to threaten that in the case of disorders in Austria, he would 'march', being unable to resist any longer the pleas of the 'downtrodden German population in Austria'. . . . Actually—as I am able again to assert without fear of contradiction—Herr Hitler delivered an ultimatum. . . . This is the reason for the complete silence on the interview which has been kept in Berlin. The table had been banged; the terms handed over; and it only remained to wait for acceptance.[22]

The *Daily Telegraph* was especially upset by this example of Hitlerian technique and printed a leading article which stated that 'Whatever changes may have been introduced into German policy by the Nazi regime, it is now evident that the method of the mailed fist has been preserved without abatement. The ex-kaiser, at the height of his career, was never more

[20] *News Chronicle*, 16 Feb. 1938, Vienna Corr., p. 12.
[21] *The Times*, 16 Feb. 1938, Vienna Corr., p. 12.
[22] *Daily Telegraph*, 16 Feb. 1938, Vienna Corr., p. 12. For the Schuschnigg interview, see *Daily Telegraph*, 5 Jan. 1938, ed. art. by Kies van Roek, p. 12. Von Papen had been instructed to ask for an explanation of some statements in the interview: 'In official quarters here,' Gedye reported, 'the publication of the interview seems to be regarded as the most disturbing incident in Austro-German relations since the conclusion of the agreement of July 11, 1936, under which Austria recognised herself to be a "Germanic State".'

absolute, imperious, and minatory than Herr Hitler showed himself to be in his Berchtesgaden meeting with Dr. Schuschnigg.'[23] And the next day the paper, in Lord Oxford's famous phrase, likened the talk of a settlement with Germany, in her present mood, to 'the twittering of sparrows in a thunderstorm'. The only settlement to which Germany would care to subscribe would be one which satisfied her full demands—and one which did not bar the making of further demands 'at a convenient season'.[24] Fodor reported to the *Manchester Guardian* from Vienna that, while the people were pessimistic, the view taken in Government quarters was one of optimism: that Austria had done her share and German concessions were now expected.[25] The *News Chronicle*'s first leader on 18 February, however, was called 'Whole Hog' and said that it would be childish to base any hopes whatever on Hitler's 'moderation' as far as his taking advantage of the present situation was concerned. 'We do not believe that Herr Hitler is ready to go to war. But he is clearly going the whole hog in exploiting Germany's ability to bluff and threaten.'[26]

From the very day on which the real story became known, 16 February, there was a striking *assumption* on the part of all the newspapers that Austria was a closed case, that war in her support would be out of the question. The *Daily Telegraph* expressed its editorial opinion on that day, that 'in this country, more easily than in others, it is possible to regard objectively the new situation created for Austria . . .'.[27] The paper stated that Schuschnigg must take Seyss-Inquart

---

[23] *Daily Telegraph*, 17 Feb. 1938, 1st Leader, p. 14. Here the *Daily Telegraph* referred to the generals: 'Fuller information now enables us to picture the ordeal to which the unhappy Austrian Chancellor was subjected—with his interlocutor, attended by a group of sabre-rattling generals, storming and shouting.' This leader blamed Mussolini.

[24] *Daily Telegraph*, 18 Feb. 1938, 1st Leader, p. 14.

[25] *Manchester Guardian*, 19 Feb. 1938, Vienna Corr., p. 14.

[26] *News Chronicle*, 18 Feb. 1938, 1st Leader, p. 10. The leader expressed, however, the somewhat contradictory hope that it did not follow that because Austria had submitted to the German ultimatum she would become as Nazi as Germany. It would be difficult to 'browbeat into compliance' the Social Democrats or the Roman Catholic Church.

[27] *Daily Telegraph*, 16 Feb. 1938, 1st Leader, p. 12. This crisis was seen as a 'manifestation of the new spirit which has been infused into German foreign policy as a consequence of the purge'. It added that it was impossible 'to mistake the meaning of the ultimatum so bluntly and so menacingly presented to her'.

into his Cabinet; and that President Miklas and the Cabinet 'must acquiesce in his decision there is no doubt. For the immediate peace of Austria there is nothing else to be done.'[28] The *Daily Herald* wrote that the days were past when, immediately after the war, because they were immeasurably more powerful than any other European State, France or Britain could impose their will upon the Continent. Now, indeed, the only solution which could avoid war would be a new European and colonial settlement not based on the 'rotten' Versailles treaty: 'The only alternative is to watch passively while Germany pursues the path of revision by act or threat: or to face a new European war of which the purpose would be to stop her, but of which the end would be—what?'[29]

The *Manchester Guardian* resignedly hoped that, with the examples of Germany and Danzig before her, Austria would not tamely submit to gradual absorption by the Nazis. 'It may be useless for her to remind England and France of the declarations they have made in the past about the maintenance of her independence; nor will it, apparently, be of any assistance from a once so diligent but now embarrassed Italy.'[30] The next day Fodor wrote from Vienna that 'The cause of the gloom in Austria is not so much the fear about her immediate future, but that the Nazis could arrange such a real mobilisation without being checked by France or by Italy.'[31] The *Manchester Guardian*, however, never mooted the policy of supporting Austria. Even Voigt wrote that since there was no access to Central Europe except through, or at least with, the good will of Italy, 'Austria was lost when the Rhineland was reoccupied and when the conflict between Italy and the League broke out.'[32] In a leading article on 'The Hitler Touch' the paper stated that whereas when hitherto Hitler had violated a treaty or undertaking he had invoked some 'intolerable suffering of the German people', Berchtesgaden was clearly a demand that a sovereign government

[28] Ibid.   [29] *Daily Herald*, 1 Feb. 1938, Leader, p. 10.

[30] *Manchester Guardian*, 16 Feb. 1938, 2nd Leader, p. 10. The next day the *News Chronicle* ran a box on p. 2, listing the five separate Anglo-French-Italian guarantees of Austrian independence.

[31] *Manchester Guardian*, 17 Feb. 1938, Vienna Corr., p. 9.

[32] *Manchester Guardian*, 17 Feb. 1938, Dipl. Corr., p. 12.

fall into line. In fact, 'by all accounts truculently and to the accompaniment of sabre-rattling generals and "manœuvres" on the Austrian border that remind one of the claim that a battleship is a defensive weapon, he has now summoned the Austrian Government to transform itself in the interests of Nazi Germany'.[33]

For the first time, on the 17th, *The Times* printed a leading article explaining its point of view. The arguments put forward in this article were held throughout the following weeks until Austria was part of Germany. Before 1933, the paper stated, Austria's desire to join Germany was clear; but even after 1933 Austria could never be anti-German: 'Ultimately this is the real strength of the Reich's claims upon it, and the real difficulty of an Austrian Chancellor when he has to define and to defend Austrian independence.'[34] Indeed, for *The Times* the roots lay deeper still: 'One of the least rational, most brittle, and most provocative artificialities of the peace settlement was the ban on the incorporation of Austria in the German Reich. One of the largest blunders in European policy since the peace was the judicial strangulation of the proposed Customs union between the two States. These crows are coming home to roost.'

On a wider policy level the article asserted that 'It can be no part of British policy to resist expansion . . . or the relations that will develop along with it. What Europe needs above all things is the freedom and the power to think of its future in these terms.' German expansion was carefully defined as the 'extension of German influence' guaranteed by its economic preponderance as a great production and marketing area, exerting a natural attraction upon complementary communities.

As far as the Berchtesgaden meeting was concerned, the paper regretted its form but insisted upon withholding judgement of its content. 'The one really disturbing addition to public knowledge concerns the method even more than the substance of the Berchtesgaden meeting. A sudden meeting is called; demands are presented along with something like an ultimatum; and the invited guest is threatened, either expressly

---

[33] *Manchester Guardian*, 17 Feb. 1938, 1st Leader, p. 8.
[34] *The Times*, 17 Feb. 1938, 1st Leader, p. 15.

or by implication, with the huge oppression of military Germany.' The leader concluded, however, that victories of this kind were self-defeating.[35]

In the *Sunday Times*, Scrutator wrote, 'No rational man proposes that this country should go to war to save Austria, and the bluff of war, however successful it may sometimes be with dictators, is always wrong for a democratic country.'[36] Echoing *The Times*'s fear, he suggested that even setting aside Austria's weak condition, and assuming that she could fight, she would probably prefer to fight on the side of the Germans than against them. He concluded by holding up the bogy of communist expansion: 'The next war will be a leap in the dark for everyone that engages in it. And war might well bring Russian influence further west.'[37]

On Sunday, 20 February, Hitler addressed the Reichstag. He said little of vital interest, especially in view of the great build-up for this, his first public pronouncement in several months. Ominously he claimed to be the protector of all Germans outside Germany. He asserted that he would never rejoin the League of Nations; he announced Germany's recognition of Manchukuo; reaffirmed the identity of German and Italian attitudes and goals in Spain; and pledged that he had no more European territorial demands upon France, and no quarrel with Great Britain apart from colonial claims.[38]

Hitler's speech was relegated to the background by another event of the greatest significance and importance. On 20 February, Anthony Eden resigned from the Cabinet over disagreements with Chamberlain concerning the latter's belief that negotiations should be opened with Italy at the earliest moment, in an effort to detach her from the Axis. Eden's resignation filled the British Press, in some cases—the *Manchester Guardian* for example—almost to the exclusion of other news. The conjunction of the resignation and Hitler's truculent Reichstag speech was unfortunate, for as Holburn reported from Berlin, 'The man in the street here is convinced that Mr. Eden resigned because of the attacks made by Herr Hitler yesterday. In consequence, a speech which had rather

---

[35] Ibid.   [36] *Sunday Times*, 20 Feb. 1938, Scrutator, p. 16.
[37] Ibid.   [38] See *Sunday Times*, 21 Feb. 1938, Reuter, p. 9.

misfired yesterday has become this morning a resounding success for Herr Hitler.'[39]

On 24 February, Schuschnigg made a speech in which he defiantly promised that Austria had gone as far as was possible and honourable in compromising for peace—'Thus far and no farther'. Until the violent German reaction to Schuschnigg's words became known, the speech was given little attention. *The Times* made it sound very mild indeed, with Reed's commentary from Vienna almost being misleading.[40] It is difficult to say whether this was because the speech really was unexceptional and only became important because of the German reaction to it, or whether attention was so focused upon Germany's next move that Schuschnigg's firmness went all unnoticed until the Germans pointed it out. Fodor in the *Manchester Guardian* perfunctorily summarized the speech and then commented slightingly that 'the meeting was accompanied by scenes such as are now common in the neighbouring dictatorships.'[41] After this, a period of comparative quiet intervened until Schuschnigg touched off the final crisis on 8 March by announcing his plebiscite for the following Sunday.

THE ANSCHLUSS

THE TIMES

'All over Europe', a leading article in *The Times* after the Anschluss stated, 'the opinion has steadily gained acceptance that the prohibition of the Anschluss was a mistake, and if Herr Hitler had set about to achieve it with the consent of both peoples, he had every opportunity to do so with international good will, or at least, acquiescence.'[42] And a few days later: 'No one in this country has ever seriously maintained that the status quo in Austria could necessarily be maintained for all time.'[43] It was, then, not the Anschluss itself which angered and worried *The Times*; indeed, 'there would have been no British protest if this process of attraction had developed

---

[39] *The Times*, 22 Feb. 1938, Berlin Corr., p. 14.
[40] *The Times*, 25 Feb. 1938, Vienna Corr., p. 15.
[41] *Manchester Guardian*, 25 Feb. 1938, Vienna Corr., p. 6.
[42] *The Times*, 19 Mar. 1938, 1st Leader, p. 13.
[43] *The Times*, 21 Mar. 1938, 1st Leader, p. 13.

naturally through growing confidence and mutual good will'.
Rather, 'What is so deeply resented here—and throughout
the civilized world—is that it was thought necessary, for the
sake of a Dictator's prestige, to reverse the whole process by
applying to it the physical strength of the bully, and in so
doing to arrest other hopeful movements towards a stable
peace.'[44]

The Times, which had consistently argued for ten years
in favour of a revision of the Versailles settlement, was appalled
by the arbitrary violence of Hitler's method. 'The indignation
of the world', the paper explained, 'is not at the thing he has
done, but at the manner of the doing.'[45] Another leading article
stated that 'If the Anschluss had been effected by legal and
constitutional methods, with due regard for the rights of a
dissident minority, British public opinion at all events would
have had no criticisms to offer.'[46]

Resentment of Hitler's method was twofold: first because
of the danger to world peace inherent in any use of force;
and second because of the set-back it dealt to the policy of
European appeasement. *The Times* saw Hitler's Government
as 'a regime which has an almost Oriental reverence for
"face" ',[47] and it was ludicrous for such a sensitive Government to bluster about the world applying force to attain ends
which could be attained peacefully by negotiation and waiting.
'Inevitably, as Germany and all the world know, and as history warns them, no limit can be set to the consequences of
any act which risks a European upheaval.'[48] Hitler would
have henceforward to take care because, 'If there is a warning
for the world in the events which destroyed the Austrian
Government, there is a warning for Germany in the instinctive
response to them over most of the world.'[49] In an important
and prophetic leading article, *The Times* wrote:

The danger of a success of this kind—and here again foreign observers may usefully remember the lost leaves of the Sibylline book—

[44] *The Times*, 14 Mar. 1938, 1st Leader, p. 15.
[45] *The Times*, 19 Mar. 1938, 1st Leader, p. 13.
[46] *The Times*, 21 Mar. 1938, 1st Leader, p. 13.
[47] *The Times*, 14 Mar. 1938, 1st Leader, p. 13.
[48] *The Times*, 12 Mar. 1938, 1st Leader, p. 13.
[49] *The Times*, 13 Mar. 1938, 1st Leader, p. 13.

is that it may encourage confidence in the methods that achieved it. But methods which succeed within the German family are certainly not applicable outside it; and there is a natural limit to the number of issues which would lend themselves to an apparently effortless triumph followed by a plebiscite in which it would be difficult for the patriotic German conscience to answer 'No'.[50]

Perhaps even worse in *The Times*'s eye was the supernal foolishness of using such methods and upsetting the natural flow of the British policy of appeasement which would eventually have satisfied the German demands without any risk of war. As the paper pointed out,

> The employment of violent means, under any conditions, to secure an end, even a legitimate end, is bound to move the British Government and people to instinctive resentment and condemnation. It denies and thwarts the essential aims of British policy by adding to the divisions and dangers of the Continent a new store of ill-will, suspicion, and alarm.[51]

The enthusiastic reception the German invaders received in Austria did not alter *The Times*'s view.[52] The reception was analysed and found to be extraneous to the nature of Hitler's act.

For many Austrians and Germans the Anschluss represented the fulfilment of an old dream; for others, an overdue assertion of German power. Hitler's reception in Austria was 'a triumphant answer to the call of racial pride and the hope of a vigorous future which was not to be assured even by the gallant but precarious endeavour of the past four years'.[53] As Holburn wrote from Berlin,

> In Austria, as in the Rhineland, Herr Hitler has achieved something which stirs the pulse of every German. The methods may have been distasteful to a few; they do not disturb the great majority of a population which feels and is made to feel that since the end of the War it has been on the receiving end of foreign big sticks.[54]

Whatever the reasons or explanations, however, the essential fact remained that Hitler's action was 'A Blow to Europe',

---

[50] *The Times*, 11 Apr. 1938, 2nd Leader, p. 13.
[51] *The Times*, 15 Mar. 1938, 1st Leader, p. 15.
[52] *The Times*, 14 Mar. 1938, 1st Leader, p. 15. 'Our correspondent leaves no room for doubt about the public jubilation with which [Hitler] and his army were greeted everywhere.' See ibid., Vienna Corr., p. 14.   [53] Ibid.
[54] *The Times*, 9 Apr. 1938, Berlin Corr., p. 12.

'an open exhibition of overbearing force', 'the latest and worst demonstration of the methods of German foreign policy', a 'display of precipitate force' the pretexts for which 'make the case no better'.[55] These were the first, instinctive words, while news of the German invasion was still pouring in. Four days later, with Hitler in Vienna, the paper printed its famous headline which Hitler found ironical, describing the Anschluss, 'The Rape of Austria'.[56]

That British policy must take a warning from these events was clear. Douglas Reed, *The Times*'s correspondent in Vienna, wrote personally to Dawson from Prague about the invasion he had just fled:

In my wildest nightmares I had not foreseen anything so perfectly organised, so brutal, so ruthless, so strong. When this machine goes into action, it will blight everything it encounters like a swarm of locusts. The destruction and loss of life will make the World War look like the Boer War. . . . From what I have seen of England in my last visits we have no chance of withstanding this gigantic machine when it is turned against us, and the vital thing to remember is that the ultimate object is precisely the destruction of England. This is a thing which nobody can understand, apparently, who has not lived with the Germans. Their real hatred is for England.[57]

Far from ignoring Reed's words, Dawson took them very much to heart. On 14 March, *The Times* surveyed 'A March and the Moral':

But there is at least a moral to be derived from the very simplicity of the story, since it admits of no other version. No country, least of all our own, can afford to be lulled into false security while these methods prevail on the neighbouring Continent. It is not untimely that they should have been revealed in so blatant a fashion just when the British Parliament is engrossed in unprecedented estimates for the Defence Services. If ever there were any doubts about the colossal and most deplorable size of these estimates, there will assuredly be no reluctance to pass them after last week's events.[58]

The call for armaments was constantly sounded now in *The Times*, which frankly stated that 'The British Government

[55] *The Times*, 12 Mar. 1938, 1st Leader, p. 13.
[56] *The Times*, 15 Mar. 1938, headline of unattributed article from Westminster, p. 14. See Hitler's reference to this headline above, p. 136.
[57] *Hist. Times*, iv. 917.   [58] *The Times*, 14 Mar. 1938, 1st Leader, p. 15.

will see first and foremost to their own armaments—that is clearly what matters most.'[59] But the need to rearm did not negate the policy of appeasement however much it might dampen it.

The Times's attitude, then, was that an unfortunate situation had been unfortunately remedied. 'Certainly in this country there have been many ready to reckon with Greater Germany— which, whoever likes it or not, is the product of inevitable forces and Herr Hitler's historic accomplishment—as one of the sure developments in Europe. With greater international wisdom it would have emerged in a different form and spirit.'[60] The moral for Britain was clear: increased armament; but the essential wisdom and necessity of the policy of appeasement was not altered. This was stated with admirable clarity the day after Hitler's plebiscite:

This consideration, and this alone, inspired British policy in the resolution of acting upon the lesson of experience and of anticipating, by steady and continuous negotiation upon differences as they arise, the realignment of balanced and implacable antagonisms. Mr. Chamberlain and successive Foreign Ministers have made it perfectly clear for their part that they do not for a moment refuse to deal with any foreign country because its social doctrine differs from our own. Apart from the methods by which it was accomplished, there has never been any public feeling in England against the union of Austria and Germany, nor is it in itself the slightest bar to an understanding between *Grossbritannien* and *Grossdeutschland*. It will no doubt increase the resources and strength of Germany. Great Britain is also engaged in increasing her strength. But it is perfectly appropriate that negotiations should be conducted from strength by both parties.[61]

DAILY TELEGRAPH

Even after several days of exciting dispatches from its Vienna correspondent, G. E. R. Gedye, the *Daily Telegraph* was still surprised and shocked by Hitler's precipitate invasion of Austria. 'The ultimate repercussions of the coup it is as premature as it is unpleasant to prognosticate. . . . Never, indeed, has the mailed fist been wielded with such dramatic

---

[59] Ibid. See also *The Times*, 15 Mar. 1938, 1st Leader, p. 15.
[60] *The Times*, 11 Apr. 1938, 2nd Leader. p. 13.   [61] Ibid.

effect as by Germany between dawn and dusk yesterday.'[62]
Although it had been printing Carleton Greene's and Anthony
Mann's reports from Berlin and Gedye's from Austria, the
paper had made little editorial comment concerning any news
from Germany since the New Year. In a leading article, 'The
End of Austria', on 14 March, its position was made clear
when it wrote approvingly of the Government's conduct:

> Welcome as is the news that M. Blum has now formed a French
> Government likely to command confidence in his own country,
> there should be no illusion that events would have taken a different
> turn had he been in power on Friday. Neither the French nor the
> British Government, nor, above all, the Government of Italy, was
> prepared to shed blood in a cause which Herr von Schuschnigg
> himself would not defend by force of arms.[63]

On the following day Chamberlain's words to the House of
Commons were used to express the paper's own attitude: 'He
denied that this country had ever given encouragement or
consent to the absorption of Austria; but he added that nothing
could have arrested this action by Germany unless we and
others had been prepared to use force. The policy of appeasement and economic recovery, he pointed out, must be re-
tarded.'[64] The speed with which Austria was Nazified was
regarded as impressive: 'Herr Hitler's mills grind not only
exceeding small but also exceeding fast . . .';[65] and Hitler's
plebiscite was considered significant not because of its result,
which was a foregone conclusion, but because of 'the crescendo
of mass delirium to which a great nation—the greatest, numeri-
cally, in Europe, barring Russia—surrendered itself during the
weeks of the campaign'.[66]

Largely thanks to Gedye, the *Daily Telegraph* led the British
Press with its hard-hitting reports of the vicious anti-Semitism
which swept Vienna. It was not particularly surprising, therefore, that he was ordered 'to be over the frontiers of Germany,
including Austria', by noon on 28 March. Despite its rather
nondescript editorial policy, then, and mainly thanks to

[62] *Daily Telegraph*, 12 Mar. 1938, 1st Leader, p. 14.
[63] *Daily Telegraph*, 15 Mar. 1938, 1st Leader, p. 16.
[64] *Daily Telegraph*, 15 Mar. 1938, 1st Leader, p. 16.
[65] *Daily Telegraph*, 28 Mar. 1938, 1st Leader, p. 12.
[66] *Daily Telegraph*, 11 Apr. 1938, 1st Leader, p. 12.

Gedye's reporting, the *Daily Telegraph* gave a particularly clear picture of the horror the Anschluss meant to Austria.

MANCHESTER GUARDIAN

In the first two months of 1938, F. A. Voigt was completing his book *Unto Caesar*. The book, as we have seen, cogently argued that both Nazism and Communism were revolutionary movements. Nazism was by far the more dangerous because it seemed the opposite—a wolf in sheep's clothing; it was the more insidious because it sought to subvert Western Christendom from within. Frequently in his Diplomatic Correspondence, and occasionally in leading articles during this time, he interpreted the developing events in terms of this thesis.

Voigt applied this analysis to the question of Hitler's ambitions for Austria. In mid-February he wrote that

. . . it would be impossible for Hitler to forego union with Austria even if he wished to, for it is only with the union that the Nazi revolution begins to have a meaning. The seizure of power in Germany was no more than a pre-revolutionary action. Germany is to the Nazis but the base from which the pan-German hegemony on the European continent can be achieved, and Hitler wills the Austro-German union with all the concentrated inflexible passion of which he is capable.[67]

At the same time as Voigt was expounding his Hitler-as-revolutionary thesis, Lambert was writing about Hitler-the-moderate, or more properly, Hitler-the-absent. The Führer seemed to be withdrawing from active politics, and control to be passing to Göring, whom Lambert described as 'a moderate and responsible leader'.[68] The *Manchester Guardian* itself was clearly of Lambert's mind in this respect. When Voigt was vindicated by events; when Hitler, as much as ever in command, intimidated Schuschnigg at Berchtesgaden; and when finally German troops began spilling over the border into Austria, then Voigt's hand becomes very clear in the paper's leading articles. But even then, the paper still would not allow the possibility of Great Britain going to war, and

---

[67] *Manchester Guardian*, 16 Feb. 1938, Dipl. Corr., p. 15.
[68] *Manchester Guardian*, 24 Jan. 1938, Berlin Corr., p. 9.

while its condemnation was clear, it offered no policy, no lead for those who sought an alternative to appeasement.

No space was wasted on distinctions between Hitler's end and his means. Only his action was considered, and that had only one virtue: it was clear.

No propaganda can disguise and no ignorance fail to understand so unconcealed a threat of armed force. This, as many have long realised, is the only foreign policy known to the present German Government. It has been used again and again, but hitherto there has always been some excuse, if not justification, and some doubt if no excuse. . . . An ultimatum was delivered at a few hours' notice, and when it expired Herr Hitler did not hesitate to send his aeroplanes over Vienna and his troops over the frontier. This is invasion of an independent State as brutal as that of Japan's into China or Italy's into Abyssinia. If it is not also war it is only because Dr. Schuschnigg preferred surrender to bloodshed. This, then, is Hitler's policy; this is the naked fist.[69]

Thus the New Germany presented itself to the world 'arrogant, intolerant, formidable'.[70] Such a confrontation would surely disabuse those in every country who 'fondly imagine that Herr Hitler will respond to reason' and 'from now on the Governments of Europe will know what to expect'.[71] Hitler had assessed the fragmented condition of Europe—France without a government, Russia in the midst of a purge, Britain irresolute—and taken his main chance. 'He confronted not only Austria but also the Western Powers with the alternative of peace or war, accurately foreseeing that they would choose the former. His tactics on this occasion are familiar and characteristic. Nor is this the last time they will be used.'[72]

But never once was the possibility of resistance to Germany mooted; indeed the paper's only 'proposal' was negative in the extreme: 'The British Government will have to consider its problems afresh. Rearmament is not itself enough. Everyone is rearming at top speed.'[73]

For the moment, British prestige was very low. Voigt called the German reply to the official British protest 'a

[69] *Manchester Guardian*, 12 Mar. 1938, 1st Leader, p. 12.   [70] Ibid.   [71] Ibid.
[72] *Manchester Guardian*, 12 Mar. 1938, Dipl. Corr., p. 13. See also *Manchester Guardian*, 14 Mar. 1938, Berlin Corr., p. 12.
[73] *Manchester Guardian*, 14 Mar. 1938, 1st Leader, p. 8.

masterpiece of cynicism. Indeed, it is doubtful whether a British Government has for generations received such a piece of insolence from any foreign power in peacetime.'[74] Lambert wrote from Berlin of the wave of enthusiasm sweeping Germany: '. . . even non-Nazis have again been swept into the current of enthusiastic patriotic fervour by the bearing and strength of Herr Hitler and the strength of the new German Army in the face of what they see to be the irresolution of Britain . . .'[75]

The farce of the so-called plebiscite remained. Hitler's plebiscite speeches revealed 'an immensely enlarged sense of power'; indeed all the Nazi campaign speeches were delivered 'with a truculence of expression surprising even to those who are used to National Socialist oratory',[76] and indicated that the Nazi leaders were becoming 'anything but more moderate'.[77] Throughout the campaign Hitler spoke of his divine mission, of the sleepwalker's certainty of his actions. At the final election meeting on the eve of polling he told his audience in Vienna, 'I believe that it was God's will to send a youth from here into the Reich, to let him grow up, to raise him to be the leader of the nation so as to enable him to lead back his homeland into the Reich.'[78]

It must have been Voigt who wrote that

... owing to this mystical view of the union, to vote 'No' on Sunday was the mark of a heretic as well as of a traitor. . . . The plebiscite was a test of orthodoxy, an opportunity for sinners to confess that they had erred, and for the outside world a revelation of Hitler's State militant here on earth. That is the solemn view of it, and the organisers meant it to be a solemn occasion.[79]

It must have been Voigt too who earlier had written that just as Napoleon had followed his star, and Lenin his inexorable dialectic, so Hitler had a 'somnambulist certainty' and this 'holy' plebiscite. It was this religious base which made him so dangerous, for he could never stop, he must be either everything or nothing. 'If a man is convinced that what he desires to

---

[74] Ibid., Dipl. Corr., p. 9.   [75] Ibid., Berlin Cor., p. 12.
[76] *Manchester Guardian*, 9 Apr. 1938, Dipl. Corr., p. 17. See also *Manchester Guardian*, 8 Apr. 1938, 4th Leader, p. 10.
[77] *Manchester Guardian*, 12 Apr. 1938, 1st Leader, p. 10.
[78] See Baynes, *Hitler's Speeches*, ii. 1457–8.
[79] *Manchester Guardian*, 12 Mar. 1938, 1st Leader, p. 10.

do is imposed on him as a mission from above what is to stop him from making the attempt?'[80]

Fodor and Lambert sent perceptive and hard-hitting stories throughout the crisis. Fodor left Vienna as soon as the German invasion began, becoming 'Our Special Correspondent', and from Prague covered fully the Nazification and plebiscite campaigns. He wrote of the Brown Terror which was generally considered to be worse in Austria than it was in Germany.[81]

The *Manchester Guardian*'s response to the Anschluss must be adjudged a disappointing one. Had it matched the spunk and spirit of the *News Chronicle* to its own ideological perception and integrity, it might have served as a standard to which advocates of opposition to Hitler could rally. In the event, it only sat back and complained.

NEWS CHRONICLE

The *News Chronicle* pursued a lively course of disagreement with those forces and newspapers which took any kind of soft line towards Germany; it stated that the broken system of collective security should be rebuilt around Czechoslovakia, and proposed its own peace plan which tended, unfortunately, to be vague. On the same day that it carried news of the Anschluss, the *News Chronicle* proffered its own alternative policy to that of appeasement which had produced such a state of affairs. It proposed:

That we should maintain without qualification the principle of international right and thereby enlist the moral forces of the nation and the world, for if international right perishes, the British Empire, which cannot be defended by British force alone, will also perish; that we should meet frankly the reasonable desires of the Fascist countries so that they shall have no excuse for feeling themselves to

---

[80] *Manchester Guardian*, 29 Mar. 1938, 5th Leader, p. 10.

[81] For five articles by Fodor tracing the history of Austria from St. Germain to the Anschluss, see *Manchester Guardian*, 31 Mar. 1938, former Vienna Corr., 'The Austrian Tragedy', p. 11; 1 Apr. 1938, p. 11; 2 Apr. 1938, p. 17; 4 Apr. 1938, p. 12; 5 Apr. 1938, p. 11. For articles on anti-Semitism in Nazi Austria, see *Manchester Guardian*, 17 Mar. 1938, p. 11; 18 Mar. 1938, p. 11; also *Manchester Guardian*, 13 Mar. 1938, Vienna Corr., p. 11; 17 Mar. 1938, Spec. Corr. Prague, p. 11; 19 Mar. 1938, Spec. Corr. Prague, p. 17.

be forced into aggression; and that the policy should be realistic, so that we shall not be misled by mere slogans.[82]

The article went on to say that Germany would not negotiate until she knew that an act of war would be met with an overwhelming solidarity of resistance. And 'this—and no nebulous idealism—is the hard practical reason why to throw over the collective principle is suicide for Britain'. Unfortunately no practical application was suggested, no indication given of the steps by which this plan might be initiated, by which the collective system might be restored.[83] The words were strong, but their application vague and very probably impossible.

The Nazi Terror in Vienna was well reported. 'Remember that what has happened in Austria over the week-end', the paper told its readers, on 14 March, 'is largely our own fault. Our hesitation had encouraged cumulative acts of aggression and treaty breaking across the world. Manchuria, Abyssinia, the Rhineland, Spain, China, Austria. Who next?' The German action would at least wash 'the last grains of illusion from the sink of contemporary history' and hasten the realization that 'only one thing will make Hitler pause—his own weapon, the threat of force'. With this in mind, the Western democracies should pledge to fight for Czechoslovakia if she were threatened by Germany.[84] This seemed to give substance to the nebulous peace plan of three days earlier. The guarantee of Czechoslovak independence was to be coupled with rearmament. The article concluded bluntly: 'There is only one thing for Britain and Europe to do in this critical hour, and the duty to do it is imperative. We must rearm to the full and couple with rearmament the most energetic efforts possible to reconstruct the collective system while there is still time.'[85] By the next day, however, rearmament was no longer so important, and the rebuilding of the collective

---

[82] See *News Chronicle*, 11 Mar. 1938, Leader, p. 10. The following month the *News Chronicle* experienced—or tried to create—a Gestapo scare, printing stories about the subversive threat this organization posed to Britain. It also took great exception to the requirement that all 'British Germans' register for the plebiscite; this requirement, the paper felt, 'comes perilously near to a claim to interference in the affairs of another State. What next? A demand for autonomy for the "British German"?' *News Chronicle*, 4 Apr. 1938, 2nd Leader, p. 10. See also *Manchester Guardian*, 4 Apr. 1938, p. 9.   [83] Ibid.

[84] *News Chronicle*, 14 Mar. 1938, Editorial, p. 1.   [85] Ibid.

system around Czechoslovakia had changed to a re-establishing of 'the rule of international law and decency'. Thereafter the paper only made occasional comments, without suggesting any course of action.[86]

DAILY HERALD

The *Daily Herald* followed the line that Austria was irretrievably gone but that Czechoslovakia must be guaranteed against the same fate. 'Aggression has again succeeded. It is too late now to save Austria. That fact—that brutal and shameful fact—we must accept.'[87] It was of course difficult for Labour's official paper to forget that Schuschnigg had supported Dollfuss in the bloody days of 1934, but the lesson of successful aggression was clear to see.

Along with the *News Chronicle* the *Daily Herald* felt that 'the only chance for the future is to rebuild the system they have shatt-ered'.[88] Czechoslovakia was the cornerstone of such a rebuilding.

SUNDAY TIMES

The *Sunday Times* recorded its view of the Anschluss mainly through the pen of Scrutator. Hitler's method was deplored, but the necessity for British non-involvement was stated in a particularly forthright manner. Scrutator, Herbert Side-botham, wrote: 'We have registered with due emphasis what we think about Germany's methods, and that is the end of Austria so far as our politics are concerned. Neither this nor any other country has any intention of disputing the union of the two countries. Austria survives in international politics only as a warning of what may happen to other neighbours of Germany.'[89] In a leading article called 'Law of the Jungle' the paper editorially deprecated Hitler's unprovoked threats and employment of brute force.[90]

Scrutator's interpretation of the crisis shifted between two poles. At one end was disgust with the German methods and fear that these 'grave happenings may be ominous of

---

[86] *News Chronicle*, 15 Mar. 1938, 1st Leader, p. 10.
[87] *Daily Herald*, 14 Mar. 1938, Francis Williams (Editor), p. 10. See also ibid., W. N. Ewer, p. 1.   [88] Ibid.
[89] *Sunday Times*, 20 Mar. 1938, Scrutator, p. 16.
[90] *Sunday Times*, 13 Mar. 1938, Leader, p. 18.

events still graver'.[91] At the other was the deep-rooted urge to settle European problems in the most fair and rational way possible—by appeasement. Despite the Anschluss, he still saw Hitler as a calculating opportunist who would like to have his way without bloodshed: 'If there were any compromise that would enable him to get equal treatment for the three millions of Germans in Czechoslovakia without war, he would prefer it.'[92] Already Austria was given up for lost and attention turned towards Czechoslovakia.

The paper expressed the wish that Hitler would at least use the one way open to him to mitigate the disastrous impression which the Anschluss had created: 'That is by using his new power in Austria to effect the change there without bloodshed or persecution.' Tracing the history of the Nazi movement, the leading article recalled that the movement's first triumph came after years of faction fighting. When the police came under Nazi control there had been a reign of terror which, 'horrible though it was', had 'some excuse in the confusion of the moment and in the absence of any strong, organised power behind the Government except that of the party "troops"'. Such were not the conditions in Austria, and there was thus no precedent for violence and brutality. Concluding on what today appears a foolishly optimistic note, the paper said that it would be 'a test of civilisation for the Nazis whether they treat their opponents in a civilised way'.[93]

The *Sunday Times* was shocked by Hitler's method but not particularly disappointed with the result, provided the Germans comported themselves like 'good winners'. The possibility of war, not over Austria or any particular case, but precisely over Hitler's methods, seems to have occurred to Scrutator, but it remained vague in his mind and was not refined beyond an initial statement: 'If by union is meant annexation which suppresses national independence, and if the method is the compulsion of force, war is certain. It may not be a war about Austria, nor should we necessarily be involved in it, but any act of this nature must inevitably increase the insecurity of the world and dangerously infect our relations with Germany.'[94]

[91] Ibid., 1938, Scrutator, p. 18.
[92] *Sunday Times*, 20 Mar. 1938, Scrutator, p. 16.
[93] *Sunday Times*, 13 Mar. 1938, Leader, p. 18.   [94] Ibid., Scrutator.

OBSERVER

In the *Observer* the battle for Austria had been conceded a month before the crisis; the paper breathed a sigh of relief when President Miklas agreed to Hitler's Berchtesgaden demands on 14 February. Thereby the Anschluss, 'a bogy that had daunted high diplomacy for many years—was given substance as an accomplished fact'. While certain elements in Britain would raise objections—mainly the communists and 'unbalanced elements' in other parties would call for war— 'the majority of our countrymen, by contrast, will recognise the inevitability of what has happened, and will calmly go about their own business'.[95] For as J. L. Garvin stated them in his editorial article of 27 February, the alternatives were negotiation or war.[96] And on 6 March he directly broached the question of British support for Austria: 'Is it imagined for a moment that Austria itself is a harmonious unit? It is riven with discord. A powerful section passionately demands closer union with the Reich. Conflict would mean civil war. It is a family issue within the German race. We have nothing to do with it.'[97]

Of the real Anschluss, Garvin, who felt that Schuschnigg was to blame for precipitating it, wrote, 'This is a mighty event. In our judgement it cannot be reversed. The moral is that the British people, while utterly refusing to be involved in Eastern Europe this time, should extend their rearmament without delay and adopt special measures to speed up without fail.'[98] The same day Francis Yeats-Brown wrote from Vienna about the surprising swing of public opinion to Hitler which many of the correspondents did indeed find 'almost unbelievable if one had not seen it with one's own eyes'. The truth was, he explained, 'that the frontier dividing Munich and Vienna . . . has always been artificial. From Munich to

---

[95] *Observer*, 20 Feb. 1938, Leader, p. 14. This leader concluded that 'For the immediate future, Herr von Schuschnigg's surrender saves Europe from something worse. If we recall the Far East, Abyssinia, even Spain, we may be thankful that this matter of Austria and Germany has been settled without bloodshed.'

[96] *Observer*, 27 Feb. 1938, Leader, p. 14. Garvin said that Anglo-Italian negotiations were of the first priority and that Anglo-German negotiations stood beyond these.

[97] *Observer*, 6 Mar. 1938, Leader, p. 16.

[98] *Observer*, 13 Mar. 1938, Leader, p. 16.

Vienna people talk alike, think alike, drink the same kind of beer. Naturally they want to be one people.'[99] On Sunday, 10 April, they voted alike as well, but by the time the *Observer* appeared again, a week later, this was hardly news and elicited no comment from the paper for which the Anschluss was a fortnight old before if happened.

DAILY EXPRESS AND DAILY MAIL

Even more vociferous in its insistence upon British non-interference was the *Daily Express* which said that Austria was not at all like Belgium in 1914—as some now claimed—but like the Rhineland two years earlier where the inhabitants had welcomed the German 'invaders'.[100] The only thing that tied Britain to Austria was Sir John Simon's pledge of 26 July 1934. This was a 'foolish promise' which 'must be withdrawn now and never be repeated'. Such a pledge to support Austrian independence, to thwart the inevitable Anschluss, was wrong and foolish; 'we have no right to do it. It is we who should get out and stay out. We have no business whatever to forbid the German peoples to unite. Our business is to unite our own peoples in our own commonwealth by a policy of Empire Free Trade and Splendid Isolation.'[101]

The *Daily Mail* saw the Anschluss as an almost unequalled postwar demonstration of 'the speed and effectiveness of power politics'.[102] The paper had carried its determined isolation from Europe to the extreme when it printed nothing about Schuschnigg's Berchtesgaden ordeal, and on 17 February commented that the settlement reached by Hitler and the Austrian Chancellor there was 'founded upon facts', and that it was a 'natural'

[99] *Observer*, 20 Mar. 1938, Major F. Yeats-Brown, p. 15.

[100] *Daily Express*, 12 Mar. 1938, Opinion, p. 12.

[101] *Daily Express*, 16 Feb. 1938, Opinion, p. 10. This was thus written *over three weeks before* the Anschluss. The *Daily Express* was more worried that Britain might guarantee Czechoslovakia than that she might support Austria. See, for example, *Daily Express*, 17 Feb. 1938, Opinion, p. 10, and ed. art. by Emrys Jones, ibid. Also *Daily Express*, 5 Mar., Opinion p. 10. The *Daily Herald* was singled out for suggesting a pledge to Czechoslovakia and challenged to a public opinion ballot on the question 'Would you fight for Czecho-Slovakia?' See *Daily Express*, 26 Feb. 1938, Opinion, and *Daily Express*, 28 Feb. 1938, ed. art. by Emrys Jones, p. 10.

[102] *Daily Mail*, 12 Mar. 1938, Leader, p. 8.

settlement 'brought about by peaceful negotiation'.[103] It was impossible to ignore the Anschluss itself, but that event only confirmed the paper's long-standing campaign: 'Arm, arm, arm! That has been the lesson of the past few years. That is the lesson which is underlined and emphasised by Austria to-day . . .'[104]

The paper was unequivocal about British involvement: 'Today the resolve of the British people will be to have nothing to do with the situation in Central Europe. Not one British soldier, not one penny of British money, must be involved in this quarrel which is no concern of ours.'[105] Britain's part was to act with dignity, favouring none of the groups whose rivalry might lead to world war. 'She must concentrate on building up her strength, ready to exert it to the last man and the last penny if her direct interests are threatened.'[106]

From the moment German troops entered Austria it was clear that Hitler's next demands would be made against Czechoslovakia. When Göring had personally sought out the Czech Minister in Berlin during the interval at the Opera on the night of 11 March and affirmed that his country had nothing to fear from Germany, no one took his reassurances seriously, least of all the Czechs. Even the most optimistic observers only dared frame their hopes in terms of a lengthy ingestion process for Austria into the Reich. As the *Daily Express* put it, 'At present Hitler has enough on his plate with his Vienna schnitzel.'[107]

As early as 18 March, Leo Kennedy had written to Dawson from Prague that during a two hour conversation with Beneš he had put forward all the arguments why Britain should not become involved in that part of the world. Kennedy himself remained convinced, however, that Germany was aiming to challenge Britain and her Empire and that 'The only question therefore for us, as I see it, is this—at what point are we going to say, "halt"? Is Czechoslovakia good ground on which to make our stand?'[108] Not everyone or every newspaper had

[103] *Daily Mail*, 17 Feb. 1938, 1st Leader, p. 10.
[104] *Daily Mail*, 12 Mar. 1938, Leader, p. 8.   [105] Ibid.
[106] *Daily Mail*, 15 Mar. 1938, Leader, p. 12.
[107] *Daily Express*, 26 Apr. 1938, 6th Leader, p. 12.
[108] Kennedy to Dawson, 18 Mar. 1938, *The Times* archives.

the perspicacity even to formulate these questions; some, however, had already answered them in the negative. The Czechs therefore were worried not only about German aggression but about the weakness the Western Powers had shown in the face of the German invasion of Austria. Opinions about Czechoslovakia differed in the British newspapers, but again all were basically united, that the Sudeten German demands should not become a *casus belli;* that there was justification on both sides; and that reasonable pressure by the British Government upon Prague to make concessions was not untoward since the proper settlement lay in negotiation.[109] The *Daily Express* was only the most outspoken when it concluded, 'So, Czecho, No! No! A thousand times *no.*'[110]

In mid-May, shortly before the important municipal elections in Czechoslovakia, Konrad Henlein, the Sudeten German leader, came to London. He spoke to many people including Churchill and Vansittart, and addressed the Royal Institute of International Affairs. Although there had been nagging suspicions that he was only Hitler's cat's-paw, Henlein's responsible and sensible demeanour in London seemed an 'eminently satisfactory proof that the leader of the Germans of Czechoslovakia is himself desirous of a peaceful solution. Of this there can be no doubt after the visit, whatever may have been supposed before he came; the London conversations were also proof, not only that peaceful diplomacy is at work, but that the importance of Great Britain's role is appreciated by all parties.'[111]

The actual events of the 'Week-end', or May Crisis of 21–2 May, were never very clear. There was an incident at Cheb (Eger) on the Friday night in which Czech soldiers killed two drunken Sudeten Germans who tried to run a barrier on a motorcycle. The *Daily Herald* fastened upon this incident as the

[109] See for example, *Daily Telegraph*, 23 Apr. 1938, 2nd Leader, p. 12, and 2 May 1938, 1st Leader, p. 12; *Manchester Guardian*, 9 May 1938, Dipl. Corr., p. 14, and ed. art. by Crozier, p. 11.   [110] *Daily Express*, 30 Apr. 1938, Leader, p. 10.

[111] *The Times*, 16 May 1938, 1st Leader, p. 15. See also *The Times*, 14 May 1938, p. 12. For suspicions about Henlein see *Daily Telegraph*, 23 Apr. 1938, 2nd Leader, p. 12, where the fear is expressed that 'under orders from Berlin, he may wish rather to maintain the grievances in order to split the Czechoslovak State'. And on 2 May 1938, 1st Leader, p. 12, the *Daily Telegraph* stated that 'A peaceful settlement is quite as much dependent on the policy of Berlin as on that of Prague.'

trigger of the crisis and found it ludicrous that Europe might have been plunged into war for the sake of two Bohemians [*sic*].[112] *The Times* seemed to view the crisis as springing from the internal tension over the first stage of the Czech elections: elections held amid racial rivalries in a neighbourhood where three countries met, with tempers already inflamed, the whole contest dominated by a minority problem, and frontier incidents actually occurring. What had turned these conditions into a European dilemma was the mobilization of part of the Czech Army on the basis of alleged German troop movements against the Czech frontiers.

It is clear from the captured German documents that there was in fact no such military action under way against Czechoslovakia. Whether Czech intelligence was simply wrong or, more likely, whether the whole affair was a ploy to test the West's resolution, will probably never be definitely settled. J. L. Garvin was suspicious and thought it 'unfortunate, though not blameable, that the British inquiries at Berlin had to be taken on the strength of alarmist information from the Czech Government, which was mistaken but, nevertheless, was immediately used to cover real military action of their own and action of a fatal kind, that, if repeated, might be fatal to peace'.[113] The *Daily Mail* stated that any kind of pledge that France would fight for Czechoslovakia would only inflame Prague which might then be tempted to take irrevocable action at other people's expense.[114]

From the British documents we know that the warnings to Germany by Halifax were far from unfriendly, and, although they affirmed that Britain would fight with France for an invaded Czechoslovakia if it came to that, the most telling point Halifax made was that only Bolshevism would be the winner of a European war. The content of these approaches was not known at the time, and their importance was considered to lie in the reaffirmation of the British Government's role as mediator—as uninvolved mediator. As *The Times* expressed it, 'The British Government's policy is clear to all

---

[112] *Daily Herald*, 23 May 1938, Leader, p. 10. For an exhaustive and colourful re-creation of this incident, see Leonard Mosley's *On Borrowed Time*.

[113] *Observer*, 29 May 1938, Garvin, p. 16.

[114] *Daily Mail*, 23 May 1938, 1st Leader, p. 10.

the world. It is to urge moderation and peaceful methods, to promote mutual understanding of difficulties, and above all to face the fundamental problem of unrest among the minorities and to press for its solution.'[115] The *Daily Telegraph* stressed that Britain was not a partisan in this case but had a right and a duty to intervene as a 'friendly interpreter'.[116] The extremes of such an outlook were represented by the *Daily Mail* and the *Daily Express*. The former insisted that Britain enter into no automatic obligation to fight for Czechoslovakia.[117] The latter stated that Britain would not, could not, and should not fight:

Don't take sides yourself yet, don't get into the frame of mind of taking sides.

There are different views about the Czechs as well as about the Germans. This present tense situation has its root twenty years old. Whatever the Germans are doing now, they had a rough ride at the peace conference which set up Czechoslovakia and carved up Germany and, however the Czechs are treated now, twenty years ago they did some of the rough riding, and have done some since.[118]

On the other side, the *Sunday Times* felt that the Czech reaction had been understandable whether or not the German demurrers had a case,[119] and *The Times* pointed out that two months earlier reports of troop movements had proved only too true.[120]

Comment in the British Press was thus restrained. Only the *News Chronicle*, the *Evening Standard*, and Voigt in the *Manchester Guardian* might be said to have treated the incident as a British victory and a thwarting of German plans. The *News Chronicle*, which had not hitherto opposed counselling concession to Prague, now accepted the Czech version completely and stated on 23 May that the immediate crisis had been ended by 'the commendably prompt and vigorous representations of the British and French Governments to Berlin and partly by the equal promptitude of the Czech

[115] *The Times*, 23 May 1938, 1st Leader, p. 15.
[116] *Daily Telegraph*, 23 May 1938, 1st Leader, p. 12.
[117] *Daily Mail*, 23 May 1938, 1st Leader, p. 10.
[118] *Daily Express*, 23 May 1938, Opinion, p. 10.
[119] *Sunday Times*, 22 May 1938, 1st Leader, p. 16.
[120] *The Times*, 26 May 1938, 2nd Leader, p. 17.

Government in calling up a class of the Army reserve . . .'[121]
On the 24th the paper's attitude stiffened further still: 'Czechoslovakia might have disappeared from the map as completely
as Austria. A material factor in preventing this calamity was
the British Government's intimation in Berlin, as the Premier
revealed yesterday, that a settlement must be reached "if
European peace is to be preserved".'[122] The lesson of the crisis
should thus be that 'The British Government, who have not
hitherto realised the power they can wield, should take a
lesson from their decisive influence in this crisis.'[123]

The *Evening Standard* viewed the week-end as a triumph not
of diplomacy, but of arms. War had been avoided because
Germany realized the strength of British arms and that they
would be used. Thus had the good of peace come about through
the evil of armaments and pointed the lesson that Britain's
strength depended upon armaments.[124]

Voigt wrote that war had been averted thanks to the 'skilful
precautionary measures of the Czechoslovak Government
tanks, to the energetic diplomatic effort made by Great
Britain, and thanks to the far-reaching collaboration between
Great Britain and France'.[125] Even this correspondence as
published was apparently considerably attenuated by Crozier
who wrote that:

I am afraid you will think I have omitted rather a lot of your
article tonight, but it's a matter of tactics. What you write about
the German plans for the conquest of Czechoslovakia is vivid, and,
I have no doubt at all, accurate. On the other hand, I don't think
that to-night, when we are hoping that we have just escaped, even
if only for the time being, from the imminent outbreak of war, is
the right time to describe the German plans for making war.[126]

The *Manchester Guardian* was generally moderate in its
comment, insisting that there was nothing in the Czech
situation which should lead to war unless Hitler was determined to push Henlein over the edge; otherwise the usual
channels of international intercourse should suffice. The

[121] *News Chronicle*, 23 May 1938, Leader, p. 10.
[122] *News Chronicle*, 24 May 1938, 1st Leader, p. 10.   [123] Ibid.
[124] *Evening Standard*, 23 May 1938, Leader, p. 7.
[125] *Manchester Guardian*, 23 May 1938, Dipl. Corr., p. 9.
[126] Crozier to Voigt, 22 May 1938, *Manchester Guardian* archives.

paper followed the prevalent line that Britain's role was properly one of detached mediation: it suggested that Britain could 'propose that international inquiry into the responsibility which is the only right solution and it can offer to play its full part in such a mission'. Voigt wrote to Crozier that 'the crisis was much more dangerous than this morning's London papers indicate (though *The Times* "diplomatic correspondent" hints at the truth between the lines.)'[127]

Thus with few exceptions the British Press treated the crisis, which was over by the Monday morning, with calm and moderation. 'By refusing to be hurried into irremediable action or promises, by maintaining steadiness and calm, Mr. Chamberlain has again revealed himself, to quote a foreign commentator, as an "exceptional statesman".'[128] Far from revelling in any kind of satisfaction over the week-end's outcome, the British Press remained sober and straightforward. *The Times* affirmed that there had been no 'vainglorious assumption here that British diplomacy has won a triumph at the expense of the Reich'.[129] The *Daily Herald* insisted that it be understood that Britain and France had acted for peace alone and 'There is no question of diplomatic victory or diplomatic defeat. The victory (if victory it proves to be) is for peace.'[130] The *Daily Telegraph* took pride in the fact that it was seldom that 'firm diplomatic action from a single quarter awakens so universal a chorus of praise as could be noted yesterday following the week-end moves made by Britain to relieve the tension in Central Europe.'[131]

Whence, then, springs the legend of the May Crisis? The legend is that the cumulative effect of diplomatic and press firmness enraged Hitler and led him to decide, almost by way of spite, to set an early and final date to his plans for destroying Czechoslovakia. Laffan writes in the *Survey of International Affairs* that

What was certain was that a most dangerous situation had existed and continued to exist. In such circumstances it was most unfortunate

[127] Voigt to Crozier, 23 May 1938, *Manchester Guardian* archives. See also *The Times*, 23 May 1938, Dipl. Corr., p. 14.
[128] *Daily Mail*, 23 May 1938, 1st Leader, p. 12.
[129] *The Times*, 26 May 1938, 2nd Leader, p. 17.
[130] *Daily Herald*, 24 May 1938, Leader, p. 10.
[131] *Daily Telegraph*, 24 May 1938, 1st Leader, p. 16.

that many newspapers in France and Britain indulged in complacent talk about vigorous diplomacy having saved the peace. Instead of saying as little as possible, they rubbed it in that Hitler had recoiled before the determined front presented to him and had abandoned, at any rate for a time, his projected attack on the Czechs.[132]

We have seen, however, that the British Press was, almost without exception, measured and moderate. After all, the catalysts of the crisis were the alleged German troop movements and the Czech mobilization in answer to them on Saturday. By Monday morning the allegations had been generally accepted as misinformed at the very least.

What kept the crisis at fever pitch after the week-end was a violent campaign in the German press against Czechoslovakia and Britain. The campaign began immediately on Monday morning and, instead of relenting as the week's events proved that the crisis was quite over, it only gained in strength and virulence. Even the most critical reading of the British Press during the Week-end Crisis could hardly justify such an excessive campaign, and the first inclination was to dismiss it: the *Daily Telegraph* stated that the embittered German press comments should not be taken too much to heart. 'Suggestions that the week-end crisis was a mere alarmist creation of hot-heads in London and in Prague are not likely to appear very convincing, even to German readers.'[133] But as the fury of the attack mounted it became impossible to ignore, and the *Sunday Times* stated the situation as it appeared in plaintive and instructive terms:

Assuming, as we do assume, that Germany does not want a European war, the Press attacks on this country, and on the Prime Minister in particular, must have been based on complete misunderstanding of British aims and policy. Our role is that of a mediator, and when our action was stiffened a week ago it was only because the danger then deepened.[134]

While the assumption that Germany did not want a European war was quite justified, it was not, as we now know,

---

[132] R. G. D. Laffan, *The Crisis Over Czechoslovakia January to September 1938*, p. 141.
[133] *Daily Telegraph*, 24 May 1938, 1st Leader, p. 16.
[134] *Sunday Times*, 29 May 1938, 1st Leader, p. 18.

the one of greatest importance. The determinative factor in Hitler's policy was that he was willing to *risk* war for whatever he wanted; this was the factor, irrational and incomprehensible, which immobilized official thinking in Britain. In May 1938, Hitler was able to look back upon successful invasions of the Rhineland in 1936 and of Austria just two months earlier. In both cases the Western Powers had objected, protested—and acquiesced. Two years had separated these two adventures and it was now widely assumed in the West that an even longer time would be required to digest all of Austria. There was no doubt that Czechoslovakia was next in Hitler's plans, and we know that on 21 April he had discussed the basic principles of 'Operation Green' (the code name for the operation against Czechoslovakia) with Keitel. The decision then was that nothing would be done in the near future. The situation in Czechoslovakia was, however, developing rapidly: under pressure from London and Paris and by the very nature of the increasing Sudeten agitation, the Prague Government was going far towards meeting all of Henlein's Karlsbad Demands. The municipal elections scheduled for 22 May and the two following Sundays would do much towards removing the few real grievances in the Sudeten case. Hitler thus faced the possibility of being robbed of his pretext for aggression by having all his demands granted.

He recognized the Week-end Crisis as another stroke of his incredible luck: while demonstrating yet again the half-hearted and reluctant nature of British and French resolution, it provided Hitler with the necessary lever against the reluctance of the German General Staff to move against Czechoslovakia. Hitler thrived in a crisis atmosphere and was thus able to see and seize his opportunity. Just as the crisis seemed to be over, a German press ramp against Britain and Czechoslovakia provided him with made-to-order arguments against his own General Staff's reluctance and served to fan the fire of appeasement in the opposite camp. It also provided justification later; at Nuremberg in the much-awaited speech on 12 September he recalled the events of the previous May: 'Germany had given way before the resolute attitude of the Czechs and the first interventions of England and France. You will understand . . . that a great Power cannot for a second time suffer such an infamous encroachment upon its rights. I have therefore taken care that the necessary consequences should be drawn.' He made similar references in his speech to the Reichstag on 30 January 1939.[135]

After the German press had expounded on British treachery and Czech perfidy for a week, Hitler signed the new directive for Operation Green and gave the latest date of execution as 1 October. The extent of the seriousness with which Hitler took his own press campaign is seen in the fact that the Operation Green directive of 30 May did not even mention the possibility of intervention by Britain or France. The General Staff continued to harbour considerable dissension—indeed, mutiny—until Hitler's judgement was vindicated once again, at Munich. Had the crisis atmosphere, which he was able to perpetuate after the May crisis, not been considered settled in the West, however, Hitler would have been hard put to it to have his way against Czechoslovakia in September.

The British Government and Press thus became Hitler's 'fall guys' and his masterful handling of the so-called May Crisis can be seen in the extent to which thirty years later we still accept his version of it.

THE CRISIS OVER CZECHOSLOVAKIA

THE TIMES

After the false alarm of the May Crisis, Europe seemed to settle down for a quiet summer. After the initial anti-Semitic excesses, Austria was fully assimilated into the Reich with almost amazing speed. Holburn reported that it had been decided to rein in the more fanatical anti-Semites during the Evian Conference on refugees which held its first session in July, and that it had been decided to ease the enforcement of the economic boycott of the Jews on the principle that 'a sweeping application of the decrees designed to drive Jews out of German economic life would produce an unwieldy crop of bankrupt businesses and have damaging effects on the economic life of the nation.'[136]

---

[135] See Baynes, *Hitler's Speeches*, ii. 1487–99, and 1571.
[136] *The Times*, 1 July 1938, Berlin Corr., p. 15.

The German railways ran an advertising campaign to encourage tourism in several British papers including *The Times*, based upon the appeal 'See Germany for yourself. You will find truth in personal contacts. A hearty welcome awaits you.'[137]

With Austria so quickly assimilated, it seemed as though Germany was at last settling down and trying to build up some systematic foreign relations. Over the week-end of 1–3 July, Germany signed new trade and clearing agreements with Britain, Poland, and Switzerland. These seemed to bode well for similar negotiations with other nations, including France.[138]

The great interest of the payments agreement lay in the possibilities it held for a general Anglo-German *détente*. Trade was naturally dear to the heart of a trading nation, and in this case, 'Common sense and a spirit of compromise have turned a difficulty which might have led to unwelcome restrictions into an opportunity for seeking ways of promoting mutual trade.'[139] On 6 July, Holburn reported a change of tone in Germany and the desire there to return to the policy of friendship with Britain laid down in *Mein Kampf*.[140]

During the early summer, *The Times*'s main concern over Czechoslovakia was that it seemed to stand in the way of an Anglo-German *rapprochement*. The Diplomatic Correspondent reported that 'it is, in fact, an open secret that the British Government are waiting for a Czechoslovak settlement to improve the prospects of a resumption of the Anglo-German negotiations'.[141] On the German side, Holburn reported that 'In the field of Anglo-German relations in general it is a question at the moment only of the possibilities which will arise once the Czechoslovak difficulty is out of the way.'[142]

The Times was thus torn between a real sympathy for the justice of the German claims on political, racial, and linguistic

---

[137] See, for example, *The Times*, 6 July 1938, p. 9; and 8 July 1938, p. 12.

[138] See *The Times*, 4 July 1938, Berlin Corr., p. 13.

[139] *The Times*, 2 July 1938, 3rd Leader, p. 13. For the favourable reaction in Berlin to this settlement, see *The Times*, 4 July 1938, Berlin Corr., p. 13.

[140] *The Times*, 6 July 1938, Berlin Corr., p. 16.

[141] *The Times*, 20 July 1938, Dipl. Corr., p. 14. He added, however, that 'at the same time they know full well that outside interference would be resented in this country as elsewhere.'

[142] *The Times*, 25 July 1938, Berlin Corr., p. 12.

grounds, and a sympathy for the problems which meeting them would cause the Czech Government. Regardless of these sympathies, however, the paper became increasingly impatient as the Czech problem seemed to stand in the way of an Anglo-German settlement. When the Runciman Mission was announced—a scoop for *The Times*—it was thus explained, defined, and defended on these grounds.[143] As the Diplomatic Correspondent had put it on 23 July, it was necessary to clear up the Sudeten dispute because 'it is simply a matter of looking facts in the face, and of realising that, lacking a Czechoslovak settlement, the premises for the [Anglo-German] negotiations must remain uneasy and shifting'.[144]

Apropos of Lord Runciman's mission, the paper stated the commonsense principle that 'So long as desired results are peacefully attained, procedure is a matter of relatively small importance. Respect for an ideal must never make people blind to the immediate issue.'[145] The definition of the Mission's nature and scope developed gradually over the fortnight following the paper's announcement on the 26th; then it was simply stated that Lord Runciman's duties would be 'advisory and conciliatory'.[146] Runciman was going to Czechoslovakia 'as less than an arbitrator and as perhaps a little more than an adviser'. He was going 'to put in a good word with both sides in favour of moderation and conciliation'.[147] The Times felt a certain pique with some Czech newspapers which appeared less than grateful for the mission and which attempted 'to discredit the intentions of the British Government, to emphasise mistakes in British policy, and to imply that the mission is only a dodge to put more pressure on the Czech Government'. It was not untoward for Czech newspapers to warn their Government against making 'undue concessions', but 'at a time when the Sudeten Germans are expressing official approval of the Runciman mission it seems curious tactics'.[148] As we have seen, it is unlikely that anyone on *The Times* knew of the real background of the Runciman mission, and

---

[143] See *The Times*, 23, 26 July 1938, Dipl. Corr., p. 12.
[144] *The Times*, 23 July 1938, Dipl. Corr., p. 12.
[145] *The Times*, 4 Aug. 1938, 1st Leader, p. 11.
[146] *The Times*, 26 July 1938, Dipl. Corr., 12.
[147] *The Times*, 1 Aug. 1938, Dipl. Corr., p. 10.   [148] Ibid.

quite properly it seemed to be fully consistent with British policy which continued to be one of 'conciliation and mediatorial action, exercised wherever and whenever possible, and backed by growing strength'.[149]

In August the German economy underwent a crisis which had been developing since the spring, and *The Times* was immediately struck with the irony of subjecting a faltering economy to a nation-wide mobilization which could not help but injure it further.[150] It seemed as though the military idol had, after all, feet of economic clay, and Funk's assurances that the German economy was sound were met with tolerant incredulity. This gave impetus in Britain to an urge for economic appeasement since both the economic crisis and the vast military manœuvres underlined the insanity of war more than ever. At the end of July, *The Times* had surveyed the world and judged that Chamberlain was 'certainly entitled to claim that the general outlook is more favourable now than it was six months ago. There is less thought of war and less fear of war.'[151]

A month later, however, as the Nuremberg Rally drew near, it suddenly became clear that questions of war and peace might lie in the Sudeten dispute. On Saturday, 27 August, Sir John Simon made a major speech at Lanark in which he reaffirmed Chamberlain's statement of 24 March that if war broke out it would be impossible to say where it would end and which Governments might not become involved. *The Times* praised the speech and was annoyed by the anti-British campaign which it unleashed in the German Press. The pattern was familiar: 'The one-sided outlook of British newspapers must, it is said, be instantly refuted, but to those who read the German newspapers day by day, it is, however, perfectly clear that in its manner of reporting news from Czechoslovakia the German Press is pursuing a systematic campaign, the object of which is evident enough.'[152] The German reaction to Lanark was based upon a 'fantastic misrepresentation' which 'could not of course survive even a cursory reading of the

[149] *The Times*, 27 July 1938, 1st Leader, p. 15.
[150] See *The Times*, 17 Aug. 1938, Berlin Corr., p. 10.
[151] *The Times*, 27 July 1938, 1st Leader, p. 15.
[152] *The Times*, 27 Aug. 1938, Berlin Corr., p. 10. See also ibid., Dipl. Corr., which expresses the hope that now the generous Czech proposals were made known, Germany would let up on the anti-Czech campaign.

speech' and was, moreover, 'quite irreconcilable with the whole course pursued by the [British] Government'.[153] In Britain, the speech had been approved 'with a remarkable degree of unanimity', and everyone realized that airing unpleasant but possible contingencies as it did, it had been a contribution to European peace. Britain, in the face of a rapidly worsening situation, was compelled

. . . to make it known in time that any development which might come to threaten an outbreak of armed conflict or of formal war itself must be a matter of instant concern to her if only because a recourse to hostilities would threaten to set fire to all the combustible material in Europe and might end by involving Britain herself, however reluctantly. If contingencies, already a little larger than a man's hand, were to grow into facts, the consequences would be what they would be, and no one should seek to be deceived. It has been the first duty of the British Government to be sure that the future shall be obscured by no deceptions.[154]

Another element of *The Times*'s attitude, as we have seen, was the conviction that Hitler certainly did not want a European war and most probably preferred having the Sudeten Germans and their grievances as a lever with which to prise concessions and propaganda gains from Czechoslovakia. Hitler would, if it were possible, avoid action which could precipitate a European war, Holburn reported, but anyway he probably found it difficult to believe that the British would go to war to prevent the Sudeten Germans from exercising the right of self-determination.[155]

As the *Parteitag* approached, however, the crisis-potential of the Sudeten situation suddenly dawned on *The Times*. While the paper still saw merit in the Sudeten claims, it was now impossible to ignore the sincere and far-reaching attempts of the Czech Government to meet them. By 5 September, although the full demands had not been met, the grievances had been substantially removed, and 'this particular problem

---

[153] *The Times*, 30 Aug. 1938, 1st Leader, p. 11.

[154] *The Times*, 31 Aug. 1938, 1st Leader, p. 11. The serious tone of this leader was somewhat offset by the day's Diplomatic Correspondence which stated that Hitler's pacific protestations were 'trusted in London'. Halifax rang Barrington-Ward to protest this, but the acting Editor insisted that it must be read in the context of trying to extract the most from the German promises. See *Hist. Times*, iv. 928–9.   [155] *The Times*, 1 Sept. 1938, Berlin Corr., p. 12.

offers no sort of reason or excuse for a war. Whatever solution is now envisaged, there can be no possible question of the Sudetens being oppressed. It may be hoped that this self-evident truth will not be forgotten at Nuremberg, where the annual rally of the Nazi Party opens today.'[156] That action was imminent was seen by Holburn, mistakenly by-lined as 'Our Own Correspondent', in an editorial page article on the 'Ritual of Nuremberg'.

And while the public of foreign countries have been able to forget on occasion that there was such a question as Czechoslovakia, the Reich has been kept continuously in a state of tension since May last. The elaborate military manoeuvres, the mobilization of reservists, human, animal, and material, may have been designed to create in London and Paris the impression that they must choose between compelling Czechoslovakia to surrender or going to war in its defence. They have also, however, given the German public the impression that their Government are determined to act as it did in Austria.[157]

Still, the Czechs were at fault—'Had the conversations now being held in the Hradcany Palace been initiated years ago, the present crisis could hardly have arisen in its present form'[158]—and Hitler had been brought into the dispute openly, 'and without the disapproval of the other party'.[159] It was with these facts in mind, with the paper's consistent editorial policy in view, and Hitler's speech at Nuremberg looming ahead, that the leading article 'Nuremberg and Aussig' was printed. Its sting lay in its tail. The last paragraph stated that:

No Central Government would still deserve its title if it did not reserve in its own hands Defence, Foreign Policy, and Finance. There does not appear to be any dispute about this principle in the minds of the Government or of Herr Henlein; and if the Sudetens now ask for more than the Czechoslovak Government are apparently ready to give in their latest set of proposals, it can only be inferred that the Germans are going beyond the mere removal of disabilities and do not find themselves at ease within the Czech Republic. In that case it might be worthwhile for the Czechoslovak Government to consider whether they should exclude altogether the project, which has found favour in some quarters, of making Czechoslovakia

[156] *The Times*, 5 Sept. 1938, 1st Leader, p. 13.
[157] Ibid., Berlin Corr., p. 13.   [158] Ibid., 1st Leader, p. 13.   [159] Ibid.

a more homogeneous state by the secession of that fringe of alien populations who are contiguous to the nation with which they are united by race. In any case the wishes of the population concerned would seem to be a decisively important element in any solution that can hope to be regarded as permanent, and the advantages to Czechoslovakia of becoming a homogeneous State might conceivably outweigh the obvious disadvantages of losing the Sudeten German districts of the borderland.[160]

It is now widely known that *The Times* was not the first to moot the plan for secession of the Sudetenland to Germany. Indeed, there is a letter in the *Manchester Guardian* archives from Crozier to Voigt in February 1938 asking 'Is there anything at all in the suggestion from the "Church Times" that Czechoslovakia would be better off all round if it lost its German minority?'[161] Immediately pre-dating the 7 September article was an editorial in the *New Statesman and Nation* (which could scarcely be tarred with the same political brush as *The Times*), which perceived two essentials in the situation. First, Berlin must realize that an attack on Czechoslovakia would mean world war. Second, it was necessary to admit that Czech authority in the Sudetenland was forever destroyed. If Hitler agreed and the Czechs made some 'imaginative offer of partnership', then all would be well. 'But if Lord Runciman reports that this is impossible, the question of frontier revision, difficult though it is, should at once be tackled. The strategical value of the Bohemian frontier should not be made the occasion of a world war. We should not guarantee the *status quo*.'[162] By neither journal was this solution considered ideal or even desirable; but it was a last resort which neither could deny existed. Immediately *The Times*'s leader was printed, the Foreign Office hastened to dissociate itself from the suggestion it made. The paper was equally quick to affirm not only its independence, but its consistency as well. 'The suggestion in question did not, of course, profess to represent the official view. But it is one that has been consistently borne in mind by this journal as a possible solution which should be considered if others were to fail.'[163]

[160] *The Times*, 7 Sept. 1938, 1st Leader, p. 13.
[161] Crozier to Voigt, 27 Feb. 1938, *Manchester Guardian* archives.
[162] Martin, *Editor*, p. 251 ff.
[163] *The Times*, 8 Sept. 1938, Dipl. Corr., p. 12.

In his diary for 7 September, Dawson wrote, 'There was a hubbub, as I fully expected, over the morning's leader—reactions in Prague and Berlin, and the Foreign Office went up through the roof—Not so, however, the Foreign Secretary, who came and lunched with me at the Travellers', and had a long talk. He is as much in the dark as everyone else, as to what is likely to happen next.'[164]

In view of the furore to which this article gave rise and its reputation as a landmark on the road to appeasement at Munich, it is perhaps worthwhile here to stress—as the paper itself stressed—the consistency of the suggestion of 7 September with its policy to that date. On 30 May 1938 the paper had stated that

The Governments which refuse even to entertain proposals of peaceful change must therefore take their full share of the responsibility if, by popular vote or otherwise, some change is shown to be desired by a majority of the population. . . . The object of national and international endeavour should be to try by all means possible to ascertain, without pressure from any side, the true feelings of the population in the non-Slav regions.[165]

On 3 June a leading article cited a letter from the Dean of St. Paul's as 'typical of many, and an effective expression of the view that the Germans of Czechoslovakia ought to be allowed, by plebiscite or otherwise, to decide their own future—even if it should mean their secession from Czechoslovakia to the Reich. With this view the majority of Englishmen probably agree'. The paper did not imagine that such a change could be made simply—for the Sudeten Germans formed an integral part of the new Czech State which was a 'well-organized State, democratic and Parliamentary'.

Nevertheless, if they could see their way to it, and to granting a similar choice to the other minorities, Hungarian and Polish, the rulers of Czechoslovakia might in the long run be the gainers in having a homogeneous and contented people, still more numerous than the populations of Belgium and Holland, and twice as numerous as those of Denmark or Switzerland. If it was an injustice that these minorities should have been included in the new Republic, that injustice would be removed; and the neighbouring States which

[164] Wrench, p. 372.   [165] *The Times*, 30 May 1938, 1st Leader, p. 15.

take a racial interest in their kinsmen would have to look after
themselves and would lose any sort of claim to interfere in the
affairs of Czechoslovakia. It would be a drastic remedy for the
present unrest, but something drastic may be needed.[166]

This leading article was immediately disowned by the Foreign
Office. Lord Halifax telegraphed to Prague that although it
seemed to indicate a change in British policy, 'you may let
it be known, as you think fit, that this is not the case and
that the article in no way represents the view of His Majesty's
Government'.[167] This was repeated to Berlin and Paris.

No solution was yet mooted but the basic principle was
reaffirmed on 15 July: 'The wishes of the nationalities themselves ought to be the determining factor, and no solution
should be considered too drastic which is desired by an overwhelming majority.'[168] By the end of August, when the situation had become more tense, while reaffirming that Britain
would not remain aloof from a European conflict over Czechoslovakia, the paper spoke of the essential wisdom of revision:

Without granting the substantial autonomy which they demand,
a composite country, ringed by nations with a direct racial interest
in these important fractions of its population, lives dangerously
indeed. The conception of strategic security must be illusory if it is
itself undermined by disaffection from national groups which have
been given too little to lose from the disruption of the commonwealth.[169]

And two days later, the paper stated that British opinion

from the left to the right of politics, is agreed in principle that a
large devolution of authority to the different racial sections is long
overdue. To reject claims for autonomy merely as incompatible
with the security of the State may itself be an impairment of that
security.[170]

In The Times's eye, this was only practical politics since

. . . a Government with as much to expect from a peaceful settlement as the British Government must be looking for the most

[166] The Times, 3 June 1938, Leader, p. 15.
[167] DBFP 3rd Ser. i. doc. 374.
[168] The Times, 15 July 1938, 1st Leader, p. 17.
[169] The Times, 29 Aug. 1938, 1st Leader, p. 13.
[170] The Times, 31 Aug. 1938, 1st Leader, p. 11.

substantial reply possible to admitted grievances and can desire to
set no limit of their own to the scope of a possible agreement.[171]

In his diary for 8 September, Dawson wrote, 'Office morning,
afternoon and night. Practically all our contemporaries had
broken out in a volley of abuse of *The Times* for its suggestion
that a revision of frontiers in Czechoslovakia should not be
ruled out of discussion—a mild suggestion, often made before.'[172]

The consistency of *The Times*'s policy concerning revision of
the Sudeten boundaries makes the authorship and emendation
of the leading article of the 7th somewhat of a red herring.
The story is well known.[173] On Sunday, 4 September, Kennedy
prepared two leaders; the first, 'Negotiations Continue', was
published on 5 September. The second was intended for later
publication, after revision. When Dawson returned to Printing
House Square—he had been away for almost a month—on
Tuesday afternoon, he found the draft of the second article
and decided to use it that night. He made a few alterations,
ordered that the incomplete last paragraph be finished, and
went to dinner. When he returned, after eleven p.m., he began
to have doubts about printing the article and called upon the
only senior editorial staff member in the office at the time for
advice. That would appear to have been generally negative
but not particularly strong. The article was sent to press at
12.05, although Dawson made some changes in the early edi-
tions. For the lines in the paragraph of Kennedy's draft which
asked whether 'a solution should not be sought on some totally
different lines, which would make Czechoslovakia an entirely
homogeneous State', Dawson substituted, whether 'they should
exclude altogether the project, which has found favour in
some quarters, of making Czechoslovakia a more homogeneous State' by secession etc. The phrase 'in certain quarters'
was the offending member indicating, as it seemed to do,
that those quarters lay in His Majesty's Government.

What Dawson really meant to say or convey must remain a
mystery. That he was acting without Government approval
or inspiration is clear. Indeed the suggestion ran counter to
Foreign Office policy and wishes. In a report to Berlin,
Theodor Kordt, the German Chargé d'Affaires in London,

suggests that Chamberlain had inspired Dawson privately, in opposition to the Foreign Office policy. This is possible, although a letter from Dawson to Astor (not to mention Dawson's diary entries) does not support such an explanation:

. . . I have little doubt that the leader in *The Times* which caused so much hubbub did good rather than harm. It was not worded *quite* as I should have done if I had had rather more time to revise it; but after all it was a very mild suggestion, and one that had consistently been made before, that no avenue should be left unexplored which might lead to settlement.[174]

This article, then, was predicated upon the assumption that war was unthinkable over the Sudeten question, and that if the Sudeten Germans wanted to remain within the Czech State then accommodation—belated at that—should be made for them; but otherwise it was only sensible to consider allowing them to rest without the State. It was ludicrous, and *The Times* knew it, to expect a group which comprised less than a quarter of the population to control the foreign policy of the other 78 per cent while challenging, internally, their whole political outlook.[175] The controlling factor was that 'the one solution that is barred by the moral sense of the whole world is a solution based on force or (what amounts to the same thing) on the threat of force'; otherwise nothing was excluded from play.[176] Hitler's part, though menacing, was as yet undefined. Here *The Times* had no illusions: 'Germany—assuming that she maintains her forward policy—can spring no surprises on the world over Czechoslovakia. She can only confirm the world's worst misgivings—misgivings entertained reluctantly in most countries but inevitably in all.'[177] Already a note of scepticism appears, and this leading article states that the coincidence of the heightening of the Czech crisis and the Hitler Nuremberg address made it 'look very much as if the Sudetens were playing under orders for time; and Germany's responsibility is increased by a manœuvre of which, whether it was artificially engineered or not, it can only be said that its German sponsors in Czechoslovakia are in a mood of irresponsibility'.[178]

Although the Diplomatic Correspondent had defended the leader on the 8th, when the Foreign Office had issued a

[174] *Hist. Times*, iv. 934–6.   [175] Ibid.
[176] *The Times*, 8 Sept. 1938, 1st Leader, p. 13.   [177] Ibid.   [178] Ibid.

statement disassociating itself from its sentiments, it was not until 9 September that the storm broke over the leading article of the 7th.[179] Holburn reported from Berlin that the leader had 'aroused the greatest interest' and that

while officials here fully realise that the suggestion contained in the article does not represent the official view, it is held to be significant that *The Times* should at this moment have touched upon a possible solution, which, if not expressed here, has long been at the back of German minds.[180]

Events now waited upon Hitler, and it struck *The Times* as being

really grotesque that so much righteous indignation should be expended on the mere suggestion, which has frequently been made in these columns before, that a revision of boundaries should not be excluded entirely from the list of possible approaches to a settlement. It is not a solution for which anyone is likely to feel enthusiasm.[181]

Further, the paper reasoned, it was an unlikely solution, to the extent that the Czechs would obviously be unwilling to lose territory and that Hitler, 'certainly, if his ultimate intentions are as sinister as is sometimes supposed, . . . might well prefer to keep them as a lever for future use outside his own borders'.[182]

Still, despite the apparent connection between Hitler and the Sudeten Germans, so loudly and frequently stressed was the Führer's love of peace that 'it would be ungenerous to assume his responsibility' for anything until his speech.[183] In the event, Hitler's speech, given the truculence of his manner, was, in content, 'essentially a moderate utterance by a statesman confident in the justice of his claims and the strength of the Reich'. It is interesting that *The Times*'s Special Correspondent at Nuremberg received a reprimand from Dawson for reporting that Hitler's speech had been a 'moderate utterance'; what he meant, of course, was that in terms of what had been expected, the speech was 'moderate'.[184]

It was Göring's speech to the *Parteitag*, the day before Hitler's, which the paper found 'boastful' and 'ill-tempered':

[179] See *The Times*, 8 Sept. 1938, Dipl. Corr., p. 12; also *DBFP* 3rd, ii, No. 271.
[180] *The Times*, 9 Sept. 1938, Berlin Corr., p. 13.
[181] Ibid., 1st Leader, p. 13.   [182] Ibid.   [183] Ibid.
[184] Interview with J. H. Holburn, 20 Mar. 1967. See also *The Times*, 9 Sept. 1938, 1st Leader, p. 13, which called the claim to self-determination by its nature 'democratic and arguable'.

It sneered at Great Britain, it reviled democracies, it referred with
vulgar contumely to the courteous antagonist of Germany in the
present racial dispute. It was in fact the speech of a bully, whose
fury makes even sympathisers with the German case forget whatever there is in that case for legitimate sympathy. It gives the
impression that Germany has both a bad case and a bad
conscience.[185]

After Nuremberg, all intelligent observers saw war looming
behind this far-away dispute. 'And the conviction is everywhere felt', the paper stated on 15 September, 'that war on
this issue would be a folly and a crime, and that humanity
would be heading for the madhouse if the nations of the most
densely populated continent of the world were really going to
bomb one another to pieces on account of the troubles of some
three and a half million folk in the pleasant land of Bohemia.'[186]
The question of method was still open, but the paper saw
that a boundary commission was required, 'rather than the
tendentious mathematics of a plebiscite.'[187]

Chamberlain's 'momentous announcement' that he would go
to Berchtesgaden was greeted with 'intense relief', and due
gratitude was expressed to Hitler for his part in making it
possible. Only those for whom 'any sort of intercourse with a
dictator is incomprehensible and anathema' would not share
in the 'sense of relief and profound satisfaction' at Chamberlain's 'bold move' which came as 'water in the wilderness and
as another proof of his courage and his common sense'.[188] The
Diplomatic Correspondent foresaw criticism, however: 'There
may be some talk, no doubt, in the usual quarters about "shaking hands with Dictators"; but the great bulk of the public,
which realises that dictatorships and democracies must live
side by side, will be thankful that something definite has at
last been done to relieve an intolerable sense of impotence and
tension.'[189]

[185] *The Times*, 12 Sept. 1938, 1st Leader, p. 13. See also the Reuter report of
the speech, ibid., p. 18.   [186] *The Times*, 15 Sept. 1938, 1st Leader, p. 11.

[187] *The Times*, 14 Sept. 1938, 1st Leader, p. 11.

[188] *The Times*, 15 Sept. 1938, 1st Leader, p. 11.

[189] *The Times*, 15 Sept. 1938, Dipl. Corr., p. 10. He continued that Chamberlain's
'momentous announcement . . . throws all other news of the European crisis into
the shade. It means that a great constructive effort is to be made to resolve the
tangle in Czechoslovakia by the best possible method—a personal discussion between the British Prime Minister and the Chancellor of the Reich.'

On the following day, while Chamberlain was with Hitler, *The Times* printed John Masefield's poem instead of a leading article on the meeting at Berchtesgaden:

NEVILLE CHAMBERLAIN

As Priam to Achilles for his Son
So you, into the night, divinely led,
To ask that young men's bodies, not yet dead,
Be given from the battle not begun.[190]

After Berchtesgaden, before detailed information became available and the Anglo-French proposals were formulated, *The Times* pointed to the greatest immediate danger: 'What is most to be feared by all is the folly which, confronting the world with a now inexcusable recourse to violence, would sweep into limbo the merits of a powerful case.'[191] For now, after the great welcome given to Chamberlain in Germany, it was 'inexplicable' that the Nazi Government should permit the violent anti-Czech propaganda campaign which filled the German Press and Radio. Operating, therefore, upon the necessary assumption of German goodwill, the problem remained that of Czech acquiescence in the Sudeten demands as now set out in the Anglo-French proposals. Secession of the Sudetenland was the only solution. In a leading article which A. J. Cummings in the *News Chronicle* called 'another priceless gem' and which was held to considerable scorn, the paper stated that

The general character of the terms submitted to the Czechoslovak Government for their consideration cannot in the nature of things be expected to make a strong *prima facie* appeal to them, and least of all to President Beneš . . . it may be hoped that the Czech Government will come to believe that the ultimate gain will be more real than the immediate sacrifice. . . .[192]

Despite the widespread dislike of the Anglo-French proposals, *The Times* could none the less see that the proposal which had aroused such indignation when mooted in the leader of 7 September was now, however reluctantly, on all lips:

[190] *The Times*, 16 Sept. 1938, p. 13.
[191] *The Times*, 17 Sept. 1938, p. 11.
[192] *The Times*, 20 Sept. 1938, 1st Leader, p. 13.

In other quarters the British Government have been criticised for
making a sudden *volte-face*. That charge is at least intelligible, for a
suggestion in these columns that a solution might perhaps have to
be found by secession was immediately disavowed by the Foreign
Office. Yet it is being eagerly canvassed today, not only by the
Foreign Office, but by the newspapers which hastened to denounce it
a few days earlier as a 'sinister blow'. The explanation, no doubt,
of the apparent change of front is that the Prague negotiations were
still formally continuing between the Czech Government and the
Sudetens—though they clearly had no longer the faintest hope of
success—and until they were formally abandoned the British
Government did not themselves wish to entertain the more drastic
solution.[193]

When it became clear that even the Anglo-French proposals
had been rejected at Godesberg, *The Times* faced the issue—
war—squarely. Before they had become known, the High
Commissioner of Canada, Massey, who had been in close
contact with Barrington-Ward throughout the crisis, gave him
a copy of the Godesberg demands. Barrington-Ward immediately wrote that the 1 October deadline alone was a
demand 'quite incapable of fulfilment'.[194] If Germany wanted
to fight, he wrote, then Britain and France had pursued the
correct course: the issue had been made absolutely clear; the
ball was now in Germany's court. The Western Powers should
publish their final solution and the methods of effecting it; 'the
resources of diplomacy on their side will then have been
exhausted. . . . The decision between peace and war would
then rest with Germany, and with Germany alone.'[195]

The Times of 27 September is an example of *The Times* at
its best as unofficial spokesman for official thought. The first
of two editorial articles appraised favourably the strength of
the Czech Army.[196] A leading article, 'The Issue', said that
Hitler had moved on to dangerous ground, since his demands
had been conceded and yet he had forced the issue to another
plane—

[193] *The Times*, 22 Sept. 1938, 1st Leader, p. 11.
[194] *The Times*, 26 Sept. 1938, 1st Leader, p. 13.
[195] Ibid. The Diplomatic Correspondent, p. 12, also pursued a hard line,
showing the nature and difficulties of the German plan.
[196] *The Times*, 27 Sept. 1938, ed. art. by Robert Leurquin, p. 13; and 28 Sept.
1938, p. 11.

The Godesberg Note reverts to the worst form of Prussianism in using the language of a bully, fixing a time limit of a few days.

—and asked the overwhelming question about Czechoslovakia, for it was

on the continued existence of this Czech nation in any tolerable shape or form that the gravest doubts are still entertained in the public mind. What are the ultimate intentions of the Nazi regime towards it? Are they determined to get a stranglehold? Are they seeking to murder a nation because it is in the way?[197]

Most important, there was an unattributed 'article' on the main news page, headed simply 'If Germany Attacks'. It said that 'It was authoritatively stated last night' that negotiations were still possible, and that the transfer claim had already been accepted. But if, in spite of Chamberlain's efforts, Germany attacked Czechoslovakia, 'the immediate result will be that France will be bound to come to her assistance, and Great Britain and Russia will certainly stand by France. It is still not too late to stop this great tragedy, and for the peoples of all nations to insist on settlement by free negotiation.'[198]

Perhaps the most galling aspect of the approaching conflict was the fact that the German people, whose peace-wish was great (as witnessed by their reception of Chamberlain), had been kept wholly in the dark concerning the crisis; were, in fact, unaware of it until only lately, when the knowledge of British and French precautionary measures had spread. None the less, the people would follow the Führer, and in totalitarian States dealings must be with the head.[199]

The Times devoted no great paeans of praise to the Munich agreement. There was gratitude to Chamberlain; but Hitler, who had entered the dispute as the devil's advocate of Sudeten rights, emerged as a fomenter of crisis for its and his own sakes. Where Sir Edward Grey had failed, the paper stated, Chamberlain had, 'for the moment', succeeded. 'It may be no more than a respite. It would be reckless to build high even upon the broad-based consultation which has now been achieved, even upon such a concentration of authority and responsibility

---

[197] *The Times*, 27 Sept. 1938, 1st Leader, p. 13.   [198] Ibid., p. 12.
[199] See *The Times*, 28 Sept. 1938, 1st Leader, p. 11; and 29 Sept. 1938, ed. art. by Berlin Corr., p. 13.

as seemed remote and impracticable at all earlier stages of the affair.'[200]

For the moment the crisis was passed. The war which neither Germans nor Italians, neither Frenchmen nor Englishmen could actually believe was imminent was now no longer so. The initial objection to war for Czechoslovakia remained and was vindicated: 'Granted that behind it is a real moral issue, which within the earliest possible period must be settled once for all, the margin of difference over the procedure proposed for the solution of the immediate problem had lately become so narrow that to start a world-wide conflict about it would be both criminal and grotesque.'[201]

The 'New Dawn' of which *The Times* wrote on the morrow of Munich was thus no idyll of satisfied appeasement. It was a hard and cold dawn in which the nation could best show its gratitude to Chamberlain, who had braved the night for them, 'by learning the lessons taught by the great dangers through which we have been so finely led—that only a people prepared to face the worst can through their leaders cause peace to prevail in a crisis'.[202] Nor did the paper, after Munich, shy from frank coverage of news or controversy relating to Germany.[203]

As Munich became increasingly the subject of controversy and also the issue in the approaching by-elections, *The Times*, in two different—and unconnected—leading articles, analysed the major objections to and criticisms of Munich. There were those—the 'most logical and consistent'—who simply wanted preventive war based solely on the chances of victory and no other considerations. Second, there were those who felt that British prestige had been irreparably damaged. Third, there were those who saw Chamberlain constructing an alliance with the Fascist States against Communism. Last, there were those who saw the British Prime Minister as a dupe.

Of the first objection, the paper said that such people had

[200] *The Times*, 29 Sept. 1938, 1st Leader, p. 13; the second Leader takes a realistically hard military line.

[201] *The Times*, 30 Sept. 1938, 1st Leader, p. 13.

[202] *The Times*, 10 Oct. 1938, 1st Leader, p. 13.

[203] See, for example, ibid., Vienna Corr., p. 15, for an exciting account of the Correspondent's arrest by the Nazis for 'telephoning information of riots'.

learnt nothing from 1914 or from 1919: the climax of their argument and the only final demonstration of its futility would have been the world war of 1938 which was precisely what Chamberlain had prevented. These were the people who considered animosity the only virtue and rejected 'even the attempt to find a bridge between two peoples living under widely differing systems of Government'.[204] As for the second objection, Britain's prestige, as the paper's leading articles had reiterated, was inestimably higher for having made the issue so clear in the crisis. The third objection seemed to be lent force by the Soviets' exclusion from Munich; but considering the state of German-Soviet relations, it would not have made much sense to include these arch-enemies at the conference table. A 'plausible case' could be made for the last objection provided one saw in Hitler 'a German disciple of Machiavelli, whose promises are designed only to ensnare'. Such might be the case—there being ample ground for caution—but 'caution is being exercised'.[205]

The most potent argument which *The Times* brought up against the critics of Munich was the fact that

If an alternative Government could be formed tomorrow it would not find the materials of a programme either in the current speeches or letters or leading articles of the critics. . . . There is no opposition to Mr. Chamberlain in the ordinary sense. No one wishes or is prepared openly to wish that he had pursued or was now pursuing war instead of peace.[206]

Part and parcel of *The Times*'s defence of Munich was the conviction that first place among the Government's tasks was 'the strengthening of our defences with an active cultivation of the tender shoots of the policy of appeasement'; the priority was telling.[207] It was Chamberlain's exciting challenge to organize militarily an unprecedentedly willing nation.[208] It had taken an extreme emergency to 'awaken the people of England to the dangers of their vulnerable state',[209] but now

---

[204] *The Times*, 4 Oct. 1938, 1st Leader, p. 15.
[205] See *The Times*, 19 Oct. 1938, 1st Leader, p. 13; and 21 Oct. 1938, 1st Leader, p. 15. [206] *The Times*, 7 Nov. 1938, 1st Leader, p. 13.
[207] *The Times*, 18 Oct. 1938, 1st Leader, p. 15.
[208] *The Times*, 17 Oct. 1938, 1st Leader, p. 15.
[209] *The Times*, 21 Oct. 1938, 1st Leader, p. 15.

it had been done, and they realized that 'British rearmament is the key to disarmament . . .'.[210] 'There can be no true or fruitful policy of negotiations except as between equals; and, unhappily, there is no final criterion of equality except that of armed strength, backed by united public opinion.' That *The Times*'s support for such a policy was unstinting was seen when it drew the logical conclusion: 'That means that the principle of "business as usual" must suffer to the extent that nothing must be allowed to prevent the Government from attaining to the full the necessary material backing for their policy in the shortest time that the vast industrial resources of this country can supply it.'[211]

On 2 October, Dawson wrote to his friend Lord Brand explaining personally the things that the paper had been stating publicly:

I entirely agree with all you say about the Nazi regime and am not in the least 'carried away' by the Hitler–Chamberlain declaration. . . . Where I probably differ from you is on the method of getting rid of the Nazi regime. I regard it as very largely the creation of ourselves and the French in the past. I am sure that it would have been immensely strengthened by a war—particularly at a moment when we are insufficiently prepared, the Russians immobilised by the murder of their leading generals and admirals, and the French positively squealing to be saved by any means from their obligations to the Czechs. (You should see some of their telegrams to our Government.) On the other hand I am convinced that Hitler has been impressed for the first time during the last few days by the hostility of the whole world to his methods and particularly by the obvious sentiments of the German people.[212]

Europe began to settle down for a stock-taking after Munich. The Christmas season approached and few saw any irony in *The Times*'s offer of Christmas cards featuring the paper's exclusive photograph of the Chamberlains with the King and Queen at Buckingham Palace upon the Premier's return from Munich. The prospects were grim, but there was peace.

[210] *The Times*, 17 Oct. 1938, 1st Leader, p. 15.
[211] *The Times*, 18 Oct., 1938, 1st Leader, p. 15.
[212] Dawson to Brand, 2 Oct. 1938, *The Times* archives.

DAILY TELEGRAPH

The issue of the Sudetenland was seen as the immediate threat to peace in the summer of 1938. The paper felt that compromise was needed on both sides, but that any kind of settlement which depended upon a double allegiance to the Czech State and the German race 'would be a continuing threat to the integrity of the country and prolong into the years the present state of acute tension'.[213] The paper apparently accepted Hitler's protests of non-involvement at face value: 'There is no reason to doubt his good faith, since the situation in Czechoslovakia is such that it is essential to reach agreement if a European conflagration is to be avoided.'[214] By the end of the month, when Sudeten intransigence was clearly originating in Berlin, the paper, while still not charging him with direct involvement, wrote that 'The final and decisive word is with Herr Hitler. If he has the will he has the power to silence those who would make mischief, to relieve the growing tension on the Continent and to aid a settlement that would give the minorities in Czechoslovakia their full part in the life of the nation.'[215] As the crisis mounted, the paper went so far as to say that 'Herr Hitler and Field-Marshal Göring cannot be held guiltless'.[216]

Perhaps this reluctance to implicate Hitler was rooted in the paper's firm belief that any worthwhile solution lay in his hands alone. For this reason, it was of the utmost importance that Hitler know and know well the British Government's attitude towards Czechoslovakia. If he knew how determined Britain was to act with France and Russia, it would surely stay his hand. As Robert Boothby wrote in an editorial article, 'The final decision lies largely in Herr Hitler's hands, and it is difficult to believe that he will not choose the right course.'[217] Events turned most dramatically upon Hitler as his address to the Nuremberg *Parteitag* approached.[218]

---

[213] *Daily Telegraph*, 2 Aug. 1938, 1st Leader, p. 8.   [214] Ibid.

[215] *Daily Telegraph*, 30 Aug. 1938, 1st Leader, p. 12.

[216] *Daily Telegraph*, 14 Sept. 1938, 1st Leader, p. 12.

[217] *Daily Telegraph*, 30 Aug. 1938, ed. art. by Robert Boothby, M.P., p. 12.

[218] See *Daily Telegraph*, 5 Sept. 1938, 1st Leader and ed. art. by J. B. Firth, p. 10. The paper was glad that Nevile Henderson had come to London before going to the *Parteitag* because he would be able to impress Hitler the more with His Majesty's Government's firmness: *Daily Telegraph*, 10 Sept. 1938, 1st Leader, p. 12.

The *Daily Telegraph* found Hitler's speech at Nuremberg violent and beside the point. It afforded a respite from the immediate danger of war, but it was not a good thing that 'Europe is apparently, in the Führer's conception, to be kept in a state of anxious expectancy during the whole time that the negotiations may occupy and beyond.'[219]

The paper continually stressed Britain's determination 'not to disinterest' herself in Czechoslovakia. The flaw in the *Daily Telegraph*'s attitude was that for all its preoccupation with firmness, it never said that Britain should fight for Czechoslovakia. Its strongest statement held little strength: 'It would be the most serious of all misunderstandings if the impression remained that we could disinterest ourselves in any attempt to coerce Czechoslovakia.'[220]

That an equitable solution was possible was patent in the paper's greeting of the announcement of Lord Runicman's mission;[221] but Hitler must know that Britain was not washing her hands by sending a mediator; nor would world opinion take any tampering with Czech independence lightly.[222] After the Lanark speech, the paper brought these two threads together in a leading article, 'An Appeal And A Warning':

The main purpose of any consultation at this moment is to discover what further help can be given in the appeasement which, as Mr. Winston Churchill said on Saturday, rests in the hand of the man at the head of the German people. As regards Czechoslovakia there can be no ambiguity about British policy. It aims at a reduction of tension giving lasting peace in Central Europe, but Sir John Simon's speech repeats the warning given by the Prime Minister in May that we could not disinterest ourselves should an attempt be made at settlement by force.[223]

It was because it seemed to indicate a weakening of Britain's position that the *Daily Telegraph* was strongly opposed to *The Times*'s leading article of 7 September of which it said that 'No more sinister blow could have been struck at the chances of settlement.'[224] It printed the Foreign Office's

[219] *Daily Telegraph*, 13 Sept. 1938, 1st Leader, p. 12.
[220] *Daily Telegraph*, 10 Sept. 1938, p. 12.
[221] *Daily Telegraph*, 27 July 1938, 1st Leader, p. 14.
[222] *Daily Telegraph*, 13 Sept. 1938, 1st Leader, p. 12.
[223] *Daily Telegraph*, 29 Aug. 1938, 1st Leader, p. 8.
[224] *Daily Telegraph*, 8 Sept. 1938, 1st Leader, p. 12.

repudiation in full and a week later printed an editorial page article by the Political Correspondent referring to the 'now notorious "Times" leading article'.[225]

An editorial page article by Winston Churchill, printed the same day as the news of Chamberlain's flight to Berchtesgaden, might well have been addressed to the *Daily Telegraph* itself: 'Only the most blunt, plain, even brutal language will make its effect. Moreover, whatever words are used must carry with them the conviction that they are spoken in deadly earnest. This is no time for bluff.'[226]

The *Daily Telegraph*'s attempt to see the best in news from Germany initially affected its treatment of the progress of the Nazification of Austria and of German anti-Semitism. In the former case, it devoted a leading article to the rumours of vast corruption in the Nazi bureaucracy in Austria and Gauleiter Bürckel's purging of it.

Herr Bürckel, to judge by his statements, and indeed by his general repute, is a man of principle, endeavouring to consolidate the Nazi regime in Austria upon legal and business-like lines. But he has found many of his subordinates turning to their own advantage the opportunities for corruption which they are afforded by the forcible taking over of private business and by the seizure of individual property belonging to Jews, Monarchists, and Fatherland Front supporters. . . .

Herr Bürckel himself, is not, of course, a moderate according to the standards of the outside world. . . . But he shows a sensible regard for administrative efficiency—which is incompatible with leave to gratify private or political spites.[227]

Two days later the Vienna correspondent reported some other lapses in administrative efficiency: eight hundred Jewish suicide attempts within a few days.[228]

Chamberlain's decision to meet Hitler personally was considered to be a courageous departure from diplomatic

---

[225] See *Daily Telegraph*, 8 Sept. 1938, p. 13; 9 Sept. 1938, 1st Leader, p. 12; 13 Sept. 1938, ed. art. by Our Political Corr., p. 12.

[226] *Daily Telegraph*, 15 Sept. 1938, ed. art., by Churchill, p. 13. Churchill called for a joint Anglo-French-Soviet note to Germany, saying that they would resist any attack on Czechoslovakia; President Roosevelt should be requested to express sympathy with such a note.

[227] *Daily Telegraph*, 4 July 1938, 2nd Leader, p. 14.

[228] *Daily Telegraph*, 6 July 1938, Vienna Corr., p. 15. See also ibid., ed. art. by Churchill on Nazi policy in Austria, p. 16.

precedents, and 'the good wishes of everybody who has the appeasement of Europe at heart will accompany Mr. Neville Chamberlain on his mission'.[229] Such a meeting would be, of course, the ultimate means for conveying to Hitler the firm resolution of His Majesty's Government, and should it fail, there could never be any question of faulty communication with the man who held lightning in his hand.[230]

The Anglo-French proposals gave considerable pause to the *Daily Telegraph*. Although it had been careful to avoid stating a commitment actually to fight for Czechoslovakia, it was not possible so to interpret its insistence upon a firm stand as covering these proposals which counselled capitulation. One just had to go along, on the assumption that it was, 'in the view of its sponsors, a concession difficult to make but justifiable as an effort to avert an immediate outbreak of war'.[231] The paper's reluctance to adopt even this attitude can be seen in its initial comment upon the rumours of what the Anglo-French proposals involved: 'if these reports prove to be substantially true it does not appear that proposals of the kind suggested will commend themselves universally—either in this country or in the Empire. There has, indeed, already been created a sense of misgiving which, if it is not justified by the facts, should be dispelled by their immediate publication.'[232]

The leading article devoted to the Anglo-French proposals was called 'Counting the Cost', and it concluded that if peace were assured and a copper-bottomed guarantee extended to Czechoslovakia then they could be—somewhat reluctantly— accepted.[233] Obviously,

The effort will not have been worth the candle if it is to bring no more than a few weeks' or a few months' respite from German demonstrations of bellicosity—if, in other words, this is but the first instalment of a Danegeld that Europe is to go on paying for ever afterwards, in ever larger sums, as the price of immunity from military aggression, any such idea is too ridiculous to merit a moment's consideration, and it must surely be doing a grave injustice not to Mr. Chamberlain alone, but to the British and French

[229] *Daily Telegraph*, 15 Sept. 1938, 1st Leader, p. 12.
[230] *Daily Telegraph*, 16 Sept. 1938, 1st Leader, p. 14.
[231] *Daily Telegraph*, 22 Sept. 1938, 1st Leader, p. 12.
[232] *Daily Telegraph*, 20 Sept. 1938, 1st Leader, p. 14.
[233] *Daily Telegraph*, 21 Sept. 1938, 1st Leader, p. 12.

Governments whose writ he carries, to imagine, as is being too hastily done in some quarters, that their peace policy amounts to nothing better than that.[234]

In his Correspondence, the Prague correspondent stressed the gallant patriotic resistance of the Czechs to any concessions.[235]

At least these proposals, representing as they did something beyond even the ultimate concession on the part of the West, would create a situation where this issue, 'the cause of so much past unrest, must be definitely determined one way or the other'. Hitler must now show how interested he was in concession or in agitation.[236] The paper sent Chamberlain off to Godesberg with the sentiments that this meeting must now either strike the pathway towards an appeasement of Europe in general, or not bring peace at all.[237]

When the nature and content of the Godesberg demands became known, the paper was aghast. What would be left of Czechoslovakia after the Godesberg demands had been met, the Diplomatic Correspondent wrote, 'would be militarily undefendable, economically broken and politically subjugated completely to German domination in all aspects of policy'.[238] If the Anglo-French proposals had posed difficulties of acceptance for the *Daily Telegraph*, the Godesberg proposals doubled them: 'The demands are as peremptory and uncompromising as if they represented, not the basis of negotiation for a peaceful settlement, but a dictation to an enemy beaten in the field—which Czechoslovakia is not yet.'[239] Everything was objectionable about them; they represented in fact an 'abject and humiliating capitulation' for Czechoslovakia. Gone was the old acceptance of Hitler's self-proclaimed detachment:

Herr Hitler must well know, the Sudeten areas could be subdued to complete calm to-morrow at a word from himself. Whatever disturbance exists has been deliberately fomented by the unceasing stream of incendiary propaganda pouring out daily from the German Press and radio. The suspicion that all the turmoil has been stirred up with the set intent of providing a plausible case for drastic intervention is now confirmed beyond a peradventure.

[234] Ibid. [235] Ibid., Prague Corr., p. 12.
[236] *Daily Telegraph*, 23 Sept. 1938, 1st Leader, p. 14.
[237] *Daily Telegraph*, 22 Sept. 1938, 1st Leader, p. 22.
[238] *Daily Telegraph*, 26 Sept. 1938, Dipl. Corr., p. 11.
[239] Ibid., 1st Leader, p. 10.

During the next few days, the *Daily Telegraph* indulged in as strong criticism as was possible short of breaking with the Government. Everyone must be finally disenchanted with the German system of 'saying "thank you for nothing" to every concession and perpetually raising the price of peace',[240] which had now gone too far. 'It can only be surmised that Herr Hitler took up this line in the hope of once more deceiving those confused minds, especially in this country, who are the habitual victims of his artful logic.'[241] Hitler's Sports Palace speech of the 26th was, with its flamboyant rhetoric 'teeming with menace and invective', seen as 'the worst possible contribution towards the pacification of minds and tempers which is so urgently needed at a time like this . . .'[242]

On 27 September the paper published the 'It was authoritatively stated . . .' statement in a box headed 'Immediate Aid For Czechs If Attacked'.[243]

From the very first, the *Daily Telegraph* was sceptical of Munich.

This nation cannot prudently afford to purchase present ease at the expense of future trouble. With the will to peace it is possible to make accommodation. It is vain to ignore the fact that throughout this crisis all the concessions have come from one side and all the extractions and provocations from the other; and that every new concession has provided the occasion for a new demand. The respite that has now been secured has naturally raised the expectation that the Czech question is about to be settled definitely, and that the Munich conference will confirm and consolidate what has been so happily begun. The danger against which Mr. Chamberlain must be vigilant is that of loosening what ought to be held fast. Already so much has been given away that there is little left to surrender if Czechoslovakia is to be left as a viable entity. All the hope and promise which the Munich conference holds out will be frustrated if such a 'settlement' is reached as results, a few months hence, in a revival of all the present trouble.[244]

Anthony Mann, in an editorial page article on 30 September, stressed the ignorance in which the German people were kept,[245]

[240] Ibid.   [241] *Daily Telegraph*, 27 Sept. 1938, 1st Leader, p. 14.
[242] Ibid.   [243] Ibid., p. 15. See p. 190, above.
[244] *Daily Telegraph*, 29 Sept. 1938, 1st Leader, p. 12.
[245] *Daily Telegraph*, 30 Sept. 1938, ed. art. by Anthony Mann, p. 12.

and a leading article stated that with the Munich settlement every conceivable benefit had been given to Hitler and if it were still rejected, 'the only possible conclusion will be that Germany regards force as an end in itself. In that event the rest of us will all know where we stand.'[246]

On the very morrow of Munich the paper wondered whether the price had been worth paying. Its answer was, generally, yes; there was still a certain euphoria on the *Daily Telegraph* over the release of the world from the grip of war. 'Peace, even at a price, is a blessing so inestimable that the first and predominant reaction to our release from the torturing fears of the past few days is necessarily one of profound thankfulness.'[247] After Munich, the paper defended Chamberlain in a left-handed way. Although no one would doubt the propriety or merit of his actions in the circumstances, no one could escape 'a feeling of profound anxiety alike as to the course of events already enacted and as to the future which hereafter confronts us'.[248] Indeed, it came close to outright criticism at one point:

Not the least ground for uneasiness is the consciousness of the impunity with which Herr Hitler has been allowed to gain his ends by the method of the threat. It was thanks to these threats that, on the day before Godesberg, and again on the day after Munich, the Czechs had to submit unconditionally to a peremptory dictate. Great as is the debt we owe to Mr. Chamberlain, it would have been greater still if he had stood out more forcefully on this issue.[249]

Within a fortnight's time it became clear that Hitler had scored a total victory at Munich. He 'obtained, through the machinery of Munich, a still larger slice of Czechoslovakia than he had sought by the method of the ultimatum at Godesberg'.[250] The lesson of Munich had been clear right away, however: Britain must arm, for, '. . . within an hour or two of a declaration of war—if indeed this formality is observed at all, we shall be exposed to a crashing attack'. The crisis when it came would be better met, and would be less likely to come at all, the stronger were Britain's arms.[251]

[246] *Daily Telegraph*, 30 Sept. 1938, 1st Leader, p. 11.
[247] *Daily Telegraph*, 1 Oct. 1938, Leader, p. 12.
[248] *Daily Telegraph*, 3 Oct. 1938, Leader, p. 10.   [249] Ibid.
[250] *Daily Telegraph*, 13 Oct. 1938, 1st Leader, p. 16.
[251] *Daily Telegraph*, 3 Oct. 1938, Leader, p. 10.

In a retrospective article at the end of 1938, J. B. Firth saw the year as having been

One crisis after another; continued bickerings; a perpetual stream of ill-natured comment and insult; floods of vicious propaganda. . . .

The rewards of British diplomacy by no means corresponded with the excellence of British intentions. Our national interests endured many grievous shocks; our national pride still more.[252]

Like the paper, Firth praised Chamberlain, who had done the right thing at Munich; 'But that the Western Democracies should have allowed themselves to be caught in such a plight is a totally different matter. The warnings they had received were quite plain enough.'[253] At least the lesson had been learned, and rearmament was proceeding apace despite shortsighted criticism in some quarters. 'Mr. Chamberlain is censured in certain quarters—happily few—for preaching appeasement and rearmament in the same breath. The common sense of the British people, however, sees no contradiction.'[254]

MANCHESTER GUARDIAN

For the *Manchester Guardian*, Czechoslovakia presented an especially difficult problem. The paper shared the generally held conviction of the geographic, racial, and linguistic validity of the Sudeten Germans' case. To deny it would be to deny justice. The essential weakness of Czechoslovakia in this respect made acceptance of the plebiscite as the instrument of self-determination impossible, since similar disruptive claims would be advanced by the other minorities. The situation was maddening and serious because although the Sudetens' case was good and no direct British interests were involved, strategically Hitler stood to get away with murder:

If [Czechoslovakia] were situated anywhere else than where she is the concern felt over her destiny here would be no more than academic or, at best, humanitarian. But, being situated where she is, her continued existence as an independent sovereign State within her present frontiers—and other frontiers are for strategic reasons impossible—is essential to the balance of power in Europe.[255]

---

[252] *Daily Telegraph*, 31 Dec. 1938, ed. art., p. 10.   [253] Ibid.   [254] Ibid.
[255] *Manchester Guardian*, 21 July 1938, Dipl. Corr., p. 6.

So although Voigt dissected the Nazi intentions with considerable skill, he never attempted to puncture the German
case over Czechoslovakia. Neither he nor his paper answered
the Germans on their own ground; rather, it seemed that
Czechoslovakia must be defended in spite of the validity of
the Sudeten demands. The diplomatic campaign to minimize
the importance of Czechoslovakia in British eyes, the inspired
anti-Czech campaign in the German Press, and the breakneck
effort to complete the Siegfried Wall—all indicated that
Germany was intent upon forcing a crisis. The German people
wanted peace, 'but the decision in the next few weeks will
hardly be affected by what the German people want or do not
want'.[256] The best answer to this was simply to play for time.
Negotiations, conferences, investigations—anything to tide
over until autumn when military action would be impossible for
at least six months.[257] This was the rationale behind the paper's
welcoming of the announcement of the Runciman mission.

While the leading article on Lord Runciman's mission
stressed that he must make clear Britain's intention to stand
by Czechoslovakia, and that unless concessions were forth-
coming from the Sudetens this very fact would tell against
them in Lord Runciman's findings, it concluded by admitting
that at the very least, the sending of the mission would win time.
Voigt wrote agreeing that although time might be the *only*
thing gained, 'on the whole the view expressed in your leader
columns today would seem to prevail'.[258]

In the meantime the crisis developed, with the Sudeten
Germans pursuing typical Hitlerite tactics: 'Extreme—indeed
wholly impossible—demands are made in Prague, accompanied
by warlike preparations that daily assume a more formidable
character, while the greatest moderation is paraded in London,
accompanied by assurances of peaceful intent.'[259] This dual
tactic produced the desired effect of generating an optimism in
England which Voigt and the paper did their best to oppose.
The British Goverment was playing right into Sudeten hands
by bringing pressure to bear solely upon Prague and, 'although

[256] *Manchester Guardian*, 15 Aug. 1938, 1st Leader, p. 8, and 17 Aug. 1938, Dipl.
Corr., p. 9.   [257] *Manchester Guardian*, 26 July 1938, Dipl. Corr., p. 6.
[258] *Manchester Guardian*, 27 July 1938, 1st Leader, p. 10, and 28 July 1938, Dipl.
Corr., p. 9.   [259] *Manchester Guardian*, 22 July 1938, Dipl. Corr., p. 7.

the Party is but one of many in the Czechoslovak Parliament',
treating the Sudeten Party 'as though it were itself a Power,
and as though it had sovereign rights of which it is itself the
only arbiter, and no duties or obligations whatever'.[260] This
was hardly reason for optimism. It was the line of least resistance which the British Government was pursuing, a line
being 'greased with official optimism'. It was difficult even
to credit the policy with being ingenuous.

While Germany remains prolific in expressions of good will, she
continues to exercise pressure on Czechoslovakia and completes her
warlike preparations. She promises 'appeasement' on the one hand,
and though her promises are regarded here with incredulity they
are broadly advertised with a view to making official optimism
more effective as a lubricant.[261]

It was indeed these German military preparations—the mobilization of the German army in the summer—which, according
to the *Manchester Guardian*, accounted for the other papers
treating seriously for the first time the growing seriousness of the
crisis.

It is interesting that the *Manchester Guardian* did not participate in the excited anticipation which surrounded Hitler's
Parteitag speech in the other British newspapers. Indeed it
pursued its own course throughout the month, reaching its
height of indignation and disappointment over the Anglo-
French proposals of 20 September, treating Munich as a
welcome respite after this initial sell-out, and then giving way,
in October, to the most serious second thoughts about the
Munich agreement and its importance.

It was considered imperative that Hitler, who was once
again being pictured in the *Manchester Guardian* as a moderate
being swayed by the aggressiveness of the Generals and
misinformed by the frustrated and evil von Ribbentrop, be
made genuinely aware of the determination of the British
Government to stand by Czechoslovakia. Voigt deplored that
the Cabinet went on holiday early in September: 'It seems
very doubtful indeed', he wrote, 'whether Hitler, and, indeed,
even German observers with some knowledge of this
country, believe that the British Government really takes the

---

[260] *Manchester Guardian*, 26 July 1938, Dipl. Corr., p. 6.   [261] Ibid.

international situation as seriously as it professes to take it (Hitler is no doubt mistaken, but it is not the reality but their impression of the reality which will determine his actions).'[262]

As if foreseeing Chamberlain's decision a few days later, the paper wrote on 12 September in the same vein: 'We are coming rapidly to the point where only the clearest intimation by the Government to Hitler himself may be effectual. We must not take the risk that, should war come, it should anywhere be said that it would not or even might not have come had Hitler known.'[263] It could therefore only greet Chamberlain's initiative as a 'bold' move which could be used to impress upon Hitler Britain's purposefulness.[264]

In many ways the *Manchester Guardian*'s spare comments on Hitler's Nuremberg speech, which was so dissected and discussed in the other papers, are instructive of the paper's misgivings and problems over its own policy on the Sudeten issue. Simply commenting that the speech was inconclusive and left open the important questions concerning the possibility of compromise, the existence of a German timetable to which the crisis was being worked, and the German will to peace, the paper concluded that: 'The British Government, for its part, must remember that it will have to convince its own people, and other peoples, that up to the last minute of the last hour it did the utmost that it could, by appeal and by warning to Berlin, to avert catastrophe.'[265]

It was not Munich that was dangerous and dishonourable, but the earlier Anglo-French proposals, which embodied the principle of direct transfer to Germany. The Anglo-French proposals were nothing less than an 'ultimatum, with a short time-limit' which would only end the crisis provisionally to the extent that they were only a provisional surrender to the Western Powers, humiliating and futile.[266]

The paper's hopes for a mighty coalition of Britain, France and Russia saying 'No' to German demands and thereby causing Hitler's downfall, and the reduction in British armaments which this would make possible—these hopes were

[262] *Manchester Guardian*, 3 Sept. 1938, Dipl. Corr., p. 11.
[263] *Manchester Guardian*, 12 Sept. 1938, 1st Leader, p. 10.
[264] *Manchester Guardian*, 15 Sept. 1938, 1st Leader, p. 8.
[265] *Manchester Guardian*, 14 Sept. 1938, 1st Leader, p. 8.
[266] *Manchester Guardian*, 20 Sept. 1938, Dipl. Corr., p. 11.

ill-founded. In the wake of the Anglo-French proposals it saw
the whole fabric of the European order rent asunder. France
and Britain were tarred with moral defeat; Russia's reaction
would probably be 'cynical and isolationist'. Instead of
courting the Soviets, the Western Powers had 'ostentatiously
ignored' them. The *Manchester Guardian* even wondered
whether Russia might not now withdraw from Spain.'[267] The
international guarantee could hardly be taken seriously, for,
including Germany and Italy, 'it is as though the viper and
the scorpion were to guarantee the well-being of the shorn
rabbit'.[268] It was hardly to be expected that Britain and
France would defend a chronically weakened Czechoslovakia
if they would not assist her when she was strong and vital.
'We may console ourselves, if we like, that in the fierce resurgence of modern nationalisms Czechoslovakia was doomed
anyway and drop a tear at her fate. But what we none of us
can get over is that henceforward the world is going to be an
infinitely more difficult place for peace-loving democratic
peoples to live in.'[269]

The forcing of the Anglo-French proposals upon Czechoslovakia was viewed as a terrific moral defeat for the Western
Powers which would have consequences 'beyond our present
range of vision'.[270] But there would certainly be immediate and
practical consequences. The entire European power constella-
tion was irreparably damaged. Poland, Rumania and Yugoslavia would now come into the German orbit; Hungary was
already there.[271] It was a 'bold man' who would not admit
that Hitler's ultimate aim was the complete subjugation of
Czechoslovakia.[272] Both Italy and Japan had announced
their complete loyalty to Germany and the paper lamented,
curiously, that now armaments would have to be greatly increased and Britain would find herself feverishly rearming 'in
something approaching isolation'.[273] One of the most important
immediate consequences of the Anglo-French surrender would
be the justifiable defection of Soviet Russia from the anti-

[267] *Manchester Guardian*, 22 Sept. 1938, 2nd Leader, p. 10.
[268] Ibid., Dipl. Corr., p. 14.   [269] Ibid., 2nd Leader, p. 10.
[270] *Manchester Guardian*, 21 Sept. 1938, 1st Leader, p. 8.
[271] *Manchester Guardian*, 20 Sept. 1938, Dipl Corr., p. 11.
[272] *Manchester Guardian*, 21 Sept. 1938, 1st Leader, p. 8, and Dipl. Corr., p. 4.
[273] *Manchester Guardian*, 22 Sept. 1938, 2nd Leader, p. 10.

German front. America too was shocked and repulsed by
this show of weakness: Britain's name was 'mud' in the United
States and the Dominions.[274] Further, there were the economic
and military losses involved.[275]

On the 22nd, the *Manchester Guardian* wrote that whereas
a week ago Chamberlain had been a hero, 'If Mr. Chamberlain
reads his papers today as he flies once again to Germany he
will see no trace of admiration for his part as the head of a great
democracy, no trust that he can save any shred of principle
from the wreck, no belief even that he can recover his country's
honour.'[276] This assessment, like that of British prestige in
America and the Dominions, was simply not true—at least not
true on a large enough scale to justify such generalization.
British and Dominion opinion of both Chamberlain's trips
to Germany was almost unanimously favourable, and it was
only after the abusive nature of the Godesberg meeting and
demands became known that disenchantment spread and
resolution to resist such bullying took its place. The relief at
Chamberlain's third trip, to Munich, was universal. It was
only after Munich that second thoughts began to appear.

The acceptance—reluctant albeit—of the Anglo-French
proposals seemed to be the end of the Czech crisis. Voigt
insisted that it was still only a prelude to an attack on the
West, but for the time being the surrender seemed a settlement.
When the Godesberg Memorandum demanded still more,
and it appeared that war must ensue, the paper was curiously
tepid in its leader columns although its Central European,
Prague, and Berlin correspondents—not to mention Voigt—
left little doubt concerning the perfidy or cynicism of Nazi
conduct or the valour of Czech resolution. The truth would
seem to be that once again, as in March 1936 and March 1938,
despite its philosophically founded abhorrence for Nazism,
the *Manchester Guardian* did not want a war, especially a war
over Czechoslovakia. When Chamberlain returned from his
first meeting with Hitler, the paper stated frankly that:

When one thinks of the intolerable price of war in lives and misery
it would be dirt cheap to pay the cost of transplanting the Sudetens

[274] Ibid.
[275] *Manchester Guardian*, 24 Sept. 1938, 2nd Leader, p. 12, and ed. art., p. 13.
[276] *Manchester Guardian*, 22 Sept. 1938, 2nd Leader, p. 10.

into Germany if there were enough common sense in the world to
do it and Germany would consent. It would be worthwhile, too, if
there were time, to give Czechoslovakia an international guarantee
of her future integrity should the Sudeten regions be torn from her.[277]

In its first leading article on Munich, the *Manchester Guardian*
said:

And whatever view we take about the policies and acts that led up
to the crisis and the character of the settlement we cannot help
sharing the common thankfulness. None of us, to be frank, can
disguise from himself that even had a European war been fought
on the deeper issues, and Germany been overcome the boundaries
of Czechoslovakia could not have remained intact . . . and great
as are the injustices that Czechoslovakia suffers under the Munich
Agreement, and they are for her calamitous, they cannot be
measured against the horrors that might have extinguished not
only Czechoslovakia but the whole of Western civilization.[278]

For the *Manchester Guardian* Munich represented 'Respite
and Hope'.[279] For Voigt, who had already reported German
optimism that the Godesberg demands might be slipped past
with the Anglo-French proposals, if the one could be made to
seem to conform to the other, the Munich Conference was from
the first a major victory for Hitler.[280] The event proved him
right: the Anglo-French proposals were the shadow and
Godesberg the substance of the final agreement. The international guarantee, which the paper had considered so
important, was rendered ludicrous by German and Italian
participation. Munich was a shambles.[281] The German rear
and flank were now all but secured, and Hitler could turn
west, demanding, say, colonies, the surrender of the Maginot
Line, or a 'plebiscite' in the Flemish districts of Belgium.[282]
Within a few days the paper had fully recovered its composure and its anti-Nazi, anti-Government line. A series of

---

[277] *Manchester Guardian*, 16 Sept. 1938, 1st Leader, p. 8. See also *Manchester
Guardian*, 15 Sept. 1938, 1st Leader, p. 8.
[278] *Manchester Guardian*, 1 Oct. 1938, 1st Leader, p. 12.
[279] *Manchester Guardian*, 29 Sept. 1938, 1st Leader, p. 8.
[280] See *Manchester Guardian*, 28 Sept. 1938, Dipl. Corr., p. 9.
[281] *Manchester Guardian*, 29 Sept. 1938, Dipl. Corr., p. 12; 30 Sept. 1938, 1st
Leader, p. 10, and Dipl. Corr., p. 11.
[282] *Manchester Guardian*, 26 Sept. 1938, Dipl. Corr., p. 9.

'second-thought' articles and leading articles lamented the tragic surrender of Czechoslovakia and especially the consequences for those non-Nazis who would be left at Hitler's mercy. After the defeat of Munich it took only the pogrom of 10 November to establish beyond doubt the danger to civilization represented by this 'barbarous apparition among modern Governments which knows neither pity nor restraint',[283] and to pose once again the basic question whether a policy of appeasement was possible 'when a necessary partner to it so flaunts the barest principles of humanity? By what system of expediency can such a spirit be made to walk hand in hand with justice, tolerance, and humanity—values which this Government is surely pledged to its people to defend?'[284]

There was no reason to doubt and every reason to expect that Germany would continue to pursue a policy of force and threat of force, and Voigt quoted extensively from *Mein Kampf* to prove this.[285] Britain must therefore rearm, as 'no Government can discharge its duty or protect its interests unless its diplomacy has behind it material strength and confidence'.[286] Although the *Manchester Guardian* questioned the 'mystery' of the Government's neglect of national defence,[287] as we have seen, it did nothing to press the need for quick and extensive rearmament—rather the opposite; it complained that one of the results of Munich would be the necessity of continuing in the arms race.

By mid-October, the paper had gone so far as to see a conspiracy in Munich:

Some day the strange story of the surrender must be forced into the daylight. With what intention was the Runciman Mission sent? What part has it played? How did it happen that England and France, posing first as friendly advisers to Czechoslovakia, then turned round and threatend her as if she and not Germany were the culprit? To what influences did the Government yield? And where is this to stop?[288]

[283] *Manchester Guardian*, 15 Nov. 1938, 2nd Leader, p. 10.   [284] Ibid.
[285] *Manchester Guardian*, 1 Nov. 1938, ed. art. by Voigt, p. 11, and 2 Nov. 1938, p. 11. See also *Manchester Guardian*, 27 Sept. 1938, 1st Leader, p. 8.
[286] *Manchester Guardian*, 29 Oct. 1938, 1st Leader, p. 12.   [287] Ibid.
[288] *Manchester Guardian*, 17 Oct. 1938, 1st Leader, p. 8.

NEWS CHRONICLE

Czechoslovakia was treated by the *News Chronicle* as a test case of British determination. Hitler must be resisted, and there was no doubt but that he was the motive force behind the Sudeten German agitation. Henlein was his 'pawn', fitted for a Seyss-Inquart role.[289] Commenting on Lord Runciman's mission, the paper said that if it were a question of Sudeten concern for their own rights, it would be different, but 'while much no doubt may be done at Prague—it is at Berlin that the real key of the problem is to be found. It was so in May last, and it is so now.'[290] The *News Chronicle* recognized the common-sense case to be made for compromise and expressed it in language similar to that of *The Times* which it treated so critically. Just as *The Times* wrote about taking seventy-five per cent instead of nothing, the Liberal paper stated that 'one thing is certain. All parties will get more from a just compromise than from holding out for impossible terms, which might well lead to a war in which the Sudeten Germans themselves would be the first to suffer.'[291]

Lord Runciman's mission was therefore greeted 'with the good will of everybody concerned'.[292] The *News Chronicle* was aware, however, of the potential danger in such a mission where 'everything depends on how Lord Runciman, and the British Government behind him, behave. . . . There is one possibility even worse than Britain's standing aloof and giving the Nazis a free hand against Prague and that is for Britain actually to help the Nazis.'[293]

From the beginning, the paper ruled out a solution in the form of an agreement between Hitler and Chamberlain which would be imposed upon Czechoslovakia.[294] It was fear of such an arrangement which informed the paper's criticism of Government policy, and this was the subject of considerable comment throughout the summer. The crux of the *News*

---

[289] *News Chronicle*, 22 July 1938, ed. art. by Gerhard Schacher, p. 8.
[290] *News Chronicle*, 27 July 1938, 1st Leader, p. 10. See also *News Chronicle*, 18 Aug. 1938, 1st Leader, p. 8.
[291] *News Chronicle*, 23 July 1938, 3rd Leader, p. 6.
[292] *News Chronicle*, 27 July 1938, 1st Leader, p. 10.
[293] *News Chronicle*, 29 July 1938, 1st Leader, p. 8.
[294] *News Chronicle*, 25 July 1938, 1st Leader, p. 10.

Chronicle's case was that Hitler would not risk a European war over Czechoslovakia, and that it was therefore necessary to combine with France and Russia to thwart Nazi expansionism and defend the democratic Czech State. Further, if adequate resistance were not mounted now, the Nazi juggernaut must inevitably roll across Czechoslovakia and beyond; so there was in fact no choice for the Western democracies. 'Playing for time', the paper stated on 22 July, 'would be justified only if the Government know that Germany is genuinely anxious to avoid a crisis and that there is more prospect of doing this if the issue is not precipitated now. But if the Government have such information they are keeping it to themselves.'[295] A week later, without any qualification, it condemned the argument that 'so long as war, and all the misery that war means, is averted, we should not be too particular about these people's "rights", or those. Rather let the Czechs suffer an injustice than plunge the world into bloodshed.' This argument, it said, 'depends' on whether such tactics would in fact prevent war. But a German Czechoslovakia would only make it more difficult for Britain in the eventual conflict because France's Eastern system and the Franco-Russian pact would in the meantime have been undermined and destroyed.[296]

The paper's policy over Czechoslovakia was set out on 29 July. Hitler, the same leader stated, did not want to face an armed coalition of Czechoslovakia, France, Britain, and Russia. 'And since we know that he *is* anxious for a peaceful solution, now is the time for us to insist in Berlin on a solution which is just and decent, and which does not jeopardize the common interests of Prague, Paris, Moscow, and London.'[297] In this sense, Sir John Simon's Lanark speech was greeted as good news for peace. 'For Great Britain to say plainly where it stands is to lessen the danger of conflict. It is not war-mongering to declare that in certain eventualities we should have to fight, but the very reverse.'[298] The urgency for an unequivocal statement of Britain's policy was heightened by the conviction

[295] *News Chronicle*, 22 July 1938, 2nd Leader, p. 8.
[296] *News Chronicle*, 29 July 1938, Leader, p. 8.
[297] Ibid. See also *News Chronicle*, 27 July 1938, 1st Leader, p. 10.
[298] *News Chronicle*, 29 Aug. 1938, Leader, p. 10.

that if her position had been made clear in 1914, there would have been no war.[299]

It was none the less true that the paper stressed, as did *The Times*, the strong advisability of a comprehensive Czech offer to the Sudetens: 'These terms must be so plainly adequate that the whole world recognizes them to be so—and, more than that, that any person or regime which rejects them in favour of violence will be branded unmistakably as a war-maker.'[300]

Hitler's speech at Nuremberg was considered a turn for the worse. Not only did it show him to be oblivious of the effects of violence, but it never even considered negotiation as a possible means of settlement. The leading article following the speech warned:

But only a madman could embark on such a policy, it may be objected. Unfortunately, Herr Hitler's savage speech last night must leave doubts whether he is fully conscious of all that he says and does. The conviction that the German people are the Chosen Race of God and that he is their divinely-appointed Leader must send a shudder down the backs of thinking people.[301]

There was never any question for the *News Chronicle* of accepting a plebiscite—and the demand for one was just a front which would collapse before a firm British statement:

In our opinion the case is clear for the support of the Czech democracy on the limit-line of concession to which it has now gone in response to the insincere demands of a more powerful neighbour which aims at its removal from the path of expansion. The democratic principle is one and indivisible, and must be defended, whether in Central Europe, in Spain, or at the gateways of the English Channel.[302]

In this half-page Editorial, the paper gave its considered opinion—which had already been well stated—on the crisis and the proper British response to it. Although it is difficult to see how the paper seriously credited reference to the League of Nations as practical policy at this late stage—and it had done little to foster the kind of rearmament needed if war were to be the issue of the Sudeten claims—it now said,

[299] *News Chronicle*, 10 Sept. 1938, Leader, p. 6, and box, p. 1.
[300] *News Chronicle*, 30 Aug. 1938, 1st Leader, p. 8.
[301] *News Chronicle*, 13 Sept. 1938, Leader, p. 10.
[302] *News Chronicle*, 15 Sept. 1938, Editorial, p. 10.

It is the Government's duty to stand firm on that positive policy, well-founded in their obligations under the Covenant of the League of Nations, and not to be content with negative calculations on the need, in an extremity, of supporting France in the purely selfish interests of survival.

If the British were willing to sacrifice the Czech democracy to keep themselves out of trouble the ultimate retribution would be overwhelming—and overwhelmingly deserved.[303]

The paper was concerned with the exclusion of Soviet Russia from the anti-Nazi camp. 'Peace can still be preserved', a leading article on 14 September stated, 'but it calls for the most resolute action by the British Government working in the closest agreement with Czechoslovakia itself and with France and Russia; and there is not a moment to be lost.'[304] On the following day, Cummings wrote that during the past few critical weeks, 'so far as I can recall, however, no British Minister has committed the indelicacy of even mentioning Russia in a public speech'. As a result of his column of 6 September to the same effect, a chain letter had begun, and thousands of post cards had been sent to Lord Halifax demanding 'an immediate consultation between Great Britain, France, and Soviet Russia'.[305]

It was in this defensive posture that the news of Chamberlain's decision to fly to Germany found the *News Chronicle*. 'This newspaper has frequently asked for the British attitude to be conveyed unmistakably to Herr Hitler, and there can be no more authentic way of doing so than by the lips of the Premier', a leading article stated. An editorial page article compared Chamberlain to Julius Caesar, Nelson, Drake, Alexander cutting the Gordian Knot, and Lady Godiva; and his flight was called 'one of the most dramatic gestures of recorded history'.[306] Perhaps the paper's attitude was conditioned by its front-page confirmation of 15 September of its earlier report, presumably obtained from the German opposition, that General Beck had

---

[303] Ibid. See also *News Chronicle*, 17 Sept. 1938, art. by Sir Norman Angell, p. 6.

[304] *News Chronicle*, 14 Sept. 1938, 1st Leader, p. 10.

[305] *News Chronicle*, 15 Sept. 1938, Spotlight on Politics, p. 11. See also *News Chronicle*, 6 Sept. 1938, p. 8.

[306] *News Chronicle*, 16 Sept. 1938, 1st Leader, p. 10 and ibid., ed. art. by Guy Ramsey.

resigned rather than participate in Hitler's plans for an offensive campaign against Czechoslovakia.[307]

The inherent danger in Chamberlain's action was obvious, however, and the paper warned that 'If the Sudeten areas were to be offered to Herr Hitler on a platter borne by the British Premier himself, the scandal would indeed be unprecedented.'[308] But thus far there were no signs of such a possibility, and on balance, even if the smaller nations were encouraged to think of Hitler as the real arbiter of Europe, Berchtesgaden was a step 'worth taking'.[309]

The paper disapproved totally of the Anglo-French proposals. Czechoslovakia was not perfect, but it was the bastion of freedom in central Europe and it was ridiculous to suppose that the Western Powers would honour a guarantee to a weak dependent when they would not fight to keep it as a strong ally.[310] Once the Czechs had accepted the Anglo-French proposals, however, it only remained to cut losses. To say that their acceptance was not a capitulation—and to say that such an accusation was slander—as did *The Times*, was 'crude editorial nonsense'.[311] Indeed, even the Editor of *The Times* had only to ask his own staff to see that opinion was hardening against Germany. The Czechs had submitted 'under irresistible pressure' and this was a great responsibility for the British Government; a responsibility which could be justified only if the guarantee were effective and included the Soviet Union, and if Germany understood that this was a surrender to avoid a greater evil, not a *carte blanche* for territorial aggrandisement.[312]

Within a few days, when Chamberlain was at Godesberg, the paper had come to view the Anglo-French proposals as 'the touchstone of Herr Hitler's sincerity'. The shoe was now on Hitler's foot, and he must wear it or else expose the real nature of his territorial claims. The paper was glad to quote its favourite 'convert' of this period, J. L. Garvin, who, long known as 'one of the most pro-German writers in Britain'[313] and 'for so long regarded as the *Observer* spokesman of the now

[307] *News Chronicle*, 15 Sept. 1938 and 5 Sept. 1938, p. 1.
[308] *News Chronicle*, 16 Sept. 1938, 1st Leader, p. 10.
[309] Ibid.   [310] *News Chronicle*, 20 Sept. 1938, Leader, p. 10.
[311] *News Chronicle*, 22 Sept. 1938, Spotlight on Politics, p. 10.
[312] *News Chronicle*, 22 Sept. 1938, Leader, p. 10.
[313] *News Chronicle*, 12 Sept. 1938, Leader, p. 10.

triumphant Cliveden Group',[314] was writing particularly perceptive and critical articles for the *Observer*.[315]

The paper had sensed a growing hardening of opinion
since the morrow of Berchtesgaden, and by the time Chamberlain was in Godesberg it could only insist upon the Prime
Minister making clear that Czechoslovakia was not about to be
carved up, and that only truly German areas could possibly
be ceded. It felt that his wireless speech to the nation and the
world, in the wake of the failure at Godesberg, was not sufficiently based upon the merits of the Czech case which was
that of the defence of Western civilization and was worth
fighting for in itself.[316]

It is not surprising that the *News Chronicle* shared little of the
enthusiasm for Munich. 'There is no one in the whole world
(except such few as may be deliberately malevolent),' it
said in a leading article, 'Third Time Lucky?' on 29 September,
'who does not rejoice that the shadow of war has been even
momentarily shifted; but just because of the momentousness
of the occasion it behooves us to weigh carefully all its implications'.[317] Looking at it in another way, the paper admitted
that whatever effects the Munich settlement might have on
Western policy and strategy, it could at least be said that 'the
Munich agreement has saved great numbers of innocent
Czech citizens from panic flight, from grievous loss of property,
from ruthless extermination from the air and from all the
horrors of military invasion'.[318]

In its very first comment on the Munich Conference, the
News Chronicle had predicated three requirements for an
adequate solution: it must remove the threat of force, settle
disputed questions by fair negotiation, and leave Czechoslovakia secure within its redrawn boundaries and adequately
guaranteed—including the U.S.S.R. as a guarantor—against
further aggression.[319] Almost immediately it was clear that
Munich would not provide these requirements. Relief was

[314] *News Chronicle*, 11 Oct. 1938, Spotlight on politics, p. 10.
[315] See below, p. 223.
[316] *News Chronicle*, 23 Sept. 1938, Leader, p. 10, and 28 Sept. 1938, 1st Leader,
p. 11. See also *News Chronicle*, 22 Sept. 1938, Leader, p. 10. for the hardening of
opinion.   [317] *News Chronicle*, 29 Sept. 1938, Leader, p. 10.
[318] *News Chronicle*, 30 Sept. 1938, 1st Leader, p. 10.
[319] *News Chronicle*, 29 Sept. 1938, Leader, p. 10.

natural, the paper reiterated on 1 October, but 'for all that, we may already begin to ask what is the price we have had to pay. That price is the sacrifice of a small and noble people; a people that have borne themselves throughout this crisis with a courage, a nerve and a restraint which have been an example to all democracies.'[320] The *News Chronicle* immediately established its own Czech Relief Fund to which it daily invited subscriptions.[321] On 3 October, the leading article stated that 'as the tide of emotion recedes, promptings of conscience and prudence force themselves to the forefront', and it would be a grave mistake to confuse the 'enthusiasm resulting from relief at the sudden removal of the threat of war with endorsement of the policy by which that removal was brought about. Distrust of this policy and resentment of the results which it has brought about are certain to be vigorously expressed.'[322]

In this leader, the paper gave vent to all the frustration of the past few months which had witnessed the inevitable course of the policy against which it had warned all the time. 'The *News Chronicle* has consistently held that the democracies could and should stand up to the dictatorships and that by doing so they could ensure without war the rule of order as against aggression.'[323] But such had not been the case. Instead, in 'one disheartening instance after another', bluff had succeeded until, just before the Munich Conference, Hitler had finally faltered: 'This was the moment when we could have won an important diplomatic victory for democracy and have decisively checked dictatorship and what it stands for. It was the hour of destiny, but the opportunity was lost.'[324] Somewhat disingenuously, the paper criticized Chamberlain's insistence that British armament would not slacken, would indeed increase in the future.

If Mr. Chamberlain has truly made friends with Germany, against whom shall we be arming? If he has not made friends with Germany, or does not trust that friendship, then the risks he has taken and the sacrifices he has made in order to obtain the piece of paper bearing his signature and the Führer's carry with them a tremendous load of responsibility.[325]

---

[320] *News Chronicle*, 1 Oct. 1938, Leader, p. 6.
[321] *News Chronicle*, 3 Oct. 1938, p. 1, and 4 Oct. 1938, 2nd Leader, p. 10.
[322] Ibid., Leader, p. 10.   [323] Ibid.   [324] Ibid.   [325] Ibid.

Throughout October the paper watched its predictions being carried out. Supporting Duff Cooper, a leading article affirmed that 'We have ourselves been urging for months past that British policy should be stated in unmistakable language. Had that been done earlier, Czechoslovakia would have been saved, Britain would have been spared the gnawing anxiety of these last days, and war would still have been averted.'[326] The Government's claims that the choice was between Munich or war were dismissed totally: 'The truth is that common and resolute action by Britain, France and Russia in the summer would not only have settled the Sudeten question peacefully and have preserved the integrity of Czechoslovakia but would have saved us from ever coming to the brink of war.'[327]

DAILY HERALD

The developing Czech crisis intruded itself almost immediately the summer began. The *Daily Herald*'s initial reaction to the Sudeten German demands was reserved. W. N. Ewer went to the Sudetenland around the middle of the month, and was impressed with the legitimacy of many Sudeten grievances. Despite the ostensible parity of languages in the area, he spoke to a Czech Post Office clerk at Eger in German and, obviously a foreigner, was replied to in French.[328] This and similar incidents made an impression upon him, and he wrote a tempered editorial page article on 22 July in which he admitted the Prague Government's good will but said that the immediate danger lay in the wild element and racial feeling on each side.[329]

Three days later the paper made Czech news a scoring-point against the Conservative Party and Press. There were 'Two Parties', a leading article explained, the Labour Party and the Bored Party. The latter affected a 'considerable fatigued indifference' to Czechoslovakia:

[326] *News Chronicle*, 4 Oct. 1938, 1st Leader, p. 10.
[327] *News Chronicle*, 7 Oct. 1938, 1st Leader, p. 10.
[328] Interview with W. N. Ewer, 28 Mar. 1967.
[329] *Daily Herald*, 22 July 1938, ed. art. by W. N. Ewer, p. 8.

That country is a very long way off—so runs the argument—it has a long unpronounceable name, and it had better be left to stew in its own juice.

Yet sensible people know that what happens in Czechoslovakia may well decide the whole issue of peace and war for our generation. And there is nothing boring about that.

As there are plenty of sensible people about, even the newspaper organs of the Bored Party feel obliged to report very fully the latest news from Czechoslovakia.

It must be puzzling to readers of those newspapers, having digested large headlines and long columns about Czechoslovakia on Page One, to learn on the Leader Page that Czechoslovakia is a matter of no interest to themselves or anybody else in the British Empire.[330]

The *Daily Herald* welcomed Lord Runciman's mission although it stressed that its unofficial nature must be understood by all parties and that 'no settlement which sacrifices future security for a temporary bridging of difficulties can be a good settlement'. One of the main components of Britain's long-range security interests was Russian co-operation with the rest of Europe; it was this which Hitler feared and would try to thwart.[331] A few days later the paper dismissed as foolish the cooling of the initial enthusiasm for the mission about to set off: 'It is too soon to talk of success. It is always too soon to talk of failure. For the time being it is wisest to wish the negotiations well and to abstain from either cheering or booing from the touch-line.'[332]

This optimistic line was pursued throughout August. In the middle of the month, Ewer wrote of the rumours of war sweeping Europe that 'nothing in politics is inevitable, war perhaps least of all. It is as foolish to think of a "European conflagration" as inevitable as to think of it as impossible.'[333] Indeed all of Ewer's German contacts indicated that Hitler had reached the end of his tether and even the enthusiasm of the young was beginning to flag. The grave question was to what means he would resort to restore himself; the impending Nuremberg rally seemed to be a logical indicator

[330] *Daily Herald*, 25 July 1938, Leader, p. 8.
[331] *Daily Herald*, 27 July 1938, Leader, p. 8.
[332] *Daily Herald*, 2 Aug. 1938, 1st Leader, p. 8.
[333] *Daily Herald*, 15 Aug. 1938, ed. art. by W. N. Ewer, p. 8.

of his intentions.[334] Would this at last be 'Twilight Over Hitler'?

This 'August attitude' ended abruptly with the month. The paper's comment on Sir John Simon's Lanark speech was strong and clear. War, if it came, would be the result of the deliberate action of some man or group of men. The only way to deter them, assuming they had not already decided upon war, was by strength clearly affirmed beforehand—affirmed, not threatened—thus precluding the possibility of the kind of miscalculation of 1914.[335] The following day the circumlocution was dropped and a leading article entitled 'Hitler's Choice' considered that stage to which the latest Czech proposal—the 'third basis' which granted almost all the Sudeten demands—had brought the issue: 'It has long been foreseen as inherent in the nature of things that such a moment must come. Conversations, mediation, and the rest of it are necessarily only a preparation for moments of decision. And moments of decision are necessarily moments of crisis.'[336] The decision, and the potential crisis, were Hitler's.

By 5 September, the world was still 'Waiting', but the terms had been still more clearly defined:

The crisis of the summer of 1938 has not been a Czech crisis or a Sudeten crisis. It has been a Hitler crisis. But for misgivings about this man, and so about the Government which he dictatorially controls, there would have been no doubt in anybody's mind that the Sudeten problem, difficult as it may be, would find a peaceful solution.[337]

Even now, however, the paper did not lay the crisis to Hitler's conscious planning, but rather to fear of his 'irresponsible emotional action'.[338]

On the eve of his speech at Nuremberg, the paper warned Hitler that if he chose war, he would find Britain united behind its commitments. The latest Czech offer would make the Sudetens the most handsomely treated minority in Europe, so there was no longer any reason to exercise the dogs of war.[339] The paper was generally satisfied with Hitler's speech

---

[334] *Daily Herald*, 26 Aug. 1938, ed. art., by W. N. Ewer. p. 8.
[335] *Daily Herald*, 29 Aug. 1938, Leader, p. 10.
[336] *Daily Herald*, 30 Aug. 1938, 1st Leader, p. 8.
[337] *Daily Herald*, 5 Sept. 1938, Leader, p. 8.   [338] Ibid.
[339] *Daily Herald*, 12 Sept. 1938, Leader, p. 8.

which showed moderation ('if such a word can be used to describe a speech which can create satisfaction only because it is less violent than had been feared') because at last he realized what his decision involved. 'No War: Hitler Is Ready To Bargain' the headline read; but in case he changed his mind even now, a leading article affirmed that 'British Opinion' was united and resolute still.[340]

By the following day the Sudeten Germans had withdrawn from the negotiations and the paper's breath was taken away by the sudden and perilous change in a situation which yesterday seemed hopeful in the extreme and today was 'almost out of hand'. There was still time, however, and that was the most important factor: 'The available time is desperately short, if indeed it still exists at all by the time these lines are in print. But, if it exists, the opportunity, slight though it may be, must be grasped.'[341] Stern warnings should be given to Hitler and, as the Labour Party Conference had resolved at Blackpool, Hitler should know that any attack on Czechoslovakia would be met by united British, French, and Russian resistance.[342]

It was in this spirit that the announcement of Chamberlain's flight to see Hitler was met. It was 'not only the bold but the supremely wise course' which, cutting through the formalities of diplomatic procedure, would firmly impress upon Hitler the firmness of British resolve. That he did not appreciate this had been a danger throughout the entire crisis, 'the seriousness of which cannot be overestimated'.[343]

In the days following Chamberlain's flight the lack of definite information hampered the formation of opinion. On 16 September the paper went so far as to say that 'It is doubtless right to concede the demands of justice, however they are put forward', although it did add 'But how much better it would have been if the peaceful nations had first of all decided what was just, offered it and stuck to it.'[344]

The following day a leading article, 'Waiting for News', expanded a principle stated briefly the day before, that

---

[340] *Daily Herald*, 13 Sept. 1938, Leader, p. 8.
[341] *Daily Herald*, 14 Sept. 1938, Leader, p. 8.   [342] Ibid.
[343] *Daily Herald*, 15 Sept. 1938, Leader, p. 8.
[344] *Daily Herald*, 16 Sept. 1938, Leader, p. 10.

peace at any price, as long as the Czechs paid for it, 'is a revolting conception'. The British people, therefore, 'should now be on guard against any attempt on the part of a clique of Great Powers to arrange a settlement between themselves and then hand it down to the Czechs with a "take-this-or-take-the-consequences" '.[345]

In the absence of news, however, Chamberlain was still given the benefit of the doubt, and if the talks resulted in the 'elimination of doubt from Herr Hitler's mind . . . they would be twenty times justified'.[346] It is curious that when their terms became generally known, the Anglo-French proposals stirred so little excitement in the *Daily Herald*. The paper's initial comment on 'The Plan' was to withhold judgement until more information was at hand and to reiterate its statement that peaceful change was good, although the right time had been long ago, before Hitler had introduced the threat of force.[347]

Indeed without commentary upon the Anglo-French proposals as the disillusioning link, the paper passed directly to resignation in the face of Chamberlain's heedless policy. The failure to bring the Soviet Union on to the scene was probably considered the Prime Minister's greatest failing and error.

In the fundamental matter of seeking not merely peace but justice, Mr. Chamberlain did not so much give up. He never really began to try.[348]

[And the following day]

All that can be known at this moment, and that with a dreadful clarity, is that in this one week a democracy has been surrendered by its friends, and that British influence on world affairs has been dealt one further almost fatal blow.[349]

Without much conviction the paper insisted that if Hitler demanded more at Godesberg, then Chamberlain must pose a British-French-Russian front by way of resistance.[350]

Public opinion had hardened since Berchtesgaden, the paper stated, as Chamberlain set off for Godesberg, and

[345] *Daily Herald*, 17 Sept. 1938, Leader, p. 8.   [346] Ibid.
[347] *Daily Herald*, 20 Sept. 1938, Leader, p. 8.
[348] *Daily Herald*, 22 Sept. 1938, Leader, p. 8.
[349] *Daily Herald*, 23 Sept. 1938, Leader, p. 10.   [350] Ibid.

although on his first visit the Prime Minister 'went to negotiate and stayed to acquiesce', such a performance could not be repeated in the light of subsequent events.[351] And indeed on 26 September the paper headlined that 'Hitler's Brutal New Demands are Rejected By Czechs'. A strong leading article stated that Hitler's clear ambition was to dominate Europe and the Sudeten dispute was only a ploy in that greater game, but it was crippled by a theoretical ending.[352] The following day the 'In authoritative quarters' statement was printed on the front page.[353]

On the 28th, as war seemed imminent, a long page-wide editorial 'By the Editor of the "Daily Herald" ' proclaimed: 'Here Are the Real Facts'. The argument was that Britain, France and Russia would continue to work for peace and if war came it would be Hitler's responsibility.[354] The paper's reaction to the Munich conference, then, was reserved in the extreme. The basic issue remained unchanged: whether or not force would be the arbiter of world affairs. And still Chamberlain had not brought the Soviets in. Or the Czechs for that matter.

At this stage in a crisis which threatened to involve the world in war before the week was out, anything which enables negotiations for a reasonable settlement of differences to continue is clearly desirable. . . . But although the relief is universal, it does not in any way absolve us from the necessity of continued clear analysis of the facts.[355]

As he negotiated at Munich, a leading article urged Chamberlain to 'Stand Firm'.[356]

SUNDAY TIMES

During the last six months of 1938 the *Sunday Times* carried to the greatest extremes what is today thought of as the classic prototype of the policy of 'appeasement'. Lord Kemsley was convinced that if he could talk to Hitler personally, war

[351] *Daily Herald*, 24 Sept. 1938, Leader, p. 8.
[352] *Daily Herald*, 26 Sept. 1938, Leader, p. 10.
[353] *Daily Herald*, 27 Sept. 1938, p. 1.
[354] *Daily Herald*, 28 Sept. 1938, Editorial, p. 8.
[355] *Daily Herald*, 29 Sept. 1938, 2-column Leader, p. 8.
[356] *Daily Herald*, 30 Sept. 1938, Leader, p. 8.

could be averted. Pending this conversation, it was incumbent upon his paper to smooth the troubled European waters with printer's ink instead of oil. In the editor, Hadley, he found a generally like-thinking and at any rate agreeable agent. But it was Scrutator who set the pace for the paper's policy, which was a kind of moderate optimism basically sympathetic to Germany.

Every event or question could be interpreted within this framework. The Anglo-German Payments Agreement was welcomed since 'it has turned a clash into a pact and given a fillip to the further talks', and where there was talk there was hope.[357] The problem of the Jews was one which deserved world attention and sympathy and one which Germany, if she wanted to be accepted as an equal in world councils, might help alleviate. But regardless, 'the gauge of the moral pressure that we can bring to bear on Germany is not the violence of denunciation, but in the efforts that we make to help the victims.'[358] Once minor irritants were out of the way, the harvest of appeasement could be reaped in the form of a better and safer life for all mankind. There were 'fruits that are ripening to be picked—an agreement for humane rules of air war, perhaps a measure of disarmament, the diversion of our toil and treasure from the ways of destruction to those that make for happiness'.[359]

Minor irritants were thus irksome; Czechoslovakia was potentially a major irritant, and was itself objectionable into the bargain. 'Most of us now recognize it as one of the mistakes of the peace', Scrutator wrote, 'that the Austrian Empire was broken up'.[360] For this reason, the Runciman mission, which would hopefully take the Czech problem out of the domain of military strategy, was most welcome. Scrutator was not blind to objections to this attitude, but had no doubt whatever about their error:

It may be that even with an independent Czechoslovakia there are larger ambitions that Germany can pursue that might later bring her into conflict with real British interests. But in the meantime we shall have killed once and for all the idea that the totalitarian states

[357] *Sunday Times*, 3 July 1938, 1st Leader, p. 16.
[358] *Sunday Times*, 10 July 1938, Scrutator, p. 19.
[359] *Sunday Times*, 31 July 1938, Scrutator, p. 12.   [360] Ibid.

and the democracies cannot co-operate for the common good, and
we shall have learned by excluding the arbitrament of force in
Czechoslovakia how it can be excluded elsewhere.[361]

Scrutator was aware of one important factor in Government
thinking, that of the role of the Dominions. Australian Ministers' statements about Dominion independence might ultimately, Scrutator wrote, 'have a greater influence on history
than anything said last week in Czechoslovakia, or even done
on the Manchurian borders'.[362]

The paper gave a weak greeting to Sir John Simon's Lanark
speech, stressing that he went, 'as he was bound to go, neither
farther nor less far than the Prime Minister had gone in
Parliament on 24 March last. He expressly referred to that
warning; specifically reaffirmed it; and subjoined that there
was nothing to add or vary in its contents.' Appeasement was
still His Majesty's Government's real policy. This did not mean,
the leading article added somewhat weakly, that Britain would
never fight. 'Her arms will never be used for aggressive purposes. But she is making herself strong in order that she may be
"a safe and effective friend of peace".'[363]

August, said a leading article on 4 September, was always
the 'danger-month' as far as European war was concerned, and
September now opened 'with a rather better prospect than
August did'.[364] Still, the Berlin correspondent reported that
he could never remember 'greater anxiety, bewilderment and
uncertainty in the German capital'.[365]

Even so sympathetic an analysis could not ignore the Germans'
inclination for queering their own pitch by constantly widen-
ing each issue: 'If the rulers of Germany did not desire
peace, if they insisted on seeking a position from which they
could dominate all Europe, then the world would know where
they stood and the challenge would be taken up. But we are

---

[361] Ibid.   [362] *Sunday Times*, 14 Aug. 1938, Scrutator, p. 12.

[363] *Sunday Times*, 28 Aug. 1938, 1st Leader, p. 12. See also ibid., Dipl. Corr.,
p. 13, for discussion of the anxiety felt in London.

[364] *Sunday Times*, 4 Sept. 1938, 1st Leader, p. 14.

[365] *Sunday Times*, 4 Sept. 1938, Berlin Corr., p. 11. He stated that all eyes were
now on Hitler but no one knew what he would do. A Special Correspondent
(ibid., p. 13) stated that 'If the German leaders arrive at the conclusion that
armed intervention in Czechoslovakia would not result in a quick victory and
could not be kept a localized conflict, there is every reason to believe that peace
will be preserved.'

still entitled to hope that wiser counsels may triumph, and that
no such fiery ordeal will be forced onto much-enduring nations.'[366] Just a week later, in the shadow of Hitler's Nuremberg speech the following day, the paper had to admit that
the Czech Government in Prague had already given the Sudetens much more than Henlein had claimed he wanted when he
was in London, and still there was no settlement. Indeed,
Germany prepared for war. 'No Power', a leading article
stated, 'could make more apparent preparations before launching a war; in fact, none even has made so many. These facts
are ominous and alarming enough. Nobody will want to
overstress them. Nobody can afford to disregard them.'

Britain's duty remained to work for peace; but a new note
crept into the *Sunday Times*'s prescription:

So far as Great Britain is concerned, the pathway is becoming plain.
To the limit of hope, and beyond it, she will persist in her mediatory
efforts for peace. But if Germany challenges Europe by launching an
attack on Czechoslovakia, then the warning declaration made by
Mr. Chamberlain last March and re-emphasised by Sir John Simon
at Lanark will be followed up.

If German uncertainty as to British policy had been a factor
in precipitating war in 1914, which the paper doubted, such
should not be the case now in 1938. Despite this apparent
firmness, a background article on the Czech crisis by Virginia
Cowles was headlined 'Czechs and Germans Ready to Part'
which was in fact the contrary sense of the article. Miss Cowles
objected and insisted that the title be changed or the article withdrawn. The piece was printed, headed 'The Czechs On Guard'.[367]

On 18 September, with, as a leading article put it, the
'Issue Still In Suspense', the paper adopted the stoical attitude
that the nation must be 'watchful and patient; to hope for the
best and be prepared for the worst, to close the nation's ranks,
and to avoid promoting disunion by flying irresponsible kites
or falling in with reckless agitations'.[368] But Scrutator indulged
some high kite-flying on the same page.

'The Czechs', he wrote, 'have made the great mistake in the

---

[366] Ibid., 1st Leader, p. 14.
[367] *Sunday Times*, 11 Sept. 1938, p. 14. Interview with Virginia Cowles, 4 Apr.
1967.   [368] *Sunday Times*, 18 Sept. 1938, 1st Leader, p. 16.

past of relying on foreign alliances for their liberties rather than
on the great Masaryk's advice to be just to their minorities.'
There were just as surely moderates among the Henleinists
as there were jingoes among the Czechs. And 'If France and
Britain are to sacrifice their youngest and best and imperil
all that modern war can imperil in consequence of happenings
in Czechoslovakia, they have a right to lay down their conditions, and Czechoslovakia a duty to respect those conditions.'[369] These 'conditions' were, of course, the Anglo-French
proposals. The following week the onus was shifted from the
Czechs—who by this time had accepted the proposals—to
France who had used Czechoslovakia 'as a pawn in her diplomatic game of encircling Germany with a ring of States that
would bar her expansion . . .'.[370] This view was supported
in an editorial page article by Lord Elton.[371] But the threat
still came from Germany, and the Berlin correspondent's
report was more to the point: 'nobody should be misled into
believing that Germany will not be ready to march whenever
Hitler issues the order. She will do whatever she is ordered to do,
because the German masses have been trained "to do their
duty".'[372]

Of all the major British Press, the *Sunday Times* gave Munich
the most cordial and uncritical greeting. 'Atticus' wrote:
'And now I am going home to take all my books on Europe,
place them in my garden trench and have it filled in.'[373]
The leading article, 'The Morrow of Peace', did draw a
'moral' from the crisis: that neither Britain nor France were
sufficiently ready to fight. But a new dawn, in which fighting
might never again be necessary, seemed to have broken across
Europe, mainly thanks to the Prime Minister. Still, three
other leaders were involved, and in Hitler, the paper stated,
'we must acknowledge the courage that dared to go back on an
ultimatum—a very difficult step, and not least so for a dictator'.[374] For Scrutator, the lesson of the danger of the crisis was
that there was 'a natural division of interest between East and

[369] Ibid., Scrutator, p. 16.
[370] *Sunday Times*, 25 Sept. 1938, Scrutator, p. 16.
[371] Ibid., ed. art. by The Rt. Hon. Lord Elton, p. 18.
[372] Ibid., Berlin Corr., p. 12.
[373] *Sunday Times*, 2 Oct. 1938, Atticus, p. 13.
[374] Ibid., Leader, p. 14.

West Europe', and where East met West, there were supposedly impregnable fortifications on both sides. 'Why not
recognize the facts of geography?'[375]

OBSERVER

The last half of 1938 saw a major change in the *Observer*'s
attitude towards Germany: a change which stands as a monument to Garvin's independence and honesty. In the spring and
early summer, no one in the British Press could match Garvin
in contumely for Czechoslovakia. He continued to insist that
the May Crisis had no basis in fact, but that 'the explosive
possibilities of the circumstances' had been seized upon by the
Czech Government to involve the Western democracies in
Czechoslovakia's racial confusion.[376] Hitler was considered to
be pursuing a policy of 'reasoned amendment' to the Czech
proposals.[377] At the end of July these proposals were deemed
late in coming, and 'more elaborate than satisfying'.[378]

Garvin greeted the Runciman mission as an 'original and
handy idea' of Chamberlain's, but felt that it would do little
to change the situation. The situation was such that it could
only be made clearer: the alternatives were a system of racial
areas or of mixed provinces. The latter had proved unworkable.

Garvin openly discounted the massive German military
manœuvres in August, and even predicted that 'by the end
of this autumn there will be a better chance of establishing
world peace for a generation'.[379] Wadsworth in Berlin seemed
to concur with this optimistic attitude.[380] Garvin set out the
Observer's threefold policy: to prevent world war altogether;
to postpone it to the utmost; and to win it if it came.[381] At
the end of August, he stressed that the British people must be as
steady as a rock during the following ten days—but prospects
were hopeful:

For well-weighed reasons, we have advised our readers to reject
completely the horrific rumours of a coming German onslaught on

[375] Ibid., Scrutator, p. 14.
[376] *Observer*, 10 July 1938, Garvin, p. 16. See also *Observer*, 28 Aug. 1938,
Garvin, p. 13.   [377] *Observer*, 24 July 1938, Garvin, p. 14.
[378] *Observer*, 31 July 1938, Garvin, p. 10.
[379] *Observer*, 21 Aug. 1938, Garvin, p. 12.
[380] Ibid., Berlin Corr., p. 17.   [381] Ibid., Garvin, p. 12.

the mixed Republic and of a world-crash in September. But if we shun the panic-mongers we are far from the school of Pangloss. Our conviction that peace can be saved does not mean that it can be saved without a hitch.[382]

Sir John Simon's speech at Lanark was not quoted with very great approval; Garvin hoped that it would be read in Germany as tranquillizing as well as impressive.[383] Britain's proper role in this controversy was to hold the balance between the disputants: 'to trim the scales; to hold a fair balance between Czechs and Sudetens in the jumbled Republic manufactured at Versailles'.[384]

On 4 September, Garvin expressly rejected the 'demonic theory' of German policy: 'We have utterly and absolutely declined to believe that Herr Hitler is a melodramatic monster with a deficiency of brains—that he is either mad or bad to the degree of precipitating an unnecessary world-war with open eyes, by a violent onslaught on Czechoslovakia.'[385] A week later, however, on the eve of Hitler's tensely awaited Nuremberg speech, the extensive Czech concessions had changed the situation considerably: 'in these changed circumstances an armed attack by the Greater Reich upon Czechoslovakia—though we still decline to believe that Herr Hitler himself has even contemplated it—would be without exception and by far the greatest crime that was ever committed in the world's history'.[386] If the speech did not turn out to be a declaration of war, it was no greater contribution to peace either.[387] Chamberlain's decision to go to Hitler was exactly right.[388] A week later, however, two visits had only produced two ultimata and no concessions. Now Britons must steel their hearts, and vow that life and goods would stand as nothing beside the issues now at stake: 'The Nazi power last week threw off the mask before the British Prime Minister and demanded in effect his total capitulation on their own soil. They counted that their armed advantage had made them already the masters of the earth. Not yet.'[389]

[382] *Observer*, 28 Aug. 1938, Garvin, p. 12.　　　　[383] Ibid.　　　　[384] Ibid.
[385] *Observer*, 4 Sept. 1938, Garvin, p. 12.
[386] *Observer*, 11 Sept. 1938, Garvin, p. 14.
[387] *Observer*, 18 Sept. 1938, Garvin, p. 14.　　　　[388] Ibid.
[389] *Observer*, 25 Sept. 1938, Garvin, p. 14.

Munich was greeted as a great event, demonstrating Hitler's 'softened and more genial humour' and 'that healing statesmanship reappears in him'.[390] The crisis had underlined Britain's unpreparedness, and henceforward, along with work for Anglo-German and Anglo-Italian agreement, Britain must rearm.[391] The *Observer*'s change to the anti-Nazi ranks was now under way. This change began in early September 1938 and was completed in March 1939; Garvin's article on 9 October 1938 was a midway piece. Hitler had boasted and threatened at Nuremberg, Garvin stated, because he now had the most powerful military system in the world. Thus in this case the threat of force had triumphed. 'As regards the Sudetenland, the Reich had a very cogent case. But the merits were one thing; the procedure by measured ultimatum quite another.'[392] Had France's and Britain's organization been equal to their principles, 'had their defence been as strong as their words, the world's recent ordeal would not have arisen at all'.[393]

Garvin continued to defend Munich, however, as the only possible course in the circumstances,[394] and to support the Government by questioning what different policy the Opposition would have pursued.[395] During January 1939 Garvin wrote about the Government's plans for National Service (which he considered inadequate) and about Britain's air strength. We shall see the full strength of his anti-Nazi conviction when we come to the occupation of Prague.

DAILY EXPRESS AND DAILY MAIL

Both papers shared a common Czecho-phobia which wholly pre-determined their attitudes, and makes them of little interest. Britain should not become involved in Europe, and certainly not over Czechoslovakia, the spawn of the Versailles system. To this end, the Runciman mission, Chamberlain's initiatives, and Munich itself were all welcomed. The *Daily Mail* combined this policy with a continued insistence upon the necessity for British armaments.

---

[390] *Observer*, 2 Oct. 1938, Garvin, p. 11. [391] See ibid., Ledear, p. 11.
[392] *Observer*, 9 Oct. 1938, Garvin, p. 18. [393] Ibid.
[394] *Observer*, 1 Jan. 1939, p. 12.
[395] *Observer*, 18 Dec. 1938, Garvin, p. 12.

Nineteen thirty-eight was the worst pre-war year for German Jewry. We have seen that the Olympic Games in Berlin in the summer of 1936 had probably spared the Jews a pogrom after the assassination of the Nazi leader in Switzerland in February by a Jugoslav Jew. Many observers feared that the Jews would suffer doubly hard once the Games were over, and some even thought that the theme of the September Nuremberg Rally would be anti-Semitism again as it had been in 1935. But the 'Olympic Pause' had continued, and in 1937 Nazi attention shifted to the Christian churches. The cruel and vicious treatment of Jews in Vienna by the Austrian Nazis during the time of the Anschluss was widely reported in the British Press— Gedye's dispatches to the *Daily Telegraph* were particularly memorable—but the persecutors were now Austrian, not German, and the situation militated against moderation: 'While it has been possible to devise measures of relief for Jewry in the Third Reich over a period of five years,' Professor Norman Bentwich wrote in the *Manchester Guardian*, 'now measures have to be devised to meet the relentless pressure in a period of months.'[396]

The 'June Days' in Berlin in 1938 saw a recrudescence of active anti-Semitism. A correspondent in *The Times* regretted the change that seemed to be coming over German policy towards the Jews:

Since 1933 the policy of the Reich towards the Jews has been summed up as emigration or annihilation; but some measure of decency was observed in enabling the Jews to prepare for emigration, to take some fraction of their property with them when they emigrated, and to eke out livelihood in the restricted callings which they were still able to practice.[397]

The *Kristallnacht* on 10 November 1938 drew the unanimous condemnation of the British Press, and sealed the failure of the crude Nazi attempts, through Schacht and the Evian conference on refugees, to turn the Jews into economic hostages.

The British Press's treatment of Nazi anti-Semitism was affected by a variety of factors, of which three were perhaps the most important. First, although there were no illusions

---

[396] *Manchester Guardian*, 13 Apr. 1938, ed. art. by Prof. N. Bentwich, p. 9. See also *Manchester Guardian*, 11 May 1938, p. 11.

[397] *The Times*, 18 June 1938, ed. art. by a Correspondent, p. 15.

about its injustice and brutality, there was a widespread recognition that, until November 1938 at least, the Jews in Germany were probably 'better' treated than Jews anywhere else in central and eastern Europe. The anti-Jewish legislation in Germany was attenuated in practice, and emigration was always possible although it became increasingly difficult for those without money or influence.

There was, second, a widespread sentiment that anti-Semitism, repugnant as it was to the British liberal conscience, was one of the central dogmas of the Nazi faith and must be accepted as such. As long as the majority of the German people supported Nazism and as long as Nazi anti-Semitism was legislative and non-violent, then Britain had no right or obligation to interfere. Hitler was generally thought to hold three things most seriously: his Versailles revisionism, his anti-Bolshevism, and the Aryan principle. That this was so, and that it did not extend to his anti-Christian activities, is seen in an article 'By a Student of German Church Affairs' in the *Sunday Times* in July 1937:

One must distinguish, clearly however, between the dragooning to which the Christian Churches are subjected and the persecution to which the German Jews have to submit. The anti-Jewish policy of the Nazi Government is a logical consequence of National-Socialist faith as embodied and set forth in *Mein Kampf*. The campaign against the Churches is a matter of tactics.[398]

Also underlying the British Press's attitude was a fundamental inability to understand the potential depths of Nazi brutality. In June 1938 the *Daily Telegraph* stated frankly that:

It is impossible to believe that the best elements of the German people can 'sympathize with a plan that aims at the extermination of a people who have lived as good German citizens and have contributed much to the higher culture as well as to the commercial importance of Germany. Nor is it possible to see in the excesses of the Austrian Nazis any reflection of the tolerant spirit of the Austrian people. The Reich will have to find some compromise by which the hundreds of thousands of Jews in the country will be accorded the right to live, for the rapid extermination by a decreed starvation

[398] *Sunday Times*, 4 July 1937, ed. art. 'By a Student of German Church Affairs', p. 8.

of people against whom is alleged no crime but their race and religion can hardly be contemplated.[399]

Unable to believe that the Nazis would allow anti-Jewish legislation and sentiment to 'exterminate' the Jews in Germany by excluding them from all economic life and thus starving them, the British Press was unable even to conceive what sinister meaning 'extermination' would assume in a few years' time. Even the *Manchester Guardian* accepted the Nazi Government's claim to be uninvolved in issuing orders for the Night of Crystal: 'No, but the Government's faithful servants carried them out while others, equally acquainted with its mind, looked on.'[400]

[399] *Daily Telegraph*, 28 June, 1938, 1st Leader, p. 14.
[400] *Manchester Guardian*, 14 Nov. 1938, 1st Leader, p. 8.

5

1939:
INTO WAR

THAT 1939 opened peacefully was about the only thing to be said in its favour. The great hopes attached to the Anglo-German Declaration Chamberlain had taken away from Munich were mocked by the Vienna Award which actually settled the disposition of the Czech territory. An atmosphere of suspicion and foreboding pervaded all the British Press; Hitler had gone to the limits of his 'justifiable' territorial claims. The worry of those who had counselled acquiescence until now was that Hitler would prove their critics right by some precipitate action. Barrington-Ward expressed this in his leading article on Hitler's 30th January speech. Hitler, he wrote, by continuing to trot out the old grievances against the Treaty of Versailles, was flailing an almost dead horse. The Versailles grievances had already been used to cover a multitude of sins: they were not, after all,

. . . inexhaustible assets and they have been swallowed up in the incorporation of Austria and the Sudetenland in the territory of the Reich. The great risk which the other signatories of the Versailles settlement have taken in assenting to its revision is that their action should be attributed to weakness or fear rather than to the reluctance to resist action and demands which, even while they seemed to challenge and invite resistance, could not be rebutted with an easy conscience. The great question before Europe now—and hanging over Herr Hitler's speech yesterday—is whether the experiences of 1938 have been tragically misinterpreted and fatally misread by those to whom they have brought the national gains celebrated yesterday.[1]

The tension was suddenly broken by rumours and reports that Hitler had prepared his next blow to fall in the West. They reached high enough and were given sufficient credence

The Times, 31 Jan. 1939, 1st Leader, p. 13, quoted in Hist. Times, iv. 954.

for Halifax to instruct the British Ambassador in Washington
to inform Roosevelt lest America be caught unawares by some
German action. On 23 January, at the same time as this
instruction, Halifax lunched with Dawson and told him of the
rumours.[2] The same afternoon Dawson noted in his diary
that Iverach McDonald had returned from the Foreign
Office with 'rather over-categorical forecasts of German
intentions. I kept them to myself, but they were disturbing,
and people began to ring up again to ask whether it was safe
to go abroad.'[3]

The rumours persisted for several days mainly behind the
scenes. None of the British newspapers gave them significant
publicity lest a war scare be created in Britain, and a situation
be created similar to that over Czechoslovakia in May 1938.
Already the rumours and their effect had had a harmful influence. As Carleton Greene wrote to the *Sunday Times* on the day
before Hitler's speech, 'Herr Hitler will be reassured by the
nervousness over the dangers of war which is apparent in the
outside world. This nervousness he will be inclined to interpret
as a sign of lack of confidence and confusion of purposes
among potential opponents. In his opinion, this must make
it easier for the Reich to pursue its own aims.'[4] *The Times*
printed a report from Holburn in Berlin, in which he stated
that what indicators there were of the trend in Germany all
pointed towards the increasing isolation of the forces of
moderation.

A period of very active foreign policy is therefore foreseen, although
whether its chief direction will be westwards or eastwards cannot
at the moment be said. . . . Eastern Europe presents a line of less
resistance and might be expected to absorb German energies in the
near future, particularly if it is the Reich's aim to make sure of its
supplies of food and raw materials before exposing itself to a conflict
with the Western Powers.[5]

When the rumours were at their height, the *Daily Telegraph*
printed a report from Berlin to the effect that the current

---

[2] *Hist. Times*, iv. 954. See also *DBFP*, 3rd, iv. No. 5.
[3] *Dawson Papers*, Diary 1939, 23 Jan.
[4] *Sunday Times*, 29 Jan. 1939, Berlin Corr., p. 17.
[5] *The Times*, 24 Jan. 1939, Berlin Corr., p. 12.

indications were that Germany's interests lay in the south and west rather than in the east.[6]

As early as 14 January Voigt had written that Germany would become 'passive' in the east and 'active' in the west, since eastern expansion was looked on as inevitable, and could be left to time—with occasional proddings, to be sure. Voigt himself thought that consolidation of an Axis position in the Western Mediterranean, astride France's and Britain's communication lines, was the German plan; Lambert supported this view.[7] Voigt, indeed, believed that the invasion of Bohemia in March was a 'consolation' for the frustrated Western European and/or Mediterranean action, for in these areas the attitude of the Western Powers had been 'sufficiently firm and their rearmament sufficiently advanced' to show Hitler that the initiative was 'no longer in his hands'. Unfortunately, it was not the case that the initiative was passing into the West's hands, 'for they do not think in terms of initiatives at all, at least not in Europe'.

In an article on 'The International Situation' on 11 March, Voigt wrote that British and French resolution had foiled German plans against the west:

The 'improvement' in the situation that is being so widely advertised is not so much an improvement in the situation itself as in the immediate outlook. The country has skirted another major crisis and has done so without the knowledge of the public as a whole.

The nature of the crisis was accurately indicated in the *Manchester Guardian* on January 27. A number of reports were current at the time—and even earlier—with regard to a German threat to Holland and an alternative, or subsidiary, threat to Switzerland. These reports were true. . . . The British Cabinet took a grave view of the situation.

Two warnings were given on behalf of this country—the first by Mr. Chamberlain on February 6, the second by Lord Halifax on February 23. Both warnings made it plain that this country would support France in all circumstances if she were attacked, and both warnings were intimately related to the immediate international situation.[8]

[6] *Daily Telegraph*, 27 Jan. 1939, Berlin Corr., p. 13.
[7] *Manchester Guardian*, 14 Jan. 1939, Dipl. Corr., p. 15, and 16 Jan. 1939, Berlin Corr., p. 12.
[8] *Manchester Guardian*, 11 Mar. 1939, Dipl. Corr., p. 13. There is no evidence, in *DBFP*, of such representations; the fear of action in the west was pretty well put to rest by the beginning of February.

Although these rumours were widespread and persistent, we now know from German documents that there was in fact nothing afoot in Germany. The only policy being pursued was that of wooing Poland. It is clear today that the crisis in March arose suddenly out of the issue of Slovak separatism; Hitler was unable to resist the opportunity it afforded him to acquire more territory on what he thought would be the cheap. In the state of tension existing in January, great attention was centred by the British Press upon Hitler's annual address to the Reichstag on 30 January.

'A guarded and somewhat puzzled sense of relief, or of respite', McDonald wrote to *The Times* on 1 February, 'seems to be the first response to Herr Hitler's Reichstag speech.'[9] The *Daily Telegraph* was not unfavourably impressed by the speech. 'Polemical in tone much of it certainly was,' the paper stated, 'but allowance has to be made for Herr Hitler's temperamental tendency to be polemical.' Indeed, 'on the whole, it is perhaps not too over-optimistic to read into Herr Hitler's latest utterance the promise of better things to come'.[10] On 9 February Winston Churchill contributed an article stating that he found insufficient justification for the 'ripples of optimism' spreading in Europe since Hitler's speech.[11]

The *Manchester Guardian* found at least something positive to say for the speech:

There is one thing that must be said about Herr Hitler: he rarely disappoints his detractors. His speech to the Reichstag last night on the sixth anniversary of his accession to power was in every way typical of the man and his policy, though set in a minor key. There was the usual historical preface, a kind of apology for the Nazi party, but now the myth has grown in Hitler's mind until it is almost unrecognizable, and Communists, Jews, and Bishops are inextricably mingled in a maze of passionate prejudice. There were snatches of his naive and astonishing philosophy, his belief in 'character' and 'vision' rather than 'knowledge' and 'intelligence', which means, in fact, a belief in those qualities which he imagines himself to have rather than in those which even he knows himself to

---

[9] *The Times*, 1 Feb. 1939, Dipl. Corr., p. 14.
[10] *Daily Telegraph*, 31 Jan. 1939, 1st Leader, p. 12. The subheading is 'A Reinforcement of the Hopes of Peace'. The speech was reported, ibid., Berlin Corr., p. 13, and given textually on p. 17.
[11] *Daily Telegraph*, 9 Feb. 1939, ed. art. by Winston Churchill, p. 14.

lack. There was the usual talent for self-deception, or, perhaps, wilful refusal to see any point of view except Germany's. . . . There were hints of that dangerous mysticism which gives him confidence in his 'divine mission'.[12]

Voigt wrote that although Hitler had probably never spoken so calmly in public as in this speech, 'he was never more fanatical in the substance of what he said'. This is an overstatement, though a defensible one.[13]

Considering what many thought it could have been— anything including announcement of a *Blitzkrieg* upon Holland or even Switzerland—the speech did indeed bring respite and relief. Very shortly in its wake the attempts at economic appeasement, which had been adopted by the Government as the best and most practical way to ameliorate conditions and prepare the way for a settlement, were once again set in motion. As early as 4 January Gordon-Lennox had written that 'Evidence of the British Government's determination to employ economic means for procuring a measure of appeasement in Europe will become apparent in the next few weeks.' Examples of this prediction were seen not only in Montagu Norman's visit to Berlin and a projected trade mission visit by Sir Robert Hudson, but also in Chamberlain's visit to Rome.[14]

February was a quiet month for news from Germany. Hitler seemed once again to have withdrawn to Berchtesgaden as was his wont after great exertion. Plans for the Hudson visit were given considerable attention, and the crisis in March developed as suddenly in the British Press as it developed on the spot, taking everyone by surprise, including the opportunist at Berchtesgaden.

THE OCCUPATION OF PRAGUE

THE TIMES

By the middle of March, the European situation looked decidedly hopeful. The fears of German action in the west

---

[12] *Manchester Guardian*, 31 Jan. 1939, 1st Leader, p. 10.

[13] *Manchester Guardian*, 31 Jan. 1939, Dipl. Corr., p. 11. Voigt wrote of the speech's attacks on Duff Cooper, Eden, and Churchill, that 'Hitler has renewed his own attempt to influence the character of future British Governments.' The speech as a whole altogether confirmed 'what has been evident for some time— the triumph of National Socialism in its most radical form'.

[14] *Daily Telegraph*, 4 Jan. 1939, Dipl. Corr., p. 11.

had proved misplaced, and the departure of the British industrial mission for Berlin, on the 13th, seemed to bode well for the first fruits of the Anglo-German Declaration of Munich and for the slowly gathering impetus for economic appeasement. Not too much could be expected from the Trade Minister's talks, but any action was better than sitting still, and even if little came of these specific meetings, the idea of conversations and negotiations was seen as a possible safety-valve for a country which, as Hitler himself had stated, must export or die. The Diplomatic Correspondent wrote that diplomatists were, indeed, trying to analyse 'the more cheerful feeling which arose as welcome as the crocuses last week'.[15]

The problems of the Slovak claim for autonomy did not seem very serious. *The Times* was inclined to be sympathetic with the central Government which, although it was taking 'drastic measures',[16] was doing so to suppress not autonomy, but separatism. The Slovaks and Carpatho-Ukrainians had taken the easy course of appealing over Prague's head to Berlin; this was unfortunate at any rate but also stood in the way of the central Government's attempts to secure national unity and thus be able to take up Hitler's promise of a guarantee of the new frontiers, contingent upon their consolidation.[17] Holburn in Berlin, however, saw the familiar pattern of a propaganda build-up, as in September 1938, repeating itself, although on the 13th it was still fair to conclude that Hitler had not yet decided what to do, or that his decision required one or two days' preparation.[18] It was necessary to remember that the German pressure for *Lebensraum* was constant and that accordingly 'it may well be in the view of the Reich that the present crisis, which took Berlin by surprise, must be made the occasion of finally clearing up in one way or another the difficulties that have developed since Munich'.[19]

The next day Holburn speculated that the Reich would

---

[15] *The Times*, 13 Mar. 1939, Dipl. Corr., p. 14. Among the reasons for the better feeling, he mentioned British determination in rearmament, Roosevelt's policy, the sale of American aeroplanes to Britain and France, and the economic recovery in South-Eastern Europe.

[16] *The Times*, 11 Mar. 1939, Prague Corr., p. 12.

[17] Ibid., 2nd Leader, p. 13.

[18] *The Times*, 13 Mar. 1939, Berlin Corr., p. 13. See also *The Times*, 11 Mar. 1939, Berlin Corr., p. 12.   [19] Ibid.

probably prefer to see three independent states, none strong
enough to survive independently without close relations with
Germany, for if such were the case, 'the territories of Czechoslovakia would be a bridge rather than a barrier to the extension of German political and commercial influence in Eastern
Europe'.[20] The paper's Special Correspondent, who had
recently travelled through Carpatho-Ukraine (which had, as
he wrote, a total population about equal to that of Norfolk),
felt that some kind of change would have to be made, for
'Judged by any standards the frontiers were absurd.' But the
paper itself was rather disappointed by the fact that not only
Germany, but also Hungary and Poland, were stirring up the
uneasy situation. The paper complained in a leading article,
'Czechoslovakia Again', that

It might naturally have been supposed that the German Government would have supported the forces of law and order in the
State, for whose new foundation and Constitution it is so largely
responsible. But in fact, whatever the attitude of the Reich Government itself, its friends and agents and the Vienna broadcasts have
steadily aided and abetted the promoters of separatism in the
chief autonomous province of the Czechoslovak Republic.[21]

When reports began rushing in during the early morning
hours of 15 March, that German troops were marching into
Prague, it was only possible to do two things: to register
outrage and shock, and to make it clear that no resistance
would be offered to this particular move. It had not been
expected 'that Herr Hitler would immediately conduct his
diplomacy once more by threat of force', but 'for the moment,
British, like French, opinion can only register their reprobation
of the ruthless treatment of a small, industrious, and friendly
nation, for the establishment of whose independence their
efforts in the War were jointly responsible. That work is now
undone, and the fact that in this case it never rested on very
secure foundations does not diminish regret at its disappear-
ance.'[22] Once again the action was considered foolish on
Hitler's part, for force, 'to put it on no other ground, was
entirely unnecessary even for the purpose, which he had

---

[20] *The Times*, 14 Mar. 1939, Berlin Corr., p. 15.
[21] Ibid., 1st Leader, p. 15.
[22] *The Times*, 15 Mar. 1939, 1st Leader, p. 15.

no doubt cherished all along, of establishing his influence over the whole area of the Republic of Czechoslovakia—which ceased to exist yesterday'. He would, eventually, have inevitably gained hegemony in the east, but had now given the Western Powers clear warning:

Herr Hitler's influence is dominant in Central Europe, as it was bound in the end to become, is proving itself consistently hostile to political freedom as the Western democracies understand it. They on their part can only continue with increased energy to look to their own security—not because they wish to prevent the normal growth of a strong Germany, but because more and more the Nazi Reich appears to be determined not only to expand to its full stature, but also to extend its domination wherever the weakness of other nations may seem to make extension possible.[23]

Hitler had thrown over his endless declarations that the union of the German people was his sole ambition, and repudiated his denials that he had aggressive designs on any other people. The Diplomatic correspondent wrote that the most recent German assurance had been 'only a few hours old' when the invasion began.[24]

The foundations of the policy of appeasement were forever washed away. It had been the correct, the only policy to follow until now,[25] but 'The invasion, occupation, and annexation of Bohemia-Moravia are notice to the world that German policy no longer seeks the protection of a moral case.'[26] Hitler's earlier coups had at least the justification 'that they brought unification to a great people from whom it had long been withheld'[27] and the tenet of racial union had 'at least seemed to be genuinely held, but it has now been cynically discarded'.[28] For this new invasion, 'no defence of any kind, no pretext of the slightest plausibility, can be offered for the violent extinction of Czech independence'.[29] The purpose was only too clear, and was 'more and more revealed as sheer aggrandisement—the brutal domination of other

---

[23] Ibid.   [24] *The Times*, 16 Mar. 1939, Dipl. Corr., p. 16.
[25] See *The Times*, 18 Mar. 1939, 1st Leader, p. 13.
[26] *The Times*, 16 Mar. 1939, 1st Leader, p. 17.
[27] *The Times*, 15 Mar. 1939, 1st Leader, p. 15.
[28] *The Times*, 17 Mar. 1939, 1st Leader, p. 17.
[29] *The Times*, 16 Mar. 1939, 1st Leader, p. 17.

countries for the sole purpose of increasing the power of the Reich'.[30]

The closest relations with the other Western powers were called for, and it was seen as fortunate that relations with France were 'never closer' than at the moment,[31] because the overwhelming question was: 'Is the recent invasion the last of a series we know or the first of a new series?'

An answer which suggests itself at once is that much depends on whether or not effective opposition is encountered. In any case this is clearly a moment for consultation between like-minded nations, and no less a moment for that reconsideration of all the measures necessary here to national safety and of the responsibilities of the individual citizen upon which the Prime Minister dwelt at the end of his speech.[32]

The strength of the British reaction must have caused considerable surprise in Berlin, and the old chestnut of 'encirclement' once again filled the German press. This time, however, *The Times* explained it as the consequence of German policy itself—which made encirclement 'a natural and even an inevitable process'.[33] It was only natural that neighbouring countries should fear German encroachment, not to say invasion, now that the logical justification of racial union was made irrelevant. *The Times* knew what German control meant to those living under it, and whereas if they were all Germans and wanted to live under 'a revolting system, unworthy of a civilized State',[34] that was their mistake but their privilege.

So long as these methods were applied only at home they might be regarded as no concern of other countries, though the principle of liberty is in fact the concern of all mankind. But when Germany begins to impose her reactionary system upon other States then every Government that values the hard-won gains of civilisation through the centuries must inevitably consider what efforts and what sacrifices it is prepared to make in order to retain them. It is a wholly natural impulse that would urge them to confer forthwith on the best means of defending together all that they are agreed in holding sacred.[35]

No longer would the paper try to explain away hostility to Germany as based upon old prejudices or unjust treaties. Now it was clear that 'the expansion of National-Socialism has come to mean the expansion of political tyranny, cruel police methods, and a new kind of paganism. . . . The reaction against these theories and these methods is entirely spontaneous and shows itself everywhere after so crude a manifestation of them as the subjugation of Czechoslovakia.'[36]

On 23 March, German troops occupied the town of Memel, wresting it away from Lithuanian sovereignty. In a leading article on 'The Case of Memel', *The Times* set out its new attitude:

The whole trouble is that the Reich shows no capacity whatever for considering the interests of any country but its own. Where it dominates, it exploits; and, where it exploits, its oppresses. The latest reports from Bohemia and Moravia tell of spying and delation, imprisonment without trial—the number of arrests is now estimated to be over 18,000—the break-up of homes, the pitiless persecution of honourable political opponents.[37]

Memel itself was one of the old German claims, and the paper pointed out that 'in regard to this particular case, it is fair to remember that the German action is not without a basis of excuse' although this by no means served to justify it.[38] In the same leading article, the new Western unity was interpreted as of the greatest significance: 'the annexation of a free non-German people has already begun to bring upon Herr Hitler the Nemesis which, if he continues in that course, must ultimately destroy him.'[39] But two days later, Holburn reported from Berlin that Nemesis seemed far away. 'The Reich', he wrote, 'is in a jubilant mood. Within 36 hours three foreign political successes—Memel, Slovakia, and the Rumanian Treaty—have been scored, while the British Government, as it is put here, reels under one rebuff after another to its "encirclement" policy.'[40]

[35] Ibid.   [36] *The Times*, 20 Mar. 1939, 1st Leader, p. 15.
[37] *The Times*, 23 Mar. 1939, 1st Leader, p. 17.   [38] Ibid.   [39] Ibid.
[40] *The Times*, 25 Mar. 1939, Berlin Corr., p. 12.

DAILY TELEGRAPH

As with the rest of the British Press, Hitler's precipitate action in Czechoslovakia came as a surprise to the *Daily Telegraph*. That he was behind the agitation in the area was clear and long known; but until the actual invasion there had even appeared to be signs of an improvement in the situation. Indeed, it was Hungary which seemed to be stirring things up to a direct purpose, whereas Germany had only 'as yet ill-defined aspirations of her own in that quarter'.[41] How far the Germans would be inclined 'to fish in these troubled waters remains to be seen'.[42] The report of the Slovak crisis from the Berlin Correspondent stated that 'Despite the aggressive tone of the German Press towards the Czechs when discussing the Slovak question, there is reason to believe that some slight lessening of tension between Berlin and Prague has taken place, during the week-end.'[43] Even by the 14th, when Hitler had intervened in the crisis, the paper stated that 'What he wants is not yet clear, though it will no doubt emerge when the terms of the ultimatum are officially disclosed; but whatever it is does not appear, on the present showing, to be the domestic tranquillity of an independent Czechoslovak State.'[44]

On 15 March the paper printed a remarkable leading article, 'Czechoslovakia In Dissolution'. It confirmed the earlier assertion that Germany's only title to intervene in this dispute was the 'title of force'[45] and that 'The truth about the Germans in Bohemia and Moravia is that they are not so much a defenceless minority in need of protection as agents provocateurs whose role is to provide the Reich with a perpetual pretext for intervention.'[46] But the paper drew conclusions similar to those of *The Times* from these common premises:

As far as Great Britain is concerned, no question of our military intervention arises, or can arise, since the Four-Power guarantee of

[41] *Daily Telegraph*, 11 Mar. 1939, 1st Leader, p. 12.   [42] Ibid.
[43] *Daily Telegraph*, 13 Mar. 1939, Berlin Corr., p. 12. He concluded that this lessening of tension was admittedly 'unlikely to crystallise until the general situation improves'.
[44] *Daily Telegraph*, 14 Mar. 1939, 1st Leader, p. 16.   [45] Ibid.
[46] *Daily Telegraph*, 15 Mar. 1939, 1st Leader, p. 16.

the Czech frontiers which was mooted in September has never become operative. But though no moral or legal obligation rests upon us to aid the victim of this aggression, we can no longer be in any sort of doubt as to the character of the Power which now confronts us in Central Europe. Germany has perpetrated an affront to the whole civilised world which will not be readily forgotten.[47]

With Britain's position thus clearly stated, the paper dealt bluntly with the invasion and its consequences. Hitler had at last 'dropped the mask' and revealed that all his grievances were only aimed at gaining power to inflict worse grievances upon other people and nations.[48] The full story of President Hacha's ordeal in Berlin—including the injections needed to revive him from time to time—was printed by the Diplomatic Correspondent on the 20th,[49] and the military, political and economic significance of the German invasion were assessed in articles from H. V. Temperley, Group Capt. Payne, and the Berlin correspondent.[50] Hitler's guarantee of the new protectorate's autonomy and sovereign rights was seen as farcical:

What all this obviously means is that in practice the 'autonomy' and the 'sovereignty' will be a derisory farce, and that the Czechs will hence-forward be the hewers of wood and drawers of water for their German masters. As a foretaste of what is to come, the Gestapo carried out a series of wholesale arrests in Prague, and was already dragging off scores of its victims to the German concentration camps.[51]

In the article published on the 22nd, G. L. Steer dispelled false ideas about colonies as far as raw materials and living-space were concerned: 'The Czech State alone, with £60,000,000 of gold and foreign securities and £250,000,000 of stocks in store, presents in 24 hours more loot than all the African colonies of Germany combined can offer during 10 years of Nazi rule.'[52]

It was clear that Hitler would not stop now. In 1938 the slogan 'self-determination' had been used to cover a multitude of sins. Now 'self-preservation' appeared to allow Hitler,

[47] Ibid.   [48] *Daily Telegraph*, 16 Mar. 1939, Leader, p. 16.
[49] See *Daily Telegraph*, 20 Mar. 1939, Dipl. Corr., p. 11.
[50] See *Daily Telegraph*, 16 Mar. 1939, p. 11; 18 Mar. 1939, pp. 9, 13.
[51] *Daily Telegraph*, 17 Mar. 1939, 1st Leader, p. 16.
[52] *Daily Telegraph*, 22 Mar. 1939, ed. art. by G. L. Steer, p. 16. See *Daily Telegraph*, 7, 8, 10, 11, 14, and 15 Mar., 1939, for Steer's series of articles on colonies.

'with a perfectly good conscience', to march in any direction where he was unlikely to meet with dangerous opposition.[53] In a leading article on 20 March, 'A Matter of Urgency', the paper stressed the importance of immediate and definite action by the British Government, and came close to proposing a coalition:

Clearly what the situation demands is a policy which is at once closely concerted between the Powers, which formulates exactly the course to be followed in given circumstances, and which is capable of instant application. In default of such a policy Europe will just crumble piecemeal before the spreading Nazi attack, and, as in the past, Herr Hitler will be left to win each new position before anyone has realized that he has begun to take it.[54]

The article continued that 'A policy that is effectively to avert such a consummation is bound to envisage new commitments for this country somewhere; without commitments, Herr Hitler will undoubtedly conclude that he can carry on with impunity as far as this country is concerned.'[55]

Hitler was on the move, and in the nine days following the invasion of Czechoslovakia, the paper recorded his German-Rumanian Trade Treaty 'which gives Germany virtual control of Rumania's principal natural resources'[56] and the occupation of Memel which might in itself 'be accounted small fry, but the manner of its absorption is none the less indicative of the unchanged character of German policy'.[57] The obvious policy lesson for Britain in these events was that appeasement was no longer possible; 'The "spirit of Munich" is dead and buried, for who can hope to "appease" a boa-constrictor?'[58] Like the *Manchester Guardian*,[59] the *Daily Telegraph* was disappointed with Chamberlain's remarks in the House of Commons

[53] *Daily Telegraph*, 17 Mar. 1939, 1st Leader, p. 16.
[54] *Daily Telegraph*, 20 Mar. 1939, 1st Leader, p. 12.   [55] Ibid.
[56] *Daily Telegraph*, 24 Mar. 1939, Berlin Corr., p. 17.
[57] *Daily Telegraph*, 24 Mar. 1939, Leader, p. 16. See also *Daily Telegraph*, 1st Leader, p. 16, in which the same line—that pursued by other newspapers—is taken: 'In itself Memel is of altogether trifling importance. . . . What is chiefly significant is the fresh evidence that Herr Hitler continues to be wedded to the method of the mailed fist. . . . But it seems that with Herr Hitler menaces have almost become an end in themselves and that anything obtained without them is by so much less worth having.'
[58] *Daily Telegraph*, 16 Mar. 1939, Leader, p. 16.   [59] See below, p. 248.

which pushed understatement 'to the point of irony'.[60] The invasion of Prague had made 'a complete and utter mockery' of Munich[61] and the assumptions upon which Munich was based. Now it was over, and Britain must look to the future.[62] This was not to say that appeasement had been wrong or was something to be ashamed of. Quite the contrary:

It has to be recognised that the policy which Mr. Chamberlain had set before himself has not been without its value. It has demonstrated to all and sundry, beyond cavil, the sincere and ardent devotion of this country to the cause of peace. It has given Herr Hitler every chance of mending his ways and withdrawn from him every excuse for not doing so. If to-day he has elected to unmask himself as an unconscionable aggressor, the policy which Great Britain has followed has removed any possibility of doubt about it in any mind. That policy has received a fair trial with an outcome which all must deplore. That does not change the fixed resolve of this country to seek peace and ensue it. What is changed is not the objective but the method; and it is to the new orientation of the method that our Government has now and henceforward to apply itself.[63]

In an editorial page article, Winston Churchill wrote of the 'veritable revolution' of opinion which had swept Britain and the Dominions.

This mass conversion of those who had hitherto been hopeful took place within a single week, but not within a single day. It was not an explosion, but the kindling of a fire which rose steadily, hour by hour, to an intense furnace heat of inward conviction. Nothing is more impressive than the outward calm which has been preserved. It has hardly been thought necessary to argue the matter. Those who have seen in these events the melancholy fulfilment of their beliefs and warnings have been exalted. Those whose eyes are now opened, have not recanted; nor need they do so. Their aims were honourable.[64]

The paper became increasingly disenchanted with the Government's apparent reluctance—or inability—to muster the new

---

[60] *Daily Telegraph*, 16 Mar. 1939, Leader, p. 16.   [61] Ibid.
[62] *Daily Telegraph*, 18 Mar. 1939, 1st Leader, p. 14.   [63] Ibid.
[64] *Daily Telegraph*, 24 Mar. 1939, ed. art. by Winston Churchill, p. 16. Churchill concluded that 'A period of suffering resulting from the air slaughter of noncombatants may lie before us; but this, if borne with fortitude, will only seal the comradeship of many nations to save themselves and the future of mankind from a tyrant's grip.'

feeling into discernible policy. 'It behoves us . . . to fix once and for all the line where we shall intervene with all our resources the moment it is transgressed. The sooner we fix it, and the more resolute our commitment to defend it, the less likely will be the transgression and the less likely the general conflagration we would fain avert.'[65] As Eden put it, every minute counted, and it would be most disappointing if Poland and the 'more exposed Powers' were hesitating to pledge themselves along with the Western Powers 'due to any weakness or ambiguity in the declaration to which they are being invited to subscribe'.[66] On the 25th, in a leading article called 'Perils of Delay or Indecision', the paper minced no words in replying to Sir John Simon's suggestion in the House of Commons that the extension of definite commitments would place Hitler's fate in foreign hands. The great lawyer's doubts only begged the whole question:

. . . for the purpose of any commitment now envisaged is to aid the victim of an unprovoked aggression, and it is surely not the victim who decides whether there shall be an aggression. In a word, we find ourselves in a situation which demands a realistic not a legalistic view of our undertakings. The firmer and more decisive the policy of the Government the more certainly will they be assured of the unstinted support of the country.[67]

The leader concluded with a pointed reference to Simon and the Inner Cabinet, by expressing the hope that the rumours would prove unfounded 'of a certain wavering or irresolution on the part of some members of the Cabinet. At a moment when the whole country is waiting unanimously for an instantaneous and vigorous lead it would be lamentable indeed if unanimity on this issue were lacking within the Government itself.'[68] The month ended with speculation upon Poland's role as next in line.[69]

MANCHESTER GUARDIAN

That there had been 'simply tremendous' pressure by Germany upon Czechoslovakia since, and regardless of, Munich, had

---

[65] Ibid., Leader, p. 16.   [66] Ibid.
[67] *Daily Telegraph*, 25 Mar. 1939, 1st Leader, p. 14.   [68] Ibid.
[69] *Daily Telegraph*, 28 Mar. 1939, Berlin Corr., p. 18.

been clearly stated in the *Manchester Guardian* since the New Year.[70] Given the situation it was inevitable that Prague must co-operate with Berlin, but the Czechs had proved themselves not easily 'stampeded', and had thus far managed to retain their own outlook 'and a certain pliant independence'.[71] Indeed, 'only the stubborn spirit of the Czech people has so far prevented an almost complete subservience to Nazi Germany'.[72] On 11 March, Voigt wrote that there were two views in London of 'The International Situation'. One held that gaining time would weaken the dictatorships as internal problems grew within them; the second held that the menace of internal collapse would only make foreign activity more needful. The second view, he wrote, was generally accepted, and it was now felt that if peace in Europe could be preserved for, say, another year, it might have been saved for many years, perhaps for a generation.[73]

On 11 March, the paper remarked that the German Government seemed at least to be holding the Slovak separatists at arm's length, and taking the view that the matter was one internal to Czechoslovakia.[74]

The first anniversary of the Anschluss was commemorated in a leading article—the only one of its kind in the British Press—which called the Hitler-Schuschnigg meeting at Berchtesgaden 'perhaps the strangest event in the whole post-war history of Europe' and surveyed the results which were now well known: all former opponents of the Nazis—Jews, Catholics, Socialists, Liberals, all 'have had to endure suffering almost beyond description'.[75]

By Monday 13 March, it had become clear that the Slovak agitation was reaching dangerous proportions and that Europe was once again being edged towards the brink by that far-away country. The paper maintained that Hitler was still undecided, perhaps even deterred, by the 'growth of courage in Eastern and

[70] See, for example, *Manchester Guardian*, 15 Feb. 1939, Cent. Eur. Corr., p. 5; ibid., Dipl. Corr., p. 11; and *Manchester Guardian*, 8 Mar. 1939, 3rd Leader, p. 10.
[71] *Manchester Guardian*, 19 Mar. 1939, 1st Leader, p. 10.
[72] *Manchester Guardian*, 8 Mar. 1939, 3rd Leader, p. 10.
[73] *Manchester Guardian*, 11 Mar. 1939, Dipl. Corr., p. 13.
[74] Ibid., 4th Leader, p. 12.
[75] Ibid., 3rd Leader, p. 12. The article did point out that the Anschluss had not been an unmixed economic blessing for Germany—that in fact the drawbacks had exceeded the benefits in economic terms.

Central Europe, an increased concern for independence' which might lead to dangerous movements if Czechoslovakia further disintegrated.[76] This referred to predatory Polish and Hungarian activity. Germany's plans for this part of Europe would not include sharing it as a sphere of influence. 'But there is no certainty; Germany has ambitions in the East, as everywhere, and only the time and the pretext for their attainment remain unknown.'

At present there is a calm, which seems to owe its existence only to Germany's indecision. She has several chestnuts on the fire in this part of Europe; her care is lest in stretching too greedily for one of them some of the others fall into the wrong laps.[77]

For Voigt, however, the trend was clear. 'Events in Czechoslovakia', he wrote, 'show that the Munich "settlement", so far from being an end, was a beginning. Czechoslovakia, having been mutilated, is now to be dismembered, although the formal union between Slovakia and Prague is allowed to remain for the time being.'[78]

The London edition of 15 March had gone to press too early to carry the reports of the invasion, and the leading article, 'Another Victory', was written with only the knowledge of Hitler's demands on Hacha. The article stated that 'in one sense, indeed, Munich had been a defeat for Hitler, for it deprived him of a "conquest" and left the stubborn Czech people still able to resist complete absorption', and this could only be seen in line with the Sudeten agitation, and the inequities of the Vienna Award, as part of Hitler's determination to attain hegemony in Central Europe.[79] The same leader referred to Hitler's timing.

In making this last stroke Hitler has shown all his old skill and ruthlessness. He chose his time perfectly, when the democracies had been lulled into a sense of security and our own Government was actually announcing the dawn of a new and peaceful era. Having masked his intentions by threatening the Western Powers earlier in the year, he completed his preparation (for one must see in this a skilful plan) with the utmost secrecy. When finally he struck

---

[76] *Manchester Guardian*, 13 Mar. 1939, 1st Leader, p. 8. See also ibid., Cent. Eur. Corr., p. 12.　　[77] Ibid.　　[78] Ibid., Dipl. Corr., p. 12.
[79] *Manchester Guardian*, 15 Mar. 1939, 1st Leader, p. 10.

he did so with speed and decision. Though it was a typical hammer-stroke, based on force and backed by 14 divisions of the German Army, by taking advantage of the simplicity of the Slovak leaders he has given it a legal and almost an altruistic appearance.[80]

This analysis erred on the side of over-estimation, but the essential point was that Hitler was again on the move—that this was only a beginning of the push for a German-controlled 'Mittel-Europa'.[81]

Speculation now turned to where the next German blow would fall. Although German public opinion had been shocked and surprised at the cavalier way in which the Führer dealt with war, indications were that no respite was intended, although a policy of lulling the West into complacency would once again be pursued.[82] But security was an illusion. 'Indeed Germany has now so many irons in the fire that it must be difficult to know which to draw out next. The South-eastern countries are alarmed, the West finds itself no more secure, and even the North—the Baltic and Scandinavian countries—feels itself threatened.'[83] The lesson was clear: 'To have the power over other people—let us not forget it—is for [Hitler] the need to use it.'[84]

The first assertion was that nothing would be done to aid the Czechs. The British Guarantee at Munich had only covered external aggression, not internal dissolution. The guarantee had, therefore, apparently never been in force and Britain had no legal obligations. The paper did not dispute this fact or propose action regardless of it.

We must, however, have a deep feeling of responsibility for the sufferings of the Czech people. The truth is that Czechoslovakia was abandoned to Germany at Munich, and what is happening now is merely the consequence of what was done then. If we would

---

[80] Ibid.   [81] Ibid.

[82] See *Manchester Guardian*, 17 Mar. 1939, Cent. Eur. Corr., p. 6; see 18 Mar. 1939, A Corr. recently in Germany, for an interesting breakdown of the course of German public opinion; and 24 Mar. 1939, 1st Leader, p. 10.

[83] *Manchester Guardian*, 24 Mar. 1939, 1st Leader, p. 10. There was a brief consideration of the danger to Poland against which a press campaign on the traditional lines was being mounted in Germany. See *Manchester Guardian*, 28 Mar. 1939, Dipl. Corr., p. 11; ibid., 2nd Leader, p. 10; and *Manchester Guardian*, 29 Mar. 1939, Dipl. Corr., p. 11.

[84] *Manchester Guardian*, 16 Mar. 1939, 1st Leader, p. 10.

not fight then, we cannot fight now; the present crisis is rather an opportunity to reflect with shame on the past and to prepare with energy for the future.[85]

And two days later, a leading article reiterated this position:

The British Government has disclaimed with relief any legal obligation to protect Czechoslovakia. It is perhaps as well, for we could not save her if we would. No one, however, can deny that we have a moral responsibility for what has happened or that it is our duty to do all we can to relieve the sufferings of the Czech people. . . . If Mr. Chamberlain has any credit with Nazi Germany for his policy of appeasement, for his forebearance towards her aggression, now surely is the time to draw upon it. If for once the British Government asserts its influence in Berlin, it may not prevail upon the German Government to show mercy (for that is impossible) but it may at least help some to escape from persecution. It would be something if the Czechs could take with them into bondage the memory of a Britain sincerely anxious to repair the damage which she helped to cause.[86]

Once the fact that there could, would, and should be no British action was established, the paper continued its familiar anti-appeasement, anti-Chamberlain, anti-Nazi line. Both the occupation of Prague, and the invasion of Memel eight days later, were simply affirmations of long-recognized Nazi perfidy. There was a difference between the two, however, which, in common with most of the press, the *Manchester Guardian* perceived. Whereas the invasion of Bohemia and Moravia had been 'without a shadow of justification', 'with scarcely even a pretence of grievances (since time did not allow of their adequate invention)', 'the most brutal as it is the most terrible of Hitler's assaults on a free and independent people', 'using a shameless pretext, to wreak on the Czechs the vengeance which he had intended last summer but had been compelled by Munich to postpone',[87] the German determination to recover Memel 'is not a crime like her decision to conquer and absorb the Czechs, but the method is the same immoral one of force that was applied in turn to

85 *Manchester Guardian*, 15 Mar. 1939, 1st Leader, p. 10.
86 *Manchester Guardian*, 17 Mar. 1939, 1st Leader, p. 10.
87 *Manchester Guardian*, 16 Mar. 1939, 1st Leader, p. 10.

Austria, the Sudeten problem, and the final destruction of Czechoslovakia.'

In a leading article on 'The Gift of Prophecy', the paper quoted statements of various Cabinet Ministers after Munich, envisaging a golden age of peace as a result of that settlement. 'Was not', the leader asked, 'Mr. Harold Nicolson's description of the guarantee at the time as "the most farcical piece of diplomatic hypocrisy that has ever been perpetuated" a juster prophecy than those of the Cabinet Ministers who thought (or tried to make us think) that they had saved Czechoslovakia from extinction as an independent State? And who was the more right about the inevitable consequences of Munich—our purblind Ministers or their despised critics?'[88]

In a leading article the next day, the paper poured scorn upon Chamberlain's statement in the House of Commons. Labelling it a 'remarkable passage' which illustrated the Premier's 'freezing gift of understatement', the leader concluded,

Mr. Chamberlain says that these events will 'administer a shock to confidence'. They will not give much of a shock to those who have never shared the crude optimism which the Government has so lavishly distributed. These terrible events should finally dissipate any illusions that remain about the character, aims, and methods of Hitler. Whatever excuses might be made by apologists for his action over the Rhineland, over Austria, and over the Sudeten Germans, there can be none for his conquest of Bohemia. He will not stop there.[89]

By the 17th, the Conservative Press itself had turned against the Munich policy—'even *The Times*, faithful unto death, has to plead pathetically that after all Munich was a "supreme demonstration of British faith and goodwill", whatever the Germans made of it. Mr. Chamberlain's complacency should be shaken if this is the best his friends feel they could do for him.'[90] But despite the influx of fresh detail of the 'brutality and duplicity' of the German action, 'our rulers even yet

---

[88] *Manchester Guardian*, 15 Mar. 1939, 2nd Leader, p. 10.

[89] *Manchester Guardian*, 16 Mar. 1939, 1st Leader, p. 10.

[90] *Manchester Guardian*, 17 Mar. 1939, 2nd Leader, p. 10. The papers listed as those which 'Chamberlain must be presumed to notice' were the *Daily Mail*, *Birmingham Post*, *Scotsman*, *Daily Telegraph*, and *Yorkshire Post*.

show few signs of realizing the character of the man with whom they have to deal.'[91]

On the 17th, the situation took an entirely new turn. Chamberlain's speech in Birmingham, reported the following day, was interpreted in a leading article as 'the gravest from any British Minister since Grey's on August 4, 1914. It marks a decisive change in our national policy. It carries tremendously grave implications, but from it there can be no going back.'[92] The Prime Minister had spoken in the strongest terms to the Birmingham Conservative Association of the need to resist Hitler. A second leading article on the same day gave a rather left-handed compliment: 'As a result of the annexation of Czechoslovakia one thing at least seems certain: not even the stupidest Government can now fail to realize the urgent danger of German expansion in Europe.'[93] There remained, of course, a vast difference between Chamberlain having his 'blinkers' torn away, and his acting upon the new understanding of German policy. He would have 'to show not only that he has seen a light but that he can walk firmly in the strength of it'.[94]

The point at the moment is that Mr. Chamberlain has learned his lesson by bitter experience, in the case of a man of his temperament the most salutary way. He feels that he has been betrayed, that the bases on which his whole structure of 'appeasement' rested have been 'wantonly shattered', that solemn undertakings have been disregarded, and that the man he had hoped to win has proved himself a brazen perjurer. The blinkers are off, and the country heard for the first time from Mr. Chamberlain his true feelings about the Nazi system, its vileness and its cruelty. The words have been said, just as President Roosevelt's have been said. They cannot be glossed over. We now stand in an entirely different relation with Germany than we did yesterday. We may have to face the dictator's early anger. . . . But we must all be glad that at last British policy is becoming honest, that we have given up make-believe, and that we can express the faith that is in us without fear of being charged with 'fouling our own nest'. For Mr. Chamberlain this is only the beginning. His old policy is dead; he will be judged by the speed

[91] Ibid., 1st Leader, p. 10.
[92] *Manchester Guardian*, 18 Mar. 1939, 1st Leader, p. 12.
[93] Ibid., 2nd Leader.
[94] *Manchester Guardian*, 20 Mar. 1939, 1st Leader, p. 10.

with which he turns to carry out the new. But of one thing he can be certain. His speech last night came nearer to expressing the feeling of his countrymen than any he has yet made. If he goes back on it he, and perhaps we, are doomed.[95]

By the end of the month the paper was again disillusioned by the 'indecisiveness' of the British effort which had taken the desultory form of attempting to make arrangements for consultation; consultation was useless since 'with Hitler the threat and the act are sudden and simultaneous'.[96] A coalition was first called for on 17 March.

If the 'Western world' is to show 'solidarity' there must be some kind of common approach, some sort of common association, which may be effective without involving us in wide, unknown 'commitments'. The least we can do for our own safety is to make the attempts to see whether any kind of 'solidarity' is possible. The most serious charge that can be brought against the Government is that it does not make this attempt, that our policy is as uncertain as ever it was, and that for all their fine words France and Britain are to-day in even more desperate isolation than they were six months ago when the great revolution in their strategic position in Europe became clear.[97]

Three days later Voigt pictured Britain 'passing from the passive to the active in foreign affairs and . . . assuming the leadership of a coalition',[98] but three days after that, when Memel had been taken, the paper saw that for the Government to construct 'a "peace front" . . . and to construct it quickly on a basis of mutual confidence between its neighbours . . . after its policy in recent times, may be no easy task'.[99]

An essential part of any coalition was Soviet Russia. So strong an anti-communist as Voigt wrote on 21 March, 'Old prejudices are at work, especially amongst Conservatives, but these old prejudices are being overruled by new enthusiasms.'[100] The day before, the paper had printed a leading

[95] *Manchester Guardian*, 18 Mar. 1939, 1st Leader, p. 12.

[96] *Manchester Guardian*, 29 Mar. 1939, 1st Leader, p. 10.

[97] *Manchester Guardian*, 17 Mar. 1939, 2nd Leader, p. 10. See also *Manchester Guardian*, 16 Mar. 1939, 1st Leader, p. 10, where the need for a coalition is set out in all but terms.

[98] *Manchester Guardian*, 20 Mar. 1939, Dipl. Corr., p. 11.

[99] *Manchester Guardian*, 23 Mar. 1939, 1st Leader, p. 10.

[100] *Manchester Guardian*, 21 Mar. 1939, Dipl. Corr., p. 11.

article, 'The Danger And the Need', in which it stated that 'However dreadful the [Red] Terror has been, it is the fact that time after time in recent years Russia has been firmer and more outspoken on behalf of honesty in international affairs than any other Great European Power; better than any other Governments she has expressed the view of the ordinary decent man and woman.'[101] At the end of the month the issue was put in its most basic terms: 'Russia, whatever the differences of opinion about her, stands against aggression, and one of the things which should be made known as soon as possible is what steps our Government has been taking during the last week to bring her within the talked-of combination.'[102]

NEWS CHRONICLE

So primed was the *News Chronicle* for a German action that when the Slovak crisis suddenly arose, the paper rushed to judgement and was caught short when the actual invasion came. At first, the extent of Germany's involvement was questioned,[103] but when Hacha went to Berlin on the 14th, the paper wrote of this as the end of Czechoslovakia. The full range of *News Chronicle* vehemence was directed against Chamberlain, whose comments in the House of Commons on the 14th 'were those of a distant spectator of a tiresome conflict in a land of which he "knows nothing" '.[104] The failure of Munich was patent:

He believed he was righting an injustice, but instead he has opened the floodgates of injustice. He believed that he was strengthening Czechoslovakia, but instead he has put that land at the mercy of the Nazis. Never at any time, whether at Munich or since, has he given Czechoslovakia the diplomatic support necessary if it was to maintain its integrity and independence.[105]

Quoting the 'notorious' *Times* leader of 7 September 1938 and its own on 26 September[106] the leader continued:

[101] *Manchester Guardian*, 20 Mar. 1939, 1st Leader, p. 10.
[102] *Manchester Guardian*, 29 Mar. 1939, 1st Leader, p. 10.
[103] See *News Chronicle*, 11 Mar. 1939, p. 1; also 2nd Leader, p. 10, and a long piece by Douglas Reed, p. 17. See also *News Chronicle*, 13 Mar. 1939, p. 1.
[104] *News Chronicle*, 15 Mar. 1939, 1st Leader, p. 10.
[105] Ibid.   [106] See above, pp. 177 ff. and 211 ff.

History has already judged between these views. In the light of current news, the claim that Czechoslovakia would become more homogeneous by the cession of the Sudeten areas stands out either as farcical or hypocritical. The acquisition of Sudetenland was the insertion of a wedge which has now completely disrupted the Czechoslovak State.[107]

The headline of the 15th, 'German Troops Take Key Czech Towns Says Prague: General Advance Feared', was shown to be somewhat premature even by the same day's Berlin correspondence. This stated that while Hacha's journey to Berlin marked the acquisition of Germany's 'first post-war colony—Slovakia', it was generally believed to end for the moment any danger of German troops marching, although a 'symbolic' occupation of Prague might be expected in a few days' time.[108]

The German invasion was treated in terms of its effects upon Chamberlain and his policy. 'The only real consolation about all this miserable business', wrote Vernon Bartlett from a convalescence in the Scilly Islands, 'is that the Prime Minister must be finding it very difficult to continue, under the attractive title of "appeasement", a policy which is destroying all those freedoms which his and our ancestors fought to win.'[109] The paper ran a box on the front page quoting its report 'from an excellent source' printed on 29 November, to the effect that Hitler had three army corps secretly ready and waiting for an excuse to overrun all of Czechoslovakia, 'an action which he is reported to have hankered for even after the Munich agreement was signed'. This had been vehemently denied in Berlin and provoked an onslaught against the *News Chronicle* from Hitler himself; now 'History has supplied the answer.'[110] Both Vernon Bartlett and the leading article drew the same conclusions from Hitler's action: 'One thing stands out of the Czech business so clearly that not even *The Times*, not even Mr. Chamberlain, fails to see it—that Herr Hitler has committed an act of naked aggression.' A new policy was needed, and if Chamberlain did not realize this, then a new Prime Minister was needed as well.[111]

[107] *News Chronicle*, 15 Mar. 1939, 1st Leader, p. 10.
[108] Ibid., Berlin Corr., p. 1.
[109] *News Chronicle*, 16 Mar. 1939, Vernon Bartlett, p. 4.
[110] Ibid., p. 1.   [111] Ibid., Leader, p. 12.

Chamberlain was an old familiar target, and although his coming round after the invasion of Prague was sympathetically reported, its desultory effect on policy soon dispelled any sympathy.

The present Prime Minister has identified himself so personally, so ostentatiously, with the policy of so-called 'appeasement', his misjudgment of the character of Nazism and of its leader has been so profound that while he remains in office nations that are our potential allies in a struggle and a large section of our own people will with difficulty be persuaded that the policy is dead.[112]

After the flagrant invasion of Czechoslovakia itself, nothing has so much outraged public opinion in this country as Mr. Chamberlain's handling of it.[113]

Chamberlain's initial remarks upon the invasion were those 'of a company chairman announcing the closure of a branch in foreign parts',[114] and even his most devoted adherents were complaining that something stronger was needed. The paper's comments on the Premier's Birmingham address were in an important leading article on 20 March: 'Mr. Chamberlain's conversion has been reluctant and painful, but there is no reason to doubt that it is genuine. He has been contemptuously tricked; and Hell hath no fury like a Chamberlain scorned.'[115]

Two leading articles set out the *News Chronicle*'s policy for a coalition—a 'Peace Front'—of Powers against Germany. The first, on 18 March, 'Unity—The First Step', dealt with Britain itself. The events of the preceding three days had 'deeply touched the emotions of the British people', and even in the eyes of its greatest proponents 'the policy of Munich crumbled to its inevitable ruin'. Consequently, 'the overwhelmingly pressing essential, in face of the barefaced menace that now threatens our freedom, is a solid unity of the national purpose to stand ready and resolved for whatever may be in store. Peace may yet be secured by sufficient strength and firmness; but peace or war, the one supreme necessity is preparedness of armed power on a scale to match whatever

---

[112] *News Chronicle*, 18 Mar. 1939, Leader, p. 6.
[113] *News Chronicle*, 17 Mar. 1939, Leader, p. 10.   [114] Ibid.
[115] *News Chronicle*, 20 Mar. 1939, Leader, p. 10.

may challenge us.'[116] The second, two days later, 'Peace Front Now', spoke of the need for co-operation between Britain, France, and America, but also with the Soviet Union which was 'an equally essential element, and the front should include Poland, Turkey, Rumania, the Balkan countries generally, Holland, and others who are prepared to pool their security with ours'.

The front formed, it must be decided where a stand will be made if necessary. To this question there can be only one answer. It would be folly to wait till Hitler has possessed himself of Hungarian corn and Rumanian oil. He must be told flatly, in a joint and immediate declaration by all the Powers of the peace front, 'Thus far, and no farther.' If he attempts to commit any further act of aggression, it will be regarded as an act of war against all.[117]

Time was of the essence since there seemed for the moment to be a pause in Hitler's 'wild bid for world dominion'.

Two days was enough to explode the illusion of meaningful action by the British Government. The desperate leading article on the 22nd, 'Peace Front—At Once', stressed that the Government 'must eradicate from its mind every scrap of latent prejudice about the Soviet Government', and move immediately to convince the other powers of its seriousness of purpose. Bartlett wrote the same day that the 'brutal and lamentable' truth seemed to be that the Governments sounded had not been inclined to place much more confidence in British than in German assurances.[118] He concluded: 'There is, in fact, a suspicion in many embassies and legations that all this talk about a strong line is not much more than an attempt to silence criticism by a show of activity on the part of Ministers, some of whom would still prefer to deal with Hitler's Germany than with Stalin's Russia.'[119] On the 27th, Bartlett expressed frustration at the Government's suggestion that plans for a Four Power Declaration be put aside until Beck's impending visit to London. 'In other words the peace-loving nations, faced by one of the most flagrant annexations of territory ever carried out in peace time, are doing precisely nothing either to

---

[116] *News Chronicle*, 18 Mar. 1939, 1st Leader, p. 6.
[117] *News Chronicle*, 20 Mar. 1939, Leader, p. 10.
[118] *News Chronicle*, 22 Mar. 1939, p. 1.   [119] Ibid.

compel Germany to reverse her action or to warn her against similar actions in the future.'[120]

The seizure of Memel only served to stress the necessity for meaningful alliance. The tendency to consider Memel as another 'justified claim' was 'the reverse of the truth. Hitler's method in seizing Memel is precisely the same as his method in seizing Austria or Czechoslovakia; and that method threatens the whole of Europe.'[121] Memel illustrated, no less clearly than Prague, the Nazi belief 'that might is right, that God is on the side of the big bombers. This doctrine, unless challenged immediately, may be used in future with equal ruthlessness against Amsterdam, Paris or London.'[122]

The month ended with speculation concerning German aggression against Poland. The paper found it understandable that the Poles were wary of Russian assistance, but thought that 'it should be the duty of British diplomacy to remove these fears. . . . The Russians of today are wholly different from the Tsarist Imperialist regime. It is very different also from the Russia which so alarmed other nations in the first flush of the Bolshevik Revolution.'[123]

DAILY HERALD

On 3 March Bernard Shaw contributed an article on Labour's foreign policy which, although it typically hovered at the Shavian extreme, spoke some common sense.

We on the Labour side have nothing in the way of a foreign policy that will wash.

We praise peace and collective security, and in the same breath revile the Conservatives because they did not make war on Japan over Manchuria, on Italy over Abyssinia, and on Germany over Austria and Czechoslovakia.

This is patent nonsense. Suppose the Labour Party had been in power with a ninety-nine per cent majority, could they have led the Nation to war for the sake of the Chinese, the Danakils, or the entirely imaginary race called the Czechoslovaks?[124]

---

[120] *News Chronicle*, 27 Mar. 1939, p. 1.
[121] *News Chronicle*, 23 Mar. 1939, 2nd Leader, p. 10.   [122] Ibid.
[123] *News Chronicle*, 31 Mar. 1939, 1st Leader, p. 12. See also *News Chronicle*, 28 Mar. 1939, p. 1; 29 Mar. 1939, p. 1; 30 Mar. 1939, Vernon Bartlett, p. 1; 31 Mar. 1939, p. 1, in which Bartlett reported the Anglo-Polish Guarantee.
[124] *Daily Herald*, 3 Mar. 1939, ed. art. by G. B. Shaw, p. 10.

Ewer saw through the Slovak crisis from the very beginning. 'A new German threat to Czechoslovakia is impending', he wrote on 11 March. 'That is the real meaning of the trouble in Slovakia, of the recent trouble in Ruthenia.'[125] On 15 March, when only Hitler's demands were known, the paper adopted Ewer's earlier analysis in its leading article, 'The Sword Rules':

No help will come to Prague from anywhere. Not from London, not from Paris, not from Moscow. Prague knows that.

. . . National Socialism was always aggressive. It always possessed a foreign policy which demanded sacrifices from others. But they were sacrifices of specific things—of treaty rights, of territory.

Today National Socialism has gone a stage further. It now demands power—power for its own sake, for the sheer pleasure of exercising it. The material concession, the instruction accepted, are secondary.

It is the act of submission, the salute of slave to master, for which Herr Hitler lusts. Munich was not enough. The Czechs gained nothing by giving the Sudetenland. They must cry 'Heil Hitler'. The world must cry 'Heil Hitler'.[126]

The next day, with German troops in Prague, and Hitler on his way to join them, the paper printed a two-column leader, 'The Plan Goes On', which said 'I told you so' with a quiet bitterness. The fault lay with the Western Powers and with Britain particularly, which at Munich had fallen into line with Hitler's technique of demanding more than he expected and then demoralizing and infiltrating, finally to take everything. The occupation of Czechoslovakia was not justified by any national claims. 'It is naked aggression, the planned and deliberate conquest of another country; an act of war.'[127] Although it seemed impossible in the face of the facts,[128] Chamberlain had told the House of Commons that what had taken place was with the agreement of the Czech Government;

---

[125] *Daily Herald*, 11 Mar. 1939, Dipl. Corr., p. 2. Ewer unfortunately overestimated by accusing the Nazis of month-long plans for such an action, quoting himself to show his foresight. The Berlin Correspondent had the facts in the next issue: he wrote that Hitler had been supporting the Slovaks for a long time but that the sudden crisis was now forcing his hand. See *Daily Herald*, 13 Mar. 1939, Berlin Corr., p. 2.   [126] *Daily Herald*, 15 Mar. 1939, 1st Leader, p. 10.

[127] *Daily Herald*, 16 Mar. 1939, Leader, p. 10.

[128] See W. N. Ewer's report of Hitler's threat of an air attack on Prague, ibid., p. 1.

'surely we, and they,' the paper stated, 'might be excused that final hypocrisy.' Chamberlain was not alone:

There are many voices today to take up once again the chorus that has followed every defeat of international justice, every triumph of Fascism, the chorus that followed Manchuria, and Abyssinia, Austria and Munich and Spain—'This does not concern us and, anyway, it was inevitable.' Let the British people not deceive themselves. This does concern us—and it is only inevitable because of our own failures and treacheries.[129]

The paper called for immediate consolidation of forces with France, Russia, and America. The purpose of Hitler's latest aggression was clear—to eliminate the chance of an attack upon his south-eastern border 'if and when the opportunity occurs—or is made—for aggression in the West'. Only the possession of overwhelming force could prevent the use of force.

Francis Williams wrote an editorial article on 'Britain's Policy Now'. Chamberlain, whose sincerely held policy of appeasement had been so tragically proven wrong, he wrote, was not the man to embody the nation's new resolution. Co-operation with Russia and America was essential—France was not mentioned—and especially in America, Chamberlain symbolized 'a policy of slavish acquiescence in the aggression of the dictators, of readiness to sacrifice every democratic principle for a temporary reprieve'. Accompanying this collaboration must go a national reconstruction under centralized control aimed at a utilization of resources of unemployed labour such as the present Government seemed incapable of effecting.[130]

The *Daily Herald*'s reaction to Chamberlain's Birmingham speech was cool. Although it was given front page headlines and quoted in full,[131] the leading article, 'A Policy In Ruins', reiterated that the necessary world-wide confidence could not be placed in Chamberlain and that the greatest service he could do would be to resign. Further, the speech itself was not considered to be outstanding.

We share his anger. But we ask, as the world asks, what now?

To that there was no answer in his speech. Britain will fight

---

[129] Ibid., Leader, p. 10.
[130] *Daily Herald*, 17 Mar. 1939, ed. art. by Francis Williams, p. 10.
[131] *Daily Herald*, 18 Mar. 1939, p. 8.

rather than yield her liberties—that is not a policy—that is a
basic principle so unchallengeable that it needs no enumeration.
. . . the policy upon which the whole career as Premier has been
based is in ruins. He has nothing to put in its place.[132]

In several leading articles the paper continued to call for
immediate action in the form of a 'joint declaration of policy
by the peaceful Powers, headed by Britain, France and
Russia'.[133] The paper was at pains to stress the consistency of
Labour's support—even in the face of critics who said that this
meant a war policy—for collective security, and that at last
'now when the danger of war comes horribly near the policy
it has advocated throughout is recognized as the only way left
of securing peace'. The conversations with France and Russia
must lead to a Peace Pact such as the National Council of
Labour had just demanded.[134]

As the days passed, however, it became clear that little
progress was being made towards any kind of united front,
and a note of desperation began to appear in the paper's
articles. On the 24th it reiterated its call of the day before for an
'Immediate Conference', and saw no reason why Poland's
understandable reluctance to commit itself should stand in the
way:

Surely in the circumstances the wise course is for a Three-Power
declaration to be issued at once by Britain, France and Russia,
to be followed immediately by the calling of a conference of Ministers in London or elsewhere.

To that conference Poland should be invited. . . . Above all
what is now essential is that the decision, whether for a Three-
Power declaration followed by a conference with Poland or for a
Four-Power conference at once, shall be taken immediately.
Aggression can only be stopped if the peaceable nations act with the
same speed and determination as the aggressors.[135]

After the seizure of Memel, and with no Government action
in view, the paper began its attacks again. The Government
was speaking with two voices, Chamberlain's at Birmingham

[132] Ibid., Leader, p. 8.
[133] *Daily Herald*, 21 Mar. 1939, 1st Leader, p. 10. See also 20 Mar. 1939,
Leader, p. 10.
[134] *Daily Herald*, 22 Mar. 1939, Leader, p. 10; also ibid., p. 1.
[135] *Daily Herald*, 24 Mar. 1939, Leader, p. 12. See also *Daily Herald*, 23 Mar.
1939, Leader, p. 10.

(which represented the feelings of the people), and members of the Government in the House of Commons, particularly R. A. Butler whose remarks concerning British sympathy for Lithuania were taken as particularly weak and offensive. The peace front was going badly: 'Can we wonder—if the tones Mr. Butler is allowed to use in the House of Commons have been heard also in the Peace Front proposals? Is the Goverment prepared to face up to the implications of German aggression and act accordingly, or is it not? It is time we had a definite answer.'[136]

The following day a leader called for 'No More Delay', and although the paper duly reported the Nazi campaign against Poland at the end of the month, the real issue remained clear: 'On the face of it the crisis of the minute may be Polish. But at bottom it is not a Polish crisis. It is a European crisis . . . and unless swiftly and without more ado Europe faces its own peril and bands together to resist the common menace then nothing is plainer than that the free States of Europe will hang separately".'[137]

SUNDAY TIMES

'Why', Scrutator asked, 'has the sky of Europe, which only a week ago seemed to be brightening, once more become a wrack of ugly black clouds? The answer can be given in a sentence. Herr Hitler has deceived us.'[138] The Germans had turned to bite the hand that fed them, and while the feeding was undoubtedly a justifiable—indeed, a laudable—action, the time had now come for severity. Chamberlain's Birmingham speech had represented 'a parting of the ways' for British foreign policy which, since 1933, had operated upon two principles: that the Treaty of Versailles needed modification, and that 'it may often be wiser in such cases to let safety valves be opened than insist on their being eternally shut'.[139] Munich had been a 'noble achievement' for Chamberlain, who had not participated in the first act of the tragedy—the

---

[136] *Daily Herald*, 29 Mar. 1939, Leader, p. 8.
[137] *Daily Herald*, 31 Mar. 1939, 1st Leader, p. 8.
[138] *Sunday Times*, 19 Mar. 1939, Scrutator, p. 18.
[139] Ibid., 1st Leader, p. 18.

Treaty of Versailles—and had had to cope with the situation as he found it.[140]

Now Hitler's mask was off, and of the possible reasons adduced for the invasion, that of a danger from Czechoslovakia 'mocks credulity', and no pretence of urgency was even made. Britain's good will could hardly have been highly valued, for no attempt was made at consultation; 'We were apparently not thought worth the trouble, or perhaps he wished to avoid any risk that Munich might be repeated.'[141] The paper printed an article by Anthony Eden stating that the situation called for unity of response in Britain,[142] and that the 'instant need' was for every man and woman involved however remotely in supply or production of the three defence forces to 'put their best foot forward. It is no good waiting till worse happens; the time for effort is now. . . . It has been Britain's weakness that tempted others to aggression.'[143]

The following Sunday, Scrutator's analysis of 'What Next?' ran the full range of the paper's spectrum of attitude. Hitler had broken his word to Chamberlain and might well continue in this aggressive manner, but: 'It does not follow that war is inevitable: we do not go to war to improve a man's principles or morals.'[144] For the moment, however, Hitler's bond was no better than his word, and even deeds would only restore confidence slowly. In any event, for peace, Britain must rearm and see who would support her: 'In war—for we cannot avoid the military idiom of thought, however distasteful it may be— it is important to know what your friends as well as your enemy will do on the other side of the hill.'[145] Russia was the most willing after France and certainly the most anxious potential ally, 'and if it became necessary to take forceful action, it would be the height of folly to disdain the help of Russia because we dislike her domestic policy.' Poland, too, would be a useful ally. The Rumanian incident however lessened confidence in that nation:

The inaccurate disclosures of the German economic demands on Rumania and their contradiction, both alike on official authority,

[140] Ibid., Scrutator, p. 18.   [141] Ibid.
[142] Ibid., ed. art. by Anthony Eden, p. 18.
[143] Ibid., 1st Leader, p. 18.
[144] *Sunday Times*, 26 Mar. 1939, Scrutator, p. 18.   [145] Ibid.

show that there are dangerous cross-currents in Rumanian politics, and the terms of the Commercial Treaty as concluded show a remarkable deference to Germany which does not promise well for Rumania as a member of the United Front.[146]

OBSERVER

The *Observer*'s conversion had come in time for it to record the real meaning and significance of the invasion of Prague. Not only had Hitler now justified those who refused to believe his protestations of good will, but he had shown his 'contempt of those who had believed in him'.[147] *Mein Kampf* could now be seen as a real blueprint for policy rather than as a youthful indiscretion.[148] Not a coalition, but a 'Front Against Menace' was called for in the wake of Prague.

The most shameful and ominous passage in the modern annals of Europe was written last week. A stark tyranny, unknown since Napoleon's time but darker than his, trod down and trampled out with great iniquity the political life and freedom of another nation and another race. The last rag of human decency was discarded this time. . . . The fate of the doomed Czechs is that they were accused like the lamb in the fable of troubling the wolf's drinking water. What remained of the Czechoslovak Republic was destroyed with every circumstance of political brutality and humiliation that could lend lust to conquest. The warning is written in letters of fire before the eyes of all the free peoples in Europe and the world.[149]

DAILY MAIL AND DAILY EXPRESS

The *Daily Mail* was not particularly shocked by Hitler's move into Czechoslovakia. It had long stressed the need for rearmament, especially in the air, and when such rearmament was completed it would matter little what happened on the Continent. Hitler had, however, by going back on his own racial claims, created speculation as to what he would do next. 'Until the weekend he had marched along a fairly well-defined road.

---

[146] Ibid.   [147] *Observer*, 26 Mar. 1939, Leader, p. 16.
[148] *Observer*, 19 Mar. 1939, ed. art. by Garvin, p. 16.
[149] Ibid. The *Observer* went too far by claiming that Hitler had long-standing plans to invade Prague.

It was a German road. Non-Germans did not march with him.'[150]

Why was there no panicky reaction in Great Britain, as there had been on the Continent, to the events of mid-March, the *Daily Express* asked itself. 'Why are our heads cooler? Not because our hearts are hardened. Not because we have no sympathy with the Czechs. No. But we are not shocked by stale news. Munich decided that Germany was the boss in Eastern Euope.'[151] There was no reason now, or ever, for a British involvement in Europe; the pledge to Czechoslovakia was dissolved. Still, the paper had no illusions about the efficacy of appeasement which remained based on 'a childish faith' and dependent upon gestures of nothing more than 'sham' and 'make-believe'.[152]

Under the stress of these events, British policy had undergone 'probably the swiftest change' ever known. But 'The *Daily Express* is an Isolationist newspaper' which continued to view armament as the only and best way to ensure splendid isolation and status as a great but uninvolved power.[153]

SUMMER 1939: INTO WAR

The German invasion of Bohemia and Moravia effected a revolution in British policy. Within a few weeks a new course had been set, its tenor struck by the unprecedented Anglo-Polish guarantee which, fittingly enough, owed much to a journalist, one of the *News Chronicle*'s Berlin correspondents,[154] for its completion. For the first time the decision whether Great Britain would fight in Europe was placed wholly in the hands of another Power. Despite assertions that the Poles were a great historical people,[155] the fact remained that Poland was a military dictatorship whose treatment of its Jews was not

[150] *Daily Mail*, 17 Mar. 1939, Leader, p. 12. See also *Daily Mail*, 14 Mar. 1939, 1st Leader, p. 12; 15 Mar. 1939, p. 12; and 16 Mar. 1939, p. 12.

[151] *Daily Express*, 15 Mar. 1939, Leader, p. 12.

[152] *Daily Express*, 22 Mar. 1939, 6th Leader, p. 10.

[153] See *Daily Express*, 22 Mar. 1939, 1st Leader, p. 10; 23 Mar. 1939, 3rd Leader, p. 10; and 30 Mar. 1939, Leader, p. 12.

[154] See Ian Colvin, *Vansittart in Office*, p. 298 ff., for the story of Colvin's part in convincing Halifax and Chamberlain of the imminence of a German attack on Poland.

[155] *Sunday Times*, 27 Aug. 1939, Leader, p. 10.

very much better, and was certainly more violent, than that of
Nazi Germany's. The Polish Foreign Minister, Colonel Beck,
had a not altogether undeserved reputation for being shady
and deceitful; he certainly neglected to inform the British
Government of the overtures Hitler had been making since
the Munich settlement. Yet it was Beck who, in the now famous
phrase 'between two flicks of his cigarette', accepted the
responsibility of determining from Warsaw whether Britain
would fight against Germany.

While the various British papers continued to comment
upon the harsh Nazification of Austria and even to demand
restitution of Czechoslovakia before any European settlement
could be made, of all the peoples against whom Hitler made
territorial claims, the Poles were possibly the least 'attractive'
in terms of their Press image in Great Britain. Indeed, had
Hitler acted against Poland earlier in his career or had he not
taken Prague beforehand, it is unlikely that serious resistance
would have risen around Danzig or the Corridor, both of
which were German and one of which was already Nazi.
Assuming that he would have been satisfied with a 'corridor
across the Corridor' and the negotiated inclusion of Danzig in
the Reich (that is, his proposals to Lipski and Beck), these were
Hitler's most moderate and in many respects most justified
demands. But such considerations became irrelevant after
15 March.

For the British Government and much of the British Press, the
new impulse was strong and clear although the vocabulary
was strange and unfamiliar; the spirit was willing but the
flesh still unaccustomed. *The Times* dealt with the guarantee
to Poland: it was occasioned by the determination that international dealings must not continue to degenerate into the
habits of the jungle as they would if differences between larger
and smaller nations continued to be settled, as they had been
on the last four or five occasions, by reliance on the threat, or
the use, of force. The leading article continued that

The historic importance of the British Government's declaration
is that it commits them to stand for fair and free negotiation. The
new obligation which this country yesterday assumed does not
bind Great Britain to defend every inch of the present frontiers of
Poland. The key word in the declaration is not integrity but

'independence'. The independence of every negotiating State is what matters.[156]

Britain had never been a proponent of a policy of 'encirclement' against Germany and had not even opposed the natural extension of Germany's economic activities and influence, and the Polish guarantee was simply a stand for a return 'to decent and normal methods of diplomacy' and was anti-Nazi 'only in the sense that Nazi methods have called it into existence'.[157]

This leader caused a great uproar as it was widely interpreted as a return to appeasement on the part of *The Times* and, even worse, possibly presaging a return to appeasement on the part of the Government. In his Diary, Dawson notes his innocence:

3 April 1939. A great deal of to-do about Saturday's leader which was suspected (quite wrongly) of watering down the British Declaration and received some self-righteous comment from the *Daily Telegraph* and malignant abuse from the *News Chronicle*. It also ran the gauntlet in the House of Commons where there was a big debate in the afternoon . . . Edward [Halifax], with whom Dorothy and I lunched alone, was more reasonable in his comments and said that both he and the Prime Minister thought the article just right on first reading and were only worried later by the Poles and others.[158]

The *Daily Herald* insisted that there must be no falling into the trap of thinking, ' "Well, Britain and France have made their gesture and it has been effective. Germany has seen the red light. That is enough. Let us now make friends with Herr Hitler again and get back to appeasement." ' This might seem an obvious trap, but the paper feared that it would ensnare many 'unless there is a vigilant public opinion to guard against such a danger'.[159] The *News Chronicle* insisted that there must be no return to such a negative and dishonourable a policy which ought never to have been begun in the first place.[160] The *Daily Telegraph* stated that some 'mischievous misconceptions' concerning the Anglo-Polish guarantee had spread in certain quarters.

It has been asserted, for instance, that the statement 'involves no blind acceptance of the status quo', and its essence is that 'indepen-

[156] *The Times*, 1 Apr. 1939, p. 15.   [157] Ibid.
[158] Dawson Papers, Diary 1939, 3 Apr.
[159] *Daily Herald*, 3 Apr. 1939, Leader, p. 8.
[160] *News Chronicle*, 3 Apr. 1939, Leader, p. 10.

dence in negotiation must be restored to the weaker party'. If that were indeed the 'essence' of the matter it would be difficult to imagine anything so well calculated to spell jubilation in Berlin and stupefaction not in Warsaw alone, but in all other capitals which may be disposed to look to this country as a bulwark against aggression.

Such an interpretation as *The Times*'s article was taken to imply would mean that if Germany tried to take Danzig or even the Corridor, Britain would

. . . assist Poland to negotiate those territories away. That obviously makes sheer nonsense of the whole guarantee. The function of our new policy is not to aid and abet in aggression, but to intervene decisively and promptly with the whole of our resources the moment Poland finds it necessary in her 'vital interests' to fight in defence of her frontiers.[161]

This was only a momentary lapse for *The Times* which soon began a series of leading articles which clearly and concisely analysed the situation and came down for complete resistance to Germany. Indeed by June many of the papers would be making an effort to stress that Britain's new determination did not *preclude* negotiation under proper conditions.[162] For the first time in Germany's relations with the Western Democracies, the latter saw that the case at issue was not limited to the disputants alone. The Rhineland had been Germany's own back yard; Austria had been an internal settling of accounts with an aberration of the Versailles system; the Sudeten Germans were Germans by their very names. Prague had been the spoke in the wheel, and now the line was drawn:

The present crisis is not a crisis over Danzig or even over Poland only but over France and Great Britain. That Great Britain is threatened now as much as she was during the Napoleonic period and by Imperial Germany is not the mere thesis of the academic observer; it is recognized and has been recognized for some time by those responsible for the conduct of British foreign policy as the essential reality of the European situation.[163]

161 *Daily Telegraph*, 3 Apr. 1939, 1st Leader, p. 10.
162 See *Daily Telegraph*, 12 June 1939, 1st Leader, p. 12.
163 *Manchester Guardian*, 21 Aug. 1939, Dipl. Corr., p. 12.

As *The Times* stated it, 'Herr Hitler is dictator inside the Reich, and exacts and receives implicit obedience. He is not dictator outside it.'[164]

If Germany could think of no other way of living with her European neighbours than by subjugating them, then the law of self-preservation demanded that they join forces against Germany, and Britain would be with them.[165]

On 1 April Hitler spoke at Wilhelmshaven; although this speech was not nearly as dramatic as the one to the Reichstag at the end of the month, it was pregnant with indications of future policies. This was Hitler's first speech since before 15 March, and it was only to be expected that it would be met with scepticism at the very least. Coming the day after the announcement of the Anglo-Polish guarantee had provided the culmination of the various attempts at a united front which the British Government had been canvassing since 18 March, the Wilhelmshaven speech was the first expression of the propaganda line which Germany would pursue until the war: the threat of 'encirclement' by the Western Powers. Even the destruction of Czechoslovakia was partially explained by the fact that she had been 'the instrument of an attack which was to be launched against Germany'. Although France was included in the opprobrium, the main burden of the speech's accusations fell upon Britain, Poland was not mentioned at all, and Hitler's attack upon Russia was milder than usual.

Even if there were any connection between Hitler's speeches and his actions, the *Daily Telegraph* felt, nothing could be gathered from Wilhelmshaven. It merely repeated, 'in the usual strident tones and for the hundredth time, the wearisome story of Germany's alleged grievances, and served up the familiar jargon about "living space", "vital rights", "the place in the sun", "encirclement" and the rest'. The fact that no mention had been made of Poland meant nothing since there had been no references to Austria in many of his speeches before 20th February 1938 or to Czechoslovakia before 11 September 1938. 'In fact, it is part of his technique to be silent

164 *The Times*, 12 July 1939, 1st Leader, p. 15.
165 *The Times*, 21 Aug. 1939, 1st Leader, p. 11.

about the thing most immediately occupying his mind until
the actual moment selected for the coup. In a word, the practice
of Herr Hitler is to act first and talk afterwards.[166] The
Manchester Guardian thought the speech more defensive than
aggressive—but then that was 'a relative distinction'.[167] The
Sunday Times found 'no encouragement, no relief of any kind,
in yesterday's speech'. Again and again Hitler had flown in
the face of the world's clear will to peace, and broken his
word so frequently and so cavalierly that his word was no
longer trusted. ' "All he wants is to be left alone"! In that we
are willing to oblige him—if he will only leave other people
alone.'[168]

On Good Friday, 7 April 1939, Italian troops invaded
Albania. Only the *Daily Telegraph* came close to appreciating
the widest implications of this action: that this putative
assertion of independence in fact bound Italy closer than ever to
the Axis. It stated ironically that 'This latest move on the
part of the axis—for there can be no doubt of Germany's
foreknowledge and connivance—is a singular contribution
towards that "long peace" which Herr Hitler professed to
foresee in his Reichstag speech of January 30.'[169] Otherwise
the opprobrium centred upon Italy for such an impious act
on so holy a day. This precipitate attack served to draw
attention away from Germany.

A few weeks later, and a few days before Hitler's Reichstag
speech on 28 April, Nevile Henderson, who had been called
back to London immediately after the occupation of Prague,
returned to Berlin. In fact he was sent back (his French
colleague followed two days later) to inform Ribbentrop of
the Government's decision to introduce limited conscription
in Britain, and also to keep the channels of communication
open and underline the fact that there was no attempt being
made to encircle Germany by Britain and/or France.[170]
Holburn reported that Henderson's return was mainly to
spread the word of Britain's serious resolve, to perform the

[166] *Daily Telegraph*, 3 Apr. 1939, 1st Leader, p. 10.
[167] *Manchester Guardian*, 3 Apr. 1939, 1st Leader, p. 10
[168] *Sunday Times*, 2 Apr. 1939, 1st Leader, p. 18.
[169] *Daily Telegraph*, 8 Apr. 1939, 1st Leader, p. 10. We know now that Hitler
in fact had no foreknowledge of Mussolini's intention to invade Albania.
[170] See *DBFP* 3rd Ser. v, docs. 288, 289.

now more than ever vital function of 'Letting Germany Know'.[171]

The Government's critics among the press, however, saw dangers of backsliding in this move. The Americans were not rushing to send their Ambassador back (no mention was made of France); the *News Chronicle* felt that Britain's Ambassador should not return until the strain to friendly relations caused by the invasion of Czechoslovakia had been removed by some action on the part of Germany giving concrete proof that she was henceforth prepared to recognize the rights of other countries.[172] The next day the paper returned to the same subject and stated that unless there was a particular reason for sending Henderson back at that time, 'then the action becomes a diplomatic blunder of the first magnitude'.[173] The *Manchester Guardian* stated that regardless of the reasons or motives, one thing was extremely likely: 'That the return of Sir Nevile Henderson will arouse fresh suspicions about the consistency of the Government's policy. There is no reason to expect any display of major weakness, but the effects of Mr. Chamberlain's former policy and of the signs of half-heartedness since then have gone deep, and especially abroad the tendency to be sceptical feeds on any seeming opportunity.'[174]

On 14 April President Roosevelt had sent a peace appeal to Hitler and requested in it a specific verbal undertaking to respect the independence of thirty specified nations. Hitler set about circularizing the nations involved, asking whether they felt themselves menaced by Germany, and announced that he would reply to Roosevelt in the Reichstag on 28 April. 'The lambs are not going out of their way to tell the wolf that they are waiting for him to attack them', the *Daily Herald* stated, and pointed out that while these thirty demurrers might provide some good debating points for the Reichstag speech, it was the frantic German rearmament which spoke loudest.[175]

[171] *The Times*, 26 Apr. 1939, Berlin Corr, p. 15.

[172] *News Chronicle*, 24 Apr. 1939, 3rd Leader, p. 10.

[173] *News Chronicle*, 25 Apr. 1939, 1st Leader, p. 10.

[174] *Manchester Guardian*, 26 Apr. 1939, 2nd Leader, p. 10. See also ibid., Dipl. Corr., p. 6, and Berlin Corr., p. 11.

[175] *Daily Herald*, 22 Apr. 1939, 1st Leader, p. 8.

Considering what it actually did, the speech of 28 April elicited remarkably little comment from the British Press. This was partly because of Hitler's masterful carrot and stick technique and partly because British resolution was now quite ready for such shocks.

Despite some menacing references to it, Hitler had not denounced the Anglo-German Naval Agreement of 1935 on 1 April; such an action, the *Manchester Guardian* stated, would only have confirmed the worst fears and united British opinion further still.[176] This denunciation was duly made in Hitler's speech to the Reichstag on 28 April.

The speech ridiculed Roosevelt's intervention, and denounced the German-Polish Declaration of January 1934 as well as the Anglo-German Naval Agreement of June 1935. It is interesting that one of the reasons Hitler gave for denouncing the latter was Britain's activities of the last few weeks and also 'the anti-German attitude of the British Press, prompted by the British Government'.[177] This clearly refers to the change in attitude of those papers—particularly *The Times*, the *Daily Telegraph*, and the *Sunday Times*—which had hitherto been either sympathetic towards Germany or restrained by their close contact with Government circles, and is important to keep in mind when considering criticisms of *The Times*'s attitude after March 1939.

Although Hitler spoke bitterly about Poland, revealing the terms which had been rejected in March, his references to Britain, unlike the violent attacks of 1 April, were more in sorrow than in anger. He had always recognized, he said, the value and merit of the British Empire as a factor of order and stability in the world. An Anglo-German war would be lamentable—'nothing but the effluence of human wanton destructiveness'—since the only outstanding issue between the two countries was that of colonies which he had always made clear would not be a cause of conflict. That the German Government expected this speech to have a strong effect on British opinion was clear from the special measures taken to assure that an accurate English translation was made and circulated to the press agencies in London.[178]

[176] *Manchester Guardian*, 3 Apr. 1939, 1st Leader, p. 10.
[177] See *The Times*, 29 Apr. 1939, p. 13.   [178] See *DBFP* 3rd Ser. v, doc. 307.

Perhaps partly disarmed by Hitler's protestations of admiration and friendship, and partly anxious to disprove his allegations that it was anti-German, the British Press treated this speech most sympathetically. Indeed the *Daily Herald* thought it indicative of the crazy state of the world that Hitler's speech in which two treaties were torn up would nevertheless be regarded by many people as a mild and even conciliatory one.[179] Even the *Daily Herald* none the less felt that on the whole the speech gave the impression of a man not ready to risk major war.

The *Daily Telegraph* stated that 'Herr Hitler gave us only the smallest inkling as to the nature of these still outstanding grievances, but the tone of mockery alike in the modulation of his voice and in the substance of his remarks left no doubt that he is as far as ever from being appeased.'[180] Seeming to ignore the two denunciations it contained, however, the *Daily Telegraph* felt that talk was cheap and since it was clear that Hitler would not accept any outside initiatives for peace or make his own, the speech would do nothing to allay 'the profound anxiety of all his neighbours, big or little, as to when and where his next blow will fall'.[181] Similarly the *News Chronicle* wrote that 'Herr Hitler has spoken, and the world breathes again. The speech was specious, and—to those who wish to find it so—even plausible. It was an attempt to fan the dying embers of "appeasement" into flame once more.' The paper's conclusion was rather more pointed: three things emerged from two and a half hours of oratory—'two more pacts have been denounced, and Herr Hitler has refused to conduct negotiations except when wearing a gun'.[182]

Voigt wrote that Hitler's speech was 'a masterpiece of skill, cunning, and eloquence' which accomplished its main purpose of convincing the German people that they were 'encircled' and that Britain was intent upon aggression. The *Manchester Guardian* itself was somewhat more reserved, feeling that the 'eagerly awaited speech has not improved, if it has not greatly changed the situation'. Surprisingly cool about the

---

[179] *Daily Herald*, 29 Apr. 1939, Leader, p. 10.
[180] *Daily Telegraph*, 29 Apr. 1939, 1st Leader, p. 14.
[181] Ibid. See also *Daily Telegraph*, 1 May 1939, 1st Leader, p. 12.
[182] *News Chronicle*, 29 Apr. 1939, Leader, p. 8. See also *News Chronicle*, 1 May 1939, 1st Leader, p. 10.

treaty denunciations, the leading article was more concerned to deny the charges of encirclement. It was Hitler himself who united those who, rightly or wrongly, feared lest they become his victims.[183]

The *Daily Express* welcomed the speech by disregarding its menace entirely: 'Hitler opens the door to negotiations. That is the crux of his speech so far as we are concerned.'[184] Perhaps the most coldly critical of all the British Press was *The Times*. Although the paper's attitude was restrained, there was a scarcely veiled annoyance in its treatment of Hitler's reference to the British-led policy of encirclement: 'The whole course of British policy—the restraint, the constructive temper, and the pertinacious good will for which it has incurred so much obloquy from some types of critic—makes nonsense of the allegations of wilful British enmity on which he bases his suspicion of the Anglo-German naval agreement.'[185] A few days later the paper even dealt with Hitler's familiar references to the reparations burden under which Germany had suffered, and concluded that 'If, in fact, there is any grievance arising out of post-War financial transactions between Germany and the ex-Allies, it is rather the latter who have reason to complain.'[186] Holburn reported from Berlin the basis of the German attitude which saw international relations as a matter 'of enforcing Germany's right to carry through by appropriate methods—the criterion is "success"—and without interference from Britain a programme of treaty revision which does not affect England directly'.[187] On 5 May the *Daily Telegraph*'s correspondent was expelled from Berlin.

On 22 May, the Italian Foreign Minister, Count Ciano, was in Berlin for the signing of the Pact of Steel between Germany and Italy. Such a Pact had been long foreseen as a consequence of the Rome-Berlin Axis, but at this point Mussolini was far from anxious to bind himself to Hitler's

---

[183] *Manchester Guardian*, 29 Apr. 1939, 1st Leader, p. 12.
[184] *Daily Express*, 29 Apr. 1939, 1st Leader, p. 12.
[185] *The Times*, 29 Apr. 1939, 1st Leader, p. 15.
[186] *The Times*, 2 May 1939, 3rd Leader, p. 15.
[187] *The Times*, 1 May 1939, Berlin Corr., p. 13.

Germany in peace or war. Ciano noted in his diary that 'It
contains some real dynamite.'[188]

Such was the aversion in Britain now to Chamberlain's
policy of trying to split the dictators, and so hardened had the
British Press's attitude become by this time, that little attention
was given to this major landmark on the road to war. Despite
her uneasy reluctance, Italy found herself drawn ever closer
into Germany's plans. Italy was reaping the ill-will of its
Albanian pluck; whereas Mussolini was indeed wisely reluctant
to hitch his cart to the German horse, he was increasingly the
prisoner of his own policies. The reserve of good will in Britain
which had followed his successful intervention in the Czech
crisis had been somewhat dissipated after the Vienna Award
in November 1938 and after March 1939, but it disappeared
entirely when he invaded Albania. Henceforward the British
Press spoke only of the opposition between the Axis—including
of course Japan—and the Peace Front or Peace Bloc which
most of the newspapers were anxious for the British Government to consolidate immediately.

The Times felt that the signing of the Pact of Steel was
'a notable ceremony rather than a notable event', cementing
so obvious a relationship that it hardly seemed necessary.[189]
Göring supposedly burst into tears when he saw Ribbentrop
invested by Ciano with the Order of the Annunziata; The
Times acidly recalled that the last two recipients were said to
have been Emperor Haile Selassie and King Zog of Albania.[190]
The Daily Telegraph said that the new Pact only served to
make de jure an already de facto relationship.[191] The Manchester
Guardian was little surprised by the Pact—if indeed it had not
already existed: 'Germany and Italy want peace, but peace
with so many qualifications and reservations that the word
reads like a printer's error in this context.'[192] And the News
Chronicle saw in the Pact of Steel 'no new cause for anxiety':
it only confirmed the futility of any attempt to separate the
Axis nations.[193]

[188] Ciano, Diary, 13 May 1939.
[189] The Times, 23 May 1939, 2nd Leader, p. 17.   [190] Ibid.
[191] Daily Telegraph, 8 May 1939, 1st Leader, p. 12.
[192] Manchester Guardian, 23 May 1939, 1st Leader, p. 10.
[193] News Chronicle, 23 May 1939, 1st Leader, p. 10.

Almost immediately there occurred the first of two incidents which showed to good advantage the new firmness of British opinion. The first issue dealt with the transfer to Germany of £6,000,000 of Czech gold assets in the Bank of International Settlements. The impact of Hitler's invasion of Czechoslovakia was such that unlike the Rhineland or Austria or even the Sudetenland before it, Czechoslovakia's fate was kept in the limelight by the British Press. Even Garvin, no Czechophile, wrote that the invasion of Bohemia and Moravia was a Macbeth business for Hitler, and that their ghosts, like Banquo's, would be a grisly apparition at every feast until restitution was made.[194] This was true, and the spectre of Czechoslovakia's fate continued to haunt the British Press.[195]

There was thus a widespread uproar when it appeared that the British Government was countenancing or even assisting the transfer of Czech gold to the Nazi conquerors. Although the Bank of England had blocked Czech assets it held directly, it appeared that neither Otto Niemeyer nor Montagu Norman, the British Director of the B.I.S., was trying to stop this other transfer. Duncan Sandys put down a question in the House of Commons but was requested to withdraw it. The following day, however, the *Daily Telegraph* printed the story on the front page, as did Paul Einzig's *Financial News*.[196] Answering Lloyd George who mentioned these reports, the Prime Minister called the affair a 'mare's nest'. The facts became known, however, and although the Government itself appeared genuinely innocent, the matter was too galling to pass over.

The *Daily Telegraph* remarked that Sir John Simon, the Chancellor of the Exchequer, in his desire to avoid any interference with the independent jurisdiction of the B.I.S. 'had rather gone out of his way to keep himself in total ignorance of the actions of that institution'. And if, as appeared to be the case, the Bank was to become 'an instrument for aiding and

---

[194] *Observer*, 27 Aug. 1939, Garvin, p. 10.

[195] See, for example, *The Times*, 29 Apr. 1939, 1st Leader, p. 15; 19 June 1939, 1st Leader, p. 13; 23 Aug. 1939, ed. art. from a Corr. lately in Bohemia, p. 13; 24 Aug. 1939, 1st Leader, p. 11; *Daily Telegraph*, 16 May 1939, 1st Leader, p. 16; *Manchester Guardian*, 19 May 1939, ed. art. by Dr. Fritz Sternberg; 25 May 1939, 2nd Leader, p. 10; *News Chronicle*, 2 June 1939, 3rd Leader, p. 8; 26 June 1939, p. 13; 12 July 1939, ed. art., p. 8; *Daily Herald*, 14 June 1939, 3rd Leader, p. 10; *Observer*, 27 Aug. 1939, Garvin, p. 10.

[196] See *Daily Telegraph*, 19 May 1939, Political Corr., p. 1.

abetting in aggression then the sooner its statutes are radically revised the better.'[197] The paper's final verdict was that the Exchequer was exonerated but possibly not the British representative at the B.I.S., and that the whole incident was to the 'extreme discredit' of the Bank itself.[198] The *News Chronicle*'s attitude was mainly the same as the *Daily Telegraph*'s.[199] The *Manchester Guardian* stated that Chamberlain's 'mare's nest' attitude would not decrease the anxiety of those who watched the progress of negotiations over the disposition of the Czech gold.[200]

The matter seemed to pass over with Simon's statement that he was not entitled to ask the B.I.S. about its transfers. Later the same evening he saw Montagu Norman, who told him that the system of accountancy of gold deposits in the Bank of England had just been changed and it was now impossible to tell to whom particular gold assets belonged. Simon told this to Henry Strakosch the next morning during a game of golf on Walton Heath. Three days later Strakosch told this to Einzig who was able to piece together a story which he published the next morning, 31 May. Bank and Treasury officials were stunned and no one could imagine how this information had leaked out.[201] Although this caused little further attention in the British Press, it undoubtedly served warning that ammunition was ready to hand should any attempt to be made to transfer the gold. For whatever reasons, the Germans let the matter drop completely. The *Daily Herald* had the last word, calling for immediate nationalization to bring the Bank of England and its Governors under Parliamentary control.[202]

The other 'mare's nest' incident was potentially more serious, involving as it did a definite, if peripheral, revival of attempts at economic appeasement. *Staatsrat* Helmuth Wohltat had come to London early in June to forward the idea that Britain should 'recognize Germany's sphere of economic interest in

[197] *Daily Telegraph*, 27 May 1939, 2nd Leader, p. 12.
[198] *Daily Telegraph*, 6 June 1939, 2nd Leader, p. 16.
[199] *News Chronicle*, 23 May 1939, 2nd Leader, p. 16.
[200] *Manchester Guardian*, 24 May 1939, 3rd Leader, p. 10.
[201] Gilbert and Gott, *The Appeasers*, p. 212.
[202] *Daily Herald*, 21 June 1939, 2nd Leader, p. 8.

South-East and Eastern Europe'. He met Sir Horace Wilson and Sir Joseph Ball at the Duke of Westminster's house in Eaton Square; and he lunched with Frank Ashton-Gwatkin on 7 June. Neither of these meetings became known. After a month in Spain, Wohltat returned to London ostensibly to head the German delegation to the International Whaling Conference held at the Ministry of Fisheries and Agriculture. R. S. Hudson, Secretary of the Board of Overseas Trade, told the Norwegian delegate to the Conference that he would like to talk to Wohltat, and a meeting was arranged for the evening of 20 July.

Word of this meeting reached Vernon Bartlett from three different Embassies, and after making an oblique reference at the end of an article on 20 July,[203] he scored what his paper called 'an outstanding journalistic "scoop" ' when it was printed in full on the 22nd.[204] It will suffice here to say that the newspapers probably never discovered the extent of the proposals made during this conversation; nor did they ever discover the more important and equally far-reaching conversation between Wohltat and Sir Horace Wilson on 18 June. While the German Press published rather more complete details of the British suggestions, Hudson gave an exclusive interview to the *Daily Express* which was the only first-hand source of information available and was the basis of most other British newspaper commentary. He said that he had insisted to Wohltat that Hitler must understand that any attempt to rule Europe by force would be resisted and that he had insisted upon such preconditions as disarmament and withdrawal from Czechoslovakia as precedents to a loan.[205]

Alternatively it is possible that the newspapers knew much more than they told, but operated on the assumptions that Hudson was, as a junior member of the House of Commons, more vulnerable but less important than the shadowy and powerful Wilson, and that one example would be sufficient to scotch the attempt without endangering public morale. The *Manchester Guardian*'s Political Correspondent pointed out that it was Hudson who had led the revolt of junior Ministers for a

[203] *News Chronicle*, 20 July 1939, Vernon Bartlett, p. 2.
[204] *News Chronicle*, 22 July 1939, p. 1, and 25 July, p. 1.
[205] *Daily Express*, 24 July 1939.

stronger foreign policy in December 1938, and that being no 'appeasementeer', he was hardly a likely instrument for an appeasement move by the Government.[206]

For whatever reasons, it was generally held that Hudson had, in an innocent unofficial capacity, suggested that if Europe could be secured against aggression, a genuine movement toward disarmament be put under way, and the independence of the Czechs restored, then 'the way would be open for those measures of economic and financial cooperation with which Europe could, if it would, attain a higher level of prosperity than it has ever known'.[207]

On the basis of this information, *The Times* pointed out that Hudson had put forward 'nothing more than might be heard with universal approval from a member of any British party on any platform'. Indeed his alleged statements were almost platitudinous.[208] In defending Hudson, *The Times* could not resist taking a swipe at some of its hypercritical colleagues:

So far there can be no censure of Mr. Hudson. Nothing that he advanced was in the least degree inconsistent with national policy as all schools of thought now understand and accept it. But, if he had known to what unscrupulous use, above all in the German Press, his talk was to be put, it is safe to say that he would never have embarked upon it—and there criticism speaks for itself. In Germany it was represented quite falsely, as a British offer to buy German 'rights' for a loan, and since there are for some reason politicians and journalists in this country whose pertinacious and insufferable self-righteousness devotes itself only too readily to the depreciation of British undertakings, it seemed likely that German propaganda would be echoed over here in allegations that British policy was 'weakening'.[209]

The *Daily Telegraph* was satisfied that Chamberlain and Halifax had removed all doubts on the matter and agreed with the Prime Minister that the greatest danger from the affair lay in its disclosure.[210] In the *Manchester Guardian*, Voigt warned against Wohltat's attempts to spread the

[206] *Manchester Guardian*, 25 July 1939, Political Corr., p. 11.
[207] *The Times*, 25 July 1939, 2nd Leader, p. 13.   [208] Ibid.
[209] Ibid. See also ibid., Parliamentary Corr., and Berlin Corr., p. 12.
[210] *Daily Telegraph*, 25 July 1939, 3rd Leader, p. 16.

notion that without financial aid Germany would crash and fall a prey to Bolshevism. 'Herr Wohltat professes to be a "Moderate" ', Voigt wrote, '—but it is always "Moderates" who are sent by the German Government to explore, to exercise an influence, and to encourage all those who are trying to promote "appeasement".'[211] A leading article on 'Mr. Hudson's Conversation' was quite critical, taking exception to Chamberlain's statement that the conversations were not wrong but their being publicized was: 'These things always get out. It was not the wicked newspapers which are to blame, but the wicked people who persist in telling them all that happens, or sometimes does not happen.'[212]

The *News Chronicle* spoke strongly against 'Hudson's Howler' as 'a grave disservice to the cause of peace', and regretted that its absurdity was not its only demerit. 'For such a scheme to be put forward, even tentatively and unofficially, by a member of the British Government can only encourage the Nazis to believe that Britain is weakening and trying to find once more the path to "appeasement".'[213] The *Daily Herald*, too, scorned Chamberlain who saw no harm in such a conversation, in which a Minister had used an official meeting for the propagation of his unofficial views: 'even though reports of those views cause world-wide confusion regarding British foreign policy at a time of international tension, what odds?'[214]

Sometimes the balance between willingness to negotiate under the right circumstances and immovable determination to resist any further German aggression tottered and had to be redressed. Symptomatic of this were Lord Halifax's two speeches in June. On 8 June the Foreign Secretary spoke in the House of Lords. He reaffirmed that negotiation was the best policy. That this was something of a trial balloon was indicated by *The Times*'s statement that the most interesting thing about the speech would be the German reaction to it.[215] The *Observer* expressed the hope that Halifax's 'most earnest

211 *Manchester Guardian*, 25 July 1939, Dipl. Corr., p. 15.
212 *Manchester Guardian*, 25 July 1939, 3rd Leader, p. 10.
213 *News Chronicle*, 25 July 1939, 2nd Leader, p. 8.
214 *Daily Herald*, 25 July 1939, Leader, p. 8.
215 *The Times*, 9 June 1939, 1st Leader, p. 17.

and decisive words' would carry far.[216] Already, however, Holburn had reported that the German attitude was negative.[217] The speech was made on Thursday, the German reaction known by Saturday, and two officially inspired statements were issued that day. The first appeared in the *Sunday Times* of 11 June. A leading article on 'Our Unaggressive Stand Against Aggression' disabused those who considered Halifax's speech as marking a return to appeasement and an abandonment of Britain's new commitments in Eastern Europe. 'No such abandonment, it can be said with authority, either was or is intended. The British Government stands firm by all its recent agreements, and is sincerely anxious to round them off as early as possible by a suitable agreement with Russia.'[218] Lest any doubt remain, the following day the *Daily Telegraph* stated that there should be no apprehension:

Some suggestion has been made that the very frankness of phrasing which our statesmen employed gives occasion to fear a weakening of the Government's purpose, a deviation from the clear lines of the New Policy inaugurated on the morrow of the March coup in Czechoslovakia, and a dilution of that policy with the familiar ingredients of 'appeasement'. Any such suspicion, it can be said at once, is completely without foundation. . . . There is not a word or a gesture in the latest Ministerial utterances which indicates the slightest intention of adopting any such deviation.[219]

At the end of the month Halifax made another speech, this time to the Royal Institute of International Affairs. While he still spoke of the 'twin foundations' of British policy— the determination to get on with the constructive work of building peace and the determination to resist force—this time the emphasis was clearly on the latter. 'The threat of military force is holding the world to ransom, and our immediate task is . . . to resist aggression', Halifax stated. 'I would emphasize that tonight with all the strength at my command, so that nobody may misunderstand it.'[220]

This speech elicited almost universal approval in the

[216] *Observer*, 11 June 1939, Garvin, p. 14.
[217] *The Times*, 10 June 1939, Berlin Corr., p. 12.
[218] *Sunday Times*, 11 June 1939, 1st Leader, p. 18.
[219] *Daily Telegraph*, 12 June 1939, 1st Leader, p. 12.
[220] For the text of this speech, see *The Times*, 30 June 1939, p. 9.

British Press. The *Manchester Guardian* deemed it the finest speech made by a Minister since the National Government began, and was content that 'the knowledge that British policy has at last been clearly defined and firmly spoken in a manner of which no man need feel ashamed will help many, who hitherto have lacked that meagre comfort, to screw their courage to the sticking-point'.[221] The *News Chronicle* felt that Lord Halifax had said the right things in the right order in 'a finely balanced speech, couched in dignified but firm language, and it will meet with the general approval of the British people this morning'.[222]

The Times devoted much of its leading article to elucidation in the form of restatement of extracts from the speech. Dealing specifically with Danzig, the paper echoed that it was an international problem only because Germany had made it such. 'Neither in the status nor in the internal administration of the Free City is there anything which in a rational world need be the cause of an international war; but if the Reich chooses to upset the present state of affairs by force and if Poland's independence is thereby threatened, then this country will fight without hesitation on the side of Poland.'[223] Only the *Daily Express* maintained its opposition and criticized Halifax's speech.[224]

After top-secret negotiations which had gone on since 17 April, a final German push secured Soviet agreement, and on 22 August, Ribbentrop flew to Moscow for the final negotiation and signing of a non-aggression pact. At the very time of its signing, the British and French military missions were in Moscow trying to find some formula for agreement with the Soviets. Hitler had placed great reliance on this sudden ideological and political *volte face* stunning and immobilizing the Western Powers into cowed submission. More practically, it would remove the threat of an Anglo-French-Soviet front aimed against Germany, and would effectively isolate Poland.

[221] *Manchester Guardian*, 30 June 1939, 1st Leader, p. 10.
[222] *News Chronicle*, 30 June 1939, Leader, p. 8. See also *News Chronicle*, 3 July 1939, 1st Leader, p. 8.
[223] *The Times*, 30 June 1939, 1st Leader, p. 17.
[224] *Daily Express*, 30 June 1939, 1st Leader, p. 10.

At this point German plans called for the invasion of Poland
on 26 August. Nevile Henderson came to Berchtesgaden on
the 23rd to deliver a letter from Chamberlain written after the
Cabinet of the 22nd, which had discussed the announcement
of Ribbentrop's departure, and determined resolutely to
honour its commitments: 'If the case should arise, they are
resolved, and prepared, to employ without delay all the
forces at their command, and it is impossible to foresee the
end of hostilities once engaged.'[225]

There were two factors most important in determining
the British reaction: nothing was known of the terms of the
Pact for three days after its announcement (knowledge of the
exchanges between Hitler and Henderson and Chamberlain
being confined to the participants), and although the Germans
openly treated the Pact as an important step towards the
partition or even destruction of Poland,[226] the Soviets, for
whatever reasons, fostered the impression that the Pact was in
no wise incompatible with the negotiations with Britain and
France then in progress. The British Press, the only source of
public information for a crucial three days, therefore assumed
that the new Pact was either a regular, if singularly ill-timed,
non-aggression pact such as Russia had in fact concluded with
many nations; or that the new Pact was a Russian ploy to 'ginger
up' the British and French negotiations,[227] and that the
Russians might well come over to the West if they were now
offered everything they demanded;[228] or that the Pact was
rather a German ploy in the war of nerves, intended to shake
Britain's resolution. The result was that the effect of what was
in fact a tremendous diplomatic coup was utterly muted and
by the time second thoughts could be indulged—around the
28th—events had moved too far and too fast for the full
realization to have any effect.

The Times affirmed on the 23rd that whatever the Pact's
terms proved, 'Great Britain at any rate has taken her stand,
and she will not draw back.' The paper's Special Correspondent in Moscow (the first *Times* correspondent ever in Soviet

[225] *DBFP* 3rd Ser. vii, doc. 200.
[226] *Manchester Guardian*, 24 Aug. 1939, 2nd Leader, p. 8.
[227] *News Chronicle*, 24 Aug. 1939, Leader, p. 10.
[228] *Manchester Guardian*, 23 Aug. 1939, 1st Leader, p. 8.

Russia) reported the Soviet claim that there was no inconsistency involved and that the Anglo-French negotiations could go on. 'In any case', the paper noted, putting the shoe nicely on the Nazi foot, 'it is morally damaging to the Nazi regime—if any moral credit remains to it—that it should turn suddenly to a Government about which all its leaders have been scathingly contemptuous ever since they came into power and against whose machinations they used to claim that National Socialism was the one strong bulwark in the world.'[229] Two days later the paper reaffirmed that Britain was united and commented that the rumours that the new Pact partitioned Poland 'only shows what brutal cynicism can credibly be attributed to States in which all vestiges of individual liberty have disappeared'.[230]

Similarly, the *Daily Telegraph* stated that Britain stood firm—'A Nation's Constant Mind'. Hitler planned everything for maximum effect, but the Poles remained nonplussed and France was trustworthy without a doubt.[231] As far as the Pact itself was concerned, even given Hitler's penchant for the dramatic, it seemed utterly impossible—as if water had begun to run uphill. Still, in spite of the circumstances and until something definite was known of the terms, it was possible to believe that the Russians genuinely saw no incompatibility with the proposed Peace Front Pact; it had been pointed out that other Soviet non-aggression pacts all had escape clauses and one could only wait and see whether this one did.[232] By the 28th, an editorial article by Robert Hield stated that 'under the name of "anti-aggression" it marks, in fact, an indispensable step in the fulfilment of a plan of unbounded aggression at the expense of individual freedom and national independence. In resisting it, Great Britain, France and their associates are defending not merely their own interests, but the fundamental conditions of human progress.'[233]

The *Manchester Guardian*'s initial reaction was mainly to wonder how the German people would react to this sudden turn-about abandonment of anti-Bolshevism and how much

---

[229] See *The Times*, 23 Aug. 1939, 1st Leader, p. 13, and Spec. Moscow Corr., p. 12.

[230] *The Times*, 25 Aug. 1939, 1st Leader, p. 13.

[231] *Daily Telegraph*, 23 Aug. 1939, 1st Leader, p. 12.

[232] Ibid.   [233] *Daily Telegraph*, 28 Aug. 1939, ed. art. by Robert Hield, p. 8.

reliance the Soviets could expect to attach to Hitler's promises.[234] None the less, until the actual text of the Pact was known,
'no one in this country will pre-judge the issue. We shall not
have long to wait, however, before events will show'.[235]
The *Manchester Guardian* adopted the curious line that, even
assuming that there was nothing sinister about the Pact, it
would none the less serve to encourage the Germans.

There are still some who, because they wish it, pretend to find
encouragement in the news, but no encouragement can be found.
On its most favourable interpretation the Russian move, coming
at such a time and in such a manner, is a diplomatic blunder which
must inevitably impair the confidence of the democratic countries
(those 'non-aggressive Powers' so recently praised by Mr. Molotoff)
and encourage the Fascist Powers in their designs.[236]

Voigt, as we have seen, was not so surprised that these two
states with their 'apparently contrasting and yet essentially
similar natures' should come together. He incorrectly stated
that the secret negotiations had begun in March before the
occupation of Prague and that ever since then Russia was
playing the West false: 'The prospective alliance was a shadow,
the German-Russian agreement was a reality.'[237] On 25
August the paper could at last comment upon the text which, it
stated, had 'none of the redeeming features which the hopeful
had assumed; its repudiation of the idea of assisting any victim
of Germany's aggression is as wholehearted as Russia's earlier
enthusiasm to assist any victim that could be found'.[238] The
Pact was thus worse than had been feared: 'It is indeed a
pact of non-aggression, but it is more: it is a pact of friendship.'[239] There was no escape clause as had been so confidently
predicted by Soviet statesmen in Moscow and by the faithful
in Great Britain so that Russia could get out if Germany
aggressed against a third party. 'There we have it in black and
white. Russia cannot join the coalition for peace nor, if
Germany attacks Poland, can she engage in war against her.
The German Press was right. The pact, which was hailed by
the British Communist party as "a victory for peace and

[234] *Manchester Guardian*, 23 Aug. 1939, 1st Leader, p. 8.
[235] *Manchester Guardian*, 24 Aug. 1939, 2nd Leader, p. 8.   [236] Ibid.
[237] *Manchester Guardian*, 25 Aug. 1939, Dipl. Corr., p. 6.
[238] Ibid., 1st Leader, p. 10.   [239] Ibid., 2nd Leader, p. 10.

Socialism against Fascism", will clearly make it easier for Germany to carry out her aggressive plans in Europe.'[240] On 26 August, Voigt guessed rightly the full infamy of the Pact: 'There is a growing belief here that, as was suggested in these columns yesterday, Germany and Russia have agreed on the partition of Poland and that the Baltic States are to be a Russian sphere of influence.'[241]

The *News Chronicle*, which had been so insistent upon Russia's inclusion in the Peace Front, and had so castigated the British Government for not achieving this, now affirmed that whatever else happened, the decision for war or peace still lay in Warsaw. One could only wait and see, and meanwhile the effect on the Axis might not be entirely without disadvantage for Hitler. Germany's Anti-Comintern partner Japan would not be pleased, Catholic France would certainly not be jubilant, and the German people would find it difficult to accept this 'sudden and cynical reversal of policy'.[242] Vernon Bartlett thought that like Munich, the Nazi-Soviet Pact might bring a postponement of war because Hitler might think that he could get whatever he wanted by threats. Bartlett wrote reassuringly that 'No man in the whole course of human history has better understood that an army is most useful if it is not called into action.'[243]

The *News Chronicle* developed a unique line of analysis the following day: that Russia now had the leading hand in European diplomacy since the Nazi-Soviet Pact was

by no means signed, sealed and delivered as was first suggested from Berlin. Nor need we suppose—until we hear the terms authoritatively —that it implies anything like an alliance. Indeed we have as yet no firm ground for saying that it involves any change in Russia's policy at all. According to one cynical view, Stalin has done nothing more than take a very drastic step to ginger up the Governments of London and Paris.[244]

Even when the terms were known, the paper held out hope against hope—'Moscow has yet to clarify the situation beyond

[240] Ibid.   [241] *Manchester Guardian*, 26 Aug. 1939, Dipl. Corr., p. 11, and 1st Leader, p. 10; also *Manchester Guardian*, 25 Aug. 1939, Dipl. Corr., p. 6.
[242] *News Chronicle*, 23 Aug. 1939, Leader, p. 8.
[243] *News Chronicle*, 23 Aug. 1939, ed. art. by Vernon Bartlett, p. 8.
[244] *News Chronicle*, 24 Aug. 1939, Leader, p. 10.

all doubt.'[245] By 28 August, the *News Chronicle* could only pettishly say that the Pact had not been as clever as the Nazis had hoped since 'its effect on our nerves has been negligible'.[246]

The *Daily Herald*'s reaction was 'We stand firm', and it shared some of the hope but none of the illusions of its colleagues. Details lacking, it was still possible to hope, 'though it must be confessed that it is the barest of hopes—that when they are known the implications of this agreement will not prove so grave as they now appear. Unless the most optimistic interpretation proved right, however, this would be a grave set-back for international relations.'[247]

The *Daily Express* had only wanted the Russian Pact to implement the Polish guarantee which it had opposed in the first place. Besides, the Poles had never wanted Russian involvement. Now the *Daily Express* was relieved and vindicated, and nothing was changed: Britain still would defend Poland. The paper seemed impervious to the obvious strategic implication of the Nazi-Soviet Pact.[248]

Although the final crisis over Poland had been long building, the really precipitate decline only began in the very last days of August. On the 29th, in the evening, Hitler demanded the arrival of a Polish plenipotentiary within twenty four hours, near midnight on the 30th Ribbentrop read to Henderson a list of sixteen proposals which had been prepared for negotiation with the Polish Government. Although Ribbentrop read them 'at top speed' and refused to give Henderson a copy, the British Ambassador's immediate impression (he was quite right) was that although they were harsh, at face value the proposals were 'not unreasonable'.[249] It is now known that the proposals were not meant to be a basis for discussion at all.

Even without the benefit of Halder's diary, however, the British Press wasted no second thoughts on such will-o'-the-wisp generosity. *The Times* considered the German methods very confusing and bluntly stated that 'The German statement

[245] *News Chronicle*, 25 Aug. 1939, Leader, p. 10.
[246] *News Chronicle*, 28 Aug. 1939, Leader, and ed. art. by J. B. Priestley, p. 8.
[247] *Daily Herald*, 23 Aug. 1939, Leader, p. 8.
[248] *Daily Express*, 22 Aug. 1939, 1st Leader, p. 8.
[249] Henderson, *Failure of a Mission*, p. 273.

does not correspond with such facts as are known to the British Government.'[250] The next day it branded the German claim that the Poles had rejected the German proposals as a 'blatant lie'.[251]

The *Daily Telegraph* deemed the German demands a mockery —an unacceptable ultimatum.[252] The *Manchester Guardian* on the last day of peace found it difficult not to believe that the German tactics were 'in the nature of by-play'.[253] Voigt saw that the German proposals revealed the familiar method: 'They are very skilful in so far as they have a certain plausibility.'[254] It hardly seemed conceivable, however, that Germany could describe as already 'rejected' terms which had only just arrived.[255] The *Sunday Times* stated that Hitler had gone into the crisis with ill-will, mirrored in his spurious, cleverly drafted 'terms' to Poland.[256] Now the *Daily Express* saw that Hitler never wanted peace with Poland and that all the diplomatic manœuvring was just a blind to satisfy the German public.[257]

At a time like this, as the world poised perilously on the brink of war, it was frustrating for the British newspapers (and especially important for us to bear in mind) that their reports of action were a day behind the events. On 2 September, however, what information there was about the German invasion of Poland appeared in all the papers. 'The long period of international tension, never appreciably relaxed throughout the summer, was ended yesterday by an act of naked aggression, which by itself exposes the hollowness of all Nazi declarations of peaceful intent and Herr Hitler's clumsy sophistries.' That it was one man's war—Hitler's war—alone was now clear beyond doubting.[258] 'Before the facts are drowned in the flood of propaganda', the *Daily Telegraph* insisted, 'guilt for the war should be fixed where it belongs.' And where the guilt belonged was clear—it was with

250 *The Times*, 1 Sept. 1939, 1st Leader, p. 11.
251 *The Times*, 2 Sept. 1939, 2nd Leader, p. 11.
252 *Daily Telegraph*, 1 Sept. 1939, 1st Leader, p. 10.
253 *Manchester Guardian*, 31 Aug. 1939, 1st Leader, p. 6.
254 *Manchester Guardian*, 1 Sept. 1939, Dipl. Corr., p. 9.
255 Ibid.   256 *Sunday Times*, 3 Sept. 1939, Leader, p. 8.
257 *Daily Express*, 2 Sept. 1939, Leader, p. 8.
258 *The Times*, 2 Sept. 1939, 1st Leader, p. 11.

Hitler 'impelled by over-mastering desire to bring off a single-handed coup',[259] and an editorial article traced 'Hitler's Grim Six-Year Record in Technique of Perfidy'.[260] The *Daily Express* felt that Britain's labours for peace and offers of negotiation had not been in vain because 'they have shown clearly that the responsibility for war rests on one man'.[261] Garvin wrote that Hitler had only used force to feed the 'fixed fanaticism of his insensate dream of racial domination'.[262]

Now, unlike at any time during the past four years, and perhaps even unlike 1914,[263] the British people were firmly united and resigned to the necessity and anxious to earn the glory of the present situation. Indeed, the *Daily Telegraph* stated that Britons were disappointed that they had to wait upon Mussolini's last attempt to secure a peaceful settlement over the weekend of 2–3 September: 'Had the mood of our people been the overriding factor in the situation, the first shot across the Polish frontier would have been the signal for British intervention.'[264] Not only was Britain determined but Poland as well, and notwithstanding the Nazi-Soviet Pact, it was envisaged that Hitler would find himself facing exactly what he had striven to avoid—a two-front war.[265]

By this time the question of war aims was both irrelevant and taken for granted: it was Hitler's war, and beyond ridding the world of him and his barbarous and crazed régime, there seemed little need for further formulation. The *Daily Telegraph* affirmed that 'Poland, France and ourselves will stand together in determination that we shall see this struggle through, not laying down our arms until we have assured that aggressive force cannot establish dominion over the world.'[266] For the *Manchester Guardian*, it was for 'the overthrow of this dictator and his system of government that we enter the war'.[267]

---

[259] *Daily Telegraph*, 2 Sept. 1939, 2nd Leader, p. 10.

[260] *Daily Telegraph*, 4 Sept. 1939, ed. art. by H. C. Baily, p. 8; also 2 Sept. 1939, ed. art. by R. Hield, p. 11.

[261] *Daily Express*, 2 Sept. 1939, Leader, p. 8.

[262] *Observer*, 3 Sept. 1939, Garvin, p. 8.

[263] *Manchester Guardian*, 2 Sept. 1939, 1st Leader, p. 8; also *Daily Telegraph*, 2 Sept. 1939, 1st Leader, p. 10.

[264] *Daily Telegraph*, 4 Sept. 1939, 1st Leader, p. 8.

[265] *The Times*, 1 Sept. 1939, 1st Leader, p. 11; also *Daily Telegraph*, 1 Sept. 1939, 1st Leader, p. 10.   [266] *Daily Telegraph*, 2 Sept. 1939, 1st Leader, p. 10.

[267] *Manchester Guardian*, 2 Sept. 1939, 1st Leader, p. 8.

Poland's fate today, if permitted to go the German way, would be that of Holland, Switzerland and Belgium tomorrow and of Britain and France the day after.[268] Two days later, with war begun, it was now felt that 'The future of the world is at stake, and for one of the great leading Powers of Europe to leave the world to its fate would be an act of abdication deadly to its good name and to its spirit and its character.'[269] It was both curious and characteristic that the *Manchester Guardian*, which wrote knowingly and bitterly of Hitler's amorality and duplicity throughout the latest crisis, should add that the agreement for the limitation of bombing, which France and Britain had undertaken, would provide 'another test of Germany's good faith whether Hitler also responds'.[270]

Other papers expressed similar resolution,[271] and all agreed with the *Sunday Times*: the issue no longer lay in Danzig nor even in Poland: 'We are dealing with a threat to the peace and liberties of the world.'[272]

[268] Ibid.

[269] *Manchester Guardian*, 4 Sept. 1939, 2nd Leader, p. 6. See also ibid., 1st, 3rd, and 4th Leaders.

[270] *Manchester Guardian*, 2 Sept. 1939, 1st Leader, p. 8. See also ibid., 2nd Leader, p. 8.

[271] See *News Chronicle*, 1 Sept. 1939, Leader, p. 8, and *Daily Herald*, 4 Sept. 1939, Leader, p. 6.

[272] *Sunday Times*, 3 Sept. 1939, Leader, p. 8.

6

CONCLUSION:
THE PSYCHOLOGY OF APPEASEMENT

THE psychology of appeasement emerged from a complex of causes and factors. It took the advent of Hitler and his Nazi revolution to make the British Government, first under MacDonald and Baldwin and finally under Neville Chamberlain, equip this psychology with an actual policy. Once under way, the policy stirred deep feelings of approval and disapproval in Britain and the world; but that it was firmly rooted in the British conscience could not be denied. Every British newspaper by 1933 was the disciple of the gospel of Keynes and Nicolson, and the wisdom of the experience of years could not be put aside when events precipitated the Hitler Government.

When the confusion of German politics suddenly crystallized into Hitler in January 1933, the British Press was little equipped to understand and analyse the real nature of this event. One has, of course, to allow for hindsight; Dr. Granzow is prone to seeing the later devil in the early demon, and strongly criticizes those papers which, before January 1933, treated the Nazis as just another party of the right and Hitler as just another demagogic politician.[1] But the fact is that the Nazis were just one among a number of radical anti-Semitic parties spewed up in the Weimar Republic. Their greatest electoral strength in a free contest was only 37 per cent, and by the time Hitler was called to the Chancellery through Papen's machinations (and hopefully surrounded in a web of 'safe' conservative Ministers), they had passed their electoral peak. The movement itself was not monolithic and although the Strassers gave up more easily, it took the purge of 30 June 1934 to settle Hitler's supremacy over Röhm and the SA. The death of Hindenburg

---

[1] Brigitte Granzow, *A Mirror of Nazism*. See pp. 119, 124, 126–7.

(whose stolid figure did much to bemuse the British Press) in August 1934 gave Hitler yet another opportunity to increase his power, but it was not until after February 1938 that the Army and the Foreign Office were effectively under his control and he could proceed more or less unheeding along his then-chosen course of aggrandizement based upon the possibility of aggression.

Dr. Granzow is, at any rate, correct in pointing out one of the great mistakes of the British newspapers in the years before the Nazis came to power. They assumed after 1930 that legality ('responsibility') would temper the Nazis and make them respectable; there was also a doubt in some papers that perhaps a disservice had been performed: surely if so many people, especially young people, suddenly began voting for the Nazis, they could not be so totally bad after all. As Crozier wrote to Voigt in July 1932, 'I have heard the question raised in conversation how the Hitlerites can be as bad as they are represented to be if they form so large a part of the people. I suppose a lot of people who are just weary of, and disgusted with, the last years have joined their ranks. However, I know you will keep the balance of justice even.'[2] There was, further, the question of untoward interference in German affairs: as Kennedy wrote to Ebbutt in October 1931 when the latter had suggested a leading article about keeping Brüning in office:

If the Nazis, therefore, are the people who really count, had they not better be the people in office? . . . Hitlerism seems in one sense to be a sort of national neurosis, and the best way of treating it may be to let it come to the surface and then treat the patient gently but firmly. I do not see that *fundamentally* the Nationalists' foreign policy can really differ much in practice from that of Brüning.[3]

Until they suddenly came to power, and even for some years thereafter, the Nazis were a party in which two or three people and elements were disputing with Hitler for control and leadership. As late as February 1933, Crozier had to caution Alexander Werth, who had just replaced Voigt in Berlin, against assuming too much familiarity on the part of British readers with things like Hitler's Twenty-five Points or with

[2] Crozier to Voigt, 22 July 1932, *Manchester Guardian* archives.
[3] Kennedy to Ebbutt, 8 Oct. 1931, *The Times* archives.

Horst Wessel. 'For instance', he explained, 'I am constantly keeping out of the leader columns reference to the "Weimar Constitution" and the "Third Reich" .'[4]

Added to this was the danger of disbelief in Hitler: bemused and isolated opinion might not be able to assimilate the knowledge of such a fantastic character. Even in 1932 Voigt feared that the driest account of the German situation and Hitler would seem like a piece of sensationalism; Crozier had slightly to alter an article 'for the reason mentioned in your letter, that we do not want anyone to think that so strange a phenomenon is by no means incredible. It is, indeed, a strange phenomenon, and your description will make people realise it.'[5] Even so, testimony was conflicting, and Lambert's correspondence from Berlin was generally more restrained than either Voigt's or Werth's; on 25 February 1934 he wrote to Crozier, *inter alia*, that 'Hitler of course is absolutely straightforward and a man of his word'.[6]

Hitler only achieved his power gradually and by overwhelming strokes which immobilized opposition by their very scale and horror (like the Jewish boycott of April 1933, and the Röhm purge of June 1934) or by their sudden daring (like his actions after Hindenburg's death and the first 'Saturday Surprises' beginning in April 1935). Dr. Granzow herself describes the problem Hitler posed the British newspapers: "The Fascist wolf had been described very often—and proved a reactionary sheep until Hitler. When Hitler came to power, the outward forms were more "democratic" than had been the case with three previous governments. The vigilance with which British observers had always regarded the deviations from parliamentary procedures slackened when parliamentary forms were seemingly restored.'[7]

As we have seen, the British newspapers formulated their attitudes towards Nazi Germany characteristically in keeping with their general political and philosophical outlooks. The conservative quality press adopted the line that Hitler's was a legal government recognized by and on at least ostensibly

---

[4] Crozier to Voigt, 6 Feb. 1933, *Manchester Guardian* archives.

[5] Voigt to Crozier, 14 July 1932; and Crozier to Voigt, 21 July 1932, *Manchester Guardian* archives.

[6] Lambert to Crozier, 25 Feb. 1934, *Manchester Guardian* archives.

[7] Granzow, op. cit., p. 67.

friendly terms with the British Government, and considerably more stable than any of the other Central or Eastern European Governments of the time. It held that the British Government had no right to interfere in the internal policies of friendly States as long as they did not interfere with Britain; British parliamentary democracy must not be considered the *ne plus ultra* of political arrangements as far as other countries were concerned. This did not mean that real news of Germany was overlooked or suppressed. In its attempt at fairness as it saw it, *The Times* had to face the criticism from its radical contemporaries as well as from the Nazis. Ebbutt was told by the Nazi Press department as early as February 1933 that they found *The Times*'s coverage very annoying.[8] At the end of March 1933 John Walter replied to a critical letter sent to him from Hamburg:

I am quite sure, from long personal observation, that our Correspondents in Berlin have done their best to give a true picture of what is happening in Germany. They have not omitted any essential facts, but I think the tendency has been to place the actions of the German Government in as favourable a light as possible. We have received privately in this Office authentic news of a large number of incidents which we have deliberately refrained from publishing, as being likely to convey an exaggerated idea of the unrest that exists in Germany . . . surely it is better for our friends in Germany to be accurately informed as to the impression that their actions are making upon English public opinion than to be placated by ill-informed or insincere compliment?[9]

The liberal and Labour press adopted a critical line. For the *News Chronicle* and *Daily Herald* this took the form of critical reporting of German news, and occasional feature articles on the persecution of the Jews or on conditions of life in Germany. The *Manchester Guardian* as a quality paper had to have a more sophisticated line for the presentation of daily reports from and about Nazi Germany. In January 1934 Crozier set out his aims in a letter to Voigt:

My aim is always, on the one hand, not to be alarmist and not to preach a 'Hymn of Hate' against Germany or the German Government but, on the other hand, to tell people the truth so far as one

[8] See Werth to Crozier, 10 Feb. 1933, *Manchester Guardian* archives.
[9] Walter to O. H. Thomson, 31 Mar. 1933, *The Times* archives.

can ascertain it about what is happening in Germany in all kinds of respects (rearmament, foreign policy, domestic tyranny, etc.) in order that whatever happens people here may not be able to say that we have kept them in the dark. I would, of course, like to treat the other dictatorships (Russia, Italy, etc.) in the same way, but obviously it is not possible on anything like the same scale for various reasons.[10]

Hitler in power meant that Germany could not be fobbed off any longer with promises of good intentions; he meant that Germany might now resort to high-handed and tactless measures using force or the threat of force to restore herself as a Great Power; but he did not mean that Germany's complaints or grievances were any less valid.

Barrington-Ward expounded this view in a letter to the Master of Balliol in October 1938:

A friend of mine said in a letter to me the other day that 'we ought not to grant to Nazism what we have failed to concede to the German republic'. It is hardly possible to state more compendiously the view which *The Times* has contested as hard as it could. This means that faith unfaithful is to keep us falsely true and that we are to spin towards disaster in a vicious circle largely of our own creating. We believe this to be a notion which plays straight into the hands of Nazism. It allows the Nazi regime to found itself upon causes that are the possession of the whole German people irrespective of view. I do not know what outside influence can be brought to bear for the eventual disruption or extinction of Nazism except in the removal of the causes which have created it.[11]

Dawson made an even more basic distinction in this regard. The follies which had 'created and endowed Nazism in Germany' were widely admitted. He could not see, therefore, as he wrote to a friend, 'how we are now to turn round and deny the force of the truths, axioms or even platitudes on which you and I would, I think, have been agreed ten years ago. When we fight, let us fight Nazism and not Germany.'[12]

This was quite the same point as the *Manchester Guardian* made when it stated that Hitler's regime was popularly

---

[10] Crozier to Voigt, 25 Jan. 1934, *Manchester Guardian* archives.

[11] Barrington-Ward to the Master of Balliol, 7 Oct. 1938, *The Times* archives.

[12] Dawson to N. Law, 4 Oct. 1938, Dawson Papers.

founded upon national grievances, and the best way to remove him was to remove the grievances.[13]

If the slaughter and futility of the Great War had not made the world safe for democracy, at least they should have made the world safe from war; none of the British newspapers suggested or would have countenanced war on ideological grounds, at least until after March 1939. As Scrutator put it, 'one would have thought that if the last war proved anything, it was that you could not fight opinion, however heretical, with guns'.[14] After March 1939, there were other reasons for contemplating war, and still 'we do not go to war to improve a man's principles or morals'.[15]

The Times felt that as neither side wanted in the last analysis to impose its system upon the other, it was common ground 'that there neither is nor should be the slightest reason for their making war upon each other, however great the contrast in outlook, merely on account of differing ideologies'. But this did not mean that 'reasoned criticism' or judgement by other nations could be stifled.

The total conception of race and State has had certain repercussions, such as the wholesale expulsion of Jews, which not only affect the interests of other countries, but challenge the general conscience of humanity; and in other ways, too, the theories of Führer and Duce, whether intended for export or not, cannot possibly leave foreign countries indifferent, either politically or morally. Yet the instinct is sound that there is in these differences of political creed alone no sane cause for armed conflict.[16]

Although many of the Nazi theories which were not repugnant to the British mentality were incomprehensible to it, it was necessary to remember, as a writer in the *Daily Telegraph* put it, that 'They may be wrong, but their enthusiasm should be understood in all our dealings with them.'[17] *The Times* stated that 'Warlike as some of the aspects of Nazi Germany may be, they answer to the needs and character of the people, and they are no proof that Germany believes herself immune from the

[13] *Manchester Guardian*, 1 Nov. 1937, 1st Leader, p. 8.
[14] *Sunday Times*, 10 July 1938, Scrutator, p. 9.
[15] *Sunday Times*, 26 Mar. 1939, 'Scrutator', p. 18.
[16] *The Times*, 2 Jan. 1939, 1st Leader, p. 15.
[17] *Daily Telegraph*, 3 Feb. 1937, ed. art. by William Teeling, p. 14.

consequences of adventure and disturbance in the world of today. Rather the contrary.'[18]

It must be the policy of the British Government, all newspapers agreed, to get along with all nations as long as they did not try to export or in any way impose their own systems of government, and as long as their policies did not create or exacerbate international problems. Unlike Bolshevism, which, despite the various fictions indulged to indicate otherwise, was sworn to world-wide revolution hastened by the means nearest to hand, Nazism was a German system for governing Germans. Only when this systematic consistency was overthrown in March 1939 was unanimous resistance possible. As long as it was possible to distinguish between Nazism's domestic and foreign policies, then its future properly lay in the hands of the German people alone: 'Even the peculiar and repellent vices of German authoritarianism could not shake the determination to leave German evolution in German hands,' *The Times* affirmed in September 1939. With other States practising other forms of authoritarianism, Britain had easy, and in some cases, intimate, relations. 'No foreign claim to dictate upon the internal affairs of Germany brings this war about,' this leading article on 'Hitler's War' stated— 'nothing but the claim of the Nazi regime to dictate to other peoples as it dictates to its own subjects, willing or unwilling . . . It is Hitler himself who has turned Hitlerism from a domestic expedient to an international menace.'[19]

None of the papers, except perhaps the *Daily Mail*, were favourably disposed toward any kind of continental arrangement with Nazism; the best policy for Britain was to avoid involvement with all systems while having friendly relations with them all. However unpleasant the Soviet dictatorship might be, it remained a fact that no stable peace could be maintained without it. This sobering realization was mingled with relief when Hitler used the 1936 Nuremberg *Parteitag* to assault Bolshevism. But, as *The Times* stated in a leading article, 'the German leaders will quite misjudge the temper of the British people if they suppose that—to adapt a famous quip of Charles II—this country would be ready to help

---

[18] *The Times*, 25 Nov. 1937, 1st Leader, p. 15.
[19] *The Times*, 4 Sept. 1939, 1st Leader, p. 9.

cut off the head of Communism in order to make Fascism king of Europe.'[20]

If there were to be lasting and meaningful peace in Europe, Germany must be a part of it: such was the basic fact of the situation. From the point of view of *The Times*, Germany was the aggrieved nation which needed to be brought back within the comity of nations; Russia was not only at Geneva but was the pace-setter of the League. *The Times* stated that British opinion was aware that there could be neither peace in Europe nor a League of Nations worth the name without Germany,[21] and the *Manchester Guardian* went so far as to say that:

Even if the worst possible interpretation is put on all Germany's actions, even if it is assumed, as some observers do assume, that she only wants to rejoin the League so as to work against it from within, even then it is desirable that she should rejoin it. If it proves that Hitler's Germany stands for principles incompatible with the League, it is at Geneva that the incompatibility must be eliminated. If Hitler's Germany stands for war, it is at Geneva that the peace of Europe must be vindicated. Indeed, the greater the German danger is the more desirable becomes the return of Germany to the League. The danger has to be faced in any case, and in different parts of Europe, but above all at Geneva.[22]

Germany was needed for peace, and there could be little doubt about the popularity of the Nazi regime in Germany—which was even negatively attested to by the inconsequence of the opposition to it. As Ewer wrote in the *Daily Herald*, the childish things of the optimistic 1920s must be put aside: Locarno and the League were dead. What remained were the Anglo-French alliance, the Franco-Soviet Pact, and the German-Italian entente. Upon these realities a strong and stable Europe must be built. War for ideology was no more justifiable than it was inevitable, for European 'ideological alignments' had been flimsy 'ever since Richelieu allied Catholic France with the German Protestants against the Empire'.[23] Not only was there no moral obligation to resist Germany, but in

---

[20] *The Times*, 14 Sept. 1936, 1st Leader, p. 13. See also *Manchester Guardian*, 14 Sept. 1936, 1st Leader, p. 8.

[21] *The Times*, 6 July 1936, 1st Leader, p. 15.

[22] *Manchester Guardian*, 22 Apr. 1936, 5th Leader, p. 10.

[23] *Daily Herald*, 22 Dec. 1936, ed. art. by W. N. Ewer, p. 8.

Central and Eastern Europe there were no military or legal obligations either.[24]

What then would Britain fight for? Aside from the obvious defence of the British Isles and the Empire, the answer, in the papers which articulated it, was clear: Britain's traditional interests. The safety of Northern France and of the Low Countries must be inviolate, but beyond that, and as long as events did not threaten Britain's safety, Europe's destiny might work itself out in its own way.[25] As Voigt wrote to Crozier on 27 March 1936, 'We *cannot* allow France, Belgium— and Holland—to be conquered. This is a matter of life and death to us. Why is there no discussion of these things? These things *are* European politics. All the rest is humbug or semi-humbug.'[26]

Two days later Voigt wrote again to the Editor on the same subject. The most important thing was that Germany be made to understand that the West must not be touched. This was not to say that Britain should appear to give, even by implication, the green light to Germany in the East; but whereas in the west Britain must show a strong hand, in the east she ought only to show a strong bias in favour of the *status quo*. Voigt went very far in this letter:

I cannot myself see that the annexation of Austria, of the Suedetic regions, of Danzig, Memel, Eastern Upper Silesia and the Corridor would be such a general catastrophe, or such a menace to our own vital interests, that we should as much as even *risk* being dragged into a war to prevent it. Indeed, it seems to me that there is a good deal to be said for the reunion of all the German speaking peoples. It will, of course, be a frightful tragedy for a vast number of individuals, but to try and save them by risking English lives would be monstrous, in my opinion.[27]

Voigt continued to hold this theory of Britain's interests in *Unto Caesar*, and as late as the May Crisis of 1938 he wrote to Crozier that 'We ought in no circumstances to commit ourselves to the defence of Czechoslovakia. But we must continue

---

[24] *Daily Telegraph*, 15 Mar. 1939, 1st Leader, p. 16.
[25] See *The Times*, 6 July 1936, 1st Leader, p. 15.
[26] Voigt to Crozier, 27 Mar. 1936, *Manchester Guardian* archives.
[27] Voigt to Crozier, 29 Mar. 1936.

to make it quite clear (as we did on Saturday), that if France goes to war, we hold the sea and Belgium and Holland, and co-operate in the defence of the French left flank.'[28]

Garvin called it 'stark madness' to speak of warlike intervention by Britain in Spain or the east. 'Never', he wrote in May 1937, 'should we thrust our hands into any of these wasps' nests in Eastern Europe. For the successful support of all the strictly unavoidable responsibilities of a world-wide Empire we have enough, and more than enough, to do.'[29] Undoubtedly a further, tacit, element in the concept of defending only Britain's interests was the knowledge that time was needed for the completion of Britain's rearmament.

To this general background of appeasement were added some special elements *vis-à-vis* Nazi Germany particularly. By the mid-1930s the only real war guilt remaining in Europe was felt in Britain: by not making better use of their hard-won victory, they had created the very Nazism which now threatened them. 'It is the doing of the men in Britain and France who, in the first decade after the war, presented the Nazis with their opportunity,' the *Daily Herald* stated in 1938. Now the Tories, 'who killed German democracy', were ready to make any surrender to Nazism; it was too sad to be ironical that 'It was only in the days when Germany was democratic and peace-loving that the Allies bled her white, that they made her sign humiliating war-guilt clauses, that Poincaré ordered the invasion of the Ruhr.'[30] Thus even those most critical of the Nazis felt that Britain must go far towards accommodating this unpleasant regime for which she was partly responsible. 'However unprofitable it may seem,' the *Manchester Guardian* stated in 1936, 'it is necessary to answer unreason with reason and to remember always that the German people are still the same as they were five years ago.'[31] And despite its bitterness over the origins of the situation, even the *Daily Herald* could not counsel a policy which would compound the error: 'Does this newspaper advocate banging the door in Hitler's face and giving him no quarter at all? No, sir. It has always

[28] Voigt to Crozier, 23 May 1938, *Manchester Guardian* archives.
[29] *Observer*, 23 May 1937, Garvin, p. 16.
[30] *Daily Herald*, 11 Apr. 1938, Leader, p. 10.
[31] *Manchester Guardian*, 15 Sept. 1936, 5th Leader, p. 10.

advocated making him just concessions as sincerely as it has opposed making him unjust ones.'[32]

Another element in the attitude towards Germany was, as we have seen again and again, the reversal of the axiom 'Forewarned is forearmed'. Quite the contrary, anticipation of German actions seemed to disarm criticism and opposition in the British Press. The *Manchester Guardian* saw it as a 'merit' of German foreign policy, which others lacked, that its aims and methods were perfectly clear. 'Knowing what Germany wants, and knowing that she means to get it, we know, when she has got one thing, what she will try to get next.'[33] But since the ambit of German ambition was well known, and as long as it was kept within the range of Versailles-justified grievances, then although there would be anger, indignation, censure, and disappointment over the timing and method of particular actions, more serious reactions were not possible because they would have been inconsistent. Further, allowances had to be made for Hitler who, though comparatively a moderate himself, was obviously not sane over the questions of the Jews or Bolshevism. The other European statesmen must seriously ask themselves 'how far is he sane and how far is he mad? Is he sane enough to negotiate with—or will the obsession always disastrously dominate his mind at the critical moment?'[34] A. J. Cummings summed this up in the *News Chronicle*: National Socialism, he wrote, 'is founded on a human volcano'.[35]

Added to all this preconditioning—especially by *Mein Kampf*—and all the allowances made for Hitler and the nature of his movement, was the fact that the most conflicting stories about life and conditions in the Third Reich continued to come from the most reliable sources. Perhaps the area of greatest secrecy in Germany, for example, far more secret than the concentration camps and even than the great rearmament, was that of the national economy. From the very beginning, the Nazi regime's downfall on economic grounds was predicted. Every time the *Reichskredit Gesellschaft* issued an annual report

[32] *Daily Herald*, 6 June 1938, Leader, p. 8.
[33] *Manchester Guardian*, 21 July 1936, 1st Leader, p. 10.
[34] *Daily Herald*, 12 Sept. 1936, 1st Leader, p. 10.
[35] *News Chronicle*, 5 Jan. 1937, Spotlight on Politics, p. 10.

or Schacht visited another country, the most dire predictions would be made, especially in the *Daily Herald* or the *News Chronicle* or *Manchester Guardian*. But as the *Daily Mail* commented in January 1939, when the predictions, backed by impressive figures, were once again being made in some of the British papers, 'These statistics are seemingly foolproof—until one remembers that they have all been seen before.'[36] The *Daily Telegraph* took a detached although not unadmiring view of the Nazi economic performance which had, after all, accomplished the impressive and undeniable feat of eliminating unemployment. A leading article in July 1936 stated that 'preoccupation with her political aims sometimes obscures the fact that Germany is engaged in a social experiment as large in scale as that of Mr. Roosevelt in the United States, and showing a more revolutionary departure from economic doctrines of the past... Herr Hitler, happier than Mr. Roosevelt, can make his own laws and enforce them by decrees'.[37] Only time would determine whether rejecting the old theories would lead to salvation or collapse. The *Daily Telegraph* was not 'taken in' by Nazi economic achievements, but maintained an attitude of interested observation. In one respect it seemed impossible not to admire the dictators, for 'They do not shirk the most formidable tasks. When they think that State necessity impels something, they do not say "Do it, if possible", but "It's possible, do it" '.[38]

Thinking about the Third Reich until the present day has tended to ignore or slough off Nazism's pretensions to, and role as, a revolutionary socialistic economic and social policy. Recent studies of life in pre-war Nazi Germany show, however, that this was possibly the most important element of Nazism's popular appeal; many of its most ardent supporters thought of it not as an anti-Semitic, racial dogma, but as a socially mobile revolutionary economic experiment.[39]

This, then, was the background and setting in which appeasement seemed possible and likely; this was the nettle

[36] *Daily Mail*, 24 Jan. 1939, 3rd Leader, p. 10.
[37] *Daily Telegraph*, 23 July 1936, 1st Leader, p. 14.
[38] *Daily Telegraph*, 21 Oct. 1936, 1st Leader, p. 16.
[39] See Schoenbaum, *Hitler's Social Revolution*, and Allen, *The Nazi Seizure of Power*.

danger from which the flower safety must be plucked, for peace's sake. At this most common denominator of conviction, all the British newspapers were in agreement. After the reoccupation of the Rhineland, when joint resistance to Germany was possible for the last time in peace, and when France pressed earnestly for it, the *Manchester Guardian* stated that:

We may assume what we will about the sincerity of these [Hitler's] proposals, and about the attempt which they and their presentation obviously make in many different ways to conciliate British public opinion. The question is whether, whatever the doubts and the difficulties, we must not try to turn them to good purpose in the face of the bitter alternative which faces Europe, and to that there can be only one answer.[40]

Three years later, with hopes for appeasement crushed under the treads of Hitler's tanks as they advanced on Prague, Barrington-Ward wrote a history of appeasement in the past tense:

Appeasement is a misleading term, even though it has had official sanction. *The Times* has declined to use it, implying, as it does, a policy of 'buns to the bear' instead of an endeavour to secure by negotiation the removal of the causes of war. . . . It was an endeavour to discover even at the eleventh hour whether the Nazis were, according to their professions, out for reasonable change or whether they were out for mere domination. Chamberlain was ready to wait for the proofs and Churchill was not. The Churchill case completely ignored the admitted blunders of the settlement of 1919 and above all the failure to give Germany a say in the Versailles settlement. A policy (Churchill's) which could have been represented as of mere frightened encirclement would have ranked every German behind the Führer and left this country with an uneasy conscience and deeply divided. The decay of 'appeasement' is the work of the Germans themselves. The occupation of Bohemia and Moravia shows that the Nazis are not bound by their own professions and that they are out for domination unless resisted. Very well, they must be resisted.

Such being (as I see it) the picture of events since 1936, I cannot understand why 'appeasement' (so-called) is to be represented as a sort of criminal undertaking.[41]

It is unfortunate that the ideological context in which the British newspapers approached each other in the 1930s

⁴⁰ *Manchester Guardian*, 2 Apr. 1936, 1st Leader, p. 10.
⁴¹ Barrington-Ward to G. V. Ferguson, 27 Apr. 1939, *The Times* archives.

made it difficult to perceive the essential similarity of their attitudes towards Hitler's Germany. The fact is that despite their disagreements on questions like colonies, armaments, and Soviet Russia, every British newspaper with the idiosyncratic exceptions of the *Daily Mail* and *Daily Express* shared an overwhelming similarity of view about Germany. Individual correspondents and contributors differed deeply and sometimes violently; and the range of editorial vocabulary on different papers varied greatly, but in terms of basic editorial policy and reporting, the differences of expectation and appreciation regarding Germany were remarkably few.

Again and again we have seen how attitudes towards other problems and issues determined newspaper policy towards Germany. On the basis of the British Press it would not even be impossible to draw a conclusion which stands the orthodox version of the 1930s on its head, and to show that it was the Left, which constantly condemned Hitler and all his works and pomps, which made resistance to him impossible, and then made it begin with the disadvantage of weakness when resistance became unavoidable. The Left had a plethora of villains in the 1930s of whom Hitler was by no means the first. It was Mussolini who had run amuck in Abyssinia in October 1935 and torn away the few illusions which still remained to the League of Nations. Here was a brutal invasion of an innocent and unoffending people; but desultory opposition led only after some time to the débâcle of sanctions, with which Britain's and Anthony Eden's prestige became involved and soiled.

After 1936 there was a fighting war in Spain which involved the Left deeply and vocally, but ineffectually in terms of British action. Similarly, after 1937, there was an ideologically compelling war in the Far East, where Britain's interests were as prominent but not nearly so well protected as in the Mediterranean. The Dollfuss and Schuschnigg regimes in Austria were considered fully as dictatorial and oppressive as Hitler's in Germany; and Poland's treatment of Jews was admittedly more violent than Nazi Germany's.

The PEP *Report on the British Press* published in 1938 saw the problem this situation represented but could not know what it would lead to:

Effective public opinion, which in specialized issues may depend on the reactions of a remarkably small number of men and women, cannot be focused on many subjects at once. To take a simple example, people find it impossible to be effectively indignant about Spain, China, Abyssinia, and Austria all at once. The Press therefore, wields an immensely powerful weapon in its power to influence the choice of the issue on which public opinion shall make itself felt at any one time.[42]

When the number of international situations over which indignation had to be kept up was added to the number of domestic problems, the problem of the radical press becomes clear.

For the Right, and for the Conservative press, the merit of the *status quo*, not so much as a barrier against change but rather against the chaos which change was likely to represent in Central and Eastern Europe, made things clearer if not simpler. The basic thesis was that Hitler was only more militantly obnoxious than most continental leaders. He had been able to mobilize German opinion behind him to an unprecedented extent, however, because of certain valid claims, arising out of the Treaty of Versailles and French action in Europe since the Great War, which could not forever be denied and which were certainly not meet cause for another war. These were essentially German claims which would exist regardless of Hitler; indeed, the way to remove him was to remove the popular grievances upon which he based his rule. The other factor in favour of temporizing even in the face of extreme provocation was the slow pace of British rearmament, of which the Conservative press was fully aware.

Very gradually we are coming to realize that even today, after several years of intense controversy, some of our strongest-held conceptions about the era and policy of appeasement are still preconceptions or misconceptions. It is hoped that this study of the British Press and its treatment of news from and about Germany has shown that then, as today, the roots of complex problems do not lie in single causes, nor their explanation in simplicities.

[42] *Political and Economic Planning Report on the British Press*, p. 33.

BIBLIOGRAPHY

A. NEWSPAPERS

The Times
Daily Telegraph
Morning Post
Observer
Sunday Times
Manchester Guardian
News Chronicle
Daily Herald
Daily Express
Daily Mail
Evening Standard
Daily Mirror
The Times Literary Supplement
The New York Times

B. REFERENCE WORKS AND OFFICIAL DOCUMENTS

Documents on German Foreign Policy, Series D, HMSO, 1949 etc.
The History of The Times, Vol. iv, Printing House Square, 1952.
House of Commons Debates, 5th Series, 1933 etc.
Political and Economic Planning Report on the British Press, London, 1938. Also, the PEP broadsheet 'Planning', Nos. 58 (24 Sept. 1935), 82 (22 Sept. 1936), 108 (19 Oct. 1937), 118 (8 Mar. 1938), 119 (22 Mar. 1938), 120 (5 Apr. 1938).
Royal Commission on the Press 1947–9, Parliamentary Papers, Cmd. 7700, 1948–9, Vols. xiv, xv, xx, HMSO, June 1949.
WOODWARD, E. L. and BUTLER, ROHAN, Editors, *Documents on British Foreign Policy 1919–39*, Third Series, HMSO, 1949 etc.

C. ARCHIVE AND PRIVATE MATERIAL

Archives of *The Guardian*, Manchester.
Archives of *The Times*, London.
Geoffrey Dawson Papers.
F. A. Voigt Papers, including *The Arrow*.
G. Ward Price Papers.

D. OTHER SOURCES

ALLEN, W. S., *The Nazi Seizure of Power*, London, 1966.
AVON, THE EARL OF, *Facing the Dictators*, London 1962.
BARTLETT, VERNON, *Nazi Germany Explained*, London, 1933.
—— *If I Were Dictator*, London, 1935.
—— *This is My Life*, London, 1937.
—— *And Now, Tomorrow*, London, 1960.
BAYNES, N. H., *The Speeches of Adolf Hitler 1922–1939*, Oxford, 1942.
BROOK-SHEPHERD, G., *Anschluss*, London, 1963.
BULLOCK, ALAN, *Hitler, A Study in Tyranny*, London (Penguin edition), 1963.
CAMROSE, VISCOUNT, *British Newspapers and Their Controllers*, London, 1947.
CHRISTIANSEN, A., *Headlines All My Life*, London, 1961.
CIANO, G., *Diary 1939–1943*, London, 1947.
COCKBURN, CLAUD, *In Time of Trouble*, London, 1956.
—— *Crossing the Line*, London, 1958.
See also Frank Pitcairn
COCKBURN, PATRICIA, *The Years of the Week*, London, 1968.
COLVIN, IAN, *Vansittart in Office*, London, 1965.
COOTE, COLIN, *Editorial*, London, 1965.
DELMER, SEFTON, *Trial Sinister*, London, 1961.
EDELMAN, MAURICE, *The Mirror*, London, 1966.
FODOR, M. W., *South of Hitler*, London, 1939.
—— *The Revolution Is On*, London, 1941.
GEDYE, G. E. R., *The Revolver Republic*, London, 1930.
—— *Heirs to the Habsburgs*, London, 1932.
—— *Fallen Bastions*, London, 1939.
GEHL, J., *Austria, Germany and the Anschluss, 1931–8*, Oxford, 1964.
GILBERT, MARTIN, *The Appeasers*, (with Richard Gott) New York, 1963.
—— *The Roots of Appeasement*, London, 1966.
GRANZOW, BRIGITTE, *A Mirror of Nazism*, London, 1964.
HADLEY, W. W., *Munich: Before and After*, London, 1944.
HAMBRO, C. J., *Newspaper Lords in British Politics*, London, 1958.
HARVEY, OLIVER, *The Diplomatic Diaries of Oliver Harvey*, edited by John Harvey, London, 1970.
HENDERSON, NEVILE, *Failure of a Mission*, London, 1939.
JONES, T., *A Diary With Letters 1931–50*, London, 1954.
KENNEDY, A. LEO, *Britain Faces Germany*, London, 1937.
KIESER, ROLF, *Englands Appeasementpolitik und der Aufstieg des Dritten Reiches im Spiegel der Britischen Presse (1933–9)*, Winterhur, 1964.

LAFFAN, R. G., *The Crisis Over Czechoslovakia January to September 1938*, Volume Two of the Royal Institute of International Affairs *Survey of International Affairs 1938*, London, 1951.

LAMMERS, DONALD, *Explaining Munich*, Stanford, 1966.

McLACHLAN, DONALD, *In the Chair*, Barrington-Ward of *The Times 1927–1948*, London, 1971.

MARTIN, KINGSLEY, *Fascism, Democracy and The Press*, London, 1938.

—— *Editor*, London, 1968.

MOSLEY, LEONARD, *On Borrowed Time*, London, 1969.

MOWRER, EDGAR, *Germany Puts the Clock Back*, London (Penguin Edition), 1938.

MUGGERIDGE, MALCOLM, *The Thirties*, London, 1967.

The New York Times, "We Saw It Happen", London, 1939.

NORTHEDGE, F. S., *The Troubled Giant*, London, 1966.

O'NEILL, ROBERT, *The German Army and the Nazi Party 1933–9*, London, 1967.

PITCAIRN, FRANK (Claud Cockburn) *Reporter in Spain*, London, 1936.

PRICE, GEORGE WARD, *I Know These Dictators*, London, 1938.

—— *Year of Reckoning*, London, 1939.

—— *Extra-Special Correspondent*, London, 1957.

REED, DOUGLAS, *Insanity Fair*, London, 1938.

—— *Disgrace Abounding*, London, 1939.

REYNOLDS, ROTHAY, *When Freedom Shrieked*, London, 1939.

ROTHERMERE, VISCOUNT, *Warnings and Predictions*, London, 1939.

ROWSE, A. L., *All Souls and Appeasement*, London, 1961.

SCHOENBAUM, D., *Hitler's Social Revolution*, London, 1967.

SCHUSCHNIGG, K. VON, *Austrian Requiem*, London, 1947.

SCOTT, C. P., *The Making of The "Manchester Guardian"*, London, 1946.

—— *The Political Diaries of C. P. Scott*, edited by Trevor Wilson, London, 1970.

SHARF, ANDREW, *The British Press and Jews Under Nazi Rule*, London, 1964

SHIRER, WILLIAM, *Berlin Diary*, London, 1941

SPEER, ALBERT, *Inside the Third Reich*, New York, 1970.

STEED, WICKHAM, *The Press*, London (Penguin), 1938.

TAYLOR, A. J. P., *The Origins of the Second World War*, London, 1961.

—— *English History*, London, 1965.

TEMPLEWOOD, VISCOUNT, *Nine Troubled Years*, London, 1954.

TOBIAS, FRITZ, *The Reichstag Fire*, London, 1963.

VOIGT, F. A., *Unto Caesar*, London, 1938.

WATKINS, KENNETH, *Britain Divided*, London, 1963.

WATT, DONALD CAMERON, *Personalities and Policies*, London, 1965.

WILLIAMS, FRANCIS, *Dangerous Estate*, London, 1957.
WISKEMANN, ELIZABETH, *The Europe I Saw*, London, 1968.
WRENCH, JOHN EVELYN, *F. Yates-Brown*, London, 1948.
—— *Geoffrey Dawson and Our Times*, London, 1955.
YATES-BROWN, FRANCIS, *Bengal Lancer*, London, 1930.
—— *European Jungle*, London, 1939.

INDEX

and von Ribbentrop, 105; Government-inspired article, 44.
Daily Sketch, 53, 55.
Daniels, H. G., 62, 116; on colonies, 29–30; on Guernica, 113–15.
Danzig, 20, 279.
Dawson of Penn, Lord, 103.
Dawson, Christopher, 3.
Dawson, Geoffrey, 35, 56 ff.; and Anglo-Polish guarantee, 264; and Anschluss, 152; and Anthony Winn, 65 ff.; and British Empire, 29, 58–9, 68; and colonies, 29; and Czech crisis, 179, 181–2, 183; and Germany, 67, 99, 292; and Halifax–Hitler visit, 101; and J. B. Priestley, 64–5; and Lord Milner, 56, 60; and Nazi religious persecutions, 119; and Soviet Russia, 26; becomes Editor of *The Times*, 56; correspondence with Eden about von Neurath's visit, 71, 117; letters to Daniels and Lothian in May 1937, 113–16; view of Editorship, 69–70, 123.
De Jouvenel, Bertrand, *Daily Mirror* interview with Hitler, 92–3.
Deakin, Ralph, 123–4.
Dell, Robert, 78, 79, 95.
Delmer, Sefton, 3.
Dietrich, Otto, 54–5.
Dirksen, H. von, 42.

Ebbutt, Norman, 62, 81, 111, 116; and Dawson, 62; on attitudes inside Germany, 13, 81, 89, 90 n., 107, 113, 289; on Nazi religious persecution, 121; on the German elections, 100–1; expelled from Berlin, 121–6; Nazi Press department and, 291.
Edelman, Maurice, 92 n.
Eden, Anthony, 44, 50, 132, 133, 233 n., 243, 260, 301; and *The Times*, 71; correspondence with Dawson about von Neurath's visit, 71, 117; resignation, 148–9.
Einzig, Paul, 273–4.
Elementary Education Act, 1.
Elias, J. S., 42, 43.
Elton, Lord, 222.
Ensor, R. C. K., 55.
Evening Standard, 35; and May crisis, 167, 168; and Poliakoff on Halifax–Hitler visit, 129.

Ewer, W. N., 43, 95, 110, 213, 214–15, 256, 295.

Financial Times, 53.
Findlay, A. A., 42.
Firth, J. B., 44, 198.
Flandin, E., 99.
Fodor, M. W., 79–80, 142–3, 145, 149, 158; *South of Hitler*, 79–80.
Foot, Michael, 3; *Guilty Men*, 3, 5.
Forbes, Sir George Ogilvie, 130.
Foreign correspondents: 1930s as golden age of, 3.
Forrest, William, 36.
France, and Treaty of Versailles, 11; anti-French feeling in British Press, 12–14.
Franco-Soviet Pact, 12, 13, 91, 93, 295; Barrington-Ward on, 25; Ebbutt on German attitudes towards, 13; *The Times* on, 14.

Gallagher, O'Dowd, 36.
Gandhi, 126.
Garvin, J. L., 35, 51–3, 63, 210–11, 273, 297; and Anschluss, 162; and Czech crisis, 223–5; and Czechoslovakia, 18, 51; and Hitler's war, 286; and May crisis, 166; and Munich, 225; and Runciman mission, 223; and Soviet Russia, 26.
Gedye, G. E. R., 46–9; and Anschluss, 143, 144, 153–5; and *Daily Telegraph*, 46–7; and France, 12, 46; and Germany, 46, 47–8; and persecution of Jews, 154, 226; *Fallen Bastions*, 46–9; *Heirs to the Habsburgs*, 12.
George V, 'attacked' by *News Chronicle*, 42.
George, David Lloyd, 55, 273; *Daily Express* interview with Hitler, 37, 103–4; on Treaty of Versailles, 11; *The Truth about Peace Treaties*, 11.
Germany: natural dominance of Central and Eastern Europe, 21–2, 235.
Glasgow Herald, 75.
Goebbels, Joseph, 100, 101, 122, 136.
Goerdeler, Carl, 41.
Gordon-Lennox, V., 44, 50, 111, 233.
Göring, Hermann, 101, 111, 126, 132, 155, 164, 183–4, 191, 272; on *News Chronicle*, 41.
Granzow, Brigitte, 288–90.